VOICES FROM THE PAST

VOICES
FROM THE PAST

Reformed Educators

Edited by

Donald Oppewal

University Press of America, Inc.
Lanham • New York • Oxford

Copyright © 1997 by
University Press of America,® Inc.
4720 Boston Way
Lanham, Maryland 20706

12 Hid's Copse Rd.
Cummor Hill, Oxford OX2 9JJ

Library of Congress Cataloging-in-Publication Data

Voices from the past : reformed educators / Donald Oppewal, editor.
p.   cm.
Includes index.
1. Reformed Church--Education. 2. Reformed Church--Education--
Curricula. 3. Calvinism. 4. Education (Christian theology) I.
Oppewal, Donald.
LC586.R3V65 1997   371.071'5'136--dc21   97-3169 CIP

ISBN 0-7618-0767-5 (pbk: alk. ppr.)

♾™ The paper used in this publication meets the minimum
requirements of American National Standard for information
Sciences—Permanence of Paper for Printed Library Materials,
ANSI Z39.48—1984

Table of Contents

Voices From the Past: Reformed Educators

Preface

Books and articles on education come and go, enjoying a brief stay in the limelight, and then they are relegated to library shelves. There they are accessible mainly to future generations of students and scholars. They are for all practical purposes lost to practicing teachers and school board members. While the presses continue to groan under the weight of new books and issues of periodicals, much that is valuable in the old tends to get lost in the process. It remains for those who believe in the value of wisdom from the past to select, often for instructional purposes, what is of most worth for facing the future.

The Reformed Christian tradition for over one hundred years has been accumulating a literature revealing an intense interest in and dialogue about schooling: lower, secondary, and higher. For the size of its intellectual and religious community it has made a considerable contribution to the thinking of not only its own group of believers, but has had an influence in the larger Protestant evangelical community.

With the proliferation of Christian groups beginning their own Christian schools, there is need for a responsible treatment of both the problems in and the potential of Christian schools. Not all groups have a scholarly community which can express the best vision for Christian schools. They would benefit from exposure to the Reformed perspective even if their own tradition is different. The Reformed tradition is rich because of a common theology, but also because various disciplines of thought have made their contribution. Not only philosophers and theologians, but also literature specialists, educational psychologists, and others with expertise in the foundations of education contributed to the dialogue. The era of domination by clergy of Christian vision in education is not reflected in these readings.

Voices from the past and no longer in print are valuable because the views have contributed to the practices of the present. New language for old issues does not obscure the likelihood that the new language and the issues find their plausibility in the older voices as well as the present proponents. This set of readings consists of chapters from books and periodical articles of this century but not this generation. They are publications that enjoyed a readership to the point that the publisher sold out the stock, and let the copyright lapse because reprinting was not commercially feasible. In the case of periodical articles permission to reprint for sale has been secured.

Selection of the representative materials was most difficult because of the risk of making a massive tome that would be daunting to all but the most diligent scholar. The opposite risk was making the volume slim but not capturing the textured meaning of multiple spokespersons. Worse still, a slim volume could well represent only the bias of the editor. The editor has tried to tread between the meager and the massive in selecting items for inclusion. He assumes full responsibility for inclusions for their respectability, and exclusions for their lack of ability to communicate to a later generation and to a broader audience than when they were originally published.

Those who use this reader instructionally should know that the authors are in no particular order, chronological or otherwise. They thus can be used in any order deemed sound by the instructor, and sections can be selected for their relevance to course content.

Most of these materials were field-tested in both undergraduate and graduate teacher education courses in both the United States and Canada. Some were omitted because the present generation of teachers and would-be teachers found them difficult to translate into their idiom. Most helpful assistance in this trying task has come from Canadian Christian school principal Jack Zondag and from educational historian Peter DeBoer at Calvin College.

It is the Editor's hope that these voices from the past send a message loud and clear that Reformed thinking on Christian education was alive and well then, and that the future is best shaped by revisions and improvements over the past, but without the ignorance of the past.

Dr. Donald Oppewal
Calvin College
January, 1997

William H. Jellema:
Editor Introduction

Jellema was a philosophy professor at Calvin College for many years. After his retirement he continued to teach philosophy for many more years at Grand Valley State University in Allendale, Michigan.

While Jellema rarely wrote or published on topics in philosophy, he did offer his insights on various social and political issues. Frequently these were on educational matters, both college level and pre-college. Some topics were as specific as the matter of appropriate textbooks for Christian education (*Reformed Journal*, October, '51) and the case for foreign language (*Reformed Journal*, July, '53). Some were on the perennial question of the distinctiveness of Christian Teaching (series in *Christian School Magazine*, January, February, April, and August, '24). He also addressed the college level question of the need for a Christian university (*Reformed Journal*, November, '55).

In all of the above he represented a traditionalist warning against modern tendencies in American education. What follows is his most thorough, as well as most specific, blueprint for a liberal arts education. It was published by the college in 1958. It was Jellema's attempt to delineate for Calvin College a curriculum that would be the norm, even if a college could not always fully exemplify it. It stands as a voice from the past that is the most eloquent and clear definition of what he and others held to be the essence of a liberal arts education. He went beyond the usual goal talk to point out what curriculum content would follow.

While the specifics are college level, the principles enunciated are intended to be applicable to all levels of schooling.

The second essay deals with the perennial question of in what way Calvinism as a thought system (called a "world and life view") demands not only Christian education but commitment to a school as an "independent institution," a school not under the authority or ownership of either the state or the church.

The Curriculum in a Liberal Arts College

by William Harry Jellema, Professor of
Philosophy, 1958

Calvin's Present Curriculum:
Its Intrinsic Idea

Architects of Calvin's Curriculum

Our present curricular requirements for the so-called "General College A.B." degree were not hammered together haphazardly. Design is evident in the structural framework.

Who were the architects ?

Not our generation. We simply inherited our curricular framework. True, within it we did on occasion introduce alterations. We shifted and sometimes removed partitions; we added a few doors and annexes and emergency exits; we may in the process have weakened some of the supports. But the structural pattern remains what it was when our present generation took over.

No more than we were our predecessors at Calvin the architects. Beginning some thirty-five years ago, the older generation gradually built our original school into a four-year college, granting the A.B. degree. But for an academic blueprint they simply went to the state university.

The University of Michigan in its turn had only a little earlier refashioned its own curriculum in accord with the style of curricular architecture then coming into vogue.

Designers of the new style were educators at the American universities at about the turn of the century. They, not we at Calvin, laid out the pattern of Calvin's present curriculum.

3

Purpose in the Minds of the Architects

No one, certainly, will wish to reject a design simply because he did not originate it. Had our present curriculum been authored at Calvin, that fact as such would not justify it; nor is the design to be rejected simply because it originated elsewhere.

As generally in the arts, when I ask whether a given pattern is appropriable, the question of authorship is in itself of no diagnostic importance. The primary question is not who the author was; it is not even what the idea which he consciously purposed; the primary question is whether the idea *which is intrinsic to the design* is or is not acceptable .

And the intrinsic logic of the design which they originated was only vaguely, if at all, evident to the educators of the early twentieth century. Their conscious intention was only to adjust curricular requirements to the accumulated social pressures and academic tensions of their day.

With the rapid expansion of industry, there came increased demand for more of "practical" education. Collateral was rebellious pressure against the existing curriculum as being insufficiently "democratic. "

The natural sciences, capitalizing on the contemporary prestige of Spencer and Huxley, were with increasing self-confidence insisting that they could curricularly accomplish all that the classics could.

There had been an extended and frequently acrimonious debate on the issue of "formal" discipline; the "form" about which the argument turned had during the years lost its concrete identity; all unconsciously, the debaters were now fighting about an abstraction as unreal as the grin on the Cheshire cat. Men were now ready to bury the grin, meanwhile thinking they were burying the cat.

The disciples of Harvard's Eliot were clamoring for student election that should be almost unrestricted.

Of such intramural and general tensions and pressures the architects of the new curriculum were acutely conscious. And historical forces such as these may serve to indicate the idea consciously in the minds of the architects; the architects intended simply to adjust educational details to the new social needs. But in this instance the purpose in the minds of the authors does not explain the idea intrinsic to the design.

Intrinsic Idea of the New Curriculum

To speak of idea intrinsic to a product as something distinct from purpose in the minds of its creators is not to suggest a wholly subjectivistic inquiry into "motives." To ask what is the intrinsic idea of the new curriculum is here to ask the simple question: "On what hypothesis does this curriculum with its omissions and requirements make sense?" True, an attempt at answer is not without hazard, but it need not be prejudiced and subjectivistic. And that the reader, being forewarned, may be critical of the analysis and argumentation of ensuing pages, I shall at once state my own answer.

Education is for wisdom. And whatever the conscious intention of the designers of the new curriculum, unconsciously their minds had been patterned by a conception of wisdom radically different from that which prevailed at the inception of the older. I submit that the current curriculum makes sense on the hypothesis that *wisdom consists very simply in the ability so to use nature as to achieve position in a society devoted to mastery over nature.* Grant this definition of wisdom and the new curriculum becomes intelligible, both in what it does and in what it does not require for the A.B. degree.

For if this be wisdom, then the single objective reality with which man has finally to concern himself is nature;—nature round about man, nature in man, nature in the cultural product, but always nature. And his concern is not simply to know about nature, but to get on the inside of nature, to have his mind so patterned by nature that when he thinks and reasons, when he judges, when he wills, it is not so much he that thinks as nature achieving the stature of reason by means of him. Wise thinking is thinking what nature would think, could it think. Hence, if this be wisdom, the curriculum will insure not merely that the student acquire knowledge of nature; it will seek to ensure that the mind with which the student judges about anything whatever is a mind that has been patterned by nature, by its content and its behavior patterns, its "laws" and its substance. Whatever else the student may pick up as he runs can be all to the good, provided only the mind with which he picks it up is a mind disclplined by the patterning content of nature; the former may be left to student election, the latter must be curricularly insured, lest the student fall short of wisdom.*

---

*"Education is for wisdom"—Man is conscious of purpose; for man, living means living for ends; for man, living is realizing ends which he sets or recognizes. And wisdom lies in having all his living, including his setting of more immediate ends, patterned by the end which fits a being that can set itself ends and seek to realize them. In short, wisdom lies in being patterned by the end which fits a human being. And formal education is the process of sifting and arranging and communicating material so as to introduce the learner to such patterning; so as to mold and shape him into wisdom

Analysis of Calvin's present Curricular Requirements

Intrinsic to the curriculum which Calvin a generation ago adopted was the new conception of wisdom. But, conceivably, during the intervening years the curriculum, more particularly at Calvin, might have undergone modifications which radically changed its nature. At once to conclude, therefore, that the notion inherently patterning Calvin's *present* curriculum is that of the new wisdom would be unfair. On the other hand, at once to infer the opposite from the mere facts that the present curriculum provides for mental discipline and restricts student election, is equally unwarranted, inasmuch as such facts are not inconsistent with the new conception of wisdom.

Any final judgment as to the notion intrinsic to Calvin's present curriculum must be preceded by further analysis; by an analysis that determines the nature of the restrictions and the kind of discipline which Calvin's present curriculum provides.

Our present curriculum imposes two types of restriction on the student's right of election:

(a) "Prescribed Work."—Certain hours in certain fields are required of all candidates for the A. B. General College degree.

(b) "Distribution of Work. Majors and Minors."—The student must distribute a large fraction of his studies among three designated "groups" in accord with certain stipulations arithmetical in character.

An analysis follows with the purpose of determining what each type of restriction guarantees curricularly.

Calvin's "Prescribed Work" and What It Guarantees Curricularly

Required of all candidates for the (General College) A. B. are the following hours (sometimes courses) in certain fields:

Bible: Old and New Testament, Reformed
    Doctrine, Calvinism.
    Five prescribed *courses* .... 10 hrs.
English: Grammar, Rhetoric, Introduction to
    Literature
    Two prescribed Freshman *courses* 6 hrs.
History: (no specific courses) .... 6 hrs.

Philosophy: (no specific courses, but excluding Logic) .... 6 hrs.
   Natural Science: General course in Physical Science
      and general course in Biology .... 12 hrs.
   Foreign Language: depending on high school
      preparation .... 0 to 22 hrs.
   Average total of "prescribed work"
   probably about .... 50 hrs.

The student with average high school preparation (i.e., with two years of Latin) will then probably spend about fifty college hours in "prescribed work", twenty-eight hours of these fifty being in stipulated courses. And the majority of students will work off most (80%) of the prescribed fifty in the first two years.

If one now asks what this "prescribed work" guarantees curricularly for the first two years of the General College Course at Calvin, one is warranted, I think, in drawing at least two conclusions.

First, the maximum in the way of common college training which the teacher may with some confidence assume Calvin juniors to have had consists of:

Enough English to write an acceptable paragraph, and the rudiments of
   some foreign language.
A general knowledge of the Bible, and a survey of Reformed Doctrine.
Six hours of History.
Twelve hours of natural, mainly subhuman, science.

A junior will, of course, have acquired more hours of credit, but these may represent work scattered over a variety of fields; beyond what has been stated there is no guarantee of common discipline and knowledge .

Second, (since Philosophy is normally postponed till senior college) essentially all that stands between the junior college curriculum at Calvin and the new idea of wisdom is six hours of history.

Consider that the English and the foreign language which every junior may be assumed to have studied are (apart from some literature in second semester Freshman English) studied primarily as tools. They are needed as implements, though of course in the mastering of them there is also formal discipline.

Except for Bible and six hours of history, then, common *patterning content* is limited to the natural sciences. But consider further that the Bible requirement follows not primarily from the design of our curriculum but from the fact that we are a Christian college, and that we would therefore have included Bible no matter what our curriculum. What is left to stand between our curriculum and the new wisdom is six hours of history. For the rest, the single type of discipline by content which the "prescribed work" insures in junior college is that which the new wisdom advocates: discipline by nature's content and laws.

"Distribution of Work: Majors and Minors," and What This Restriction Guarantees Curricularly

In senior college, every candidate for the A. B. degree (General College) has to include two hours of Calvinism and (as far as the curricular requirement is concerned, *any*) six hours of Philosophy; he will then have finished the "prescribed work. "

But there is a second type of restriction imposed, that denominated "Distribution of Work: Majors and Minors" (cf. pp. 45-6 of *Bulletin,* 1955-56).

Just *how much of liberal education* is ensured by this second restriction may be illustrated by a few wholly random examples. And now under consideration is not merely junior college, but the whole curriculum leading to the General College A. B. at Calvin.

Example 1. Suppose the student chooses as his major Greek. To fulfill requirements for the A.B. he must have 24 hours of Greek and 12 hrs. of another subject in the same Group (in this instance, in Group 1). He must then choose one of the two remaining groups in which he completes a sequence of 12 hrs. in some one subject and of 6 hrs. in some other.

So then in fulfillment of this requirement he presents the following program, completed during his four years:

Group I: Greek .... 24 hrs.
                  (and eight of these hours may be first-
                  year; i. e., certainly of Greek as tool only)
                  English .... 12 hrs .
                  (and most of the first six are tool)

Group II: Natural Science .... 12 hrs.
                  (and these may be the 12 hrs. "prescribed"though I do not
                  find Physical Science listed)
                  Human Anatomy and Physiology .... 6 hrs.

Example 2. Suppose he chooses to major in Psychology. He may present the following as an acceptable distribution:

Group II: Psychology .... 24 hrs.
           Natural Science (the "prescribed" course) .... 12 hrs.
Group I: Latin (may include 8 hrs. Freshman Latin) .... 12 hrs.
           English
           (may be "prescribed" Freshman English) .... 6 hrs.

Example 3. Again, he might elect to major in Philosophy, and then present this program:

Group II: Natural Science (prescribed) .... 12 hrs.
           Psychology .... 6 hrs.

Group III: Philosophy .... 24 hrs.
           Bible (10 hrs. of which "prescribed") .... 12 hrs.

Example 4: Should the student elect to major in Biology, Chemistry, or Physics, he will have to take a total of some 48 hrs. in Group II; two-fifths of his time will be spent in Math and the sub-human sciences. With two extra hours (of Bible) beyond the work already "prescribed" in Group III, he has fulfilled requirements.

The examples are random. But the same type of program may be presented by a major in any field. And the canny student, looking over the "prescribed work" may note that fulfilling this requirement already guarantees him:

Six hours of English, and usually 14 hrs. of Foreign Language, all in Group I;

Twelve hours of Natural Science, presumably all in Group II; but he is certain to be able to use at least six (Biology);

Six of History, six of Philosophy, ten of Bible, for a total of 22 with which to play around in Group III.

In determining how much of liberal education is ensured by this added restriction ("Distribution of Work: Majors and Minors"), one should, with such examples in mind, ask such questions as these:

(a) Does this second type of restriction materially add to the restriction of "Prescribed work," beyond the fact that the student must show he has "majored" (acquired 24 hrs. during his four years) in some one subject?

(b) Assuming for the moment that the division of subjects into three "groups" is meant to represent division into three types of subject matter of equal importance for discipline (or at least equally indispensable), is there any guarantee that the student will receive discipline in all three types ?

(c) Taking *both* types of restriction into account, is there apart from Bible and (any) six hours of Philosophy and (any) six hours of History, any guarantee that the Calvin graduate will have been subjected by patterning other than that furnished by
(1) his acquiring some elementary mastery
over linguistic tools;
(2) the natural sciences.

(d) Apart from Bible, is there any curricular guarantee that the student who receives an A. B. (General College) degree, has been disciplined by anything other than modern mind? Or even (cf. b, above) that he has been disciplined by all of *modern* mind?

And if the answers to these questions are negative, then the conclusion would seem to follow that the idea intrinsic to our curriculum is the "new" idea of wisdom. Our "major and minor" restriction no more than the restriction of ' prescribed work" can serve as disproof of the contention that curricularly Calvin insists on no more than does any other school, except that it demands Bible. Curricularly Calvin does not even guarantee general education, let alone liberal.

An Alternative Approach with the Same Result

Or, having in mind analysis of our present curriculum, one may approach evaluation in yet another way.

High school preparation of the student is deservedly censured as being far below what it can be, to say nothing of what it ought to be. But our curricular design being what it is, is there any *curricular* guarantee at Calvin that the student graduating as Bachelor of Arts:

— knows anything of classical literature? of Greek science? of classical architecture? of the classical mind?
— can draw a rough map of the Mediterranean? (can even correctly spell Mediterranean?) knows anything of Goethe ? has any knowledge of articulated medieval mind?

— has any knowledge of mathematical pattern?
— has any scientific notion of the nature of evidence, or even of relevance?
— has any reflective idea of Christian ethics?
— can connotatively comprehend an expository paragraph?
— can think what needs to be thought in order to define even common concepts like nature, soul, moral, humanism, social, animal, equity, reason, evolution, etc., beyond being able to furnish a memorized verbal definition for the narrowest of technical purposes ?
— though he may readily speak of "antithesis", has any knowledge of a concretely articulated difference between Christian and e.g. "pagan humanistic" and "modern" minds?

The question is not whether we graduate some students who are liberally educated, nor whether the staff members are making devoted attempts, each in his courses, to emphasize Christian interpretations. The question is whether the idea intrinsic to our curricular design reflects our Reformed convictions.

Intrinsic Idea of Calvin's Curriculum: Summary Statement

Analysis of our present curricular requirements with the purpose of determining what our curriculum guarantees has yielded the following conclusions:

(a) As for Junior College, except for Bible and some training in the handling of linguistic tools, there is no dependable common patterning save that furnished by natural science. And this is the foundation on which senior college teaching is to be built.

(b) The curriculum as a whole, including all four years, makes sense on the hypothesis that its intrinsic idea is that of the new wisdom: "Wisdom consists, very simply, in the ability so to use nature as to achieve position in a society devoted to mastery over nature. "

That Calvin exists to furnish Christian education we are hardly in danger of forgetting. My present emphasis is on the fact that in the measure that we do not *curricularly* insure *liberal* education we withhold from the student the medium indispensable to *Christian* education. And this raises the question of the definition of liberal education.

It should perhaps be added that a negative evaluation of Calvin's present curriculum need not be interpreted as a pronouncement of censure on the earlier generation at Calvin. Calvin needed accreditation, or thought it did; it had still to make its way academically; it had no experience of its own; it could not simply copy European models; under the circumstances, what to do but borrow the curricular pattern of our state university?

The Aim of Liberal Education

There can be no question that to think liberal education it is necessary to think its aim. And, stated as briefly and traditionally as possible, liberal education aims at the *man* in each individual; at the *man*, intellectual and moral. It proceeds on the assumption that while man is always individualized, to speak of each such individual as man makes concrete, objective sense.

Hence liberal education is not overwhelmingly concerned, curricularly, with "individual differences," or with transient individual student "interests"; these are, at best of tertiary importance.

And liberal education aims at man intellectual and moral; ultimately, at the intellectual for the sake of the moral. The definitions of liberal education which emphasize development of ability "to think" or "to judge" or which employ terms like "integrated personality" or "the free man," though too purely psychological, do to some degree reflect the aim of liberal education.

To think liberal education it is necessary to think its aim. But to think its aim, and its conception of wisdom, more is needed than the simple statement that liberal education aims at the man in each individual. How shall we think the concept man ? Can man be defined simply by reference to nature? or simply by reference to nature and himself? or by reference to psychology (have we said much, saying man is "psycho-somatic,"e.g. ?). Is rationality self-contained? What ought man to be ? Is there an objective purpose set for him ? And where shall we go for answers to all such questions?

Definition of aim at once involves all the basic issues of theology and metaphysics and ethics; questions that cluster about concepts like creation, image of God, sin, redemption, the nature of society, the place of religion in life, the importance of the economic and the physical, the meaning of history, divine revelation, —such questions immediately arise.

Happily, among us one may assume substantial agreement on such fundamental matters. One can hardly over-estimate the importance of this agreement; it means that we have a concrete and well rounded definition of the aim of liberal education.

Nonetheless, one can over-estimate. And if one devotes all one's energies to reiterating the aim and to polishing one's statement of it, and to insuring that all the teachers are in agreement with it, one is indeed over-estimating its importance. For *liberal education is not defined by its aim alone.* And the same holds for Christian liberal education. To know that education aims at the man, and then further to know that the man is "the man of God completely furnished, etc." is to know what educationally is of capital importance; and at Calvin this we know. But there is still the question how one best goes about the business of "furnishing" him. Our real problem at Calvin is that of translating into concrete (and, just now, concrete *curricular*) terms that on which we all agree; a problem all the more pressing if our present curriculum is basically designed to express an ultimate aim quite opposed to that which we profess.

Translating Aim into Curriculum

Among us, familiar as we are with Reformed anthropology, statement of the aim of education is no real problem. The really difficult problem confronting us, and one which we prefer to avoid, is that of translating aim into curriculum.

What I mean by the difficulty which translation involves may readily be illustrated. Assume, then, that one has a satisfactory definition of the aim of liberal education. Even if for the moment we disregard the specifically Christian qualification, would a liberal educator equipped with no more than a definition of aim be able at once to say what as liberal educator one ought to say in answer to or in comment on such typical curricular questions and statements as the following?

Isn't German or French or Spanish as good a medium for liberal education as Latin is supposed to be?

Liberal education means survey courses.

Is not the native ability of a matriculating student more important than the pattern of his high school training?

Is there any sense to requiring students to go on in mathematics beyond arithmetic? Are not many students constitutionally unable to learn mathematics?

Liberal education does not square with terminal education; at most one could argue for its suitability only as preparation for graduate school.

Does it make any difference what history a man studies, as long as it is history?

A "major" is a form of undergraduate specialization.
Is it realistic to talk liberal education in the face of the demands made by professional schools, science associations, etc. ?

Does not a laboratory course teach a student how to think as well as does a course in history?

Liberal education is based on the theory of faculties and formal discipline; and this idea is already long discredited.

We should not teach subject matter, but the pupil.

It makes little difference what the curriculum is, if only it is taught by good teachers.
American education must be democratic; liberal education is for an aristocratic leisure class.

Unless a student is interested in a subject, most of the time he puts into it is wasted; hence a curriculum should not attempt to insist on a common pattern.

Liberal education may be good for a select few; but what are we doing for the rest?

Our students are not liberally educated? But old examinations from the days when liberal education was in vogue, when given to our students prove these latter better educated.

What is the practical sense talking liberal education on the college level when everybody knows high schools teach no Greek and barely two years of Latin?

Never mind the curriculum; important is only that the college should graduate well-integrated personalities.

A liberal curriculum is loaded with bygones; rather, the student should be made acquainted with the modern world, so that he may be able to interpret current events.

Students learn by doing; a liberal curriculum assumes that students learn by reading books.

A student is liberally educated when he has some knowledge of every field and a more specialized knowledge of one.

Survey courses are incompatible with thoroughness, and liberal education therefore means a smattering of all fields with mastery of none.

Nothing much matters in education, just so it is Christian.

Mere statement and restatement of the aim of liberal education does not yet yield curriculum, nor does it answer questions of the types illustrated, questions that have directly to do with curriculum.

To the definition of liberal education, statement of aim is indispensable. But it is not enough. Those definitions which emphasize general education and the classics contribute elements which are equally necessary, and which are directly related to the problem of translating aim into curriculum.

General Education as Protest

The new idea of wisdom implicit in the contemporary curriculum manifests itself in the increasing trend in recent decades to curricular fragmentation. The wise man is a specialist, the wise student is he who specializes as early as possible in the field of his interest; the ideal curriculum, therefore, is fractionated, offering as wide a variety of courses as may be from among which the student is free within very loose and largely mechanical restrictions to select as he pleases, provided only he develops a specialty. "The student's individual interests and abilities are entitled to that much consideration"; "After all, why be so traditional and jealous about the A. B. as we have been?"; "Your good students, so-called, can still select a solid and general curriculum, and meanwhile you are not implying undemocratically that the student who makes other selections is somehow of inferior status; all will receive the same degree"; "In our day no one can hope to cover all knowledge anyhow; there are not enough school hours in four years, not in forty; why not be realistic"; "Even conceding that every student should have a course in history, does it make any difference which course he takes ? "; "The main idea is that the student do intensive work in some field, so that he knows it well; only specialists can hope to get ahead in our age"—so run some of the theses. And the ideal curriculum, accordingly, makes it possible for a student to graduate with an A. B. degree who presents a concentration of a third of his hours in a narrow field, e.g. chemistry, the rest having been distributed over largely unrelated and fragmentary courses in a motley distribution of fields; he has, e.g., taken a course or two in English rhetoric, a semester of Schiller, three hours of economics, a course in Mexican history, and another in

Egyptian art, etc.

Against such splintering of the curriculum the advocacy of general education is a protest. Graduates of such a curriculum come out ignorant of the pattern of Western culture, unread, hopelessly provincial; fit at best for a narrow vocation in a competitive society; unfit for citizenship in a republic, to say nothing of unfitness for discharging responsibilities with reference to moral issues.

The remedy is, for the advocate of general education, a curriculum that will ensure that no student graduates without cross-sectional acquaintance with all fields of knowledge. Such cross-sectional acquaintance must be guaranteed curricularly. And since not too much time is available in the student's program, such acquaintance will have to be got in some six to twelve hours of survey courses. Very commonly a curriculum which includes such prescription is then considered to be a curriculum for liberal education.

The Protest Justified

The advocate of general education is right in his contention that college graduates of the last decades all too frequently are quite ignorant outside some narrow field of specialization. Most of them would flunk a general, comprehensive examination. And the evil is compounded by the fact that most of our teachers today are themselves products of such training. Even on the high school level a teacher of history may be unable to assist a pupil who is having difficulty with a sentence in Caesar or with a problem in algebra; such matters are "outside his field." Nor would many a teacher of American History be abashed at his own ignorance of the battle of Marathon, even though he teaches in college.

The advocate of general education is right also in contending that the education against which he protests is a poor servant of democracy. It is also a poor servant of Christianity. The business of a college, we sometimes forget, also in seeking to serve democracy, is not simply to produce leaders; its business is no less to produce intelligent followers, individuals who though perhaps lacking either ability or leisure to advance ideas do possess the disciplined ability to discriminate between program and principle, between the conventional and the right; in other words, individuals who can distinguish between demagogues and prophets. And such individuals are not educated by mere specialization. Disraeli once described one of his characters as "distinguished for ignorance; for he had only one idea and that was wrong." Worse, perhaps, are A.B. 's "distinguished for learning," who have only a single idea, and that one right. In his protest against the trend toward early specialization and its effects, also on curriculum, the advocate of general education is justified. Whether his suggestion that the curriculum be made to ensure inclusion of a cross-section of all modern knowledge is adequate remedy is a further question.

Insufficiency of the Suggested Remedy

There are likely to be at least two things wrong with his prescription for rectifying contemporary curricular un-wisdom.

In the first place, too frequently the advocate of general education himself still believes that knowledge is simply a collection of specialties; that there is no real knowledge except as it is highly specialized. True, he insists that one specialty is not enough, there should be something also of totality. And since in our day no one can be a polymath, which today means a specialist in all specialties, his survey course gives each specialty a lick and a promise.

And if this is his approach, as it too commonly is, the graduate of his curriculum may not be much better off than the kind of graduate he is lamenting. Too often the student comes out a specialist in one field with some vague idea about atoms and molecules, evolution, Freud, "Avogadro (they grow pears like that in California), man is social by nature, communism is dangerous, racial segregation is something I don't ascribe to, I believe in keeping the negro in his place, Luther founded the Christian church, and since everybody has to take something for granite why not Christian faith; modern history started in 1815 when Congress met in Vienna with a man named Maeterlinck; he specialized in bluebirds; no, I guess it must of been somebody else; anyway it was in 1815 and I remember that date because before I came to college I always use to think 1492 was the important date because then we got the declaration of Independance; no, 1492 was when Columbus discovered America; let's see, when was the declaration of Independance then, was that before or after 1492? I just have no head for dates, history isn't my field though. . ."

A second error, distinct though not necessarily unrelated, generally underlies "survey courses" in the present meaning. It is the assumption that the body of knowledge with which the student is cross-sectionally to make acquaintance is that content which the modern mind thinks, and as it is thought by the modern mind. The assumption is that history is one continuous process, with today's facts and evaluations a necessary and quite superior precipitate, so that even history is to be taught from the viewpoint of modernity. Or again, the "cross-section" is, despite attempts at "historical approach," still a horizontal section only; it is a section through objective modern mind. And by so much, too, the remedy falls short of being liberal education.

Contribution to the Notion of Liberal Education

Although general education as commonly understood is not yet liberal education, its advocate does nonetheless make an important contribution to its definition.

His notion of the aim of education may be largely negative ("not to turn out mere specialists"), but at least he attempts to translate aim into curriculum. And to this extent he takes education more seriously than does a liberal educator whose protests never get beyond pitting aim against aim.

Moreover, translation into curricular terms which makes use of the idea of cross-section represents an important step toward an intelligible definition of liberal education. Curricularly, liberal education *does* involve something of what may be called cross-section, something of "general" education.   And as to the errors which the preceding section depicts as being rather generally prevalent among advocates of general education, the critic should remember what ought to be said in extenuation. A survey course if taught by a man himself liberally educated can in actual practice be an instrument of liberal education. A liberally educated teacher has learned to recognize something of the pattern of objective rationality that repeats itself, though with theme variations, in all knowledge because present in all creation; for him science is not a mere collection of specialties, nor man a mere collection of specialists. That is to say, a survey course need not become the excuse for dilletantism that, with the wrong assumptions underlying, it invariably becomes .

As for the second error (the assumption that all knowledge is knowledge from the viewpoint of modernity), the advocate of general education frequently does make some effort at correction by seeking to accompany his survey course curricularly with the study of great books. At the same time, study of these is intended to supplement the extensiveness of the general survey by emphasis on intensive analysis. So much is all to the good. And if the study of classic texts is undertaken with the idea of getting into the *thinking* (not merely the psychological) *mind* of,e.g., Materialism by way of, e.g., Lucretius, one may be on the road to abandoning the false assumption with which one began, and to that extent on the road away from illiberal education.

It is at this point that a most significant contribution to the definition of liberal education is made by the educator who insists on the importance of classical languages and literatures,—by the educator whom we have become accustomed too summarily to dismiss as advocate of "Greek and Latin. "

Classical Education: Contemporary
Misapprehension of the Issue

For centuries mastery of Greek and Latin was intimately associated with liberal education. During the last hundred years this association was increasingly under attack, and from several sides."Realism" and the natural sciences arrayed themselves against the "humanism" of classical education; the notion of formal discipline supposedly basic to classical education was on the one hand ridiculed and on the other claimed as prerogative of the sciences ("the sciences teach careful observation, cautious inference from data, objectivity, etc. "); Greek and Latin were held to be dead languages, and "if languages are to be studied, study the living; it is even a question whether study of grammar and inflection and construction is not a waste of time, whichever the language. And as for classical literatures, we now have translations of all that is important. . . "

Underlying all these public disputes was something else, the insistence of modernity, of modern mind, that to it belonged sovereignty. And the capital mistake of the classicists was to agree with this assumption, as they had been doing ever since the Renaissance; in their nineteenth century apologies for the study of Greek and Latin, they are constantly seeking to establish that the traditional education in the classics fits in with the modern mind. The real argument in its favor, I should say, is rather that it does not. Let me add that I should not think a thesis far-fetched which maintained that historically it was the break with Christianity that meant death to appreciation of classical civilization.

And so we now educate wholly in and within the modern mind.

But, someone may say, why all this fuss ? we reject the imputation that all we teach is modern mind; we refer you to the fact that we still teach courses in history. And, if you like, we are quite willing to insist on the student's knowing ancient history too; we ourselves, no less than anybody else, recognize that the past lives on in the present, that we got our jury system from medieval England, e.g., and that the buttons on our coat sleeves have a history. Nor have we serious objection to requiring that students read some of the ancient classics in translation; while Herodotus is not a scientific historian, he is an entertaining old gossip, and after all he is called the father of historians, and we certainly believe it good for students to learn that to be scientific one should go to the sources, and Herodotus and Thucydides are sources.

Indeed, instead of lamenting the claim to sovereignty of the modern mind as though its claim meant failure to understand or to present the past, should one not rather gratefully acknowledge that it was the nineteenth century which first gave rise to scientific historiography ?

Aye, all true; and itself only re-emphasizing that we still mean to educate in and within the modern mind. At issue is not at all whether history, including ancient history, should be included as one of the fields of cross-sectional knowledge.

So, too, the issue is not whether Latin is useful for understanding and using English, and Greek for the spelling and understanding of technical terms. Time spent in high school (or earlier) on Latin or Greek, and under a good teacher, would save time in the teaching not only of English but of all other subjects on the college level .

I should also concede the point that liberal education is not synonymous with six years of Latin and five of Greek; a fortiori, if these are taught by philological pedants. Among men who have learned the languages merely as languages there are some who are nonetheless barbarians, "Barbaroi," aliens to the classical mind. In other words, simple ability to read Greek and Latin does not guarantee liberal education.

Also I agree that the modern development of the natural sciences means that room should be provided curricularly for natural science, as indispensable both for understanding of the modern mind and (may one hope?) for proper assessment of its myopia.

Nor is the present issue whether liberal education means general education. For, as previously suggested, general and cross-sectional education may still be in and within the modern mind.

Contribution of Classical Education to
Definition of Liberal

The real issue presented by the old classical education is whether there is in Occidental culture another *mind* besides the modern. The old tradition had hold of the idea that there is at least one other mind, that of pre-Christian culture; and a concretely articulated mind it is. The classical tradition had hold of the further idea that to get on the inside of this other mind the student had to master the languages,—an idea that may not be nearly so ridiculous as contemporary educationists assume. But the second of these ideas is also secondary; one may debate it while convinced of the first; and to disprove the second is not to have disproved the first.

What the classical tradition, therefore, contributes to the notion of liberal education is most importantly the thesis that the modern mind is not the only significant and respectable objective mind, and that there is no a priori reason whatever for supposing the modern mind intrinsically superior.

Since the Renaissance it has become increasingly necessary to insist, quite apart from one's own religious committment, a third major objective mind, the Christian; it, too, a concretely articulated mind, not to be confused with either of the others, and certainly not to be assimilated to either. To consider pagan and Christian, ancient and Medieval-Reformation, minds as simply historical stages in the development of the modern, is a prevalent way of assimilating them to the modern, and thus of obliterating their distinctness and significance.

The aim of liberal education is to develop the man. And one truth we should learn from the tradition which insisted on the classics is that modern and human are not synonymous. The principle suggested is that to the development of judgment, to the development of the individual mind, intimate acquaintance with the major objective minds is indispensable.

Far more important than *what* the individual happens to think about this or that is the *mind with which* he thinks, the mind to which he is religiously committed. And for intelligent commitment and articulation, the individual needs acquaintance *from the inside* with what are by this time three or four objective, well-articulated, major minds.

"From the inside"; I know not how else briefly to suggest that the familiarity with each of the three or four minds should be more than what the individual customarily obtains from a contemporary textbook in History. Of course familiarity with what we today call historical fact and historical method is indispensable; but contemporary textbooks customarily proceed on the assumption that for the rest historiography is only a kind of sociological description and tracing of "causes " by a spectator convinced of the infinite superiority of modern mind; at best the historiographer adds to his sociological description an attempt at psychological "Einfuehlung. " My concern is not to minimize facts and natural and social causes, nor to minimize the attempt imaginatively and psychologically to identify oneself with persons studied, etc., but only to emphasize that this is not yet liberal education. The student must learn what it means to think, and to choose, and to define God and man, and right and wrong, and reality and appearance, and state and society, and justice and mercy, and the ends of science and business and all the rest, when one thinks and believes with the mind of e.g. pre-Christian culture. And, speaking broadly, all the facts he learns in ancient history and all the conclusions and opinions he reads in ancient authors should help to get him on the track of that objective pagan mind. He is to become familiar with it in all its articulate concreteness as a mind by which men did, and can do, and do, their thinking and living and choosing and believing and hoping; a mind, commitment to which is ultimately religious in character.

No student is liberally educated who is not familiar from the inside with the Pagan (or Pre-Christian, or Classical, or "Ancient") Mind, both on its idealistic and its materialistic side; with the Christian as represented by, e.g., the Middle Ages and the Reformation (nor simply with the Christian ecclesiastical); and with the Renaissance Aufklaerung-19th Century-Contemporary Mind; and with each as objective mind. (Nor, though I should deny that history is spiritually a mere continuum, do I affirm that these minds are cut off from each other as with a hatchet). Hence general education is not enough.

And Christian education on the college level falls short of being liberal and also falls short as Christian education to the extent that the distinctiveness of Christianity in its antithesis to paganism, to modernity, and to the errors of medieval and Reformation culture is not in this way made capable of concrete articulation. The Christian mind as the mind with which we think and evaluate and choose and believe and hope is more important than isolated opinions that we think or learn. But how is one to know it? By learning Christian ideas and principles with a mind that is modern? Or by reading perhaps Aeschylus with a mind that is modern, here and there adding a detached Christian homily? "But surely we Christians ought to be up to date."— For that I am pleading; we must know the modern mind also; and to know it we must know the others as well. "But Christianity means antithesis."— Again, for that I am pleading; to make the "antithesis" articulate, to make it concrete, to make it more than merely verbal, to make it mean more than simply insisting on our occupying a separate suite in the same mansions of modernity, we must know the objective minds of paganism and of modernity.

I must get on, and so must leave the thesis as it is. There is one possible misunderstanding which I do wish to mention. I anticipate it would take some such form as this: "So you want the Christian student to betray his Christian commitment and to become a pagan; then again to divest himself of Christianity and to become modern; and finally also for, say, one-third of his time to be Christian. " Of course I wish nothing of the sort; nor is anything of the sort implied or required. And this reply must here suffice;

any other reply to be brief would have to be brutal.

A Second Contribution of Classical Education: Trans-Natural Law

Associated with classical education is a second important constitutive of liberal education

Classical education is rightly denominated humanistic But modern mind has reduced this essential feature of liberal education to one area in the cross-section of modern knowledge. We think we have done justice to the old "humanistic" element by including in the curriculum what we call "the humanities"— literature, philosophy, religion—as viewed by the modern mind.

Just as a curricular insistence on history alongside the natural sciences may mean no more than an abetting of positivism, so too an insistence on further addition of some "humanities" to the curriculum. Neither addition need at all indicate curricular break with the new notion of wisdom.

Involved in classical education at this point is not merely curricular inclusion of "humanities," but recognition of another objective system or set of laws besides the system of nature, a second system no less indispensable for disciplining of the individual mind. This second system is not evidenced in the facts of nature, nor is knowledge of it acquired by the study of nature, whether nature outside man or in man himself. This second system is the system of the necessary patterns of intelligent discourse, of the necessary patterns of aesthetic creation and appreciation, of the objective patterns of the moral universe, of philosophic reflection, etc.; in short, it is the objective system of the human as "rational," of the human as distinct from the rest of creation.

There are "two laws discrete" said Emerson. And the facts and system (or law) of nature are not alone that by which the individual mind is to be formed, "informed" disciplined, patterned. There is another system (or law), equally objective, and certainly no less significant.

But how get at this second system? What "facts" make this system concrete ? Where find the patterned content which will teach me literary tastes? which will mature my mind so that I can distinguish between a genuine lyric and sentimental salivation? or will develop my sense for mathematical pattern? or will make my mind alert and sensitive to implicit moral contradictions? or will enable me to distinguish the relevant from the irrelevant in a demagogic argument? or will train me in recognizing the presence or absence of principle in a proffered program?

Once more, not in nature round about man nor in the natural facts and system (physico-chemical, physiological, psychological, etc.) within man. Immediate source of the facts and system which here concerns us is books. Of course, books only express rational activity, reflection, insight, judgment, aesthetic genius, moral intuition, etc. of the authors. And of course, institutions, works of art, states, laws, polities, mores, etc. also express such activities of man. But generically and immediately, books are the road by which we get at this second system.

Classical education has often been ridiculed as being an education in books instead of in realities, in words instead of in facts. Before we add our own voices to the chorus of derision, we do well first to weigh whether the contemporary advocate of the natural sciences who ridicules "education from books" understands what a book is. Certainly one who uncritically assumes that the only objective system is the system manifested in the facts of nature, the system which involves matter, space, time, and perhaps a divine geometer or originator, is, irrespective of his field of specialization, whether physics or biology or history, unable to understand the meaning of a book. Education in books is not what he supposes it to be; and ability to read a book is not what he means by ability to read.

The reflective activity which is expressed in books is the medium in which the trans-natural disciplinary system objectively manifests itself.* The student is to have his mind patterned by this system, by these objective laws, surely no less than by the objective system found in the world of natural fact.

This is a second element in liberal education which the classical tradition represented. And like its suggestion that there is more than one "mind" so this suggestion of "two laws discrete" is of capital importance to anyone seeking to translate into curricular terms the aim of liberal education (to discipline the man). The educationist who assumes that all that is involved is the question of whether to include Latin and Greek among requirements for graduation is not addressing himself to the basic issues. The lesson to be learned is that a curriculum which is to serve liberal education must ensure, must curricularly guarantee, that the student will be disciplined by the trans-natural objective system or laws; more immediately, must insure that the student learns how to read books, reads books, and is patterned by the objective system to which they introduce him.**

A Third Contribution of Classical Education

A further element in the definition of liberal education, and in the solution of the problem of translating into curriculum which is contributed by the classical tradition, has already been touched on, but is significant enough for separate underscoring.

I have in mind what is implicit in insistence on the study of classical languages. The contribution associated with this insistence is the importance to liberal education of intensive work with texts One need not just now argue the worth of Greek and Latin as subjects of study, nor even the value of translating from a foreign language when it is properly done, much less the usefulness for the understanding of English of a knowledge of Greek and Latin roots; I mean only to underscore the indispensability to liberal education of the discipline of close study of first-rate texts . If laboratory work with the microscope is indeed necessary not simply to see some things that cannot be seen with the naked eye, but to teach the student careful observation, etc., intensive study of classics is even more necessary to teach the student how to read and assess.

The second contribution of classical education to liberal involves this third as necessary corollary. There is no sense in requiring discipline by the trans-natural system unless the curriculum also guarantees that the student will have been subjected to intensive study of texts, i. e., guarantees that he will learn how to read.*

Application to Problem of Liberal Curriculum

Calvin's present curriculum, we have contended, is essentially an embodiment of the new idea of wisdom, and is not a fit instrument for liberal education.

It has also been contended that liberal education is necessary if Christian education is to come to its own; with a curriculum other than liberal, Christian education is seriously handicapped; in any adequate definition of itself, Christian education is thwarted, and made impossible.

What then to do? In the American college world there is nothing but apparent confusion as regards both curriculum and the definition itself of liberal education.

Calvin has, under these circumstances, the following major options:

(a) Do nothing. Retain the present curriculum. Retain it intact at least until pressures from the outside demanding changes become too strong longer to resist. In a word, be conservative in policy, and talk distinctive "aim. "

(b) In general, still do nothing and be known only for conservatism and aim. But here and there, now and then, try to doctor up. Counseling of individual students will at once recommend itself, since it does not involve curricular changes.

(c) Throw out the present curriculum and substitute for high school and college a Gymnasium or Lycee curriculum, retaining much of the present senior college curriculum.

(d) Attempt concrete definition of liberal education and of Christian liberal education; i. e., attempt a curriculum that will serve as fit instrument of Calvin's own aim.

Arguments can be adduced in favor of each of these courses. Doing nothing has in its favor arguments so obvious that they need not be reviewed. And the same arguments favor meanwhile talking distinctive aim .

Adding counseling of individual students so that they e.g. take logic instead of psychology, can also be argued favorably. But again the arguments are obvious.

Substituting the curriculum of the Gymnasium would at least insure curricularly that the student had at graduation acquired something of liberal education and in a form that has been historically influential and successful.

And for the fourth option one can obviously argue that it would seem to be most consistent with the principles of Christian education.

On the other side, against the fourth option is that it is not easy, and that it may seem presumptuous, perhaps even arrogant. Besides, it might mean changes in course offerings and organization that would not be applauded by all teachers.

Against substituting the Gymnasium curriculum is that we then neglect the American factors, will have to revolutionize our high schools, and will be ignoring inadequacies in that curriculum which are lately beginning to trouble even European educators.

Against the first and second options, to do nothing or at least to do nothing but move a partition now and then and enlarge the room devoted

---

*"Trans-natural system": Trans-natural only in that it goes beyond, is of a different order than, what we today mean by nature. I do not mean to imply bifurcation of objective system; actually the two orders are not separate; grammar, e.g., involves both; so does politics; etc. At the moment my concern is only to main-tain that the systems are distinct; that the second, to put it mildly, is no less objective than the first; and that wisdom is not gained through discipline by the first alone.

to counseling, there remains the fact that the architectural plan is wrong; its intrinsic idea is that of the new wisdom; it is designed in no sense to turn out graduates who understand the meaning of Christian faith. Either of these first two options, moreover, means practically that having enlarged the faculty and having filled vacancies in terms of the present curriculum, we increase the difficulty of future curricular remedy .

I suggest we do make an attempt to set forth a curriculum designed to make liberal education concrete, and Christian education curricularly meaningful. And I suggest that we begin now, before our enrollment and staff commitments make the move impossible, and we have also meanwhile not trained teachers to do the work.

In what follows I have ventured on the road. And I have tried to keep in mind the lessons one may, before venturing, learn from contemporary discussion of and even from contemporary confusion about liberal education and its definition. It may serve some purpose to summarize a few of these lessons as succinctly as possible.

(1) Liberal education is defined by its aim; it aims at the whole man; at the individual as man.

(2) Liberal education presupposes that the individual mind comes to maturity, intellectual and moral, only by discipline, by taking over into itself the objective systems of nature and trans-nature.*

(3) Such discipline is by *patterned content;* not by abstracted system, but by system-in-content; not by fragmentary facts nor by frag-

---

*The reader will anticipate me in noting that the first and second contributions of classical education, taken together, at once suggest an important problem, more particularly for the Christian educator. Its nature may perhaps be indicated by formulating this question: If the difference between major minds is granted, will this difference not also affect the interpretation of what has been denominated the trans-natural system ? Or, if there is a Christian mind, and if e. g. the norms of good lyric poetry are to be learned from study of books, from study of so-called literary classics, what happens?—A dogmatic answer must here suffice. The question is not to be dismissed, it is a serious question, for the Christian educator especially, but any answer which would result in rejecting this second contribution of classical education is, one may be sure, wrong.

mented knowledges, but by content exhibiting the pattern of the whole.

(4) Liberal education is not vocational in the usual sense of the term; nor is it professional; nor is it "useful."

(5) Liberal education is "general"; but "general" must then not mean a collection of specialized knowledges.

(6) Nor must "general" mean simply a horizontal cross-section through knowledge as organized and understood and interpreted by the *modern* mind.

(7) A liberal curriculum must ensure that the student is made acquainted from the inside with the major Occidental minds, of which the "modern" is only one.

(8) A liberal curriculum will not only recognize some grouping or other of the various fields of knowledge, but will also ensure that the student is disciplined in both of "the two laws discrete," in both the natural and the trans-natural system.

(9) A liberal curriculum will therefore also ensure that the student has done intensive study of texts.*

* Someone may object "But a good humanist might well also subscribe to these nine statements." No doubt he might. My point is that a Christian educator must.

Proposed Curriculum, A.B.

---

* Educationists currently are also much concerned with the problem of reading. And, we are told, we should all learn to read much more rapidly. Hence the study of eye movements, the advice to read phrases rather than words, etc. Doubtless all this concern with the mechanics of reading may yield significant results especially for grammar school teaching. But even though it yielded all that it can, we should be little helped on our college problem. Something of what is tied up in this latter may perhaps be suggested by the statement that no one can learn how to read rapidly who has not first learned how to read slowly. Or, less indirectly though more paradoxically, no one can read who does not to his reading bring a mind disciplined by the trans-natural system; learning to read, in our present sense, is learning the nature of that system. And for the rest, perhaps it is true that we all should learn to read very rapidly the most of what we read; it might be asked, however, whether it were not better then to learn how not to read such material at all.

In the light of the foregoing I am venturing to suggest a curriculum for Calvin that, so far as curriculum can, would more nearly implement Calvin's own educational ideas and standards.

In making these proposals, I am not setting up an ideal curriculum. In constructing a curriculum one has to consider more than statements of college purpose and proper definitions of liberal education. One has to consider and weigh the so-called demands of modern life, the educational tradition in the Occident, the American college and current college trends, the quality of pre-college schooling, and not least the existing curriculum at Calvin and the inertia which always accompanies established practices. In short, in constructing a curriculum one must be "realistic."

The proposals are, therefore, adjusted "realistically" to existing conditions around us and within our institution; that is to say, the proposals make least possible demands on institutional inertia; require the least possible introduction of new courses and make the greatest possible use of present offerings; as far as possible preserve and utilize the familiar notions of majors and minors, of groups, of hours and honor points, and the like; do not require immediate radical revision of high school curricula; provide a large measure of flexibility, also in the form of guided student choice, etc. Stated briefly, the proposals follow the principle of using what we already have but remolding to the purpose of Christian liberal education.

While our primary official concern happens at present to be junior college curriculum, and even more specifically curriculum in the sophomore year, since such junior college curriculum should be seen in the context of the whole four years of liberal education on the college level and should be defined in that context, the present proposals concern themselves with the *whole* curriculum leading to the *General College A.B.*

It may at once be noted, however, that a distinction is envisaged between junior and senior college at Calvin, and is part of the proposals.

Outline of Junior College Curriculum
Freshman Year
First Semester

(1) Required of all, ten hours, as follows:
English 101 3
Bible 101 2
Classical Mind* 2
Ancient History, *or* Greek *or* Roman History 3

(2) *Choice* permitted between the following options (A, B, C, or D):

   A. Natural Science 3

      Latin or German or French or Greek .... 3 (or 4)

      (For a sem. total of 16 or 17 hrs.)

   B. Chem. or Physics 101 4

      Lat. or Germ. or Fr .... 3 (or 4)

      (For a sem. total of 17 hrs.)

   C. Natural Science 3

      Additional Classical Mind 2

      (For a sem. total of 16 hrs.)

   D. Chem. or Phys. 4

      Addit. Class. Mind 2

      (For a total of 16 hrs.)

*Some explanation of what is covered by such courses in "Mind" (Classical, Medieval-Reformation, and Modern) will follow later.

Second Semester

(1) Required of all, ten hours, as follows:

   English and Speech 3

   Bible 102 2

   Medieval & Reformat. Mind 2

   Medieval History 3

(2) *Choice* permitted between four options: (As for first semester, but substituting Med. & Ref. Mind for Classical) (For a semester total of 16-18 hrs.)

Sophomore Year

First Semester

Required of all:

   Bible 2

   Nat. Sc 3

   Hist. Renaiss. and After 3

   Lat ., Germ ., or Fr 3

   College Math. or Logic 3

   Modern Mind .... 2 or 3

   (Semester total 16-17 hrs.)

<u>*Second Semester*</u>

Required of all:

    Bible 2

    Nat. Sc. 3

Lat., Germ., or Fr. or Greek. 3

Modern Mind

    (which may include e.g. Lit., Psych., Econ., Soc. etc.)* .... 8 or 9

    (Semester total 16-17 hrs.)

Concerning the Courses in "Minds"

A. The Three Major Minds

The suggested junior college curriculum includes courses in "Minds." The general connotation of this term I have already suggested , as also the three or four major minds that have become historically concrete and articulate in Occidental culture. They can, *roughly*, be associated with the traditional divisions of Occidental history into Ancient, Medieval, and Modern. I know that so to tie them in with chronological periods is to run the danger of being misinterpreted, as though, e.g., the medieval mind disappears in the 15th century, or at best lives on as a mere precipitate. By the tie-in I mean no more than this: the Medieval Period is, together with the Reformation period, the time in which the Christian mind achieved articulate historical concretion; and so with the Ancient and Classical; and so in turn with the Modern .**

Briefly, then, I think of the Minds with which the student must become acquainted "from the inside" as:

    (1) The "Classical", or Pre-Christian, or Pagan (Occidental), or "Ancient'' And here the opposition between Materialistic and pagan Idealistic .

    (2) The Medieval-Reformation, or Biblical, or Christian (with no suggestion, of course, that it is perfectly articulated, etc.). And here the differences between Roman Catholic and Protestant, etc.

    (3) The "Modern," or "Renaissance-Modern~" with the emphasis again not on mere chronology but on the Mind. And here again opposition between Naturalism and Modern Idealism.

It is to be understood that if one takes the term "Modern" in the purely chronological sense, as I here do not, all three Minds are modern; in the sense, namely, that all three minds can be found today.

It is also to be understood that each of the three Minds makes use of the facts and laws and potentialities of the natural order, and likewise makes use of the facts and laws and potentialities of the rational order. Or, from another angle, there is something of the inescapably human in each.

And so, too, it must be understood that besides the pedagogical problem of understanding each Mind in its contrast to the others there is the certainly no less difficult problem of disentangling the "human" from the Mind with which it has historically become interwoven. Nor is this quite the same problem as that of disentangling historical accident from essential principle. For example: How much of ancient rhetoric is humanly inescapable? Or of ancient (classical) philosophy? Or of the organization of the Roman family under the Republic ? Or again, there is modern science; the phlogiston theory, let us say, is historical accident; but is resort to mathematics simply modern or is it inescapably scientific?

B. General Nature of Courses in "Minds"

The purpose of each course in Mind is to get at the inside of the given Mind, and comparatively and critically to consider how Christian Mind in its articulation differs, etc.; that is, the purpose is always not simply specialized information as such, but an understanding of the spiritual forces and beliefs imbedded and expressed therein.

The curriculum suggested prescribes a minimum of 14 hours of courses in Minds; of these at least six must be strictly in texts. By a "text" I mean e.g. Cicero's *De Senectute* (in translation), or Rousseau's *Emile*, or Boethius' *Consolation*, etc. Such textual courses are intended also to teach the student to construe, not only verbally, grammatically, etc., but connotatively, reflectively, discriminatingly. Background reading in the library should be required. Short incisive essays weekly. Classes should not have over twenty students.

Nor do I think that in the Classical Mind only one or two text courses should be offered in a given semester, each with the necessary number of sections. Theoretically, there is no reason why there should not be as many different texts studied as there are groups of twenty students. Nor need they be offered by only a few departments.

In the second semester of the Sophomore year there is provision for including under Modern Mind courses very like some of our present offerings; indeed, our present offerings in "Principles of" or in "Introduction to" e.g. Psychology, Economics, Literature, etc. could well serve with little revamping. Equally, however, a course in a text (e.g., Adam Smith) might be substituted for its equivalent "Principles" course (in this instance, Economics). And certainly we should not limit our offerings in Modern Mind to analytic and systematic "Introduction" or "Principles" courses; we should also offer text courses.

There is a further requirement that as to content or field at least six Mind courses concern themselves with Social and six with Moral Sciences. The distinction need not be elaborated at this point; the grouping of the sciences is suggested on a later page.

For the present, no text courses are contemplated in the Natural Sciences. We already include twelve hours of Natural Science; this means, essentially, twelve hours in Modern Mind.

One more remark. The courses in Minds as discussed are courses in Junior College. Text courses in Minds on the senior college level are of course not excluded, but are not now under discussion.

C. Illustrations of Possibilities

As to the kinds of texts contemplated, let me suggest a few by way of example.

For Classical Mind, in its materialistic and its idealistic aspects , and of varying degrees of difficulty: Lucretius, Homer, Cicero, Thucydides, Aeschylus, Plato's Apology, Longinus, Sophocles, Epicurus, Demosthenes, Seneca.

For Medieval Reformation: Paul, Augustine, Boethius, Anselm, Thomas, Luther, Calvin, Dante (also De Monarchia), Newman, Kuyper,

---

*For the second semester of the Sophomore Year, many of the present "200" courses in "Principles" or "Introduction" etc., essentially analytical rather than historical in character, and reflecting the modern mind in content or approach, may be used to satisfy this requirement. Such courses should, naturally, be so designated.

**The Renaissance humanists who first suggested the three-fold division into Ancient, Medieval, and Modern were justified; there is an essential difference of *Mind*. This is of course not to say that their estimate of the significance of each (cf. the disparaging term "Middle Ages") is justified.

Bavinck.

For Modern: Hobbes, J.S. Mill, Fichte, Goethe, Nietzsche, Machiavelli, Locke, Lessing, Herder, Dewey, Spinoza.

Just as we already offer courses in Modern Mind which with slight adaptation can serve to meet requirements in the second semester of the sophomore year, so we now offer some courses that are readily adaptable as text courses in one or the other Mind; a course in Lactantius, e.g., or a course in Romans, or in Chaucer. Obviously, however, there are not enough now offered if we were to require text courses in the Minds, and of all junior college students.

D. Why Such Courses in *Minds* ?

Let me list some aspects of the idea behind these suggested courses in the "Minds," and especially text courses.

Intensive work on texts is as indispensable to the "humanities" etc. as is laboratory work (not merely the acquisition of technical proficiency) to the natural sciences. Indeed, reading is more difficult to teach than is observation and inductive reasoning from and around an experiment.

We must have some substitute for the intensive discipline afforded by the old classical education, also for the discipline which when it was done well came from translation and construing of Greek and Latin.

If we can teach such textual courses as they should be taught we can do much to prevent purely "historical" interest in history (history of literature, of philosophy, of theology, etc. as well as history in the sense of a college subject).

Textual courses in Mind are intended to teach students to construe, not only exactly (grammatically, verbally, etc.) but connotatively, reflectively, discriminatingly; what is the thesis ? How qualified? What is the supporting argument? Is it sufficient? What are the presuppositions? Are they essential or could the thesis be maintained on other presuppositions as well? And would a difference in presuppositions materially affect thesis ? And what kind of "presuppositions" are you discussing? Chronological, circumstantial, "accidental," "historical;," even merely prejudicial, or ultimate, religio-philosophical, constitutive of Mind?—The emphasis should be on wholesome intensive work; i. e., on intensive work that will serve to delineate the Mind represented, to understand it from the inside, enabling critical and intelligent and concrete articulation of the Christian Mind.

The student will become familiar with at least a few classics. Curricularly, these courses should help to prevent the modernistic parochialism of the contemporary college graduate.

Much practice in the short expository essay.

Concrete comparison and assessment of the three Minds.

The teacher will be taught by the teaching.

E. Some Problems Entailed by Offering Text Courses in Minds

The chief problem which the offering of such courses in Minds would immediately raise is that of finding teachers. Other problems are minor.

On the one problem that matters, I present a suggestion later.

Student Choice and the Curriculum

The curriculum leaves room for some election on the part of the student, but within a definite framework.

In the first semester of his Freshman year, the student may elect either Ancient History or Greek History or Roman History, and if he has had a good foundation in high school, I think I should advise him to elect one of the latter two.

In this same semester he has a choice between four options. He may within the field of natural science elect either straight Physics or Chemistry, or he may elect three hours of Physical Science. And he may elect foreign language or take an additional course in Classical Mind. If he elects a foreign language he has a choice between ancient and modern; which he chooses depends on his high school preparation in foreign languages. If he wants no foreign language in his Freshman year he must take additional Classical Mind, so that he gets something of a substitute by way of close study of a text etc. (In order to keep matters simple, I am assuming we shall continue to operate under our present foreign language requirements; except that every student will take, in his Sophomore year, one year of a foreign language beyond the elementary level).

In the second semester of his Freshman year, the options are similar. In general, the student will carry on with his first semester option .

In the first semester of his Sophomore year, the student may again exercise option as to foreign language. He may also choose between college math and logic.

In his last semester as Junior College student he may exercise choice with regard to eight or nine hours, provided they are courses designated in the catalog as suitable for this option. He might e.g. elect a course in Principles of Economics, or a text course in Adam Smith, or a course in

Introductory Psychology or in Matthew Arnold or in Victorian Poetry or in French Romanticism or in Principles of Sociology or in Karl Marx or in Hobbes' *Leviathan,* etc., provided the course had been designated as an option.

I should add that I have supposed we might offer courses in e.g. Classical Mind during a single semester in various texts; e.g., Cicero, Sophocles, Demosthenes, Plato's Phaedo, Thucydides, Homer, etc.; the student would then have choice here also.

But the curriculum is in its outlines and general framework prescribed. The student is not free not to obtain the nearest we can under present circumstances give him in the way of a junior college education that will serve him whether he continues in senior college or terminates his schooling.

Some Analysis of the Proposed Junior College Curriculum

This proposed curriculum is, as I said earlier, a realistic accommodation to the existing situation (the American college, the high school, the existing curriculum at Calvin). But it makes a beginning at least of translating liberal education into curriculum.

It has shortcomings, because of the need for adapting to present day education. An analysis will serve to make clear e.g. that in the matter of trying to insure that every student is familiarized with other objective minds than the modern, it is still the modern mind which receives the lion's share. The fact is due in part (though only in part) to the present existing allotment of a minimum of twelve hours to natural science. And yet, as between the three Minds, it is in the light of his previous education exactly the modern mind which we need have least fear will be under emphasized.

There are other shortcomings, intentionally permitted to remain in the interest of ready adaptability to the existing situation. Consider a breakdown of the *minimum* curriculum in terms of the objective minds:

(1) Classical Mind: Ancient History, 3 hrs.;
   Classical Mind, 2 hrs. .... Total 5 hrs.

(2) Christian or "Medieval and Reformation" Mind:
   Bible, 8; Med. Hist., 3; Med. Mind., 2 .... Total 13 hrs.

(3) Modern Mind: Nat. Sc.,12; Mod. Hist.,3;

Mod. Mind,10; Engl. Lit. 3 .... Total 28 hrs.

(4) Formal Sciences: Logic or Math., 3; say half of English, 3, and here place also the first two years of any foreign language.

To improve the proposed curriculum would not be too difficult, and perhaps I underestimate our venturesomeness. Let me then suggest a slight modification that would do much for the student: Reduce the requirement "Modern Mind" in the second semester of the Sophomore Year by two hours, and make the study of Plato's *Republic* (two hours) mandatory in this last semester of the Sophomore Year; and in this *last* semester.

But less than the proposed minimum curriculum we should not have. And such a minimum would guarantee that every General College student would at the beginning of his junior year have had at least:

Two years of a foreign language (and he should not be admitted to the Freshman Year without at least two years of another)

Logic or else one course in College Math

One year of English

Physical and Biological Science

History: Ancient, Medieval, and Modern

Bible and Reformed Doctrine

Either by way of text study or by way of "Principles" courses, an introduction to at least six hours of Social Sciences and to at least six hours of what have usually been called the Humanities

He will in text courses have been drilled in writing and in reading; he will have been introduced to the major Minds; he will have been disciplined by patterning content. And at the beginning of the junior year all students will have a fairly extensive *common* background.

The curriculum proposed will insure, also, that every graduate from the first two years will have been disciplined by the *ordo rationalis* as well as by the *ordo naturalis*.

Curricular counseling of the student at registration will be limited to advice with regard to the larger options (Freshmen especially) and options *within* stipulated requirements for Mind courses. But even without counseling or with ill-advised counseling, the student cannot escape the minimum of a liberal education on the junior college level .

"Graduation" from Junior College

The Junior College curriculum proposed is envisaged as a unit. The student is to "graduate" from it; better, perhaps, cannot be promoted to Senior College without it. Otherwise stated, the student is not to apply Junior College credits toward fulfilling the requirements of the two years of Senior College, nor can he graduate from Senior College (receive the A.B. Gen Coll. degree) except he has not only 60-odd hours of credit for Freshman and Sophomore years, but can fulfill the requirements of the Junior College curriculum.

Proposal regarding Finance

If we should wish to introduce text courses in Minds and should wish to limit the size of classes especially in such courses, we should need additional staff; we should probably also need seminars of and for such staff members. Even the limiting of class size will mean financial outlay.

I suggest that an attempt on our part to revise our curriculum in the direction proposed might be of interest to some Foundation, and that we might submit to it a request for not less than $25,000 annually for not less than four years to try the venture as an experiment. Of course staff members should be themselves liberally educated if they are to teach; we cannot simply add a few "assistants" for text courses in Minds. Nor do I envisage turning over such text courses to a few new staff members. I mean that introduction of such courses with their paper work (frequent short essays are required), their class sections strictly limited to say 20-25 students, etc. will mean over-all additions to staff, and hence additional outlay.

In any event, we should attempt to translate our ideals into curricular terms, also in order that we may know where our staff needs lie. Preparation of a budget for presentation to some Foundation could then follow.

Senior College

The junior college curriculum proposed is sufficiently unified so that if the student so chooses it can be terminal. And it is also intended to serve as preparation, both by way of content and by way of discipline, for senior college.

The term Senior College refers to the two years (Junior and Senior) before graduation. Measured in "credit hours" Senior College means 60-65 hours of work.

Requiring emphasis, perhaps, is that the distinction between Junior College and Senior is *not* that junior college work is "liberal" and senior college work is "specialized. " *All four years* should aim at liberal education. Junior college should furnish the common background or basis for all students. In senior college the student should use his "major" as springboard for further liberal education.

Admission to Senior College

To be admitted to Senior College, a student:

(1) Must have completed, must have "graduated from'' the Junior College curriculum; and,

(2) Must have been accepted by some department as major.

Graduation from Senior College
(with a "General College" A.B.)

Toward graduation from Senior College (60-65 hrs.):

(1) No "100" courses will be credited. This means also that no credit toward graduation will be given for the first year of any language. Provision can be made for exception in an occasional instance at special request of the student's major department if the department is willing in such student's case to deduct the equivalent from the hours of departmental study usually required of its majors.

(2) No more than 12 hours of "200" courses will be credited.

(3) The candidate must present a total of 60-65 hours with an equal number of honor points.

(4) The whole of the candidate's Senior College program (not only courses within the major department) must have been outlined to fit his individual needs and promise, to fill the lacunae in his individual preparation, and to meet the graduation requirements of the Senior College. It is the responsibility of the department in which the candidate majors to outline his program at the beginning of his junior year (or during second semester of his sophomore year), and in such a way as curricularly to insure that the student receives a liberal (not merely "general") education. The program should be re-examined and may be revised at the beginning of each new semester, but is always subject to approval by the dean.

The major department recommends (to the dean) for graduation .

(5) In addition to the restrictions concerning "100" and "200" courses, the only formal restriction that must be observed by the department in outlining curricular programs of its majors is that the minimum pattern of "Group Distribution" be observed.

Group Distribution

Departments are grouped into three fields; in choosing a major department, the student automatically chooses to major in the "group" to which that department belongs.

It should be borne in mind that the "group restrictions" apply to Senior College; there are no "majors" in Junior College, only options.

The groupings proposed attempt to take into account both subject matter and the current educational set-up.

I. Mathematics and the Natural Sciences. *Mathematics, Physics, Chemistry, Biology*
Minimum requirement for a major in this group: 30 hours in this group, of which a minimum of 18 hrs. in his major department.
18 hrs. in Groups II and III, with not less than six in either.

II. The Anthropological or Social or Intermediate Sciences. *Psychology, Sociology, Economics, Political Science*
Minimum requirement for a major in this group: 30 hours in this group, of which not less than 18 in his major department.
18 hours in Groups I and III, of which not less than 12 in the latter.

III. The Moral or Ethico-Religious Sciences. *Bible, History, the Literatures, History and Theory of Art and of Music, Education, Philosophy*
Minimum requirement for a Major in this group: 30 hours in this group, of which not less than 18 in his major department.
18 hours in Groups I and II, with not less than 12 in the latter .

IV. The Practical Arts: Practice in Speech, Music, Art, Drama, Education, etc. Total credit toward the General College A. B. degree permitted in Senior College not to exceed six hours. No credit toward fulfilling group requirements.

It is the primary responsibility of the major department so to outline the student's program as to give him maximum possible distribution between Classical, Medieval Ref., and Modern Minds.

It will be noted that of the 60-65 hours in Senior College, distribution requirements cover 48 hours; furthermore, requirements as to group distribution apply only in Senior College.

Numbering of Courses

Assignment of numbers to courses serves not only as a convenience in bookkeeping, but also as a ready way of indicating the "level" at which a course is taught. Though the subject concerns all courses of the four years, I introduce it at this point because the "level" of courses has much to do with fulfilling requirements for graduation from a curriculum such as proposed.

Retaining the numbering plan at present in use (100-300), the proposed curriculum assumes:

(1) That all first year language courses, and all prescribed Freshman courses are "100" courses;

(2) That all prescribed Sophomore courses, and all courses of the type which are elementary systematic "introductions" or elementary surveys, or, in sum, all courses that can be taken by the average second semester sophomore are "200" courses;

(3) That the "300" numbers are reserved for courses which presuppose:
   (a) Completion of junior college; *and*
   (b) An elementary course in the field. (This restriction has nothing to do with admitting students to a "300" course; it has everything to do with the level of instruction set for the course).

What This Proposed Curriculum Guarantees

Earlier I selected arbitrarily a few instances to illustrate what our present curricular requirements can guarantee in reference to our graduating "majors." The proposed curriculum is, as I have said, not ideal, and is constructed to meet existing conditions and practices as far as possible. But take the same examples of graduating majors that were considered on the earlier page, this time graduating from the proposed curriculum:

Example 1. Major in Greek. As *minimum:*

A. He will have had the prescribed Junior College curriculum, else he could not have entered Senior College.
B. He will have had above his elementary 8 hours (a 100 course), 18 hours of Greek.
C . He will have had another 12 hours in Group III of mainly 300 courses.
D. He will have had 12 hours in Group II, senior college level.

E. He will have had 6 hours in Group I, senior college level.
F. His work will have been done under the direct supervision of his
   major department, responsible also for insuring distribution between ancient, med-Ref., and modern minds

Example 2. Major in Psychology. As *minimum*:

A. He will have had the prescribed Junior College curriculum .
B. He will have had 18 hours of Psychology on the Senior College
   level. (He may of course have had more, at the insistence of his
   major department)
C. He will have had another 12 hours in Group II, Senior College .
D. He will have had 12 hours in Group III, Senior College.
E. He will have had 6 hours in Group I Senior College.
F. As above, 1 F.

Once more, Junior College does not count toward graduation, except
that like high school it is of course presupposed. Tool subjects are assigned
to the junior college level, together with the curriculum prescribed for
Freshmen and Sophomores.

Of course no mere curriculum guarantees education. But a poor
curriculum can do much toward obstructing education.

Corollaries and Suggestions

I append a few comments on the proposed curriculum, by way of
corollaries and suggestions.

While the curriculum distinguishes junior and senior colleges, it does
not intend two distinct faculties.

Courses for Seniors should require that students *use* one foreign
language .

In general, departments with the advice of respective divisions should
insure that courses are offered on 300 level servicing liberal education and
other departments, open to students graduated from Junior College, not
restricted to departmental majors. Or, from another angle, e.g. senior
college students who are non-philosophy majors, ought to be able to take
a course in Kant; non-lit majors a course in e.g. Matthew Arnold; etc. The
course level should not be lowered, but we should not encourage the idea
that a student can do senior college work only in his "specialty. "

It is intended that responsibility for liberal (not simply general education) of the senior college student fall on the department in which the
student majors. The department lays out his program, insures that he

knows and uses his foreign languages, is not simply specializing, knows his doctrine and Calvinism, reads and writes intelligently, has the required familiarity with the significant books, is making progress from semester to semester, is not lopsidedly concerned with e.g. only modern mind, will be ready for graduate school if he plans to continue his studies (or for professional school, if such is his plan), etc.; in general, the department takes responsibility for the academic development of its majors. Hence, too, the department has certain privileges. It may orally or otherwise examine a junior college sophomore who applies to the department for permission to major; it does not have to accept an applicant; it recommends to the dean for graduation; etc.

No student is admitted to Senior College as candidate for A. B. degree (General College) who has not been accepted as major by some department.

Should we wish to take our own words regarding the distinctiveness of Calvin College (see Catalogue) seriously, we ought to cut the hours of every teacher by two or three, using the equivalent time for divisional seminars; working seminars, I mean, requiring serious research on the part of each faculty member, the writing of papers with no attempt to scale down or to popularize; assigned topic weekly on which all division members do research, though only one reads a paper on some narrowed aspect of it; discussion in which also some line may be obtained on promising younger faculty members; etc. The division chairman or some one chosen from within the division should act as director of such divisional research and seminars. Emphasis should of course be on study of first-hand source material.

A student's major is not his excuse for specializing; it is his springboard for liberal education. That is to say, his philosophy e.g. should lead him into German Romantic literature (whether or not he takes a course in this latter), into economics, into etymology, into law, into astronomy, into mythology, into mathematics, into Demosthenes, etc. Of course, no student can cover everything; and of course no teacher knows everything. But it makes all the difference between liberal education and non-liberal whether my notion of a major is after the analogy of "In junior college I had to scuttle around from one room to another in the mansion of knowledge; now, thank goodness, I am a major and can rest my weary legs; I stick to one room, intending only to scrutinize more and more closely everything within it, or at least everything in my corner," a spatial analogy of course; *or* after the analogy of one who says "Intellectually two years older than when I entered college, I still count nothing human alien to myself; as a major I study with increasing maturity, with more sureness of orientation, with more definiteness of intellectual purpose. "

Just as the college senior should be making actual use of at least one foreign language in his course work (other than his course directly in a foreign literature), so the student throughout his four years should be making use of the discipline acquired in his text courses in Minds; that is to say, in every course he should be sent to classic sources, as in perhaps many instances he now is. And in order to prevent his graduating in ignorance of too many, I suppose we should indicate, at least to our colleagues, which classics are required in each course .

It will be observed that some of the courses at present offered are already courses in one or another of the Minds not only, but text courses. Random examples: Romans, John Milton, Corneille and Racine, Chaucer, Lactantius, Kant, Plato. Rather generally, these are on the senior college level. And it is contemplated that the senior college curriculum should include more such, once we provide every student with junior college foundation, rather than a multiplication on this level of "Introductions" etc. to one field or another. But at least we have some by way of a beginning. As for Mind courses in texts on the junior college level, these would in general be new courses. Many of our present "Introductions" etc. would be offered as options to fulfill Sophomore requirements in Modern Mind, second semester of sophomore year. In other words, *over all,* and with the exception of the text courses in Minds required in junior college, the suggested curriculum would not mean additions to the staff total, and would mean corresponding reduction in student-teacher ratio in many present courses .

However, should we move along the curricular lines proposed, that fact would have some bearing on the kind of men we should be adding to the staff in the future.

Incidental would be a shift in the whole matter of academic counseling. Freshmen would require little but explanation of the difference between the four options; and this little could be stated simply and clearly in the catalog; in general, once made, the choice holds for second semester also. Sophomores have no choice, first semester; second semester they exercise choice within Modern Mind; they could seek counsel if they wished; but no matter what a student chose, he could not get far out of line. In senior college, academic counseling becomes the responsibility of the major department, and the weighty part of it comes during the semester *preceding* the student's admission to senior college.

Curricula Other Than A.B. in Liberal Arts

The proposed curriculum is intended as the nearest approach at present possible to a norm. Other curricula should not vary from it except unavoidably. Indeed, I think that generally the student can by exercising proper options within the suggested curriculum prepare himself for any of the vocations our present curricula are meant to serve.

A Pre-Law student, for example, would, having been promoted from junior college, select a major in either Group II or Group III; a Pre-Engineer in Group I; a Business Adm. in Group II; a prospective teacher in Group III; a Pre-Med in Group I.

Pre-Seminary students certainly need a curriculum like that proposed, majoring usually in Group III. The single complication they present is the foreign language requirement. However, to substitute elementary foreign language study for college work ought simply to be out of the question; both for academic reasons and for the sake of doing right by the church. We should not allow more elementary foreign language than the one year provided in the junior college curriculum to be accredited. Two things follow, I think. (1) A student who wishes to prepare for the Seminary must get his elementary foreign language (i. e., all but one; e.g. Greek) in before his junior college work or else extra- curricularly; except that (2) he will take his *Dutch* during one or more summers devoted to it exclusively (cf. Army courses). There is also the possibility, of course, of providing elementary courses in foreign languages for such students as need or wish them; provided only it be remembered that during the four years of college no student receives credit for more than one year of elementary foreign language, whichever language that be.

If we should wish to graduate in four years teachers who, if they are to get in the 16-18 hours of courses required for certification actually cannot fulfill the requirements of the curriculum for the A. B. such should be given a distinct degree.

And what about other students who cannot be fit into the curriculum proposed?

Nothing prevents the organization of other curricula by way of declensions from the proposed curriculum, provided:

(1) There is need for such declensions, and money to pay for them;
(2) Such curricula are understood not to lead to the A.B. degree;
(3) Such curricula retain the basic idea of the proposed curriculum.

However, discussion of such curricula lies outside the intent of this paper. Of primary importance is the construction of a curriculum that merits an A. B. at graduation; we need to know the nominative case before we can attempt declension.

The Christian School a Prerequisite for and an Outgrowth of the Calvinistic World and Life View

by William H. Jellema, from Fundamentals
In Christian Education,
edited by C. Jaarsma, 1953

Does a world and life view really have "outgrowths"? Does a world and life view after all make any difference in practical life ? Does a world and life view ever determine or even influence human action ?

This subject assumes that the Calvinistic world and life view will have as one of its natural and inevitable outgrowths the Christian school. And in expressing this assumption our subject compactly expresses a fundamental conviction of us of Reformed faith who believe in and maintain what we mean by Christian schools. That this assumption is very commonly made in our argumentation for Christian schools and in our feelings on the matter hardly needs proof. We often, for example, voice our amazement at the fact that many share our Reformed faith and profess to be Calvinists and yet are not to be won to active support of our distinctive educational system. May we not expect the Calvinistic world and life view to grow into enthusiasm for Christian schools? we exclaim. Well, so we might; provided the assumption is correct that world and life views ever do have outgrowths. But do they?

There are, as you know, many who would answer in the negative. World and life views, they say, are purely theoretical abstractions. They are painted pictures that neither produce nor change anything. Life goes its own way, both in nature and in man himself, indifferent to all our theorizing, unaffected by our pretentious "views." Does it make a particle of difference in their motions, for example, whether I believe the sun turns about the earth or the other way around? Did not men's blood circulate long before Harvey discovered its theory? Are not the facts of history facts quite independent of the fashion in which they are construed? Do not the natural forces of supply and demand mock all our economic theories? What is the whole history of philosophy but a series of just such ineffective "world and life views" to which the stream of life was blindly indifferent? And, once more, is the fact that many professed Calvinists are indifferent to Christian schools not itself proof that theory has nothing to do with life and its outgrowths ? We are to understand that only life itself lives; only the forces of life itself are productive. Theory is bloodless; it is in itself dead and has no outgrowths. Man, too, acts as life forces him to act; he is driven by all sorts of instincts and impulses and circumstances; by these his practical conduct is determined. And if a man thinks that his world and life view has in it the power to alter either himself or the world he is as foolish as the courtiers of King Canute who suggested that the king's command could stop the ocean's tide. This negative contention one can, of course, airily wave aside. As a matter of fact, most of us are in the habit of making short shrift of it. Aside from calling attention to its obvious confusion of natural and human behavior, there are especially two ways which we have of summarily dismissing the unwelcome thesis.

One way is very simple: to charge the contention to the ignorance and ill will and bias of opponents; to label them materialists and pragmatists and to suppose that in some mysterious fashion you have thus justified yourself. But this is hardly the way of honesty. For with many of the statements alleged by your opponents as evidence you will find yourself agreeing; some of them—- let us say the statement concerning the futility of philosophical systems— you have yourself on occasion made. We all have our moments when, skeptical of its vital effectiveness, we strongly discount theory. And it is fair to expect of a man who agrees with much of the alleged evidence but refuses to adopt the conclusion that he give some account of himself.

The other way may seem more ingenious. It is to make an exception of our Calvinism. It is to admit that all philosophies are abstractions, but that the Calvinistic world and life view is not. But this way, too, offers no thoroughfare. If all philosophical systems, all systems that give fairly coherent answers to the basic questions which man cannot help asking, if all such are fruitless abstractions, then the Calvinistic world and life view is by its very pretense also a fruitless abstraction.

If then we are to be consistent and honest, we especially who insist on the practical importance of a world and life view, the negative contention is not to be dismissed superficially.

Nor is this issue a purely academic one; the issue has important bearing on our activity in behalf of Christian schools.

We shall, in consequence, have to devote some attention to the question whether a world and life view can and does have vitality, whether it can and does actually have "outgrowths" in practical life. If it cannot, if the assumption implied in the wording of our subject is false, then certainly much of our argumentation for Christian schools has been mere beating of the wind, much of our activity has proceeded on premises that were mistaken. Most of us have fundamentally, but then falsely, supposed that if we built up a truly Calvinistic world and life view the Christian school would follow naturally or, otherwise put, we have supposed, but falsely, that the surest guarantee of the maintenance of Christian schools is a Calvinistic world and life view. If on the other hand a world and life view can and does have issues in practical life, then we should have some knowledge of the conditions under which it does, lest confusion make our activity ineffective or even paralyze it.

Does a world and life view possess vitality? Does it make any difference in practical life? Can we actually trace to its productivity such an institution as a school, for example? Life itself, we all agree, is productive; but is there anything of life in a world and life view? Anything that will in any sense determine human behavior?

In attempting an answer to this question we shall proceed most profitably if we seek some clearer formulation of that on which we all agree. What do we mean by this "life" which is by common agreement productive of practical outgrowths ? What factors, more particularly what inner factors, what factors actually live within me, determine my behavior?

Though it is of course impossible to split up human living into separate adjustments, yet we do use the term life in more than one meaning; and if we are to dispel some of the confusion about world and life views and their vitality, we must distinguish the main senses in which we use the term. In thus distinguishing the main levels or ranks of human living we shall unavoidably also be making distinctions within the objective world to which man adjusts himself. Our concern is primarily, however, with the levels or kinds of living that make up the "life" which a world and life view does or does not have. Recognizing that human life is always some kind of unified process, we want nevertheless to consider whether among the inner factors influencing behavior on each of its levels we also find world and life views, or whether a world and life view must remain on each level or in each meaning of life an otiose abstraction, a system of propositions as dead as the multiplication table.

The term life may have, first of all, a meaning which is very obvious. Life may mean a process of adjustment which is biological, which is not essentially rational, which is much like that of the animals. Eating, breathing, fighting the forces of disease within our bodies, even sensing lights and sounds and pleasures and pains, and being impelled by instincts and urges, and manifesting what look like rudimentary forms of judgment—all this may be called living. Here we all live; here there is vitality and productivity; here there are "outgrowths." But so long as we remain here the decisive inner factor is instinct; if the term life could never mean more than biological living, world and life views would not only be unproductive, they would not even exist. Animals live and act, but never because some world and life view is productive in and through them; and if human behavior were purely biological we should have to concede that the assumption of our subject is false.

But there is another level or type of life, one of which only human beings are capable. Here life means our production of and individual reaction to the social institutions about us—the family, the state and its laws, society's conventions, group habits and customs. This is what living means when I play my part in buying and selling, in banking, in owning property, in voting, in shaking hands, in driving an automobile through traffic, in establishing a system of currency, in practising medicine or law, in maintaining school. On this level we all live. And how vitally we all live here ! No mere abstract theory, this social adjustment, but vigorous, productive, practical life.

Such social life is not found among the animals. To create such a social environment and for the individual to live a life of such social adjustment is characteristic only of man with his rational and moral nature Such living requires reason, it requires symbols—a ten dollar bill is a symbol; so is a word; so our gestures —it requires intelligence; it requires some insight into causes and consequences. And such living also requires morality; man must inhibit his biological instincts; he must make choices; he is under obligation to adjust himself this way rather than that; he is under law. In short, here is not only living; but in contrast to life in its merely biological sense, here is rational moral living. Here appears a new determinant of behavior— not instinct, but moral reason. And (we should be disposed immediately to add) that proves the assumption that world and life views have "outgrowths." For if social living is rational, if it requires reason to live socially, then surely it requires a world and life view; and then surely the different modes of social behavior are the "outgrowths" of differing world and life views.

But can the assumption be proved quite so easily and superficially? The conductor who punches your ticket, the grocer who sells you food, the banker who loans you money on a note, the man who reads your gas meter these are all people to whom you adjust yourself, people with whom you live socially. Do you need a world and life view to do it? The state legislature, the traffic courts, the English language, the United States post office, the schools, the newspapers, private property — these are all institutions or traditions, adjustment to which makes part of what you mean by social living. But do you need a world and life view for that?

Suppose we answer in the affirmative. Suppose we contend that social behavior in response to all these does in the final analysis imply at least some kind of life view. The contention could probably be established. The question is still whether we have now proved that a world and life view in the sense in which our subject intends the phrase is actually a moving factor, does actually make any practical difference. For, even leaving to one side as of lesser consequence the objection that the tracing of direct and conscious connection between a specific act and a life view is often well-nigh impossible both for the actor himself and for the observer, there is the consideration that the "reason" in social life may be no more than group reason; in other words, that what we think is a "world and life view" may be no more than mere group custom. And this consideration is of definite importance to our subject.

It cannot be denied that the "reason" involved in social institutions and in socialized adjustments of the individual is to a great extent the implicit reason of historical processes. Language, for example, is rational, yet it is not consciously and deliberately sought. Language is the product not of world and life views but of the forces of social life that seem to go their own way within us as individuals, the product of life that seems to live itself in spite of us, the product of a rationality that seems to be at best a group rationality acting through me. And so with our choices. They seem controlled by custom and convention. Even my choice of group seems controlled by the group in the training it gives me. Both reason and morality seem conventionalized; group pressure would seem to be the determining factor in social behavior. There are "outgrowths" on the level of social living; and hence there are, of course, changes. But these changes are not brought about by world and life views; rather, the basic life force assumes a variety of group forms: racial, economic, vocational, and so on, and the constant interaction and conflict of these various groups prompts social changes. All "outgrowths" are the result of the slow pressure of group life, of group rationality; it produced the institutions and groups, and acting within us the same force determines our behavior. World and life views even on the rational moral level are not causative and motivating factors; they are implied if at all only as grammar is implied by language. Grammar did not produce language and neither do world and life views produce behavior; when we assume they do, the superficiality and ignorance and bias are all on our side.

I have sought to state an ancient position which is maintained today not only by economic and other determinates, by some evolutionists, and by a certain school of historians but which seems to find a good deal of support from an unprejudiced analysis of our actual behavior.

Have we who maintain the assumption basic to our subject anything further to say?

First of all, I think we shall concede that group pressure is a factor in behavior, just as we concede the biological. We shall have to concede more. We shall have to admit that this factor is one of a strength and of an importance we all usually fail to recognize; we shall admit that the conflict of group pressures determines practical "outgrowths" in every man's life to a far greater degree than individualists and radicals and all of us live to acknowledge. Take, for example our attitude toward private property, or toward bankers; or take our notion of what "success" means.

Further, from the admission we shall draw a lesson of great importance to our Christian school movement. It is this. To the extent that the Christian school is the outgrowth of the pressure of group forces, to that extent the Christian school cause will have vitality only while the custom from which it issues has vitality. As long as we remain Dutch or middle-class or immigrant, or whatever the right word to characterize the inner vitality of our group life, as long in other words as a specific custom can retain its hold on coming generations, so long the Christian school may continue. And though we meanwhile flatter ourselves and each other that the Christian school is the "outgrowth" of a world and life view, we shall some day awaken to the fact that we were mistaken. When the vitality lent by life to our group custom is spent, the world and life view will appear in all its native though gilded poverty. My world and life was spending borrowed money. And while it is going bankrupt I shall have to twist and squirm and resort to intellectual contortions and be obsessed by fear and attempt coercion— in short, behave as I usually behave in analogous situations in the financial world—only to find that the collateral has lost all value. Or shall we be more literal. If such is the status of our world and life view and of the Christian school, if they are no more than the "outgrowths" of the vitality of a group custom, then when group or individual encounters other groups and customs, the world and life view will lose even its false appearance of inherent vitality and the Christian school will cease to be. If one adds that as time goes on such group conflict is inevitable for our people, but little foresight is needed to predict the inevitable outcome.

And now, the concession made, and its lesson drawn , what we defenders of the assumption have still to say stands out the clearer: The term life has a third and hitherto unmentioned meaning; thus far we have treated life as though nowhere in it is there freedom, responsibility. But socialized living is not the only grade possible only to men. Man's rational moral nature is not limited to it. There is a form of life beyond, and there is probably no man who does not in the inner recesses of his own soul experience something of it also; who does not, shall we say, on some occasion hear the voice of transcendent duty, in some measure respond loyally to the universals of science, sometimes sense the pain of accusing conscience, sometimes glimpse the eternal depths of love, sometimes yearn after a beauty not of this world, and who does not on such occasion recognize and in some way adjust himself to a reality beyond nature and beyond society? He does not question its control over him, he borrows life from it; he finds responsibility for and life in yielding and sacrificing self to it. Such life is life beyond group and custom though not necessarily subversive of them.

In short, if we remember that the forms of false religion are legion, we shall insist that there is besides biological and social life a third type or meaning of life which is always implicitly religious. We need not here attempt a complete definition of religion. Sufficient to our present purpose is the fact that man on this level finds his god. That fact makes this living religious. It is personal and selfconscious. It is, of course, a life in and of faith. And every man has in this sense a faith of some sort, a faith in some god.

And in finding his god, man finds his perspective for judging all of reality and finds his absolute value for all living. In other words, in finding his god man finds the germinal principles of his real world and life view. Your world and life view is here alive with the personal vitality of your religion; alive with what for you—be it falsely, even —is life from and with God. And because the two, religion, and personal germinal world and life view, are bound inseparably, your personal world and life view will necessarily be vital, cause changes, have "outgrowths" in behavior. Once more, that holds of false religions as well as of the true. If Socialism or Naturalism or Modernity or Art or Science is your religion, if in any one of these you find your god and your basic perspective, then it will have "outgrowths" as well as will any of the forms of what we popularly mean by false religions.

A world and life view is productive if it be one's personal, one's religious world and life view, germinal or embryonic as this may be.

But will the vitality of such a view extend to social living? Or is it not perhaps a vitality manifesting itself only in our individual consciousness? When we say that this level is personal, do we not limit its scope to just the individual's heart? Have we not implicitly admitted that it has no effect on education and schools, for example, and on institutional and social behavior generally ? Must we not still leave the determination of the latter to the pressure of group rationality and group life ?

To many an interpreter such practical ineffectiveness not only is in fact characteristic of religion, but is actually the boast of Protestantism. The Reformation and Protestantism generally are to be construed as an insistence that religion belongs wholly to man's inner consciousness.

A little reflection, however, will show that religion as the revelation of my absolute interest and value will and does necessarily affect social life. It will do so either by adding interest and value to social life or by detracting value and interest from social life. If Art is my religion, for example, the result may well be that socialized living loses value; if so, my practical behavior will be affected not only through but also in spite of group pressures. Likewise if Science is my religion. Likewise in certain periods of the Middle Ages; man's interpretation of Christianity and of the social corruption of the day being what it was. If on the other hand, Socialism or Nationalism, for example, should be my religion, or any other that makes of an institution or custom its god, then socialized living will have increased value and religious life will flow into social channels. Personal world and life view affects social behavior either negatively or positively—which, depends on the religion—but necessarily in some way.

You will recall that our analysis was to be interested primarily in the inner factors determining behavior in order to discover whether among these we could find a world and life view. If the analysis is correct, a world and life view borrows an apparent vitality from social living, and this vitality is vigorous while the custom or tradition or institution lives; no longer. A world and life view obtains real vitality from religious faith.

To this point we have left out of consideration the objective truth of the world and life view in question. I wish now to turn to the view I believe the best presentation of objective truth.

Our previous general conclusions apply also to it. The Calvinistic world and life view is a view with group pressure behind it and to that extent shares whatever vigor our social custom still has. But happily it is more. It is rooted in the Christian religion, in God's having revealed Himself to you and me through Christ. Here, in this life from God, lies the real spring of its vitality. And only in the measure that in your case or mine what is called the Calvinistic world and life view roots here will it necessarily have "outgrowths" and is there any guarantee that it will continue to bear fruit. And only as it is rooted here is it rooted in true liberty, is it free from narrowness and tortuous intellectual twistings—as no mere institutional rooting ever is—is it free from the obsessions and phobias of mere group psychology, is it free to grow by all truth and to nourish itself on all truly human experience, is it aggressive and forceful and the transmitter of conviction also to the next generation. This, I submit, is another important lesson.

And will the Calvinistic world and life view, even when religiously rooted and necessarily affecting practical behavior, also of necessity issue in the Christian school?

Calvinism is, of course, a specific world and life view, even within the group of Christian world and life views. I shall select aspects of Calvinism pertinent to our present subject. Two important facts should be borne in mind, however. The first is that an organic world and life view cannot be split up into separated propositions—no more than life can be split; the other, closely related, that the further we get away from the center and from the germinal principles of a personal world and life view, the less apodeictic and categorical we can be. The following statements lose significance except they be taken together as a living unit in a vital organism.

The Calvinistic world and life view characteristically insists on the indispensability to right living of a life view—a view of what man's duties and obligations are, of what are the true values of living, a view of what man's life ought to be. This emphasis places us in opposition to a popular attitude which, in its reaction to hypocrisy, would minimize all theory or view and would one-sidedly emphasize mere conduct, which may even deny that a life view can have any "outgrowths."

It insists that such a life view is personal, is religiously rooted, that its conception of duties and challenges is the result of personal loyalty to what are considered absolute standards. Life views are not only social habit.

It insists that a life view, religious as one's real life view basically is, is the result of a view of God and is therefore, at least germinally, a world view as well—a view regarding nature, man, and God in the relations.

It insists that integral to right living is the explication of this world view in as coherent and systematic fashion as possible. In other words the development of the germinal principles is not a mere academic luxury; it is of the essence of our living in obedience to the will of God.

It insists that such a world view is to be intelligible and coherent and morally satisfactory and true, its center must be the God who revealed himself in the Christ of the Scriptures the source of the ultimate principles for our world and life view. Since He is the one true God, the true world and life view is the expression of his will.

It insists — and in organic relation to the previous statements this is of prime importance to our subject—it insists that if I am to realize with intellectual assurance the truth of the Christian world and life view and if I am to live obediently to the will of God. I must hear in every contact with reality the ringing challenge: Search till you find in me also a witness to the truth of Christian world and life view; search till you find in me a revelation of God.

No argument is needed, I take it, to show that such a world and life view rooted in the Christian faith will issue in Christian education. That it must necessarily issue in what we today mean by the Christian school is not so obvious A personally accepted world and life view, though it always takes precedence over institutional life and if, like Calvinism, it be of the positive type seeks to express itself in social action, need not necessarily create its own social instrument. The practical situation, socially, the institutional situation to which I must adjust myself, must be pondered, evaluated.

As concerns schools, then, the practical situation is important that as a result of various modern movements American group life has issued in schools which seek to limit themselves to neutral territory, territory not affected by nor directly affecting world and life views. Schooling has become secularized. Those who defend the institution need not be people who despair of any objective truth whatever nor who are indifferent to all world and life views; every man has some 'religious" world and life view. But whatever a defender may hold, the institution is an historical product. If we could conscientiously be satisfied with it, if we could express ourselves through it, we should. One must have serious reasons for resisting the pressure of one's group, for breaking with history. There is little if any glory in the mere independence of our schools.

Now our inability with our Calvinistic world and life view to be satisfied does not arise from maintaining that there is nowhere the possibility of what is meant by neutrality. Of course there are many "neutral" facts—that is to say, facts accepted by all, whatever their world and life view; indeed what are really facts must be accepted by all; thus certainly least of all a Calvinist objects to the facts of modern science, even though arrived at by all impersonal method.

Why not, then, assign such neutral facts to the school, leaving the question of their significance and other disputed points to other agencies like home and church? Here is the crucial question. There are different ways of answering, but the one basic and determining consideration is, I believe, that education to us as Christians, as Calvinists who are religiously persuaded to the truth of our world and life view that education to us means more and something other than we can in justice expect the customary schools to give.

The pivotal difference is not that we believe education should also include training in religion; the home and the church might provide that element. Nor is it that we believe the school should supplant the home or the church or both; we accept a division of labor between the three. Nor is it that we believe theology the only science our children must learn; on the contrary, we should be nearer the truth in emphasizing our catholic acceptance of the importance of all the sciences.

The point lies rather in something more basic than any social institution—in our religious life as Christians and in our view of life and the world which is there rooted. Not to repeat all the characteristics, it lies particularly in the Calvinist's characteristic (though not novel) insistence that God is not only the object in the narrower sense of religious faith and devotion but is also the ground and end of all existence and truth and value; or, to say the same thing as it affects man subjectively, that religious faith is confirmed by and itself furnishes the ultimate explanation of and motivation for all human experience and activity; in short, that religion and reason and morality are inextricably interwoven. Now such a conviction means in the sphere of intellect and knowledge that there is to be not a mere deductive development within my head of theoretical conclusions from the germinal principles of my personal, my Christian world and life view but such a development of the germinal principles that every widening of my intellectual horizons, every deepening of my insight, testifies in its moment of existence to the absolute reality and worth of God; a development such that in every new intellectual contact I find confirmation of my Christian world and life view; a development such that there constantly grows within me the intelligent certainty that only in the light of that view can my bits of knowledge become intelligible. And in the sphere of morality and character building this conviction means that my every experience of worth strengthens and deepens my appreciation of and loyalty to God; and again that the worth of God and loyalty to Him is experienced as the value of every bit of human living. The cutting edge of our view is that intellectual or moral growth and the religious life are in each specific instance and at that moment inseparable; they are aspects of one and the same event, of one and the same step in the process of my growth.

That is what our world and life view means for our thinking and acting to us who have long left school behind; that is what it means for what we may rightly call your and my education. But that is also what it means for the education of our children. Because we are religiously persuaded of the truth of our view we want our children trained in it as a personal, as a religious view of life and the world. And if it is to be "their personal" as a Calvinist must interpret that phrase then this view must be for them one whose truth is increasingly witnessed by all that they learn as they learn it, by all with which they become acquainted as they make its acquaintance. Religion and truth and right education unite in this demand. Our children are to he trained in so knowing and so acting.

And if education is to mean that, we cannot in obvious justice expect the customary schools to give it. Just as obviously if the parent or the minister is somehow to provide this element he will not only have to be constantly present in the classroom and have the knowledge which the teacher possesses but will himself have to do the teaching.

Such I take to be the real reason why a Calvinistic world and life view demands not only Christian education but, under the circumstances, what we mean by the Christian school as an independent institution. You may state the same point in other language. I have throughout had in mind the implications of my subject.

That is why the Christian school is "outgrowth" of our world and life view. And that, too, is why the Christian school is prerequisite. Of course you will want an independent school if you want in the most efficient manner to preserve distinctive group ideals merely as such. But then you might be better off with, let us say, a Dutch school. The Christian school is prerequisite if you mean to maintain a world and life view which has vigor because based on personal living and because to its truth and value all of life and experience and contact with reality and all growth increasingly witness. If we intend our children to be strong in their possession of our world and life view, if we intend that with them too it shall be a matter not of mere custom but of living on the level of personality, if we intend that with them also it shall bind itself in with religious faith and be productive, then the Christian school is prerequisite.

To know what we mean when we state that the Christian school in our sense of the term is both "outgrowth" and prerequisite of our Calvinism, one must on the one hand know our world and life view as germinally present in our Christian faith and one must on the other hand appreciate the strength and importance of social and institutional pressure. I have attempted to suggest something of what is involved in both these aspects.

Henry Zylstra:
Editor Introduction

Henry Zylstra, professor of English at Calvin College (1941-56) died at the early age of 47 while serving as senior lecturer in English and American Literature at the Free University of Amsterdam as a Fullbright scholar.

In his capacity as a Calvin Professor of English he took a particular interest in education, and often gave speeches at teachers conventions or wrote articles in the *Reformed Journal*. After his passing many of these speeches and articles, both on literature and on education, were published under the title of *Testament of Vision*, 1958. In it were included seven on education. Several of these have been included here to capture for the next generation of teachers and would-be teachers the eloquent expression of a self-proclaimed traditionalist and believer in liberal education at all levels of Christian schooling.

The first essay on "Modern Philosophy of Education" contains clear theses about what curriculum and what goals characterize traditional education. It also contains his clearest statement of the nature of human beings when he says "man is an horizon in which two worlds meet." Grounding this in his own list of Greek and Christian thinkers, he represents well the dualistic tradition in anthropology. The remaining essays put flesh on his affirmations, as well as, especially in "The Contemplative Life," reveal his biblical and creedal grounding in both Old Testament and New Testament sources.

These excerpts are reprinted with permission of Wm. B. Eerdmans Publishing Co.

Modern Philosophy of Education

by Henry Zylstra

If an ardent progressivist, or experimentalist, or functionalist, were to describe a traditionalist, he would, particularly if he had just been nettled by another book, say, from Mortimer Adler, probably come through with a picture something like this. He is a medievalist. He arrogates authority to himself because of something he calls reason. But you must know that this reason of his is anything but the scientific verification of evidence. It is a sort of hypostatization of his own *a priori* and factually unsupported personal opinion. He is also a blind conservative whose attitude towards all proposals for social change is *caution*. He talks such jargon as mental discipline, formal discipline, memory, faculty psychology, transfer of training, ancient languages, and good grammar. He talks also about the training of the mind, as though the mind were an isolable entity which, like the blade of a knife, can be sharpened by repeating the paradigms of Greek verbs. He thinks of that mind, not as an active principle of dynamic energy, but as a warehouse that must be stuffed full of data. He holds that it makes sense to teach a boy Latin, though the language is dead. Apparently, therefore, he wants to teach it on the ground that the boy hates it, and that it so constitutes excellent frictional material for generating what he calls discipline. He is an intellectualist. In blunt imperviousness to modern psychological inquiry, he seems never to have discovered along with the late Professor Dewey that "mind is primarily a verb" if, indeed, it be distinguishable at all from experience itself. He makes much of individualism, having apparently never heard that man is a gregarious animal whose natural habitat for growth is society. He holds to a sort of archetypal model of ideal education which he considers just as suitable for a kid in Chicago in 1953 as it was for an uppercrust Greek in Plato's Athens or an English gentleman in the reign of Elizabeth. He is always talking books,

63

great books, classics—paragons of excellence, apparently —most of them ancient, and recommends these as the best medium for education. So he ignores the environment, the situation, and our actual needs for life-adjustment, and for swift adaptation to the changing needs of a changing society. He likes to quote the old-timers: Pope, for instance: "The proper study of mankind is man," or Roger Ascham: "Learning teacheth more in one year than experience in twenty." He is the sort of fellow who might have had a place in the closed universe, the closed society, and the closed mind of Medieval Europe. But since modernity has opened these up, we shall have to abandon Ascham in favor of Pater who said, "Not the fruit of experience but experience itself is the end."

Such the *cartoon* that a nettled progressivist might draw of traditionalism in education. What is the *portrait* like, what is such traditionalism really like?

Its main feature, I think, its leading idea, is its idea of man. That idea is, frankly, a religious and philosophical idea. It assumes man's relationship with an eternal, and it is not entirely verifiable in sense experience. It represents more than a linking together of observable and measurable data, and presents man, consequently, as more than an assembly of physical, biological, psychological and other phenomena. Traditionalism knows, of course, that man is natural, and that in this nature he is a creature subject to the laws and circumstances of the natural order. It knows, too, that in this nature, man is as suitable and rewarding an object for study by an empirical scientific method as any.

But traditional education is insistent that man is an horizon in which two worlds meet, the natural and the spiritual. And It holds that it is in his spiritual character that man's characteristically human nature consists. This is his uniqueness. It gives him his independence and his wholeness. It constitutes him a self. He is not, therefore, accounted for as a piece of the continuum of nature. He is a whole, a little universe, a microcosm. He has consciousness, rationality. He lives in two orders; he can penetrate phenomenal reality, sense experience, get behind them to universals, laws, principles, causes, and ends. This it is that makes knowledge, science, philosophy proper, satisfying, exuberant and possible to him. In fact, he seeks his freedom, his fulfillment as a human being, precisely in such progressively realized knowledge of reality. It is this uniqueness of the human being in the created order that we Christians know as man's lordship, or sovereignty, owing to the endowment, at creation, of the image of God. Such human freedom is the thing that gives culture its large importance, it being only mind that can make culture.

Something like that, presumably, is the idea of man which governed his education in its essential structure, from Plato and Aristotle, on through Augustine, and Calvin, into the Renaissance of Bacon and Milton, and beyond that to Matthew Arnold and his kind in the last century, and to Sir Richard Livingstone, Jacques Maritain, and, yes, Mortimer Adler in ours. Maritain, at least, thinks that he can give out a definition of man which could serve as a basis for the civilization of our Western World, and be accepted by Greek, Jew, Protestant, and Catholic Christian. This is his definition: "Man is animal endowed with reason whose supreme dignity is in the intellect; he is a free individual in personal relation with God whose supreme righteousness consists in voluntarily obeying the law of God; and man is a sinful and wounded creature called to the freedom of grace, whose supreme perfection consists of love."

If this idea, an idea which, in short, I shall call the idea of the freedom of the mind of man, is the leading idea of traditional education, be it as assumption or as articulated philosophy, then traditional education will object to experimentalist, progressivist functionalist, or the New Education, only in proportion to the extent that it no longer makes that assumption about the nature of man. That at bottom is the only question I am asking about the New Education: does it do justice to the freedom of mind to the fulfillment of man's characteristically human destiny to know?

Some of us think that it does not. It is the sort of thought one of my colleagues at the College had when he said, in reference to the title of Mr. Randall's book, *The Making of the Modern Mind,* that he would like to write a book with the title *The Modern Unmaking of Mind.* What he was thinking of also was the threat as he supposed, in modern educational thought, to the specifically spiritual character of that mind, to its naturally human aspirations to freedom, and to its progressive fulfillment in the knowledge of reality.

I for one, together with many observers, see something of such a threat to man's humanity in the educational philosophy of the late Professor Dewey. This thinker, following in the wake mainly of William James, is of course regarded as the key figure in the New Education. What goes on for a human being when a person learns is something like this for Mr. Dewey. As an experiencing creature a man runs into a difficulty. This disturbs his equilibrium, his poise, his sense of well-being. He then makes use of something he has in his organism, which is called his intelligence, to take the measure of the obstacle and find resources for removing it. He emerges from the problem thus solved, ready for another embarrassment, another difficulty of the situation, another rub in the environment, and another solution. Now this sort of use of the intelligence can hardly be called, as Maritain puts it, a "progressive grasping of the object of knowledge," or as Plato puts it, "an inner beholding of the truth." This testing of validity by consequence, by the degree of success attained in adjustment to environment (and such is the notion lying behind the phrase, "education for life adjustment") is to make of the mind a means, a technique, and a tool. There is no freedom here, no rationality, no possibility for recognizing, determining, and judging ends. It assumes that experience is self-vindicating, and that education can only assist the human organism to grow, as Brubacher puts it, "in whatever direction a novelly emerging future renders most feasible." The second term of that phrase, "the human animal," seems appropriate now, for animal growth is nothing more than morphological development along fixed lines, and animal growth is assisted also by resources native to the organism for coping with obstacles and taking advantage of opportunity, whether by sharp quills as in the porcupine, or swift feet as in the rabbit. This notion of cleverness owing to intelligence in the struggle with nature for life is therefore exactly described as evolutionary, in that there is no fulfillment in ends, as pragmatic in that the test of intelligence is consequence, as skeptical in that there is in it no such thing as philosophical proving, and as deterministic in that the situation, the environment, whether natural or social, is the real governor of life.

To revert now to the idea of traditional education—the idea of the free human mind by education progressively realizing the truth of reality, I call attention to some of the major traditionalist emphases, some of those, namely, in which there is often a clash with the emphases of the New Education. Let me put the first one this way: *Knowledge is more important than ability.* Because it is by truth, by reality, by revelation, that man's mind is formed, is patterned, is fulfilled, traditional education holds that content is important, that subject matter matters. Now this idea that an organized program of studies, representative of reality, representative, too of a hierarchy of importances, should be followed out in schools and colleges, is an idea which is under very formidable threat in American education. We in Michigan have in recent years got a phenomenon, known as a college agreement plan, by which the colleges of the state are asked to agree that they will admit students from high schools irrespective of the content and organization of courses pursued. The idea is: not what a student has had, nor in connection with what he has had it, but what ability he generated in handling it. That's animal training—you can do it with a horse. History? No, couldn't see any use in it. Foreign languages? Look, I'm going to be a business executive. I can hire a Mexican if I have to know Spanish. Science? A little physiology. English? Yeah, I had some of that. But the grade is good. The boy must have handled his social attitudes skillfully. What can you do with him in college? Why, whet some more ability, of course.

Traditional education never operated that way. "The crucial error," says Mr. Hutchins, "is that of holding that nothing is more important than anything else, that there can be no order of intellectual goods . . . nothing central, nothing peripheral, nothing basic, and nothing superficial." Nothing but method, technique, ability, and training, without any mastery of basic instrument-knowledges, without any discipline in either scientific or philosophical-theoretical thinking, and without any confrontation of the student by that world of history and culture in which the mind can realize and universalize itself and fulfill its humanness "In such conditions," says Hutchins, "the course of study goes to pieces, because there is nothing to hold it together." It does. Lacking the principle of the underlying unity of all knowledge, the curriculum breaks the bounds of rational system and spreads out over phenomena. Scales, hierarchies of importance go by the board. Mr. Tenenbaum, biographer of Kilpatrick, exponent in turn of Mr. Dewey, records this experience: ["I have] seen a class of 600 and more graduate students in education, comprising teachers, principals, superintendents, vote their opinion in overwhelming numbers, that Greek, Latin, and Mathematics offered the least likely possibilities for educational growth; and with almost the same unanimity they placed dancing, dramatics, and doll dressing high on this list in this regard." The curriculum goes to pieces. I suggest that traditional education with its imitation of nature, its intrinsic respect for reality, rightly insisted on a rationally determined content and organization of courses. It was right in preferring natural philosophy, moral philosophy, and divinity to courses in practical skills, in social attitudes, in community values, and in "character education." It is reality that patterns the mind; it is truth that forms and fulfills.

That takes us to a second emphasis, a corollary of the traditionalist insistence that content matters. It is this, also greatly threatened by the contemporary educational theory and practice: namely, that *the object of education is more important than the subject in the training of the teacher.* I mean that in the training of the teacher, history is more important than Johnny. Modern education owes a great deal to the psychological study of the pupil and the correspondingly required methods most effective in teaching him. I, too, blush for some of the crimes committed by stupid traditionalists on the dawning intellect, and the spiritual intuition, and the creative reach, and the aspirations to the freedom of understanding, of the young schoolboy. Shakespeare suffered it out, and spoke afterwards of "the whining schoolboy with his satchel and shining morning face creeping like a snail unwillingly to school." We have learned from some of the moderns that interest is indispensable to learning, though many an ancient, Socrates, for example, including that old Roger Ascham, had guessed as much. But the source of the interest is not the pupil, nor the teacher, but the truth. A man has an affinity for the truth. The teacher must stand before the pupil in the authority of the truth. He begins with insights, not merely with difficulties. He must be educated in truth before he is trained in teaching. Johnny, as an object of known man, is not as important a subject as Homer, and the teacher should know Homer before he knows Johnny, and indeed, in order to know Johnny. The tendency and the fact in our time of some teacher training schools to segregate people who plan to teach from other people, to give them psychology limited to empirically observable data about pupils, and to support this by as many methods courses as there are subjects in the modern curriculum is well calculated to produce teachers who do not have the authority of mind. For it is the object of knowledge, rather than the pupil, the teacher, or the method, that must do the education.

A third traditionalist emphasis is its predilection for what are called the humanities. As I see it, traditional education considers culture a more important medium for education than nature. It also fosters natural science, of course, for natural science richly rewards the student with a human knowledge of phenomena and of the principles which explain them. But nature as an object of knowledge can be regarded as standing lower in the order of reality than culture as an object of knowledge, for the reason that in this subject the human, the moral, the free, the rational element is itself present. The substitution, therefore, of an exclusively scientific education for a humanistic education, or the subordination of the humanities to the sciences, or the teaching of the humanities as natural sciences—and one or another of these possibilities obtains in many schools—can represent an abandonment of the traditionalist idea of man. The last is perhaps the greatest threat, namely, the naturalization of history, society, politics, law, literature, and the like, by transforming them into studies of natural, cultural, or social circumstance.

That point, too, as a fourth consideration, has a corollary perhaps, in the traditional insistence on the educational value of books, letters, humane letters, great books, classics. These seem to traditionalists to have authority, to be their own embodiments of what a colleague calls the "funded wisdom" of the ages, vital, quickening, redolent of truth, the sort of thing to which mind leaps up in recognition of mind, in which mind enlarges and deepens itself, realizes itself. Of course you can ask on whose authority they are so great. Arnold called them the best that has been said and thought. Huxley in philosophical skepticism turned away from them as being matters of opinion. Huxley said, "Science appeals not to authority," as humane letters do, "but to nature." He identified nature with phenomenal, empirically observable reality. He was wrong. First, because nature is not science until mind has intervened. Next, because good mind is a good authority to appeal to. Now the classics are precisely large and comprehensive human readings of life. They chart the course of the human spirit, and exhibit alternative answers to man's religious and philosophical quest. In , them, as Wordsworth said, there is the breath and finer spirit of knowledge, the soul of science, the steady and whole view the harvesting of history in its concrete actuality. It is just the thing to quicken the mind's yearnings for fulfillment, to satisfy the inner beholding of truth. To supplant them by experience life, laboratories, or textbooks, though they may well be supplemented by these, is to denominate something other than knowledge the end of education.

One is not, naturally, going to have access to such funded wisdom in the classics unless one can read. I make it a fifth point. The traditionalist holds that the three R's make sense. Consider then whether there be not some departure from an idea of the uniqueness of human nature in such an utterance as this, which was addressed by a principal to the National Association of Secondary School Principals. He was being progressive with a vengeance: "When we come," he said, "to the realization that not every child has to read, figure, write, and spell . . . we shall be on the way to improving the Junior High School curriculum. We shall some day accept the fact that it is just as illogical to assume that every boy must be able to read as that each one must be able to perform on the violin, that it is no more reasonable to require that each girl shall learn to spell than it is that each one shall learn to bake a cherry pie." Certainly it would seem that when the doctrine of individual difference, of unique aptitude and interest reaches such a point, it cuts itself off from that common core of studies so long held to be the *sine qua non* of the education of democratic people.

The traditionalist, to make another point now, wants foreign languages in education as part of his learning the first R, that is reading. He wants them not for reasons of trade and holiday. He wants them not solely for their utility in research. He wants them mainly because he thinks that an adequately philosophical mind is not possible unless it is disciplined by the rationality or logic of the literature of our civilized West. It wants foreign languages, and particular foreign languages, for Arnold's reason when he said: "The civilized world (the only kind in which mind can be educated and community is possible) is to be regarded as now being, for intellectual purposes, one great confederation, whose members have for their proper outfit a knowledge of Greek Roman, and Eastern antiquity, and of one another." Presumably this knowledge is not just a knowledge about, but a knowledge of. It is not just information. It is a sharing of mind unified by something like a common idea. This idea forms us. We need it for our self-fulfillment. The best cultures represent that idea best. They would seem to be the Greek, the Roman, the German, and the French. And this too. Language, unless one abstracts it from reality to the point at which it becomes a mechanical signal system, is one of the spiritual arts. It reveals reality, truth: it speaks to mind, mind responds to it. But then there must be no divorce between the sign and the thought signified. Traditional education thought of the two as a unit, so that as Shakespeare said, language can be called the discourse of reason. "I endowed thy purposes with words that made them known," said Shakespeare. There is rationality in language.

A final emphasis. The new education makes so much of the social situation. That is good. The older education made much of the social in man also. But at this point we must be careful lest the social become again nothing more than a conditioning environment, such as the soil is to a plant. One does not get humanity, in the sense of the freedom of the human spirit, back into education by simply assuring himself that the environment is not natural but social. For the social is hardly distinguishable from the natural if one does not acknowledge that society, human society, as distinguished from instinctively gregarious animal groups, is achieved by free consent. There must be interiority of the personal self, personal conscience, deep-seated independence if there is to be society. Hence, as Maritain puts it, the essence of education does not lie in adapting a potential citizen to the conditions and interactions of social life, but in first making *man,* and by this very fact in preparing a citizen. Otherwise society is a force, and man is its victim.

But I must be breaking off this talk, till you probe me for explanation. My drift is that an idea of man is at stake in the difference between the older and the new education.

Address, Principals Convention, September, 1950.

Christian Education

by Henry Zylstra

My subject tonight is *Christian Education*. Perhaps I ought first of all to give you in a single sentence what it is I mean to say. It is this: Christian education must be both education and Christian if it is to justify itself and successfully meet the secular challenge. That is the thrust of what I have to say. Our schools must be schools—that for one thing. And then they must be Christian—that for another thing. And in making these two points I shall want to insist, of course, that they must be both at once.

I speak of these obvious considerations again, because it is easy to have the school without the Christian. All we should have to do then is a fairly competent job of handling the curriculum as it is done in any good school, and do it in what we might call a Christian atmosphere, and so justify ourselves. That would be easy. It would be easy, further, to have the Christian without the school, that is, to make what we call the "devotional" element the principal thing, and to pay little more than lip service to the subjects of the curriculum. Either of these would be easy. What is hard is to have the Christian and the school in vital and vigorous interdependence with each other all the while. But that is precisely what we are trying for, and what we must have, if our schools are to solve the problem which secular, neutral, or public education cannot solve.

Our schools must be schools. Let us look at that first. It is worth a good deal of attention. I hope, in fact, that you will think it hardly less important than the other point, namely, that they must be Christian. It is well, I think, to be reminding ourselves constantly that ours is an educational enterprise. It is not, at least not primarily, an evangelical enterprise. We call this work of our schools kingdom work, and rightly so, and the kingdom of Christ is, of course, a spiritual kingdom, and it is most certainly the business of our schools to train our boys and girls, our young men and women, for responsible citizenship in it. But to say that it is the function of our schools

71

to train for citizenship in a spiritual kingdom is not to say that the schools ought so much as possible to be churches. They are not churches. They have their own function, and it is a different function from that of the church, although, happily, not unrelated to it. It is at church and not at school that our children are by the grace of God made members of the covenant in baptism. It is at church and not at school that the offer of salvation is presented, the word of truth is preached, the communion of the saints is exercised in the sacrament. These things, and more, are proper to the church as church. They stand high in our hearts, higher than anything else. We think them the most important things. In this we are right. However, it is by no means an implication of this that we can think of the schools as Christian and important only insofar as they extend into the week-days the offices of the church.

There are Christians, though usually not Reformed Christians, or at least not mature Reformed Christians, who cannot get very excited about Christian schools as schools. They are so eager for the honor of what they call the religious and the spiritual in life, that they hesitate to think anything else of much importance. Such Christians are as likely as not to be comparatively indifferent to the curriculum, to the cultural subject matters. We understand such Christians, feel something of the attraction of the same idea, perhaps, in ourselves. The Christian, after all, finds himself called to the Christian life in the midst of the world. When regeneration, conversion, sanctification begin to operate in him, he finds himself, particularly in some times and places, estranged, opposed to, the culture, the whole complex of life, that presses in upon him from all sides. It bears down upon him mercilessly from every quarter from the business, the social, the political, the military, the scientific, and aesthetic worlds. We therefore understand the Christian who is inclined, especially at first, to apply his faith in negative ways, and to look upon science, and culture, and history, and the rest as things alien to his religion. There is, I say, something appealing about it that those who seem sometimes to be the most saintly among us, who prize a close walk with God in mystical communion with Christ, should not only by-pass culture, but even attack it as a worldly idol. Then texts begin coming to mind, and beckoning for distortion, like that one "but not many mighty and not many noble," and "If thy right eye offend thee, pluck it out," and "Seek ye first the kingdom and its righteousness," and "Sell all that thou hast," and many besides.

Such Christians are rightly aware of an antithesis between Christian and world. They see the line of it running between Cain and Abel, between

Noah and those drowned in the flood, between Abraham and Lot, Jacob and Esau, Israel and the peoples around her, between Christ and her persecutors, and they hear their Master saying, "My kingdom is not of this world. Not as the world giveth, give I unto thee." And this antithesis such Christians are as likely as not to interpret as an antithesis of Christian versus culture, Christian versus learning, Christian versus science, Christian versus reason, Christian versus literature and art, and so, wittingly or unwittingly, Christian versus school. In the end religion becomes something isolated from life, and in the name of religion the school as school is sacrificed to something not a school: be it a Biblical institute, an evangelical agency, a center for religious instruction, a place of worship, or a missionary enterprise.

We understand, I say, and are sympathetic. All the same, it is not our view of either Christianity or education. We, too, insist on the primacy of the religious, the spiritual, in life. Ours is also the conviction that regeneration, that the choice for Christ, that the turning from sin and self to God and his kingdom, that this is the primary thing, without which indeed nothing else matters, from which everything else issues. We, too, have our special revelation: Christ, and Bible, and church, and sacrament, and worship, and soul, and we refuse resolutely, of course, to identify these with any natural or mundane thing. They are spiritual, they are the one thing needful, the pearl without price.

But we are Calvinists. Our Christian conviction is a Reformed conviction. And it is part of that conviction that the religious and spiritual cannot exist in a void, in isolation from life. It is part of the Reformed conviction that the spiritual in us requires human fulfillment, human embodiment. It is part of the Reformed conviction that the religious in us is part and parcel of the rest of us. We maintain that, so far from identifying science, and nature, and culture, and literature, and history with the world, and so expressing the antithesis of Christian and world in ignoring them, we must know, judge and appropriate these all, and express the antithesis of Christian and world through them. We are not Barthians in this sense that we think God's will is unknowable to man, "wholly other," as the phrase is, and virtually irrelevant to history. We are not Manicheans: the world is not the Devil's; the earth is the Lord's and the fullness thereof, the world and they that dwell therein. True, we know the kingdom is spiritual, and not to be identified with any historical cultural product; but we know that we have no means of building for the spiritual kingdom except by cultural means as human beings living on this earth at this point in history. Hence we are not anxious about civilization as though in this life only we had hope. We are not liberals, identifying the task of the church with, and losing the Gospel message in a preoccupation with cultural concerns. We are not monastic. We neither retire into monasteries, nor into small scale social orders of our own. As a matter of fact, ours is not the facile dualism between church on the one hand, and practical life on the other, the practical life construed then as a way of making some money to continue the work of the church. For us something stands between the church and practical life, and this something is the school. Motivated by Christian conviction, it can, if it is a school, keep religion from becoming a disembodied ghost, and can keep practical life from becoming an irreligious, secularized, and commercialized thing. We take the Calvinist challenge seriously, namely, that the Christian must bring the whole range of life—science and art and society and government —under the sway of Christian principle and purpose as an expression of the kingly rule of Christ.

I repeat: the schools must be schools. It is the very strength of the Reformed profession of Christianity not solely in the isolatedly religious but in the religious commanding the naturally and culturally human. It is as human beings that we are Christians, in our human nature expressing itself in a natural environment, expressing itself also in cultural activity of all kinds, and, further, in a particular historical situation here on earth. Our being called to be saints does not exempt us from being human, nor exempt us from cultural activity, nor exempt us from social and political obligation, nor render reason superfluous, nor permit an indifference to art and literature, nor lift us out of history. On the contrary, it is in and through these things that our moral and religious choice for the spiritual kingdom of Christ becomes concrete, real, and meaningful. And that is why our schools must be schools, our education education.

Or put it this way—a kind of figure of speech. Quite apart from the religious question now, we could all manage to become some sort of men and women presumably without ever going to school. It is by virtue of our birth that we become human beings. What the school does, then, is that it takes this humanity, this humanness of ours, and makes it more intelligent, more aware of itself and its environment, makes it, so to speak, more effectively and more consciously human. It does not, in short, give us our humanity, but it develops, disciplines, and matures it, makes our choices and actions more significant, and equips for ampler and better oriented cultural activity. Just so the Christian in his Christian education. The education does not in the first instance make us Christians. It assumes, as it may assume in what are Covenant schools, that the Christianity is ours by virtue of the grace of God in regeneration. And the education now, the school as school, addresses itself to the task of making this Christian humanly significant. I say humanly significant. I have no objection to saying spiritually significant, if it be understood that it is through all of reality—natural, cultural, historical, and supernatural—that this must happen. The school addresses itself to the task of taking the Christian pupil and making his profession of Christianity a significant profession. The school, in short, teaches the pupil how he can express and gives him the means to express a responsible human citizenship in the kingdom of Christ.

You know that the public schools often designate this as the function of their education: to train for responsible citizenship. They mean, in our democracy. We have that same duty, of course, but we think it is best performed when we denominate the purpose of education, as, yes, responsible citizenship, indeed but in the spiritual kingdom of Christ. Our responsibility in society inevitably issues from that.

But then our schools must be schools. If it is at church that we make our choice for Christ, it is at school that we keep making that choice always more humanly and culturally and practically significant. Citizenship in the kingdom requires this kind of education. Else we should be dwarfed, stunted, meager, and only partially-conscious Christians. The question after all is not one of how little we can get by with and still be essentially Christians. The question in education is one of how strong, how aware, how full, how rich we make this profession. And, as I say, we have no choice, since we are the kind of creatures that we are, but to do this in our human nature, in our natural environment, by means of cultural activity, in a particular moment of history, and always in reference to a spiritual kingdom. The materials our schools as schools must use, therefore, are not ecclesiastical, or devotional, or always primarily Biblical materials. Our schools are not in this sense Bible schools. We ought not to regret this or proceed unconfidently, as though the cultural curricula of our schools are regrettably necessary for practical reasons, but a kind of interference really or at best addenda to the religious work. Nor ought we even so one-sidedly to prize, shall I say the *devotional* element at school, the religious atmosphere, as we say, the chapel exercises and such, that we suppose the distinctive part of the school inhered in these, and the rest were neutral or religiously indifferent.

You will understand me at this point, I take it. I think that devotional exercises, Bible reading, prayer, meditation, the service of song, and Biblical study seriously pursued, pursued also with evangelical emphasis, and not merely as so much scientific data—I think that these are very precious. Without them a school could hardly be designated Christian. But my point now is that they do not constitute the school a school: for this precious devotional element is just as proper to the home, to Christian industry, Christian recreation, places of Christian mercy and the like. Understand me further in this insistence of mine that the schools must be schools. I honor the teacher who, when she has reason to suppose that a pupil or student is not a Christian, drops whatever she is doing, her arithmetic, or geography or history lesson, to press the Gospel message upon him. That teacher has her values in the right order. She puts first things first. So much is absolutely true. But we ought not to go on to infer from this that a Christian school is a Christian school because it offers such wonderful opportunities for church or missionary work. It is a precious by-product. It is a true description of our schools to say of them that they come up out of the church, are supported by Christian parents, conducted under Christian auspices, taught by Christian men and women, include in their curriculum more than the public schools by virtue of Bible study, church history, and doctrine, and are carried on in an atmosphere of worship guaranteed by devotional exercises. Every one of these things is important. No school could be effectively Christian without them. And yet the essence of the distinctive in our schools lies not in these important circumstances but in the character of the education itself.

Our schools must be schools. They must subject the Christian student to as thorough a discipline as he is capable of in the natural, cultural, historical, and spiritual life of man. It is as human beings that we are Christians. All that is human concerns us. That gets us into all the subjects of the curriculum. It involves us in the whole of reality. Unawareness of any part of it, the failure to appropriate any part of it, to know it, and to judge it, and to refer it to a spiritual kingdom for justification, this by so much impoverishes our human expression of our Christian choice.

Now this humanness of ours in which we must be educated, through which we must express both our opposition to the spirit of the world and our choice for the kingdom of Christ, includes a lot. It includes, for instance, that part of us which we share with inorganic and organic nature. We are chemical and physical and biological in part, and so is our environment. Thence the natural sciences in our curriculum. We have, further, a nervous organization, akin to that of an animal, and yet differing from it, and so we learn psychology And at that point the uniqueness of the human creature among created beings asserts itself rapidly. We are conscious. We have mind. We can think. We are moral. We can make choices. We have creative freedom. We can make things out of things, expressive of higher things. You will remember that second chapter of Genesis: "And God formed every beast of the field, and every fowl of the air, and brought them unto Adam, to see what he would call them." There lies the human uniqueness, the gift of reason, the expressiveness of language. And it is in this area of our humanity that most of the subjects lie: science, government, history, mathematics, literature, social studies, and the rest. There are the materials proper of school education. By means of these, religious man enters into scientific man, aesthetic man, social man, practical man, and the rest. All of these are involved in the shaping and maturing of the Christian choice for God. These are the main business of the school as school.

And it is the teaching and learning of these that must be Christian. That is my other point. For insisting that the schools must be schools I do not mean to imply that ordinary academic competence is all that is required. No, no, the education as education must be Christian. The quality of it, the character of it, the soul of it—that must be Christian. In this lies the distinctiveness of our schools.

The fact is that education is a human affair. It represents a human awareness of reality and a human appropriation of it. And this is a further fact: whatever is human is religious. The religious in us is as natural and as real to us as the moral, or the rational, as the scientific and aesthetic, as the biological and psychological, as the social and historical. This religious in us, I say, is a part of our being a creature; it is, I say, natural to us. And this continues so in spite of the pervasive presence of sin. Just as we continue to be human beings now that sin has invaded us, so we continue to be religious beings. We say sometimes that man has become a beast because of the presence of sin, but that is only a way of speaking. Man cannot escape being human; if he could, his approaching the bestial would not be a gross disgrace to him. And so he continues to be religious, though to be sure, except for the intervening grace of God, the religion will be false. We sometimes say of people also that they are irreligious. We understand each other when we say that: we probably mean that they are profane, or pay no attention to the things of the church. But there are no irreligious people. The question is one only of a false or of the true religion. And, again, we sometimes say of a book that it is a godless book, or of a nation that it is a godless nation. There, too, we understand what is meant, and there can be no particular objection to such a way of speaking: we mean of course that the god who is served in the book or the nation is not the one true God. But that is the limit of the figure of speech. The fact is that wherever there is a man, there a God is worshipped. All men require a God for the vindication of themselves, the justification of their thoughts and actions, the justification, too, of their cultural activity.

To be human is to be scientific, yes, and practical, and rational, and moral, and social, and artistic, but to be human further is to be religious also. And this religious in man is not just another facet of himself, just another side to his nature, just another part of the whole. It is the condition of all the rest and the justification of all the rest. This is inevitably and inescapably so for all men. No man is religiously neutral in his knowledge of and his appropriation of reality. The preamble to the Decalogue does not read, "Thou shalt serve a God," as though there were any choice about that. It is a natural reality, even now, that we shall serve a God. No, the preamble to the Decalogue and the foundation stone of our Christian schools is this: "I am the Lord Thy God . . . Thou shalt have no other Gods before me." Belief is a basis of all learning, faith is inevitable in man, men are fundamentally dogmatic. All this I know is rank heresy to the secular mind, but it is the secular challenge I am trying to answer. And the answer I think very satisfactory is this answer: Christian schools in which the God behind the reality there explored is the one true God.

You see, though, that this makes of Christian education a much harder thing than that other method of conducting curricular affairs secularly and neutrally and then bringing in the distinctively religious by way of chapel exercises and the devotional element. It is hard work to prove the spirits whether they be of God. It is hard work to be in the world, really in it, I mean, fully aware, that is, of the religious and prophetic tensions and pressures of it, the ultimate loyalties and allegiances of the various cultures in it, the religio-moral choices of men in the past that make the cultural challenge of the present what it is; I say, it is hard work to be in the world that way, and then not to be of it. And yet this proving or testing or trying of the spirits whether they be of God, this being in the world and yet not of it, this, precisely this, is almost the whole business of liberal education in our schools. That is really what we are always busy with in the classroom. That makes our schools distinctive.

One hears such strange stories sometimes of how far afield an occasional teacher will go in his eagerness to establish the distinctiveness of the

Christian school. Understand, I honor and reverence them all for wanting to be distinctive. The whole burden of what I say here is to establish the need of it. I hear of teachers who suppose they are making arithmetic Christian by having the pupils take dimensions of the local church instead of a farmer's corncrib. There are others who refuse to give a pupil an A for excellent work on the ground that according to the Christian view man is imperfect, and cannot therefore be excellent. It is reported of a teacher of geography that he spends more time on the geography of Palestine than of any other country including our own, and of a teacher of drawing who will have the pupils draw nothing but the animals in the ark. There are teachers of literature who choose only novels which treat of ecclesiastical subject matters, and have nothing to do with poetry unless it be a rimed version of the judges of Israel or the names of the apostles. You will have heard your own stories: I report these, salute these teachers for their manifest eagerness to be distinctive and yet say unreservedly that this is not getting at the essence of the Christian in education at all.

Christian teachers, Christian friends: it is so easy in the name Christianity to turn one's back to art, to science, to politics, to social problems, to historical tensions and pressures, in one word to culture, if you will. But once the conviction seizes on you that these all, precisely because they are cultural realities, exhibit a religious allegiance and an ultimate loyalty, that none of them is neutral but rather that all of them are faith-founded, all laid on an altar, all dedicated to a god, then you realize that they are at the very least important Then you realize, too, that the true discernment of the God behind the culture, the assumption underlying the thought, the dogma beneath the action, the soul in the body of the thing, are precisely what it is the business of our schools as schools to disclose and to judge. In that lies the strengthening of the moral sinews of our young Christians. It is so that their choice for Christ and God can become a meaningful human choice. Christianity versus culture: no, it is the fundamentalist heresy. Culture alone: indeed not; it is the liberal heresy. Christianity through culture: the religious in man governing, shaping, determining the scientific, artistic, social in him precisely; it is the Reformed truth.

But if this kind of education is to be accomplished in our schools, then it is an implication of Christian education that it be not merely general education but also liberal. By this I mean that our passion should be not so much to try to get everything in that has cropped up on the face of the earth, as to get everything in which exhibits alternative gods, alternative moral choices, alternative beings and principles of cultural vindication. Our education, in other words, must be liberal in that it ministers to the freedom of moral choice. For us that means that it ministers to the choice for Christ already made before we come to school, reinforcing it all the while and making it always anew and always more consciously and more maturely. Devotional exercise plus vocational training is not Christian education ! I do not think this is possible if the sum total of our education consists of shop, home economics, typing, stenography, hair-dressing, pile-driving, book-keeping, accounting, mechanical drawing, and similar vocational skills. I have no objection to the inclusion of these in the schools, provided they are not regarded as adequate substitutes for what are called the humanities, sciences, and social studies. For if this sense that I speak of, the sense of the religious in man, and the religious in every cultural product, and the religious in the various cultures and epochs of history is to be borne in upon us, we shall have to be shaped and disciplined in the spiritual history of man, that inheritance in which and over against which we choose for Christ and against the world. An educated person will then know, for instance, how a Greek looked at reality and to what God he appealed for its vindication, and how a medieval Catholic looked at it, and how a renaissance humanist looked at it, and how an eighteenth-century deist, and a romantic pantheist, and a modern naturalist. It is only so that the student will learn that all things human are religious, that human culture, while inevitable, is not in itself enough in that it requires religious justification. And it is so that the Christian student will be taught and confirmed in his conviction that the religion of Christianity is the only adequate religion. Some equipment, some skills, some tools for the better making of a liveli-hood, my dear Christian friends, that has a little, but only a very little to do with the Christian in education, and it has very little to do with education. And it is justified in our schools at all only if it is a subsidiary part of a major program of studies in what we call the cultural subjects.

As to that secular challenge, I can, happily, be very brief about that now. Very brief, for it issues from what I have said already. You know that it is the going theory of secular education in public schools that education must be neutral. I do not say that the advocates of secular education, of public education, deny that man is fundamentally religious. They probably acknowledge that he is, some of them at least. But they are forced from their position to take the stand that this religious claim cannot be allowed in public schools. They must leave it, therefore, to private, and personal, and individual choice of the student, and deal with the curriculum, as they say, neutrally, that is, without exhibiting a religious allegiance or loyalty. This is the Achilles' heel, the vulnerable spot, of public education. I do not gloat over their predicament; far be it from me. These schools are necessary in such a society as ours, and we require a society to live in also, and so we are too involved in their predicament not to share even a sort of responsibility for it. Predicament it is, though. Professor Trueblood said of it: "In our democracy we proceed on the assumption that it is illegal to teach the faith on which it rests." That, in a word, is the predicament our idea of Christian schools avoids. We hold that the education being a human enterprise is inevitably religious, that except it be religious it is not education, at least not moral education, and that the alleged neutrality of the public schools must—if their education is to be real education— turn out to be a mere allegation. Our answer to the secular challenge is this answer: Being neutral is impossible for man as man, certainly impossible in so fundamentally human a thing as education. It is this answer: We believe in order that we may know, for belief is the condition of knowledge. As for those secularists who maintain that the thing to do in education is to adopt scientific method, to adopt an hypothesis and then refuse to adhere to it until the facts make it impossible to disbelieve it, we say that this is making doubt and skepticism the basis of knowledge. And it is not to be so objective and neutral as it sounds. It is a protestation made in the name of a god, the god of scientific method. That, too, when you come to examine it closely, is a profession of faith. The god is false. We know whom we have believed, and in His name we appropriate the whole of His reality in our schools.

Address, Teachers Convention, September, 1951.

"Interests" and Education

by Henry Zylstra

A number of ill-considered ideas about education threaten sometimes to filter into our Reformed community. One such idea that we should
take pains to counteract is the idea that school is a place to coddle people's
interests.

Interest is most certainly a condition of learning. Interesting subject
matter, the interesting presentation of it, and an interested student—these
are the very culture, perhaps the only culture, in which education can
thrive. Even so, however, in speaking of interesting subject matter, we
should distinguish between a natural and a disciplined interest. We like the
colored comics until we discover the *Reader's Digest,* and the *Reader's
Digest* until we earn our way into *Harper's.* This represents a kind of
progression from a natural to a disciplined interest, and "interesting
subject matter" is therefore not entirely an instinctive affair. All the same,
interest is a condition of learning, love a condition of insight. It makes
sense, therefore, to take some account in our schools of the individually
differing interests of students.

But there is a point at which this idea of "interests" invites anarchy. It
is getting so now, for instance, that some high schools and colleges
advocate paying no mind at all to what a student takes, and in combination
with what else he takes it, provided only that he takes something, and does
well in it. This, in educators' phrase, is called "ignoring content and
pattern" of courses, and "stressing achievement." Just what alien principle
this notion is an expression of, I cannot say, though it seems to blend well
with that other modern excrescence, the doctrine of "pupil-centered
education," and with its corollary, "the elective system." All three of these
ideas seem to me the last infirmity of naturalism. Reality being so very
bewildering—such the underlying dogma —maybe we can get somewhere by identifying it with its victims, and studying them. I say again that

this extravagant preoccupation with interests should not occur where the Christian idea of man and his education is operative.

I feel keenly about this again just now, fresh as I am from a tour of professional duty at assisting students in their registering at college. We have a green book there, called College Catalogue, in which there is a tabular listing of the courses offered. In the front end of this book there is also some advice about what the students ought to study, and in what order, and in what combination with other subjects. This advice is a distillation of traditional sense, and has been mediated through a good many educators' minds. It outlines a considerable range of possibilities, makes allowance for individual differences, is flexible, and undergoes revision when new occasions teach new duties. All the same, there is insistence in it on "content and pattern" of courses. So far, indeed, from being mere advice, it lays down the conditions for graduation.

Many a student, when he comes to register, chafes under the restrictions of a prescribed course of that kind. He has his eye on the second half of the Catalogue, that is, on the offerings. He pores over it like a kid at the confectioner's with a nickel to spend, pointing to the delicacies he's been pining for. He wants some of this, a little of that, and, look, could he have a couple of those? When he encounters resistance (because I am sitting there) he looks at me as if to ask whether this is not a free country. This, then, is an instance of someone who looks upon school as a place to have his "interests" tickled.

Many a student, too, be it said, comes well-girded, and seems of his own volition, and not perforce, to select a content and order of courses such as the most veteran counsellor would recommend. There is also the occasional one who makes out a program of studies that is surprising in its quality. I recall one such a year ago. It was a model performance, heartening to any teacher with some Reformed sense in his system. I looked at the name. It was not Dutch. The man had "fundamentalist" antecedents.

There are, however, those too many others. Fresh from high school, hardly emerging from a semester at college, the "natural science" and "foreign language" limping in on a "D" or an "E,' they are eager, now that they have "worked off some requirements," to get at their "interests." "I made a little schedule," says the girl, and there it is crumpled in the purse:

Music Appreciation
Story Telling

Interpretative Reading
Art
Contemporary Poetry

Clearly that will not do. There is of course no objection to any one
subject as such. There is nothing wrong with Music Appreciation. Music
has always been expressive of spiritual man, and the appreciation, form,
and history of it are as good a way as any to reach through to that moral
education which turns out in the end to be the purpose of life. Story Telling,
too, the art of story, was fundamentally significant well before Moses
could say of life that we spend it as a tale that is told. Interpretative Reading
the art of expression, is that discourse which, in well-regulated schools and
lives, goes inseparably paired with the spiritual reason. So Shakespeare:

Sure, He that made us with such large discourse,
Looking before and after, gave us not
That capability and god-like reason
To fust in us unus'd.

Music, story, speech, and those others, laid in God's reality for
discovery, use, and praise, belong in the curriculum. But what bothers me
in my student is that her "little schedule" is top-heavy on the aesthetic side,
and that it provides little opportunity for historical discipline. I fear, too,
that she looks upon herself as a creature mainly organic, and full of
sensibilities which she now wants coddled, entertained, and at best
"refined." This is nice, but is it moral education?

The student is not so much, not solely, to be blamed for a still disordered
and immature sense of what man is, what life is, and what education is.
What I wish for on such occasions is a more generally active idea of
Christian education in the community as a whole, an idea going out from
the center to the periphery, from the periphery to the center, and involving
everybody—teacher, minister, board member, pupil, and people. We have
such a fine chance for maintaining the spiritual dignity of man and his
education by way of nature, culture, and history. There is the first question
and the first answer of John Calvin's *Genevan Catechism* to challenge us:
What is the chief end of man? To know God and enjoy him forever. The
thrust of that, when we come to reflect upon it, is that man is spiritual and
moral, not merely natural and organic. There is also the counsel of the
Ecclesiast: The fear of the Lord is the beginning of wisdom. That makes
education dogmatic; it does not make education unnecessary.

We shall insist then on "content and pattern." Our object is morality, not efficiency. We want character more than calibre. We have no objection to the term "development" as an aim in education, provided it means moral development, and not merely a refinement of crude sensibility, or a better organization of impulses and instincts. We are not so bewildered by reality as to find ourselves adrift on the stream of nature. We cherish "personality" because of its "interests," yes, but even more because these lead us to the moral decision of spiritual freedom. Hence we shall want content, want to be disciplined by reality as it is. That reality must be representative reality. The curriculum will therefore include nature, culture, and history. And it will provide historical discipline. Else there will be no opportunity of showing that man in his life chooses for God or against him, and that this choice is the significance of life.

That takes me back to the solid advice at the front end of the Catalogue. I explain to the girl, and give her the usual:

Bible
Biology
Latin
Grammar, Rhetoric, Composition
History.

"Okay?" I ask.
"Okay !" she says. These students are susceptible to ideas.

The Reformed Journal, March, 1951.

The Contemplative Life

by Henry Zylstra

Contemplation is a word which sounds badly out of key with the noises of our time. It savors, even to us religious folk, of hymn-book archaism. It suggests old Plato, the Pagan Orient, and the Catholic Middle Ages. A good many of us, it may be, are content to leave it to Athens, Buddah, and the monks. We have no right to do this. The contemplative life is the God-conscious life. It is the life that knows its end and can rest in that knowledge. The Psalmist spoke of it: Be *still,* and *know* that I am God. We read of it in Hebrews: There remaineth a *rest* for the people of God. John Calvin put it into the first question and answer of his *Genevan Catechism.* His question was fundamental: What is the chief end of man? And his answer was crystal-clear: To *know* God and *enjoy* Him forever. That is the eternal Sabbath which begins here: *Delight* in the *knowledge* of God. Modernity, by its neglect of God, has idolized the active life. John Dewey, lately deceased, was typical of this idolatry. He glorified process. He deified experiment. He championed evolution. His action lacked its reason. His reason lacked its worship. His worship lacked its object. Such action is not contemplative. It is blind. It is activism. The punsters teased him with their "learn to do by Deweying," and the jest fitted him. Well before Dewey, the German Goethe had set the pace for the modern activism. He put his Faust to work translating the prologue to the Gospel of St. John. That meant finding an equivalent for the Greek word *Logos.* Faust experimented with several possibilities. He tried *Thought,* and concluded it would not do. He tried *Word,* and rejected it as inadequate. He tried *Energy,* felt he was getting closer, but remained unsatisfied. Then he hit on it, and ushered in modernity: *In the beginning,* he wrote, *in the beginning was the Act.* The creature had taken over, and God was an exile from His world. Such has been the modern temper. Service, humanitarianism, the second table of the law divorced from the first, evolution,

process, change, experiment, motion—those are the keywords to the age.
Carlyle, a disciple of Goethe and a rebel to Calvinist doctrine, applied it all
to religion: "Whatsoever religion," he said, "is not work, may go and dwell
among the Brahmins . . . or where it will; with me it shall have no harbour."
The result of this neglect of the contemplative life has not been satisfying,
even for moderns. There has been no *rest* and there has been no *enjoyment.*
Ernest Dowson spoke of its endless activity:

> I cried for madder music and for stronger wine,
> But when the feast is finished and the lamps expire....
> I am desolate and sick of an old passion
> Yea, hungry for the lips of my desire.

That old passion, were Dowson and others honest in analyzing it, is the
human passion for the knowledge of God. It is the longing of the creature
for communion with his Creator. The whole story of the sinner's pitiful
flight from the grace of a satisfying communion with God is told in Francis
Thompson's poem *The Hound of Heaven.* There is no poise in such flight,
no shelter, no harborage, no contentment. There is only the blind activism
of the panic-stricken outlaw from God. You remember the lines:

> I fled Him, down the nights and down the days;
> I fled Him, down the arches of the years;
> I fled Him, down the labyrinthine ways
> Of my own mind; and in the mist of tears
> I hid from Him, and under running laughter....

And as his panic increases, the fleeing sinner hears his Lord:

> Lo! naught contents thee, who content'st not Me.

Mr. Eliot, the contemporary English poet with the Catholic temper,
summarizes the modern predicament:

> Endless invention, endless experiment
> Brings knowledge of motion, but not of stillness
> Knowledge of speech, but not of silence;
> Knowledge of words, and ignorance of the Word....
> Where is the Life we have lost in living?
> Where is the wisdom we have lost in knowledge?
> Where is the knowledge we have lost in information?

Action must spring from thought, from thought that is seated in
worship, in worship that is worship of God.

The knowledge of God is proper to us as creatures, and it satisfies. That is the finest fruit of the contemplative life: to know and enjoy God. No one will care to ask what such enjoyment is for. It is enough for us. So far from being caught in the web of natural process, snared in the fatality of endless busyness, we can rest in that knowledge.

For man is a creature who can know. Animals cannot, though animals can be magnificently efficient. We people cannot for all our years fall as gracefully as a kitten at two weeks, or fly as well as a bird at its first attempt, or build a house in the ground as competently as an ant. True, the ingenuity and skill with which men in our time have learned to do things is amazing. But such efficiency, skill, or power does not make a man a man. We see that at once back there in Paradise. When God had done making the animals, we read this: "And the Lord God formed every beast of the field and every fowl of the air, and brought them unto Adam to see what he would name them." There we have it: a mind to know and to name. The capacity for conscious appreciation. The leisure, the spiritual freedom, to enjoy. Man, conscious reflector of the glory. *Homo sapiens*, man knowing, not quite submerged in *homo faber*, man doing. *Homo ludens*, even, man as artist, man playing. The knowledge of God, which begins in the saving knowledge of Grace through faith, makes for rest and enjoyment. That is the finest fruit of the contemplative life.

Contemplation itself, of course, is not indolence; it is not idle. The saints work hard. Mary's effort at the feet was no easier than Martha's in the kitchen. Gethsemane is unique for its ardor. Jacob wrestled in prayer. Contemplation represents not an escape from drudgery into entertainment, but the positive education of leisure. Some people are too lazy to engage in it, too bored to be still. It embarrasses them, the confrontation in solitude of self, and God, and destiny. Robert Louis Stevenson, perhaps with tongue in cheek, once wrote this of such persons: "There is a sort of dead-alive . . . people about, who are scarcely conscious of living except in the exercise of some conventional occupation.... They have dwarfed and narrowed their soul by a life of all work, until here they are at forty, with a listless attention, a mind vacant of all material for amusement, and not one thought to rub against another while waiting for the train."

In its deeper levels this of Stevenson is a kind of boredom too, a boredom springing from neglect of the contemplative life. For boredom also is an earmark of life in our day. The poets have seen it and are good reporters. "Ennui, ennui, ennui," says Christopher Fry, in a recent drama, and he toasts the vanity of a purposeless life with a yawn. It had been Oscar Wilde's final dread. "The only horrible thing," he had said, "the only horrible thing in the world is ennui." It is horrible, of course. When we cannot find God, we cannot find his world and his wonders. Or finding these, we can only use and exploit them; we cannot appreciate and enjoy them.

I thought of that when we crossed the Pacific, some of us, on military duty during World War II. There were five hundred of us crowded into the bowels of a hold in the ship. It was hot there. We travelled on or near the equator the better part of a month. Some of the men played cards all day every day. Finally we caught the first glimpse of our tropical island. It lay there sublime in its splendid beauty. Those men landed. . . and began playing cards. I remembered some lines I had once read. This was one of them: "He is an uneducated man who is fettered to a process." This was another, Thompson's again: "'Tis ye, 'tis your estranged faces, That miss the many-splendour'd thing." And these from Wordsworth also came to mind:

> The world is too much with us, late and soon,
> Getting and spending, we lay waste our powers:
> Little we see in nature that is ours;
> We have given our hearts away, a sordid boon !

If the neglect of the contemplative life can lead to such an abuse of nature, it can lead also to an abuse of work. Few will deny that work in our age needs the sanctifying influence of contemplation. The harshness of secular exploitation must be taken out of it, the tenderness of religious purpose restored to it. Men have made their work their end. Their work is therefore their fate, and they are victimized by it. No wonder: work that is not free, that is not oriented to final purpose, that provides no knowledge of God—such work violates the spiritual nature of man who was born for this end that he should know and enjoy Him.

Ruskin in romantic longing for the old religious poise said as much in the last century. We take a lovely landscape, he said in effect, breath-taking in its beauty, and exploit it. We put the belching chimneys and ugly factories with their accompanying slums and smoke into it. Then, when we see what we have done, we clear an acre or two, and decorate it as a public park. We take the freedom of individual expression out of the work on the conveyor belt and at the buffer wheel, and then, when we see what we have done to the artist in us, we hire a group of people to make art for us, and pile it up in museums. We take the positive leisure, the contemplative quality, the education out of our work, and then we tire ourselves on holidays and holydays laboring hard at our recreation. We try for a civilized house, with all the trimmings of a machine civilization—the garage, or garages, have of course supplanted the library—and then, when we have the house, radiant heat and all, we plan for a summer cottage where we can rough it for a while. There is some divorce of work and worship in all this too, and not enough consideration, not enough purpose.

Contemplation can sanctify work, provide its reason, give it purpose, harvest its fruits. I have seen it in a farmer. He was a good farmer, he enjoyed farming, but he was not a soil-grubbing, money-mongering farmer. For him the purpose of work was not to make money. It was not even to provide food, shelter, and clothing. Those were but the means. What he got from his work was the knowledge of God. After supper, evenings, he liked to saunter around his fields (that word *saunter,* incidentally, once meant going on a religious pilgrimage to St. Terre). He did this not to satisfy his "acquisitive instinct," as if to say, "This is mine; I own this." Those evening jaunts of his were a kind of Sabbath journey in which he placed his effort on the altar, and gleaned its spiritual benefit. How different, such leisure, from the entertainment we moderns have provided as an escape from the drudgery of work.

The neglect of contemplation results also in the long run in an abuse of art. On this count, as I see it from my present vantage point, Puritanism has a burden on its conscience. It has sometimes ignored art, sometimes opposed it, and sometimes bent it to practical uses. Art is in this respect like religion: it does not want to be vindicated by its usefulness. It wants to be itself. The songs, the psalms of David, are fruit of the contemplative life. They express the enjoyment of the knowledge of God as He is revealed in the Word and the world. Such indispensable leisure is the condition always for the production and the enjoyment of art.

If we have not yet a literature, and an audience for the enjoyment of literature, comparable to that of the Catholics, or comparable to that of our kind in The Netherlands, this is to be ascribed in large part, perhaps, to the comparatively greater neglect of contemplation among us. We do not *enjoy* knowledge so much, and we *use* it more. And thought—in so far Carlyle was right—thought without Reverence is barren.

The point in this connection is not, of course, that we should engage in the contemplative life for the sake of the arts. The point is rather that the presence or absence of the production and appreciation of them is an index to the quality of our enjoyment of God. For art is precisely the kind of thing which, disengaged from the processes of work, stands by disinterestedly harvesting its spiritual fruit. And the enjoyment of art, like the enjoyment of other kinds of knowledge, is at bottom not a practical but a contemplative affair. We shall sometime have to become concerned, as they in The Netherlands are already concerned, about what is there called the *manco* (it has almost become a technical term in Reformed circles there) or *lack* of a convincing Protestant-Christian literature.

We shall have to cultivate the contemplative in life, finally, if we are to maintain our respect for education. We have sometimes dealt too cavalierly with knowledge. We have talked too much about knowledge *for,* and too little about knowledge *of.* If we see to it that our knowledge be knowledge of God, we need not be so greatly concerned about what it is for. Knowledge for effective citizenship, knowledge for power, knowledge for efficiency, knowledge for social usefulness, knowledge for economic competency, knowledge, even, for service—these have crept into our defenses of education also, and they are not warranted.

Sometimes at college we get students who are always chafing at their seats because they cannot see what all the Bible, philosophy, history, literature, language, and science are for. They want—sometimes, one guesses, by parental prompting—a fast course in business correspondence, double-entry ledger keeping, shop techniques, secretarial etiquette, and the like. Such an attitude, it should suffice to say now, is hard to relate to the first question and answer of John Calvin's Catechism. They have not fathomed the question, What is the end of man?, nor its answer, To know and enjoy.... They do not understand the Psalmist's injunction: Be still, and know....

Our life is not a treadmill, but a journey, and we should be sometimes arriving. Essence of the contemplative life is delight in the knowledge of God. Because it begins, as I said, in the saving knowledge of faith, I am minded to reproduce here a poem which comes up out of a contemplative age, the eleventh century. It is the 410th number of the *Psalter Hymnal:*

> O Jesus, joy of loving hearts,
> Thou fount of life, Thou light of men
> From fullest bliss that earth imparts,
> We turn unfilled to Thee again
>
> Thy truth unchanged has ever stood;
> Thou savest those that on Thee call,
> To them that seek Thee Thou art good,
> To them that find Thee, all in all.

We taste Thee, O Thou living bread,
And long to feast upon Thee still;
We drink of Thee, the fountainhead,
And thirst our souls from Thee to fill.

Our restless spirits yearn for Thee,
Where'er our changeful lot is cast,
Glad that Thy gracious smile we see,
Blest, that our faith can hold Thee fast.

The Reformed Journal, August, 1952.

Nicholas Wolterstorff:
Editor Introduction

Nicholas Wolterstorff, for many years a philosophy professor at Calvin College, turned his philosophical talents and publication efforts in many directions beyond philosophy. Among the many political, social, and ecclesiastical questions that he addressed was the matter of Christian education. Chief author of *Christian Liberal Arts Education*, a committee document on Calvin College curriculum, he also wrote journal articles on education in periodicals like the *Reformed Journal*. His major publication in education is *Educating For Responsible Action*, published in 1980.

Reproduced in the following pages is the out-of-print monograph "Curriculum: By What Standard?", originally a 1966 speech given at a conference of Christian school administrators. In it he gives in non technical language a Biblical anthropology and epistemology, which for him was the "standard" for reforming Christian education. It has become the rallying cry for many progressives in the Christian school movement, justifying among other curriculum matters a serious attention to physical education and the direct teaching of moral and social problems, like racism and family relations.

It remains a classical statement, however brief, of a philosopher's contribution to Reformed thinking on education.

The second entry, also a speech, called "Looking to the Eighties" was delivered in Canada in about 1978 and published by the Curriculum Development Center in Toronto. It calls for even more dramatic change in the goals and curriculum of Christian education.

Curriculum: By What Standard?

by Nicholas Wolterstorff

By reference to what standard, what criterion, what measuring stick, should the curriculum of a school be determined? How must a school set about selecting what it shall teach?

Man is a creature for whom education is inescapable. His created constitution and his situation in the world make learning and being taught unavoidable for him. They are ineradicable and indestructible threads in the fabric of his existence. For man is surrounded and encompassed by change; every day brings something new under the sun which shines on human affairs. Of this change which surrounds and encompasses him, man finds he is conscious and aware. But man is also a creature of ignorance, deeply and profoundly ignorant and unknowing of what tomorrow will bring. Thus man learns, unavoidably and inescapably, wholly apart from whether he wishes to or not, yet finding delight and satisfaction in so doing. Unlike bugs and stones, unlike God, man learns—learns what is the case.

Man, as well as being a creature of consciousness, is a creature of action, of free, reasonable action. In respect to action, too, man is deeply and profoundly unknowing and ignorant. He is thrust into the world knowing how to do almost nothing. Yet, in order to stay alive and reach fulfillment he must know how to do a legion of things. Thus, under the pressure of his situation in the world and his own inner constitution, man learns-learns how to do things. In this way, too, man is unlike bugs and stones, and unlike God.

So *learning what* and *learning how* are, for us men, inseparable from life. Yet not all of what a man learns is inescapable and unavoidable, determined. For we are *free* agents. We can set ourselves to learn, we can choose to learn. Our freedom rescues our learning from being all inevitable and determined. But never can we *merely* choose to learn; always we must choose *what* to learn. Always we must select. For no one of us, nor all of us together, can learn everything. Omniscience is forever beyond us. If we would choose to learn at all, we must perforce prefer some knowledge to other, regret some ignorance less than other. Few of a man's decisions are of more consequence than his decisions as to what he shall learn and what he shall remain ignorant of. Few of a man's responsibilities are heavier than his responsibility for his knowledge and his ignorance.

Not only do I decide what I shall learn, and you, what you shall learn. Each of us also decides what the other shall learn, I what you shall learn, you, what I shall learn. We set about teaching each other. The freedom of my fellow man, as well as my own freedom, rescues my learning from being all inevitable and determined. But we can also never *merely* choose to teach. Always we must choose *what* to teach. Always we must select. For no one of us can teach everything, nor can all of us together. And within what is selected, we cannot give equal emphasis to everything. Some things must be stressed and brought to the fore; others must be allowed to recede into penumbra. If we would teach at all, we must perforce prefer that our fellow man know certain things rather than others, we must perforce regret less that he remain ignorant of certain things than of others. Few of a man's decisions are of more consequence than his decisions as to what he shall teach to his fellows and what he shall not. Few of a man's responsibilities are heavier than his responsibility for the knowledge and the ignorance of his fellow man.

A school curriculum is the outcome of decisions as to what shall be taught to our fellow man and what shall not be taught, what shall be stressed and what shall not be stressed. What we want to discuss is how, properly, to make the decisions which result in a school curriculum. From among the mass of things which *can* be taught in schools, how is one to decide which *shall* be taught? From among the mass of things which *can* be emphasized, how is one to decide what *shall* be emphasized?

Of course, what often happens in the schools is that nothing deserving the title of "decision" is made on such matters at all. Incredible as it would surely seem to an outsider, should any discover it, teachers often have no conscious and reflective reason whatsoever for selecting one thing to teach rather than another, no conscious and reflective reason whatsoever for emphasizing one thing rather than another. Of the actions that human beings perform, one would surely expect teaching to be among those done most reflectively and with the clearest perception of goals. But what a deluded expectation. For vast numbers of teachers *just teach,* teaching as they were taught, unreflectively exercising their ingrained habits, enslaved to custom, no more deciding what to teach and what to emphasize than the crow decides what song to sing. The thesis that this is indefensible and irresponsible needs no defense.

Scarcely better is something else that often happens in the schools: We teachers decide to teach those things which happen to be of greatest interest to *us,* and we choose to emphasize those things which happen, for whatever reason, most to excite *our* fancy. We make of teaching a self discourse, I communing with me, permitting others to overhear. We conduct our teaching for the sake of ourselves, giving not a fig for what it does to the student. Surely the thesis that this is indefensible and irresponsible also needs no defense.

Teaching in the schools, I suggest, must always have its face toward the student. It must answer to his needs. It must seek an outcome; and the outcome it seeks must be an outcome with respect to the student. It must aim for some effect; and the effect it aims for must be an effect on the student. The curriculum of a school must be set by reference to what one is aiming at with respect to the student. It must be determined by reference to some conception of when one has succeeded with the student and when one has failed, when one's goals for the student have been attained and when they have not, when the results hoped for in the student have been secured and when they have slipped away.

The student, however, is more than a student. He is a person, who happens to be spending some few of his waking hours undergoing school education. In view of this, what I wish to suggest next is this: School education must be of worth and significance to the student in his life outside the school as well as inside. The needs it answers to must not be needs, confined simply to his hours in school. There must be a carry-over, a significant, deliberately aimed-at carry-over, from life in the classroom to life outside the classroom. The school must inculcate those excellences which are of worth for life outside the school as well as inside. School must not be an end in itself. Schooling must not be undertaken just for the sake of schooling. It must be undertaken for the sake of life as a whole. The school acts irresponsibly when the excellences it strives to inculcate are limited in relevance to the classroom.

Possibly this point seems utterly bland and truistic to you. Yet it seems to me a point of immense importance for the content of school education, and one repudiated in principle or practice by large numbers of educators. It is repudiated in principle by those progressivists who insist that the school must not seek for aims outside itself but must simply provide the student with an experience which in itself is of interest to him—with an engrossing slice of life no more referential in its character than any other slice out of a child's life. Equally it is repudiated in principle by those traditionalists who contrast the world of the intellect and culture with the world of commerce and utility, insisting that the school is to concern itself solely with the former, seeking to make the student a learned and cultured gentleman, cognizant of the best that has been thought and said, ignorant of what men must do to make a living. And it is repudiated in practice by all those of us who assume that our teaching has been successful with respect to a given student if he passes our test, answers our questions about the material, repeats what we have said—in short, by all those of us who slip and slide into the belief that by observing and examining a student in school we can discover whether we have been successful, by all those of us who resent the request that we show what bearing our teaching has on life outside the school. What I want to suggest is that if teaching has its proper aim, then we can never discover in school alone whether our aim has been achieved. We shall have to look at the life of the student outside the school as well.

But *which* life of the student—his future life or his present life? In school education to be viewed as preparation or fulfillment? Is its content, its curriculum, to be determined by reference to what *will be* of worth and importance to the student's future life, or by reference to what is of worth and importance to the student's present life? Is its focus to be on the life and world of the adult, or on the life and world of the child?

It seems to me that the proper answer to this question, is, "Both." School education is maimed and distorted, and its effectiveness reduced when either of these is stressed to the ignoring or downplaying of the other.

It would be irresponsible, I think, for the school to provide the child with an education which did not have, as one of its aims, to prepare him for his future, adult life. Equally, it would be futile for the school to try. For whether one likes it or not, the traits that one develops and inculcates in the student inevitably carry over beyond his childhood into his adult life. So the issue cannot be *whether* we should provide him with an education which is significant for his adult as well as his child life. We *will* do so, unavoidably. The issue is only what *kind* of adult life we should aim to prepare him for.

But school education must also be of worth and significance for the life of the child. The child is not merely a lump of clay which we adults have the right to fashion as we please until, lo and behold, we breathe the breath of life into him when he leaves our hands at commencement. School education must be of meaning and significance to the child's life as well as to the life of the adult. For in the Christian view, the child is already a person, demanding love and respect. But his needs are not those of the adult. Accordingly, love and respect for him must assume different forms and colors from what it does for the adult. We must, for our schools, resolutely seek for those curricula and those pedagogical techniques that will make what is learned of worth and significance both to the student's present life and to his future life—to his life as a whole.

At this point in our discussion we come to an enormously important parting of the ways. What I have said so far pertains, it seems to me, to all school education—whether it be the education provided by the public school, by our Reformed Christian schools, by the Catholic Christian schools, or whatever. But now the road before us has many forks; and we must choose which to travel. The aim of the school, I have suggested, must be to equip the child for life—for life outside the school as well as inside, for life in the future as well as the present. But men do not agree on what human life should be. They are of different minds as to the true, the genuine, the authentic, the well-formed human life. And so they are of different minds as to what, concretely, should be aimed at in the schools. At this juncture in our discussion, then, we must make a choice. We cannot, any further, discuss curricula for the schools generally. We can only discuss curricula appropriate to this, or that, perception of authentic human existence.

You and I are interested in Reformed Christian schools. We are interested in a school educational program which aims to equip children for the Christian life, as this is understood by Reformed Christians. Thus our question becomes: How is one to go about determining the curriculum for such a school? What considerations are relevant? What consequences for the curriculum flow from the aim of equipping children to live the Christian life?

Suppose someone says that the Christian school should eliminate all teaching of sport. Is he right or wrong? Suppose he says that the Christian school should concentrate on the humane subjects, consigning the natural sciences and mathematics to a secondary position in the curriculum. Is he right or wrong? Is he right or wrong? Suppose he says that the Christian school should teach the Bible and only as much as is necessary to preach the Biblical message to others. Is he right or wrong? Suppose he says that history has no place in the Christian school. Is he right or wrong? Suppose he says that literature should be studied, but only Christian literature; art, but only Christian art. Is he right or wrong? Suppose he says that painting and sculpting and singing and playing of musical instruments have no place in the Christian school. Is he right or wrong?

I am sure that you all have views, very definite views at that, on these matters. But could you justify them by reference to the proper aim of Christian school education? Are your curricular convictions the result of a clear perception of the nature of the Christian life, and a resolute, imaginative, courageous attempt to make the curriculum of the Christian school serve the end of equipping the student for living that Christian life?

Let us delineate some of the principal features of the Christian life and draw out a few of their implications for the formation of a Christian school curriculum.

The Christian life, in the first place, is the life of a man, a human being. I dare say that this seems utterly obvious to you. Let me, however, state the contrast of what I have in mind; and then, perhaps, it will seem less obvious. The Christian life is not the life of a pure spiritual soul which happens, for some God-alone-known reason, to be attached to a body. It is not the life of a mind, a rational-moral principle, which happens to be imprisoned in a chunk of flesh. Rather, it is the life of a creature who is soul *and* body, inner man *and* outer man, a conscious personal being *and* a biological being.

It was Plato's view that what I am, and what you are, is simply a rational moral soul. Thus, strictly speaking, I do not walk, I do not swim, I do not eat, I have no weight, no size. I am, however, attached to a body which does and has all these things. This attachment to the body is really a kind of imprisonment. It is a sentence on me, a judgment, a punishment. In addition, the body is the source of evil in human affairs. Thus man's chief duty is to die away from his body, repudiate its desires, stifle and repress its drives. Death is man's friend. The mind, on the other hand, is the source of good in human affairs. Man's duty is to cultivate the life of the mind.

The Platonic understanding of what we are has been enormously influential in Western thought and culture. It has lodged itself firmly in Christian as well as non-Christian patterns of thought. Yet it is, at almost every juncture, an anti-Biblical conception. There is nothing at all in the Biblical perspective to the effect that we are really angels who have been attached to bodies. We are, on the contrary, physical and biological creatures who are at the same time conscious, personal creatures. There is nothing at all in the biblical perspective to the effect that this physical and biological existence of ours is a curse and a punishment, and that we should long for death. On the contrary, life is a great and good gift, whereas death is a curse and a punishment, not at all a friend, but rather the last enemy to be overcome. There is nothing at all in the Biblical perspective to the effect that man's root sin lies in succumbing to the desires of the body. On the contrary, man's root sin lies in alienation from God and man, an alienation which is effected and manifested throughout his existence, personal as well as bodily.

Accordingly, Christian education must not be conceived of as the development of the rational and intellectual capacities in the student, as the cultivation of the life of the mind. Not that it should not do this; for we are, after all, creatures capable of rational thought. But this cannot be its full character. A curriculum which operates on the assumption that the students are nothing but rational moral souls, or on the assumption that the only capacities genuinely worth cultivating in the students are the rational-moral capacities, is not a curriculum for Christian education. Christian education must educate for the full life of man.

I am sure that you are better able than I am to trace out all the concrete curricular implications of this position. But one thing that it will certainly mean, I think, is that a physical education program—conceived as a program designed to educate every student in the proper use of his body throughout life—will occupy a significant place in the curricula of the Christian schools.

The Christian life is, secondly, the life of faith; by which I mean not that it is a life which *includes* faith, but that *as a whole* it is the life of faith. A curriculum for Christian education will aim at equipping the student for living the life of faith.

Seen in the Biblical perspective, the situation of every man is a confrontation between God and man. Through His works and deeds God speaks to man. He sends forth His Word. And man, through *his* works and deeds, answers. God asks of man that there be fellowship between them—fellowship based on an honest and humble acknowledgment of the relative positions of both. To this call, man answers "Yes" or "No," affirmatively or negatively. The Bible calls man's affirmative answer to God's call for fellowship, "faith," or "belief." His negative answer it calls "unbelief." It sees the issue of belief or unbelief as the basic issue in human life. A man's choice of faith or unfaith has ramifications throughout his existence. It determines, and is exercised in, his entire way of life.

If we are at all to comprehend how faith and life can be related in this comprehensive manner, rather than merely to accept it as a bit of pious mystification, it is imperative that we see clearly what faith is. What

model—to borrow a term from the scientists and the mathematicians—
shall we use in thinking about faith?

You are all aware of the fact that some things we know, whereas some
things we merely believe. I know that I am now standing and talking. On
the other hand, I believe, without really knowing, that my car will start
when I am ready to leave here today. This familiar contrast between things
that we know and things that we merely believe has played, it seems to me,
a fundamental role in the thought of Christians about the Christian life.
Faith has been thought of as belief in propositions that we do not know,
belief in propositions on the basis of authority rather than evidence.
Thomas Aquinas, in fact, defines "faith" this way: Faith is assent to
divinely revealed propositions. Now I do not deny that living the Christian
life entails believing various propositions. But to take the faith to which
God calls us as consisting, in its essence, in assent to propositions, is to
commit a radical, wrenching distortion of the Christian proclamation. It is
to make the gospel a philosophy, an intellectual system. It is to make utterly
obscure the connection between faith and life.

How, then ought we to think of faith? I suggest that the model we must
have in mind is not that of believing propositions, but rather that of
believing in a person. You all know, from your own experience, what it is
to believe in a person. It is to trust him, to be loyal to him, to serve him, to
give him one's allegiance, to be willing to work for him, to place one's
confidence in him. And you also know, from your own experience, how
pervasively one's allegiance to a person can affect one's whole life. When
faith is conceived as belief in a person, there is no problem at all as to the
connection between faith and life. For it is with one's life that one exercises
such faith.

This is the model that we must use in thinking of that faith which is the
focus of the Christian life. The object of such faith is not propositions. It
is rather a personal God. To have faith in this personal God is not to believe
various propositions about Him. It is rather to give Him one's loyalty,
one's allegiance, one's service, one's confidence, one's trust, one's
obedience. The call to faith is the call to be trusting, loyal, devoted,
obedient servants of God.

What is it like to be such? It is to be like Jesus of Nazareth. He was the
completely obedient man. He was the man who gave God undiluted
service. Thus it is that in Him God's Word is focused. In Him, preemi-
nently, we see what it is to reply to God's call for fellowship with the
answer of faith. So it is that, in this new day of the Lord, to have faith in
God is to have faith in Jesus Christ. To believe in God is to become one of

His band of followers. It is to become one of His disciples. For us, now, the call to faith is the call to be disciples of Jesus in our entire lives. It is the call to be conformed to His model in the whole of our existence—in the whole framework of our beliefs, in the whole complex of our feelings and attitudes, in the whole gamut of our actions.

In so far, then, as Christian education fails to educate for comprehensive faith, in so far as it fails to educate for life discipleship, it fails to be fully Christian education. In so far, for example, as it educates for the passive contemplation of God rather than the active service of God, it fails of its true end. In so far as it confines its Christian content to separate courses in the curriculum rather than putting everything in Christian perspective, it fails of its true end. It is not faith added to understanding that we are after. It is not faith seeking understanding that we are after. Rather, it is faith realized in life.

Again, you are probably better fitted than I am to see the concrete curricular implications of this position for the schools. But let me point out two things which seem to me to flow from it. In the first place, in social studies courses there must be a good deal of emphasis on the Christian approach to contemporary social issues. I remember that in my own social studies courses in a Christian high school we studied a good deal about such phenomena as introversion and nomadism. But there was nothing at all about the racial problem seen in Christian perspective, nothing about family relations seen in Christian perspective, nothing about a Christian view of work and recreation and private property and the welfare state. In short, I and my fellow students were not very well equipped for living the life of faith.

Secondly, in all those courses in which the works and institutions of men are studied, there must, I think, be a persistent effort to show the student how the diverse responses of men to God become articulated in their cultural endeavors. In literature, for example, we must try to penetrate beneath the surface of rhymes and rhythms to perceive the ultimate loyalties and fundamental perspectives which are there at work.

The Christian life, in the third place, is the life of someone who is a member of the Christian community. It is not the life of an isolated self-sufficient individual. Accordingly, Christian education must aim at equipping the student to be a member of the community of believers.

A man, in becoming a disciple of Christ, takes his place as an organic member of the community of believers, of the household of faith. The restoration of harmony between man and God is inseparable from the restoration of harmony between man and man. The church, understood not as the ecclesiastical institution but rather as the fellowship of believers, is always the context and fulfillment of the Christian life.

The bonds uniting this community of believers are not psychological bonds; the church is scarcely a group of people all of whom like each other. The bonds are not social bonds; kings and commoners, wealthy and poor, ascetics and harlots, all are present. The bonds are rather the bond of sharing a common faith and the bond of depending on each other for the performance of a common task.

The Christian community consists of those who have made Christ their Lord. They have renounced their own pretensions to sovereignty, and sworn allegiance to a common master. They have jointly confessed that it is in love and fellowship that man realizes his true nature and finds fulfillment. They are united in the focal point of their lives.

But they are also united by virtue of the task which they must jointly perform. Christ has departed from His earthly existence. It now remains to His followers to be a light in a darkened world, a healing balm in a diseased age—in short, to witness to the world of the renewed life available to men in Christ. This they do by trying to live that renewed life. But St. Paul, especially, makes it clear than no man can do this fully by himself. The talents and the skills of each are limited, and only in cooperative endeavor can the task of the Christian on earth, in its full scope, be fulfilled. St. Paul compared the fellowship of believers to a body in which each member must perform its own proper work if the entire body is to remain alive and healthy. St. Augustine compared the fellowship of believers to a republic, which he called the City of God. In this city all the citizens together, united by a common love and mutual need, strive to bring the whole realm of legitimate human activity into captivity to Christ. All together, each doing his particular task, they strive to make Christ the Lord in every legitimate area of human life.

Christian education, accordingly, must be viewed as a project of the Christian community, designed to train its young members to become mature citizens of the community, so that the community may perform its full-orbed task on earth. The goals of Christian education must always be pursued in reference to the multiform needs of the Christian community for the fulfillment of its program on earth.

One consequence of this position for the curriculum is, it seems to me, that we must attempt to make the student aware both of Christian tradition and of contemporary Christian thought and activity. For it is imperative that the school do all it appropriately can to insure that there be genuine understanding among the various members of the community. And in speaking of the Christian community here, I mean the Christian community as a whole, in all its ecclesiastical divisions. The Christian school must not be guilty of perpetuating or increasing the inability of Christians to understand each other.

Another consequence is, I think, that we must seek to develop that which is unique in each student. We must not try to turn out every student from a common mold. Christian education has suffered immensely from the pressures of conformity. In the Christian community, where men ought to be rejoicing in their freedom, they have instead suffered under the tyranny of social conformity, and then, in hostility, have brought the same pressures to bear on others. Our schools must lend every effort to the elimination of such pressures. They must develop and encourage and prize that which is unique in each student. The body of Christians is a community, an organism. It is not a collectivity of identical atoms.

Yet another consequence is that our curriculum must not exalt some professions at the expense of others—the life of the scholar and the minister, say, above all others. In the Christian community there are no inferior and no superior occupations. Every occupation is a vocation, a calling. It is only by diverse specialization of its various members that the Christian community can carry out its full program. Thus the Christian schools must beware of becoming college prep schools. The curriculum of the Christian school must equip its students for their future lives no matter what occupations they eventually choose.

The Christian life, fourthly, is a life which is to be lived in the midst of ordinary human society. The body of Christians is not to take flight from the society in which it finds itself, but is rather to exercise its common faith in the midst of that society. Accordingly, Christian education must equip its students for life in contemporary society.

For one thing, flight never does any good. The world is within as well as without. "That which I would not, that I do." But also, to take flight is to fail fully to live the Christian life. We have said it is the task of the Christian community to be a witness to the world of the renewed life available to men in Christ. To some extent the church, by sending out missionaries and evangelists, has always recognized this. But if our earlier point is correct, that in Christ we find a new life and not just a new set of dogmatic beliefs and ritual practices, then the church can never identify its witness with its sending out of missionaries and evangelists. On the contrary, Christian life and Christian witness, Christian vocation and Christian mission, will have to be seen as opposite sides of the very same coin. And since our witness must be in the world, so must be our life. The community of believers lives not for its own sake; it lives for the sake of the world. As Christ was a servant to us, so are we to be a community of servants to those about us. We are called to follow Christ on all the concrete roads and into all the grimy houses of our civilization, being of loving service to our fellow men—giving clothes where clothes are needed, giving water where men are thirsty, healing the sick, giving comfort to those of troubled spirit, aiding those who are victims of the law, freeing men from false gods, shedding the light of truth on the world about us, teaching the ignorant, proclaiming that there is freedom. We are called, in short to seek the welfare of our fellow men. We are called to be men for others. This is our life; and in being our life, it is our witness. When the Christian life is lived in isolation, so that it is no longer a witness, then it is no longer the Christian life. It is no longer the life of service to God and fellow man.

Christian education, accordingly, must not be based on those withdrawal tendencies which have so often invaded the church. Equally, it must not be based on accommodation tendencies. Rather, the aim of Christian education must be to prepare the student to live the Christian life in contemporary society. This means that he must understand this society: its sources and roots, its values, its aims and ideals, it allegiances. Hemingway and Sartre must be read, Stravinsky and jazz must be heard, Picasso and Dubuffet must be viewed. This is not to say, of course, that students must be dropped into this forest without a guide. But the Christian school, without flinching, must acquaint the student with the world in which he will have to live out his life. There can be no denying that this is a dangerous business. To acquaint the student with the ultimate loyalties and allegiances of contemporary men in their cultural manifestations is to run the risk of his succumbing to their beckoning attractiveness. But the Christian knows his business.

The Christian life, finally, is a life engaged in helping to carry out man's task of cultural dominion. The legitimate tasks of the Christian community are not just those of preaching the gospel, relieving suffering, and doing whatever may be necessary to stay alive. The Christian school must take the whole realm of human culture for its domain.

Philosophers, since the time of the Greeks, have sought for what is most important and significant about man. They have sought to find in man that capacity which distinguishes him from the creatures surrounding him, and whose exercise gives to human life its chief meaning and significance. Some have seen man's capacity for reason as being this; others, his capacity for art; yet others, his capacity for language. What is striking in the Biblical conception of man, from the opening chapter of Genesis onwards, is that it shuns this quest altogether. For, according to it, what is distinctive about man and gives to human life worth and meaning is not some capacity in man. Rather, it is a task assigned to man—assigned to man by God. Of course, what is thereby presupposed is the presence in man of various capacities which make possible the carrying out of this task. Yet, in the Biblical perspective, what is unique and significant about man is that to him and to him alone is assigned the task of putting all creation at his service in living a life of fellowship with God and neighbor. Man is not to worship and fear his surroundings. He is to make use of them. The writer of the first chapter Genesis puts it this way: "And God said, let us make man in our image, after our likeness: and let them have dominion over the fish of the sea and over the birds of the air, and over the cattle, and over all the earth, and over creeping things that creep upon the earth." And the Psalmist expresses the same line of thought in these words: "Thou makest him to have dominion over the works of thy hand; thou has put all things under his feet."

There have been those in the Christian community, almost from the beginning, who have thought that they perceived an antithesis between Christ and culture. They have thought that the sole tasks permitted a Christian, beyond those necessary for continued existence, are the proclamation of the gospel and the performance of simple acts of mercy. They have thought that they had to choose between Christ and culture. Even the great Augustine, for example, insisted that man ought to turn his eyes away from this changing mutable world and, in so far as possible, focus his gaze solely on the eternal and immutable God revealed in Christ. And Tertullian was so impressed with the way in which culture had been laid at the altar of false gods that, rather than saying that it ought to be rededicated to Christ, he said that we ought to keep ourselves separate from all but the most rudimentary cultural endeavors. I think it is clear, however, that this is a distortion of Biblical thought. Christ did not abrogate the God-given task of having dominion. The redemption of man in Christ is the restoration of God's creation to its intended ends. The life of the redeemed is a life of serving God in the whole range of cultural tasks. Not Christ or culture. Not even Christ and culture. Christ *through* culture is what we must seek.

Thus any curriculum founded on a dichotomy and disjunction between Christ and culture, between serving God and having dominion, is not a

Christian curriculum. Any curriculum which teaches the Bible and only as much else as is necessary to stay alive and proclaim the gospel, is not a Christian curriculum. Mathematics and natural science belong in the curriculum of the Christian school as surely as do theology and moral instruction. For the task of the Christian community in this world is to build a Christian culture, different members of the community specializing in the performance of different aspects of this whole task.

An important consequence of this for the curriculum and the pedagogy of the schools is, it seems to me, that we must lay a heavy stress on creativity. By this I do not at all mean that we must seek to make every student an artist. Rather, I mean that instead of merely lecturing and drilling our students we must encourage them to discuss; instead of giving them pat answers to every social problem that the Christian faces we must encourage them to think matters through; instead of asking them to color paper plates for their mothers in art classes we must get them to express their feelings and ideas about the gospel and life with the media of the artist. In science we must encourage them to compose experiments; in Biblical studies we must get them to think through the Biblical message for themselves; and throughout the curriculum we must avoid merely acquainting our students with what has been thought and said and done by others, and get them to think and speak and act for themselves, as Christians. It is nothing but a pious wish and a grossly unwarranted hope that students trained to be passive and non-creative in school will suddenly, upon graduation, actively contribute to the formation of Christian culture.

Today, I have made but one point. It is this: That the curriculum of a Christian education is for Christian life. It is not for the training of theological sophisticates, not for the continuation of the evangelical churches, not for the preservation of Christian enclaves, not for getting to heaven, not for service to the state, not for defeating the Communists, not for preserving United States or Canada, not for life adjustment, not for cultivating the life of the mind, not for producing learned and cultured gentlemen. Christian education is for Christian life.

Looking to The Eighties: Do Christian Schools have a Future?

by Nicholas Wolterstorff

Signs Are Mixed

Does the Christian day school movement, and in particular the Calvinist day school movement have a future?

When I participated in a Christian school convention last spring in Birmingham, Alabama, and got a sense there of the fantastic flowering of Christian day schools — not racist schools, but authentic Christian schools — in the American South during the last five to seven years, then I said, "It most certainly does have a future." But when I go to some of the old, well-established, Christian day schools in the heartland of the U.S. and there witness the lackadaisical attitudes produced by middle-age respectability, then I say, "I wonder." When I participated, recently, in a conference of the non-public schools in Illinois, and there listened to Black people from central Chicago "chew out" the Calvinists and the Lutherans and the Catholics for having been so quiet about their schools all these years, then I said, "It most certainly does have a future." But on the other hand, when I listen to some of the graduates of the Christian schools pour out their resentment over how they were treated in those schools, then I say, "I'm not so sure." And when I hear, as I do now and then, about the lack of shared vision in some communities and schools, resulting in school systems flying apart into splinters, then I've got to say, "Well, I'm not so sure."

The evidence, in short, is mixed. There are hopeful signs and discouraging signs: promising signs and negative signs. My own guess, for what it's worth, is that the excitement of those new schools springing up will begin to invade some of those old, complacent schools, so that, by the end of the 80's, the combination of those new excited schools with those old, resource-rich schools, will have produced significant new impulses in

111

Christian education. What can also not be ignored is the growing sense in North America of a society adrift. Already this is driving more and more people to see the need for Christian education. In fact, the best statistics indicate that two new Christian schools are being formed every day in the U.S. So though the signs are mixed, the future seems to me promising.

The Challenge: Alternative Education in a
Non-Isolationist Setting

But tonight I really don't want to engage in prophecy and prognostication. Rather than offering predictions as to whether the Christian school movement will flourish I want to talk with you about the conditions under which it can flourish. For over those conditions you and I have some control. An whether or not the movement flourishes in the future depends on how you and I deal in the present with those conditions.

The great challenge facing the Christian school movement today is the very same challenge that has always faced the movement. That challenge is this: Is it possible to conduct alternative Christian education in a non-isolationist setting — that is, in the midst of ordinary North American society? Is it possible, without isolating the child and his family from the surrounding society, to conduct genuinely alternative Christian education? You see, I'm assuming that nobody in this room is seriously persuaded the course we ought to take is that of isolation. It's clear that alternative education is possible for the old order Amish, under the isolationist conditions which they have chosen for themselves. But the question I want you to think about along with me is this: Is it possible in a non-isolationist setting to conduct a genuinely alternative Christian education?

Let me begin by explaining what I have in mind by that question - explaining what I mean by 'alternative education' and what by 'non-isolationist setting'.

I grew up in a Reformed community on the prairies of central U.S. My memory of what was said about the goal of the Christian day schools, which I attended for part of my lower school education, is that their goal was to communicate to the child a Christian world and life view. I'm sure that formula has also been popular here in Canada. Now what was the impulse behind that formula? What were those who used it driving at? Quite clearly, in adopting that formula they were giving expression to one of the fundamental features of any authentic Reformed vision of Christianity, namely, to its passionate concern with wholeness, with integrity, with the totality of things. What they were saying was this: The Christian gospel does not speak just to our theological thought. It does not speak just to our ethical thought. It speaks to all our thought about the world and life. And Christian education must reflect that "totalism" of the Christian gospel. What they were deliberately avoiding was any formula which says the goal of Christian education is simply to imbue the child with Christian theological perspective. They didn't want to say that. And what they were also deliberately avoiding was any formula which says that the goal of Christian education is simply to imbue the child with a Christian ethical perspective. They didn't want to say that either. Instead, the goal of Christian education is to imbue the child with a Christian world and life view. Behind that formula lies the conviction that Christ's Lordship is to hold sway over all our thought, not just over some theological or ethical corner of our thought. With that, let me say that I profoundly agree.

But now I want to listen once again to the phrase, as I emphasize its last word: "A Christian world and life view." Traditionally the Christian schools have seen their goal as that of imbuing the child with a certain view — a view pertaining to all of life, indeed, but a *view*, nonetheless. They have seen their goal as above all a *cognitive* goal. Their concern has been with the thought of the child. They have wanted to shape thinking. Seeing that the question comes at once to mind: Doesn't that very same impulse toward wholeness, toward integrity, toward allowing everything to come under the Lordship of Jesus Christ, lead us beyond saying that the goal of Christian education is to impart a *view*, toward saying that the goal of Christian education is to shape a way of living? A Christian way of life includes, of course, a way of thinking. But there is more to the Christian life than thought. Christian education is a project of the Christian community. And it's goal is to induct the child into the life of that community, not just into its thought — into the life of discipleship.

And that — this is my next point — is an alternative mode of life, is it not? Isn't the significance of Pentecost in part that the life of the Christian community will always, until the end of age, be an alternative mode of life? Once upon a time God's chosen people was a natural grouping of people, a race. It's true that others could enter it, and that members of the race could defect. But nonetheless God's chosen people was Israel. After Pentecost, no longer. No longer is God's chosen people to be identified with any natural grouping. No longer is it to be identified with any nation, any social class, any sex. Now it is a transnational, a supranational, grouping with all the profound implications that has. The gospel tells us to expect that always when that new people, the church, finds itself present in some nation, it's going to find itself living, and called to live an alternative mode of life. For this new people trusts ultimately in God in Jesus Christ. And natural man always trusts in other things.

Now every society and every community educates its members for life in that community. American society does so, Canadian society does so. The community of Christians does so as well. And keeping in mind the point made just above, I come to the conclusion that Christian education must be alternative education. It's education for a mode of life which is an alternative mode of life. The Christian community is an alternative community. And its education of its members must correspondingly be an alternative mode of education. In so far as the Christian school genuinely educates for Christian life, it conducts an alternative mode of education.

Of course that's the ideal. In fact, it all too often doesn't go like that. When I survey the Christian schools of the Calvinist tradition I see, over and over, that the supporting community constantly urges its teachers to be, in effect, rebels and reformers, but fails to hold out the same challenge to others. It constantly urges of its teachers to reform sociology, philosophy, physics, chemistry. It urges that those all be rethought and reconstructed so that they can be taught in Christian perspective. In short, the Reformed community constantly asks of its teachers that *they* work out an alternative mode of thought, and conduct education in an alternative manner. But it seldom makes the same demand on others. The lawyers of the community act pretty much like other lawyers, and little is said by way of challenging them to acts as rebels and reformers in American law. So too for MD's and farmers, and businessmen. But of our teachers it is asked that they work out a genuinely Christian alternative.

How is this paradox to be explained? As follows, I think: We expect of our MD's, and our attorneys and our farmers and our businessmen that they *think* like Christians, plus acting piously and morally; but for the rest we expect them to go about their business like everyone else. You see, in my judgment it really is the case that the Christian school and its community have concentrated on a view. They have concentrated on getting the thoughts of the student straight. The Christian businessman acts pretty much the same, but *thinks* differently. And those alternative *thoughts* it is the business of the Christian school and its teachers to provide.

But that is all confused, isn't it? Christian education, to say it once more, is for Christian life, not just for Christian thought. The Christian life is an alternative mode of life. Consequently Christian education will have to be an alternative mode of education, not just in the sense of communicating alternative thoughts but in the much more radical sense of equipping the student for an alternative way of life.

A Difficult Challenge

I trust you see now what I meant when I said that the basic challenge facing the Calvinistic day school today is the same one that has always faced it: can an alternative Christian educational program succeed in a non-isolationist setting?

But why do I see that as a challenge? Wherein lies the difficulty? Well, if you agree with me that the school aims at life and not just at thought, then the school cannot be concerned just with knowledge. Nor can it be concerned just with knowledge plus abilities. It has to be concerned with what the student does with this knowledge and abilities. It has to be concerned with how the child acts. Now of course neither the school nor anyone else can guarantee that the child will act a certain way. What it can do, though, is shape what he tends to do, what he is inclined to do, what he is disposed to do. So I come straightforwardly to this conclusion: If what I said concerning the goal of Christian education is correct, then Christian schools must be concerned with shaping how the child tends to act - concerned not just with knowledge, not just with abilities, but with tendencies to act in certain ways.

Psychology and the Wisdom of the Ages

And that leads to this large next question. How can teachers and parents effectively and responsibly shape how children tend to act? I add the word "responsibly" because there may be effective ways of shaping how people tend to act which are irresponsible ways. So both words are needed, "effective" and "responsible." If you are concerned with how the children are going to live and not with just how they're going to think, how do you exhibit that concern? What do you do?

Over the last twenty years a great deal of information has been accumulated by psychologists by way of an answer to this question, most of it, in my judgment, confirming the wisdom of the ages, but interesting and valuable nevertheless. Now in the brief time available this evening I can't run through the highlights of this psychological literature. All I can do is single out just one of the most important conclusions.

The wisdom of the ages tells us, and contemporary psychology elaborately confirms it, that if you want to shape how the child tends to act, it helps for you to act that way. You all knew that anyway. But if for some reasons you're suspicious of the wisdom of the ages, then all you have to do is read what is by now a massive psychological literature on the phenomenon that psychologists call *modelling*. The idea behind the use of the word is clear. Someone serves as a *model* for the child. And it has been shown, in dozens of different kinds of situations, that this powerfully shapes in the child a tendency to act as the model acts.

Let me give you a brief indication of some of the situations which have been studied. It's been shown that you can increase a child's tendency to yield to temptation of one sort and another by confronting him or her with models who yield to that temptation. It's been shown that you can increase the tendency of a child to act aggressively by presenting models who act aggressively. It's been shown that you can increase a child's altruistic and generous actions by presenting models who act generously. It's been shown that you can induce a child to raise his or her standards of performance for one task and another by presenting models who exhibit high standards of performance. It's been shown that you can induce a child to lower standards of performance in some task or other by presenting models who have low standards of performance. And so on and on and on. You get the point. If you want a child to act a certain way it helps for respected and loved people in the environment to act that way.

Questions About "Modelling"

Floods of questions come to mind at this point. Let me pose and answer just three. What happens if a model preaches one way and practices another? The experiments are stunningly unanimous. What shapes the practice of the child is the practice of the model and not the preaching of the model. We all knew that already didn't we? As the old saying has it, "Actions speak louder than words." However, the full description of the situation is this: If a model preaches one way and practices a different way, the child tends to preach the way the model preaches and act the way the model acts. Hypocrisy perpetuates hypocrisy. Hypocrisy, like everything else, is communicated by models practicing hypocrisy. So where there is discrepancy between the preaching and practice of models, the child will preach that way and practice that way.

A second question, again directly relevant to our topic tonight, is this: What happens if people whom the child regards as models act inconsistently? That is, not if a given person practices one way and preaches another, but if one model acts one way and another acts in some way inconsistent with the first? The answer is this: you can't predict the results. Some children will follow one model, some, the other. And when you average out the behavior, it becomes unpredictable. I want to return to this result, since it seems to me to be of enormous importance for the Christian schools: when a child is confronted by inconsistent, conflicting models, you can't predict what he will tend to do.

Here's a third question, also immediately and directly relevant to our concerns tonight. What if the model in question is presented on TV or film instead of live in the environment? It makes virtually no difference. It's been shown in a great many studies that people are just as much influenced by what they see on film and TV as by what they see live. The aggressive behavior of children and adults is increased just as much by presenting them with models on TV or film as by presenting them with live models who act aggressively.

Do you now begin to see why one of the great challenges facing the Christian school is how to educate for an alternative style of life in non-isolationist surroundings? Your children and mine are not reared in isolation. Consequently they are repeatedly presented with models which contradict what you and I try to model, on film and TV if not live. They are repeatedly confronted with conflicting styles of life. And what we have learned from the modelling experiments makes one wonder how the goal of training and educating them to live the Christian life can ever succeed without isolation. How can this project that Calvinists have set for themselves, of not isolating themselves from the surrounding society while yet educating their children for an alternative mode of life, possibly succeed? Haven't we just been living with illusions all these years? Don't we have to flip one way or the other, give up as illusionary this project of an alternative education, or go the Amish way of isolation?

Before I give you some answers, I want to make one more point. I put the situation as if the child was confronted by teachers and parents who consistently model the Christian way of life, and then in addition by people on film, TV, etc. who act in contradiction with that. But that's not really the situation, is it? We have to confess that we don't consistently model for the child the Christian way of life. The life of the Christian community is not, in many respects, all that different from that of the surrounding society. So the challenge to be faced is this: How can the Christian school possibly succeed, when not even its supporting constituency is consistently presenting the child with a model of the new life of Jesus Christ? The school can preach that alternative mode of life, the parents can preach it, the church can preach it, but we know that if those who preach don't *practice* what they preach, we'll only perpetuate hypocrisy.

Doomed to Isolation?

It's time for me to present some answers. For answers there are. The situation is not really as bleak as I have pictured it.

Let me make two points. The first, is this: We really can succeed, in general, only if the church, the home and the school are living that alternative mode of life. There is no way around this hard truth. So let me say it once again. The school can expect to succeed in its goal of educating for an alternative mode of life only if the church, the home and the school model that way of life for the child. To suppose otherwise is to live with illusions.

What that means, concretely, is that the church and the home and the school must themselves be communities of love if the school is to succeed in its educational goals. For what we know is that children tend to model themselves after people whom they love or respect. A supporting, loving community has a powerful formative impact on the members of the community. So, if someone lives with great responsibility in ecological matters, but treats his children without love, all his ecological endeavors will be of little effect. When students come to me and complain bitterly about their Christian education, what they complain about is seldom its inferiority, but rather about its hypocrisy and the lack of love that they sensed. In so doing, they are pointing at an absolutely decisive defect. If the Christian school is not a community of love it cannot succeed.

But secondly, there is now a large body of research which shows that it helps immensely in shaping how a person tends to act if you give him reasons for acting that way. When the child is confronted by violence and aggression on TV, the effects of those models can be diminished by giving him reasons for not acting that way. The inarticulate model who says nothing is much less successful than the model who explains. The Christian parent who explains why he is acting as he does is the truly effective model. To counteract the discrepant, the inconsistent, the dissonant, models in the surrounding society, the Christian school must do what the Christian parent must do and what the Christian church must do: give the child reasons for acting in the right way.

And here, at last, we get into curriculum. I am convinced that if we want to make Christian education succeed, we must first ask what kind of life we want the child to lead when he leaves school. And then we must back up from that point and construct a curriculum. Forget what secular educators in Ontario and Michigan are doing. Instead, ask yourself what's necessary to equip the child to live the Christian mode of life. And then frame a curriculum in terms of that.

This means that we will have to get into the hard controversial issues that face the Christian in the living of his life. It's not sufficient to throw abstract sociology and philosophy and psychology and so forth at the child. We have no right to expect that the child is going to act responsibly on ecological matters and matters of war and matters of poverty, on matters of how he spends his money and so forth, if we just throw at him abstract academic disciplines. The school that wants to succeed must give the child detailed reasons for acting in definite ways in surrounding society. I confess, to my embarrassment, that ten years ago I was under the illusion that it was sufficient, at least for college students, to give them these abstract disciplines, and they would put them to use. I now see that that was naive nonsense. It won't work. It never has worked and it never will work.

In its curriculum the school must not just give abstract interpretations of history and so forth, but concern itself with the difficult, hard, controversial areas of Christian living, working out answers and offering to the student reasons for acting in what the school judges to be the right way.

So, in conclusion, here is what I see as our program for the 80's. To acknowledge, as I think we have not up to this point, that Christian education is for Christian life and not just for Christian thought. Secondly, to come to realize that Christian life is shaped by the entire conduct of the school, its teachers, by how they act, by how they comport themselves, and not just by what they say, not just by the curriculum. And thirdly, to begin to work out a curriculum in which we give the child articulate, soundly based Christian reasons for acting the way in which it seems to us they ought to act. If we manage to do this, then not only will the 80's be an exciting decade for educators, but at the end of that decade Christian education will be more exciting, and vastly more effective, than ever it has been before.

Nicholas Beversluis:
Editor Introduction

Nicholas Henry Beversluis retired in 1979 from the Education Department of Calvin College after a long career of work and writing in Christian education. More widely educated and experienced than most Reformed theoreticians, he brought both to bear on his writing. His academic training embraced both seminary degrees and a philosophy of education doctorate, with a master's in history as well. His extensive teaching and administration experience was at both secondary and college levels.

The fruit of that combined experience is captured in brief form in the following excerpts from his latest publication, *Christian Philosophy of Education*, 1971. Chapters 3 and 4 are reprinted with permission of Christian Schools International. The strong theological undergirding in chapter 2 is not included, as it is the work of both Nicholas Beversluis and Wolterstorff. It is in "the Two Sides of Christian Education" that he identifies past tensions in Reformed thinking, with Jellema and Jaarsma as primary representatives of the two sides. In the rest of the chapter, and in "Major Learning Goals" he lays out what view of the learner, what goals of education, and what curriculum design will bring closure, or resolution of previous conflicting views.

The whole book, but expecially these excerpts, deserve a place in the list of classics of Reformed thinking on education for their ability to communicate with both pre-service and in-service teachers in language they find meaningful.

Major Learning Goals in Christian Education

Nicholas Henry Beversluis

If choosing major learning goals is as important to articulating the school's religious vision as preceding discussions have asserted, how does a Christian school go about choosing them? Of the many kinds of learning growth it could promote, how does it decide which it should mainly aim at? To *plan* Christian educational growth, and not merely act situationally, or pragmatically, or in terms of personal preference, teachers must face these questions. They must agree not only on their choice of learning goals but also on the reasons for their choice. How should these decisions be made? Thoughtful educators from earliest times to the present were guided in their decisions by their assumptions about the nature and needs of man. Christian teachers should do no less.

Image of God and Learning Goals

To determine the school's major learning goals Christian teachers should ask *empirical* questions: Who is man? What is he like? What are his needs? But they must also ask *theological* questions—questions that cannot be answered by observing man: What ought man to be like? Why is man here? What is he called to do in the world? They must ask: What is it that God wants for him and of him? And then, in the face of those questions and answers, too, they must ask: What are his needs?

Christian teachers must believe that the nature and needs of man, and therefore of a child in school, are determined above all by his relationship to God. They should believe that the school's learning goals, chosen with a view to that nature and those needs, are to be defined not in one way but in two ways: by studying young persons empirically, in their life situation, but also by asking about their religious calling in and to the world.

Christian education must accept the wholeness of young persons and choose learning goals that will mature them as whole persons.

Thus to ask about a Christian school's major learning goals is to ask again about its religious vision and the view of man presupposed in it. It is to ask how the school should embody that religious vision in its program, a program that includes choices about preferred curriculum, but before that, choices about kinds of human growth which curriculum should help promote.

When the above questions about the nature and needs of human persons are taken seriously, Christian teachers should select their learning goals within a perspective that differs radically from the religious perspective of either the educational behaviorist or the educational rationalist. They should select learning goals in reference to the biblical doctrine of man as image of God. This doctrine illumines not only man's relationship to God but also his endowments for living in that relationship. From that biblical point of view Christian teachers should reject the behaviorist's assumption that human nature can be understood mainly by empirical methods and his tendency to limit learning goals to instrumental competencies or functions. They should also reject the rationalist's assumption that human nature can be understood mainly by some sort of speculation or introspection and his tendency to limit learning goals to intellectual power or otherworldly contemplation. Christian teachers should choose learning goals within a theological perspective.

Although educational discussion has often been weighted down rather than helped by unrelated theologizing, there are many points at which theology must enrich and control Christian educational thinking. Certainly, one of these points is the doctrine of man as image of God. This doctrine presents a far more imaginative and productive perspective for defining a school's major learning goals than does either the behaviorist's or the rationalist's view of human nature.

Man as image of God, according to biblical representation, should be understood in at least the following ways, all of them of great importance to education: (1) he is a physical-spiritual person, not two parts joined, but both at once, undivided and unseparated; (2) in that wholeness he is given unique endowments for thinking, for choosing, for creating; (3) with those endowments he is called, as Genesis says, to live in social relationships and to do the world's work; (4) in those social relationships and work, he is to hallow his person and his endowments in religious stewardship—by offering them to God in obedience and in worship. Of course, the depravity and guilt of sin radically disoriented and estranged man, estranged him from God, and thus also from himself, from his fellow man, from nature, from his work. But forgiveness and renewal through Jesus Christ restored man, not just what is sometimes called personal salvation, but also within all those relationships; so that it is again as image of God, in all its fullness, that man becomes a disciple of Jesus Christ and a steward of God in and to the world.

A Christian school should accept this biblical word about man, especially also its implications for man's life in the world. If it does, Christian teachers should above all promote the growth of those endowments in the learner that most directly prepare him to understand and accept his life in the world in all of its fullness and to obey God in it. Selecting major learning goals that promote such growth is the school's best way of meeting the nature and needs of young persons.

This emphasis on the learner's *religious* nature and needs should not, of course, become an evasion by teachers of their responsibilities to *unique* individuals in their classrooms—individuals whose situational needs, interests, fears, and differences require close attention. Those responsibilities both chapter 3 and 5 emphasize as crucially important to educational closure. They have to do with professional excellence in the teaching-learning process. In pursuing the major learning goals discussed here, a Christian school should all along the way utilize the great amount of empirical data by which physiology, sociology, and psychology clarify what a young person is like, how he learns, when he should learn this or that, what inhibits learning, what motivates him, and so on. Christian teachers would fail if the findings of those sciences were not carefully heeded. What is emphasized here is that whatever teachers learn about young persons in those ways must be made to serve, all along the way, the transcendent relationship of a young person to God, a relationship that unites, simultaneously and uniquely, all the worlds of a child's physical-spiritual existence. This is to say that teachers should honor the learner's nature as image of God.

Learning Goals for Religious Growth

What then should be a Christian school's major learning goals? Given the school's articulated and fleshed-out religious vision; given also the concern it shares with Christian parents for a child's social and psychological growth; and given especially its unique calling and competencies as a *school,* toward what sort of *educational* growth should its curriculum be mainly pointed?

The answer proposed here is that the learner's intellectual, moral, and creative growth should be given special prominence. It is these kinds of growth that can best prepare young persons for the social and psychological maturity they need in order to live knowledgeably, committedly, and productively in their Christian life—in their present and in their future adult life. Accepting these goals requires that from earliest grades on teachers will progressively guide young persons through intellectual understanding and insight to *know,* through moral awareness and commitment to *choose,* and through creative self-acceptance and freedom to *participate in* the life appropriate to a Christian human being.

Of course, distinguishing these learning goals conceptually does not imply parts or compartments within learners. The wholeness of persons forbids this and requires instead that teachers assume that these and other kinds of learnings will be interacting and simultaneous all along the way. Interrelated with all sorts of supportive and collateral development in young persons, whether social, psychological, or physical, these three major learnings are also interrelated. Thus *intellectual* growth includes morally accountable as well as creatively divergent thinking; *moral* growth includes intellectual analysis as well as creative dispositions; and *creative* growth includes the controls of both the true and the good. Even so, to keep learning goals sorted out conceptually and to *plan* educational growth, it is of utmost importance to examine these classes of learning separately and to let them function as prominent reminders of what the major outcomes of Christian teaching and learning ought to be.

It should also be clear that these learning goals ought in all respects to aim at religious growth. When these goals are thoroughly understood, when they are promoted by Christian teachers through appropriate curriculum, when they are regularly pointed toward the knowledge, the love, and the service of God, and when in these ways young persons are prepared for life in what Reformed Christians have long called the City of God in the world—then the result could well be superior Christian education. For then religious growth, rooted in personal faith in Jesus Christ, will begin to reach out beyond simple piety and simple covenant nurture. It will become a response by young persons to their appointment by God to the fullness of life: to life's complexity and variety, its mysteries and wonders, its gifts and opportunities, its needs and problems, its work and worship.

Such religious growth a Christian school should aim at through its major learning goals. Teachers should progressively lead young persons to understand, accept, and respond to the school's vision of the Christian life: that work and worship ought to hallow each other; that God's command to subdue the earth and have dominion over all things forbids exploiting the earth, but also requires resisting evil and promoting the good within all the ordinary conditions of man's social and cultural existence; that human calling requires declaring and exhibiting the reconciling love of God, but also doing the world's work; that in these ways both the creation mandate and the gospel mandate are to be responded to by man in his history, in his life.

To make that all-encompassing religious vision productive *education-ally,* in its program, a Christian school must foster in the life of all its pupils their intellectual, moral, and creative growth. On the other hand, to make these kinds of growth productive *religiously,* a Christian school must neither distort them nor pursue them only as educational growth.

What are these kinds of growth like and how can they promote Christian maturity? Some clarification of what each is here taken to mean is presented in the three sections following.

Intellectual Growth

To rise above some of the confusion that perennially stalks intellectual education, Christian teachers should be wary of a major pitfall. That is the notion that to avoid the intellectual irrelevancies and cruelties practiced by fanatical catechizers of former days, they need to accept the de-intellectu-alized curriculum of latter day progressive educators. They should choose a better way than either of these, the way of intellectual *growth.*

But if the aim of Christian education is to propel persons into *living* a life, should not the role of intellect be de-emphasized? Should not practical Christian involvement in life, rather than books and ideas and thinking, be accented—practical things such as the concerns of business and commerce, of social justice and reform, of personal attitudes and conduct, of preparing for jobs, and the like. A Christian school should reject such an implied separation of action from thought with its threat of personal and social chaos. It should believe that while far more than intellectual growth is needed for Christian living, without such growth neither a person nor a society would be fully human. Alert to the dangers of intellectualism and remembering that this learning goal has an aim beyond itself, the school must nevertheless prominently emphasize as one of its major concerns the intellectual life of all young Christians.

Avoiding the caricature. Opponents of intellectual education, and sometimes its friends, have crudely caricatured it as consisting almost entirely of fact-gathering, fact-memorizing, and a stuffing of something called the mind. What is it really like?

Most significantly, intellectual growth has to do with man's capacity to know, to know and understand what things are like, to know and understand the truth about things, ultimately to know God in so far as man can know him. Human rationality is not merely, as behaviorists suggest, an instrument of intelligence such as squirrels and elephants also possess. Nor, on a higher level, is it merely as rationalists suggest, the capacity for intellectual systems and symbols, such as all human beings uniquely possess. Including these, of course, human rationality is also more: it is above all the capacity ultimately for responding to and loving God. This the Old Testament calls *knowing* God and the New Testament calls *faith*. Derivatively, it then also includes man's ordinary behavioral intelligence as well as man's extraordinary capacity for a rational appraisal of and response to life.

Stressing intellectual growth on all of these levels and recognizing that such growth must be fostered for the sake of moral and creative response to God within life, the Christian school should give close attention to the educational skills and disciplines that foster such growth.

Schooling and intellectual growth. Because life is complex, some sort of intellectual education, whether Plato's kind or John Dewey's kind, has always been at the core of a school's concern. In the Christian perspective, education clearly requires that young persons master many assorted facts; a school believing that truth and reality come with their own claims must stress this. But intellectual growth requires much more than facts. It requires all that psychologists mean by cognition, comprehension, memory, divergence, discovery, judging, evaluation. It includes understanding things in relationship, discovering patterns and unities within life's "buzz-ing and booming," and, above all, progressing towards insight and wisdom. It includes thinking, understanding problems, forming hypotheses, drawing conclusions, testing conclusions. It includes imagining, enquiring, exploring, analyzing, probing for meanings and comprehension.

Christian teachers should ask themselves whether they are capitalizing on the vast opportunities the curriculum offers for such growth. Is the curriculum focused on understanding man's age-old problems and frustrations, as well as his great achievements in the arts, in science, in politics? Is it focused on understanding his pride, hatred, and indifference, as well as his faith and courage? Is the understanding that is fostered in science, history, literature, or whatever, brought to bear on complex social and personal issues today so that the necessary closure between what seem to be remote matters and what seem to be more immediate and urgent matters is in fact achieved? Are all sorts of contemporary issues analyzed, clarified, and understood? Are their moral aspects examined so that solutions that are both imaginative and desirable are offered in class discussions? In discussions about race and poverty, about communism and Christianity, about biblical events and Christian doctrine, about improving education or public worship, are young persons prodded, not just to talk, but to talk thoughtfully? Not just to propose action, but to do this knowledgeably? Are discussions, whether in social studies or religion class, in 4th grade or 11th grade, directed toward answers only after the questions have been understood and accepted as questions by the learner? Are the methods of inquiry, of discrimination, of discovery emphasized?

Intellectual growth is indispensable to normal human growth. In a school such growth should be the organizing center for many other sorts of development that all young persons need, not just the talented few. It is essential preparation, moreover, for responsible adult Christian life: to vote intelligently, to read newspapers critically, to rear children successfully, to disagree with fellow Christians or other fellow citizens productively. It is necessary in order to see through the deceit of modern advertising, to take positions on civil liberties, to judge the morality of a given war, to understand labor-management disputes, to have opinions about Supreme Court decisions. For the Christian life, not only the facts and tools for thinking but also understanding and insight are indispensable.

Christians must not act as though they believe that faith and the Bible, plus skill in a job and faithful religious routines in home and church, make solid intellectual growth unnecessary. Through the use of his thinking powers, every young person in Christian schools, insofar as his normal endowments make this possible, must come to intellectual terms with his environment: its physical, social, historical, and spiritual dimensions. He must come to *know* the world and its life in their variety and complexity, to know himself and other people and institutions and forces and movements. Above all, he must come to discern, to understand, and to judge the ideas and the allegiances of his fellow man. For all of this growing insight and understanding, the Bible and his faith are indispensable but not a substitute.

Intellectual growth for freedom. A Christian school should help young Christians, each on his own level, progress toward the freedom that intellectual growth brings: freedom from confusion and disorientation, but also from the easy solutions that the intellectually lazy person prefers to disciplined thought. Whether in formal subjects like natural science, art, and history or in the more immediate areas of race relations, contemporary politics, and denominational differences, young persons must come to rise above the easy way of opinions and prejudice, of half-truth and conventional thinking, and make progress toward the more difficult but rewarding way of deliberation and analysis—and of openness to the thought of others. They must take account of things as they are in order to get on with how they ought to be.

Certainly, living the Christian life as described in Chapter 2 requires more than intellectual growth, but it is inconceivable without it. To caricature this sort of growth and then to give it a kind of third class status would deprive the Christian life of some of its major moorings and Christian education of one of its most strategic roles in Christian human development.

Moral Growth

In their concern to rise above the confusion about moral growth in education, Christian teachers should reject the notion that to avoid the pitfalls of moralism and legalism they must settle for little more than something called a general religious influence in the school, leaving it, as is sometimes said, to the home and church to change attitudes and dispositions and conduct. They should choose a better way than either of these, the way of moral *growth*. Aiming in intellectual growth at the learner's developing insight into what things are like and in his creative growth at his growing participation within life, a school should aim in moral education at his growing commitment to what things ought to be like. Moral growth, rooted as it must be in understanding and culminating as it must in choices and behavior, is at the core of the Christian life. What is such growth like? What is it that a school should aim at in such growth?

Beyond rules and codes. Because the Christian life entails far more than *simple* conduct, the moral development a school aims at must go beyond the observance of rules and codes. Initiated in the miracle of God's grace, the learner's *commitment* to the good and the right must be carefully tended. It must also be strengthened. For this to happen, that commitment must grow—from simple behaviors to complex choices. In its concern for the pupil's expanding moral awareness and growth, a school must emphasize outward behavior, but also far more, it must especially emphasize attitudes, values, discriminations, choices, all below the surface of outward behavior.

Rules and codes must, of course, guide and undergird human life, and schools must strongly support homes and churches in stressing their observance. But because teachers must help parents and ministers make clear that a maturing commitment requires more than such observance and more also than the moralism and legalism it could lead to, a Christian school can in moral education offer one of its greatest services to young Christians. It can help them learn that when the Christian life is *equated* with the observance of rules and codes, that life is diminished and stunted. For then it is forgotten that such guides are but stations in a longer journey, a journey toward responsibility and freedom. It is forgotten, as St. Paul says, that Christians must move toward a freedom beyond law, the freedom of a higher allegiance of persons to the Person of Christ. In a life of such freedom, rules and codes, important though they be, are transcended; motivations are internalized; a wider, deeper, more momentous life of moral awareness and choice marks the maturing Christian.

Schooling, options, and moral growth. Such Christian progress requires a gradually widening range of moral options. This being so, the school's curriculum must become a strategic means to such growth. This curriculum must induct young persons, each appropriately to his readiness, into the complexity and variety of moral obligations, choices, ambiguities, tensions, allegiances, and behaviors that human life presents to all observant persons, and especially to observant Christians.

Of course, life apart from schools and curriculum also brings its challenges to growth: a child's good habit of church attendance becomes the army recruit's choice of attending or not attending the chaplain's Sunday worship service; the young adolescent's indifference to persons of the opposite sex becomes the older person's choice of controlling or not controlling sexual desire; the college student's relative poverty becomes the business man's choice of being honest or not being honest in his income tax returns.

But through its curriculum a school both accelerates and guides the growth deliberately. Often by imaginative projection, but nevertheless in real educational encounters, the subjects studied, the books, the discussions, and the observations become a prod to sharper awareness of moral options and of the need to make responsible choices. Because in such moral development the young person gradually learns that simple rules and codes are inadequate, he will, within his Christian commitment, learn to seek personal and internal resources for moral decisions at the deeper level of what the Bible calls his heart.

Moral growth and ordinary experience. The school's curriculum should clarify moral issues in the ordinary experience of young persons. In striking ways this can be done through studies in science, literature, social problems, history, as well as in religious studies. Such studies can help young persons understand, for example, that the simple judgments that Americans are good and Russians are bad, that Protestants are Christians and Catholics are something else, that Republicans are right and Democrats are wrong are not only inadequate, but are also morally irresponsible. In a Christian school young persons must learn to distinguish between persons and beliefs, between labels and realities, between responsible evaluations and conventional opinions, prejudice, or plain error. The intention of such clarifications is not that young persons stop making judgments, but that they become more knowledgeable and responsible in making them, that, seeing the real issues and differences between opposed principles or actions, they come to make real choices, Christian choices.

A school's curriculum presents opportunities to explore, without moralizing, conventional but defective attitudes about many things in ordinary life: simple honesty, neighboring black people, the importance of clothes and cars, violence in the streets, regard for wildlife on camping trips, the turbulence of sexuality, demagoguery in politics, and the like; to explore them in terms not just of actions but of attitudes and values and justification. Through their studies, young Christians must be brought to understand that right and wrong, better and worse, good and bad are frequently not simple but complex matters. They must come to see and to accept the moral tensions and ambiguities of life, and at the same time attempt to understand and to choose for themselves the Christian way within these tensions and ambiguities.

Moral growth and new experience. The curriculum must stimulate moral awareness and choice also through new experiences, through induction into unfamiliar issues and crises. Gradually, the school should introduce concerns and problems that young persons *ought* to be thinking about. Appropriate to their levels of maturity, their studies should introduce them to such ethical concerns as acquisitiveness and stewardship, love of country and chauvinism, poverty and affluence, law-and-order and law-and-justice; also modern warfare, pre-marital sex, pseudo-Christian fiction, civil disobedience, and so on. History study, so often a dull affair, bristles with educative moral issues and should bring the student to all sorts of confrontations: King David choosing adultery and murder; Christians choosing the catacombs and death; St. Frances choosing voluntary pov-

erty; Luther choosing religious dissent; Hitler choosing racism and geno-
cide; President Truman choosing the A-bomb. They should learn by
probing all sorts of situations and options that such dramatic choices, as
well as countless other choices by ordinary persons in ordinary life,
disclose man to be above all a choosing and responsible being. Under
careful teaching and through imaginative reconstructions, young persons
can learn that their life as human and as Christian inescapably requires
moral commitment and the willingness to make vexing choices. They can
learn that they must make such choices at times with the help of rules and
codes, but more often with the help of only a sensitive conscience, vitalized
in personal allegiance to Jesus Christ.

Moral growth and personal freedom. Increasingly, as the motivation
for attitudes and actions is internalized, a young Christian grows in moral
freedom. Such freedom is not lawlessness, but the capacity for knowledgeably and committedly choosing God's way in his life. Needing intellectual
freedom from ignorance and mere opinion, he needs moral freedom from
sin, but also from simplistic morality. Tempted as he is to live by prejudice,
by convention, by legalism, and attracted to those as he is by insensitivity,
by pride, by moral myopia, the young Christian must come to live the
examined life. He must learn that the examined life can foster the free life
and that a free life is characterized mainly by a growing willingness to
make decisive Christian choices, choices that express internalized and
vital commitment to Christ.

Progressing from grade to grade in such freedom, young Christians will
need to struggle, to agonize, to live with their failures and guilt. They will
also, however, learn in new ways how to repent and how to receive God's
renewal into their lives. Such renewal can bring Christian growth so that
increasingly they will come to choose truth over falsehood, goodness over
evil, beauty over ugliness, communion over alienation, constructive work
in the world over either exploitation or rejection of the world. Prodded by
good curriculum, good teaching, and the grace of God, they will learn that
such choices, made day by day and throughout their lives, constitute their
choice of God and their rejection of alien gods. They will learn that this is
what it really means to accept Christ and to live the Christian life in the
midst of the world. It is in these ways that a Christian school can help
prepare young persons for what we call making profession of faith. For this
is what gives substance to the profession—and to the faith.

A Christian school must aim, in its learning goals and in its curriculum,
to free young Christians in and for the religious moral life, one in which
piety replaces pietism, ethical awareness replaces legalism, conscience
replaces conformity, and allegiance to God's will replaces sectarian

withdrawal from life. Young Christians must be frequently unsettled in a Christian school, wisely, carefully, pedagogically, in order that they may be brought to greater moral maturity. Such growth, along with intellectual growth, can help young persons grow also in the disposition and competence they need for creative participation in the Christian life.

Creative growth

In their concern to rise above the misunderstanding surrounding creative growth, Christian teachers should reject the notion that to avoid uncontrolled permissiveness or a denial of the learner's sinful nature, they must choose the way of repression, of authority, of conformity in their classrooms. They should choose a better way than either of these, the way of creative *growth.*

Creative growth is, in a sense, the end-product of the educative process, giving focus and substance and expression to a young person's intellectual and moral growth. It has to do with his active response to life as a unique person, a response to life's openness and possibilities. Taking account through intellectual growth of what things are like and through moral growth of what things ought to be like, the learner in his creative development begins to be a participator. He begins to *express* himself. When this expression is not a mere reaction but a response, bearing his personal signature, it is a creative expression. Very young children in the home bubble over with such expression. Because schools must not snuff out but foster this great endowment in human nature, teachers must understand it.

A disposition, not subjectivity. Just as intellectual education can be distorted as mainly fact-gathering and mind-stuffing, and moral education can be distorted as mainly rule-learning and moralizing, so creative education can be distorted. This happens when it is supposed that creative growth is only for future artists, scientists, poets, or musicians. Of course, specially gifted persons will and should through such education be stirred up. But what is referred to here is the need and potential not of the gifted few, but of all young persons in a school.

Creative growth is more crudely distorted when it is understood to mean the encouragement in young persons of undisciplined, whimsical, romantic self-expression. Of course, creative growth calls for and encourages self-expression; it requires and fosters freedom and spontaneity and innovation. But what is referred to here is expression in reference to something; it is a response to and a reordering of some deeply perceived experience. Taking account of the realities of life, as they are and as they ought to be, self-expression in this sense is an individual person's apprehension of those realities and his response to them *within* his own life and situation.

The self-expression fostered by creative growth is not self-generated, nor is it a mere reaction to either inner impulses or outer stimuli. It is a reply, a reply to life, ultimately to human calling and to God. It is not an unaccountable boiling over at the surface of life, but the taking account by a person of an engagement at the depths of his life. Self-expression in this sense is the response, as someone has said, to a mania not from below but from above.

And so creative growth is not growth in raw subjectivity; it is not even growth in activity first of all, although it must become that. It is the growth of a disposition, a spirit, a creative intent, an intent first of all to *be* and after that to act. It is an intent to be, as in the biblical story, not a Martha, all action and motion, but a Mary, seeking strength and wisdom for action through the inner renewal and disposition of her life. Irresistibly leading out into expression and action, creative growth is fostered through self-awareness and self-acceptance. The expression and the action follow the personal freedom such growth nourishes.

A young Christian caught up in such growth and accepting the reality of God's sovereign control within all of life will be learning also to accept that other reality of the Christian paradox: Christian man's responsibility and freedom to act. He will discover that life is open-ended and that therefore all sorts of things are still possible, that they are possible, moreover, not abstractly, nor just for other persons, but for him as an individual and unique self. Creative growth takes place when such a young person becomes aware that he has it in him to live a personal life, that within all sorts of objectively real claims made upon him by God, by community, by daily work, he is nevertheless not required to reproduce in his own life the life-styles of people around him, but is free to fashion his own. When he begins to accept this about himself, such self-acceptance can foster authentic self-expression. A growing disposition to such self-acceptance can, under careful teaching, make him an active learner and can also help prepare him to live a productive life of Christian discipleship.

Schooling and creative growth. Through suitable curriculum a Christian school should foster such self-acceptance and such a disposition in all its students. It should do this in the basic three R's, but also in art, music, speech, writing, and physical education, previously described as *developmental* studies. But the school should also promote such a disposition and

such self-acceptance by the early detection and encouragement of spontaneity and originality in all subject areas. In all sorts of ways, teachers
should prod young persons to do, to say, to make things that require
imagination, innovation, experimentation, self-expression. This can happen in the second grade and in the twelfth grade, in the so-called creative
arts and in the social sciences, in a history class and in a mathematics class.
The creative expression can be writing a poem or a paragraph, making a
sculpture or a painting, proposing a solution to a social problem or
conducting an experiment with mice, reconstructing a historical setting or
playing games with numbers—or taking part in any sort of class or group
discussions. What is needed above all is that such expressions be original
and that the originator have the freedom, inside himself and in the
classroom, to do or say what is in him, to bring it out before others to see
or hear.

In fostering this sort of personal self-acceptance and expression, the
school's ongoing concern with the learner's *social* and *psychological*
development coincides with its commitment to his creative growth. Those
collateral learnings, so crucially important in Christian growth, are both
supportive of and promoted by all the concerns of a school in which
creative participation and self-expression are especially fostered: in class
discussions, group projects, laboratory experiments, art creations, as well
as in bands, choirs, contests, debates, and physical education. Creative
growth promotes openness, not only to life and the world, but also to other
persons. This is because it frees persons for the kind of life they were
created to live. A school committed to graduating young men and women
willing and competent to participate in adult Christian life should prominently emphasize the creative growth of its students. Better Christian
schools all along have stressed, more or less adequately, good intellectual
and moral education and doubtless expected that such education would
promote also the creative disposition and participation stressed here. To be
more successful in this regard than they have been, Christian schools will
need to be more concerned to promote creative growth deliberately—not
indeed as a substitute for intellectual and moral education, but rather as the
culmination of such education.

Creative growth for freedom. If what goes on in the classroom does, in
fact, culminate in such growth, it will nourish the personal freedom a
normal Christian life needs. Such freedom can help young persons come
to terms with life, life illumined by a wisdom born of accepting, but also
responding to, God's world. Evidence of the school's success in fostering
such freedom and such response should be measured in the progress young

Christians make from grade to grade—progress in their inter-personal relations, in their classroom participation, and above all in their courage to be themselves. Teachers should ask themselves: Are the young persons in their classrooms overcoming their fears of the unknown, the untried, the unusual? Are they breaking out of the inaction and passivity such fears produce? Are they becoming the unique and free individuals they were created to be, unique and free in spite of the artificial restraints and inhibitions by which establishments often stifle spontaneity?

Young Christians need such freedom, and schools should help them achieve it. Surrounded by the structures and mechanisms of organized life, by its forces and pressures to conform, and tempted by the easy security that comes with not being an individual, growing persons need the sort of schooling that helps them become the individual persons God intended them to be. They need education that will *release* them from the anxiety and self-rejection that often cause them to choose an automatic instead of an individual life.

But they need education that also promotes productive freedom, freedom for learning and living. Here too the school can measure its success. Are young persons learning to give themselves, in love and with purpose, to their daily work, to other persons, to their aspirations, to God's love and bidding? Do they dare to imagine, to experiment, to invent, to innovate? Are they, through growth as free persons, gradually finding true security and acceptance, acceptance with other persons, but first of all with themselves? Believing that such freedom and security are indispensable also to individual and personal response to God, Christian teachers should ask themselves whether such growth in fact takes place on the playgrounds and in the corridors, and also whether they are deliberately promoting it through appropriate subject matter, imaginative class procedures, and a variety of formal and informal co-curricular activities.

Related to the freedom of the mind from confusion and to the freedom of the will from easy morality, this freedom of the heart from fear—or inaction or mere conformity—becomes an opening upon life that can lead to the acceptance not only of life, but of Christian calling in life. For through this opening students can above all learn new ways to know and love God and to fulfill themselves as unique persons in their relationship to him.

A school could not be a good Christian school if it did not promote the growth of self-accepting and self-expressing free persons. For through such growth the school helps young Christians, who are coming both to understand and to choose the Christian life, to translate that knowledge and commitment into the good works of obedience—an obedience that is creative, participatory, and productive in the service of God and man in the world.

A previous chapter asserted that a school's religious vision ought to be more than a preamble to Christian education, that it ought, in fact, to embody that vision in its *program*. While that program must include matters like those touched on in the postscript following, namely, overall curriculum pattern, graded courses of study, and the teaching-learning process, what that program must above all include is the school's careful choice of its major learning goals. For in that choice it selects the major sorts of *changes* in young persons that its curriculum pattern, its courses of study, and its teaching-learning process must try to bring about—the changes, that is, that the Christian world and life view requires.

It has been argued in this chapter that the three kinds of educational growth proposed here can most directly and most suitably promote those changes, and in this way also meet the real nature and needs of young persons. Given their physical-spiritual wholeness; given also their calling in and to the world, as well as their unique human endowments for that calling; and given the insights that both empirical and theological perspectives provide for understanding young persons, it is such intellectual, moral, and creative growth that must mature the religious life of young Christians.

Of course if such growth is, in fact, to take place, all sorts of other conditions must exist: imaginative, professional teaching; regard all along the way for the readiness and ability of the learners; regard also for the learner's normal psychological, social, and spiritual development; and a careful selection of the curriculum pattern that will most directly promote these kinds of growth. Given these conditions, Christian teachers ought to believe that the kinds of religious-educational growth described in the foregoing can meet the deepest needs of the young persons in their classrooms—for growing up and for their adult life as Christian men and women.

If it happens, such Christian education will also greatly benefit the Christian community—by preparing its future leaders but also those many others who make up the solid core of that community. For whether young persons become salesmen, tradesmen, doctors, nurses, housemothers, or teachers; whether they go on to college or take jobs after high school, all need almost more than anything else to understand the Christian life, to choose that life, and to live it obediently. Its complexities, challenges, and opportunities come to all. The degree to which all future members of the

Christian community take their places knowledgeably, committedly, and productively in their homes, in their vocations, in their professions, in their churches, and in ordinary human society depends in good measure on the Christian school's success. What has been urged in this chapter is that much of that success depends on the school's choice of its learning goals.

The Two Sides of Christian Education

Nicholas Henry Beversluis

How can the comprehensive religious vision of Christian education just described become more than a preamble? How must that vision come to control decision-making in a school's educational program? The difficulties and hazards of making this connection doubtless explain why only rarely in the past attempts to do so were made, and why, when they were made, they left most teachers and parents confused or unconvinced. Despite the risks, if the terms *Christian* and *education* are in fact to enrich each other and if the worth of Christian education depends finally, on that interrelation and mutual enrichment, the task of bringing religious presuppositions to bear on the educational program must be undertaken.

In which areas of a school's program should those presuppositions come to bear directly and strategically? It will be argued here that they should be the two areas of *learning goals* and *curriculum pattern*. That is to say, after the school has asked and answered the religious question, it should ask, *first:* What sorts of growth, what changed abilities, performances, behavior, insights, attitudes, values, dispositions should the school emphasize as most appropriate to its religious vision? and, *second:* What curriculum pattern, what subject matter, what areas of study, should a school emphasize as most appropriate to its religious vision and to those learning goals? A school may err in choosing its learning goals and its curriculum priorities and should therefore remain open to new insights; but given its claim to have an educationally relevant religious commitment, it cannot avoid these questions. They have to do with the basic strategies of a Christian school.

Education as Vital Learning and Disciplining Curriculum

Christian educators ought not to let these two questions be wrenched apart. Almost from the beginning of modern schooling, in what has come to be the great debate in education, teachers have tended to choose between them, to emphasize either the objective side of education (the content of curriculum) or the subjective side (the changing person). Whether arising in the soil of philosophical systems or in the practice of perceptive teachers who sought to counteract trends they judged to be miseducative, this polarization has often led to a short-circuiting of genuine education. The great debate comes to its baldest expression when so-called curriculum oriented teachers callously consign all but the highest IQ students to a sort of educational wasteland and when so-called learning-oriented teachers solemnly intone the syntactical and educational nonsense that they teach pupils, not subject matter. Christian educators should avoid such educational dichotomy.

Christian educators should also go beyond the more responsible versions of the great debate that have illumined and enriched past discussions of Christian education, most notably in the writings of W. H. Jellema and C. Jaarsma. Accepting their fair-sighted and durable contributions and disregarding at this point the rather basic differences between them, especially regarding the school's comprehensive religious vision, Christian teachers should seek to direct the respective contributions of these men into the advancement of contemporary Christian education.

Thus teachers should accept as sound doctrine Jaarsma's major thesis about education as *response:* that education will fail unless it is suited to the learner, to his previous learnings, to his emerging self-awareness; that nothing is learned, educationally or religiously, until it is learned in the *heart,* until it is understood, appropriated, and responded to deep down where a person lives; and that even the best of curriculum will be unrewarding and oppressive unless the learner's response to it is vital and cumulative in the ongoing *process* of personal growth.

But teachers should also accept as sound doctrine Jellema's major thesis about education as *encounter:* that the right things, the most educationally rewarding things—the things that a school as *school* must teach about the wholeness of life and truth as given must be studied; that as all education is by and for a kingdom, demanding ultimate allegiance, so Christian education must serve the *civitas dei;* and that even the best of both method and aim will be short-circuited unless they are joined to a *required* curriculum whose well-taught content disciplines young Christians for living the full-orbed Christian life.

Of course, in theory almost no one deliberately separates these two sides of education. In practice, however, the difficulty of keeping learner and subject matter in range of each other and the failure to make programmatic provision for such closure lie at the center of the age-old educational debate.

Christian schools must go beyond taking sides in this debate. They should accept the best of the learning-oriented approach and the best of the curriculum-oriented approach and refocus them for the sort of educational closure a Christian vision of human calling and of human endowments requires. The Christian school's model should be not the reductions born of teacher preferences or philosophical systems but the Bible's view of God and man in relationship. Somewhat as closure in religious growth requires both God's disciplining encounter of man in his Word and world *and* man's vital response to that encounter in the biblical sense of knowing (as including also loving and serving God), so it is in educational growth: the objective and the subjective are alike indispensable. For both religious and educational reasons, Christian schools should keep the two sides of education together.

If the commitment to keep them together is made, subject matter will find its place in the school as the indispensable *means* to human growth in education. Fallible and liable to error as a curriculum structure may be, in a Christian school it nevertheless aims to come with a unique authority, the authority of objective truth and reality as given. On the other hand, authoritative as a curriculum may be, it remains a means, a means to nothing else than evoking the young person's response in vital educational growth. A school's curriculum must be organized for learning, and a young person's learning must be in response to curriculum. It is through the two together, not through either alone, nor through both separately or alternately, that a school must aim at educational closure.

If the commitment to such closure is made, the teacher will above all aim at personal changes, development, growth in young persons. To achieve this, pupils must be interested, motivated, involved; they must be active in the educative process. They must be moved and must be in motion. They must grow. They must *learn*. But the teacher will remember that this change and growth must be in reference to, in response to something. To what? To what the teacher brings. The teacher is there: he arouses the pupil, engages him, stimulates him. He *encounters* him. How is this done? It is done with curriculum.

It is not just anything at all that the young person in a schoolroom must be vitally active about; the schoolroom is not the playground, the school bus, the family dinner table. It is the schoolroom. It is the place where the teacher brings new, significant, disciplining experiences into the lives of young Christians. A wise teacher will, of course, all along the way promote schoolroom learning by means of all sorts of out-of-school experiences. But in the schoolroom even such experience must be reconstructed and expanded. It is reconstructed and expanded when new experience enriches and expands familiar experience. Such new experience must be imported, must be introduced. Carefully planned, measured, and organized by the teacher, this new experience must elicit *responses* within the learner to what for him are new encounters with reality, new encounters, that is, with the objective world of nature, society, culture, history, and, above all, God—to whom all of it must be related. To such encounters with all sorts of things that normally do not come up in ordinary experience, the learner must be guided by the teacher.

Relating such new experiences conceptually to the pupil's ordinary experience, to his previous learnings, to his expanding awareness and concerns, the teacher aims at the *enlargement* of the pupil's life. These new experiences may include the geography of China, the music of Gershwin, the processing of milk, the politics of the Civil War, the poems of Keats, the ideology of the New Left. They may include studying the crusades, painting in water colors, experimenting with air pressure, comparing sixteenth century plays, analyzing race relations, memorizing Psalms. They include whole blocks of matters that do not come up on a playground or in ordinary life. The teacher sees to it that they come up in a school, in its curriculum.

It is as response to the fullness and excitement of *curriculum* that the wise teacher promotes the interest, activity, participation, discovery, and freedom that constitute learning. And it is to encounter the human *person,* his capacities, experience, readiness, needs, that the wise teacher organizes, shapes, and introduces curriculum. One concern without the other would lead to far less than half of good education. When the necessary *interaction* between subjective learning and objective curriculum has been accepted by a teacher as the nonnegotiable major condition of educational growth, then the next questions may be asked with appropriate seriousness: What should be the major learning goals and what should be the preferred curriculum pattern of a Christian school?

Selecting Major Learning Goals

Of the almost limitless kinds of learning a Christian school could promote, which should it mainly aim at? This question should be distinguished from the question that asks about the intricacies of the learning *process;* those intricacies are many and require careful analyses and prescriptions in a philosophy of the teaching-learning process. What the present question asks about is the important intermediate step between a school's religious vision and the teaching-learning process, a step that needs more separate, prominent attention than it often receives in Christian schools. This question asks about the *changes* in young persons that a school's teaching-learning process ought mainly to aim at.

Which kinds of changes, of learning growth, should these be? As developed more fully in Chapter 4, they should be the kinds that most directly take account of the learner's nature and needs. In the Christian perspective that nature and those needs are to be determined in two ways: *empirically,* by carefully studying human persons in their life situations, but also *theologically,* by asking about the religious calling and endowments of human persons. Understood in both these ways, a young person's nature and needs require above all his *educational* growth as a knowing, choosing, and acting person. From within his personal, worldly existence and in response to the wide range and variety of life that a curriculum introduces him to, every young person must progressively grow in the competence and disposition to *understand* the Christian life, to *choose* the Christian life, and to *live* the Christian life. Such growth is indispensable if by Christian life is meant the full-orbed life described in Chapter 2.

These three kinds of learning growth correspond formally to what many modern educators are again distinguishing as cognitive, affective, and activity growth. They are here designated intellectual, moral, and creative growth. Remembering that boundaries cannot really be set between them and that in any case the growth of young persons takes place in all these ways interrelatedly, Christian teachers should nevertheless mark such growth off for distinguishable learning goals—for unit studies, for semester courses of study, and for the overall program of the school.

Intellectual growth. Acceptance by teachers of these learning goals means that they should constantly ask how they can help young persons *understand* things as they are; how they can foster in the learners a growing insight into the natural, social, cultural, historical, and religious conditions of human existence—within whose complexities and opportunities they must seek out the truth about things and live the Christian life. Teachers should recognize that for such growth young persons need *intellectual* education through suitable curriculum.

Moral growth. Teachers should also ask how they can guide young persons by means of their growing understanding of life and the world toward a deeper *commitment* to the way things ought to be, to the true and the good; how they can promote increased sensitivity to and more careful discrimination between right and wrong, particularly as the learner is coming to understand the complexities of moral life in the world; how, through the learner's expanding awareness of the moral options that life presents, they can guide him to choose Christian options, based on Christian commitment. Teachers should recognize that for such growth young persons need *moral* education through suitable curriculum.

Creative growth. Teachers should also ask how they can help free young persons from fear or inertia through growth in self-acceptance and self-expression; how they can help them grow from an inward beholding of the truth and an inward commitment to the good toward a disposition to *participate* in life; how they can guide the growing understanding and commitment of young persons toward both a unique personal life and a loyal life within human community; how they can guide young persons to express both their freedom and their obedience in a productive Christian life. Teachers should recognize that for the nurture of such dispositions and self-expression they must provide education for *creative* growth through suitable curriculum

Selecting Curriculum Priorities

Of the almost limitless sorts of subject matter a school could teach, which should be its priority subject matter? Apart from its electives, which should be its core subjects required of all normal young persons? This question must be distinguished from questions about graded *courses of study.* The latter, having to do with grouping, fusing, and integrating subject areas for suitable teaching and learning, certainly need close and careful attention. But the present question asks about a prior matter. It asks about major areas or patterns of subject matter; it asks about the school's curriculum *commitment*—something that must be settled before course of study writing can proceed.

Which curriculum areas should a Christian school mainly emphasize? It is held here that they should be those, first, that most directly and suitably promote the sorts of learning growth discussed above and, second, that most directly take account of the wide range and variety of the world in which God has placed man. This is to say that religious growth and therefore learning growth should be in *response* to curriculum encounters that present the wholeness of life and reality—the wholeness presented to man in the physical world, in human society, in human culture, in the continuity of history—all of it in its relationship to God.

Although names given to major curriculum areas will vary with different educators, what is proposed here is that on levels of complexity suitably adjusted to the readiness of the learner and in courses of study suitably organized for various grade levels, a Christian school's required core curriculum should prominently include the following groups of studies.

General Development Studies. These studies, concurrent with and important to all the others, must meet the young person's developmental needs as a *responder* to his education. They include the all-important verbal and mathematical masteries of the three R's, but also, as part of the same class of basic learnings, continuing studies in music, art, speech, writing, and physical education. These all are developmental in the sense that each promotes, in its own way, the sorts of responses and dispositions that are indispensable to the learner's self-acceptance and participation, both in the learning process and in his ordinary life outside school.

Natural Sciences and Mathematics. These studies present man's own physicalness as well as his natural environment. Through mathematical understanding and through the disciplines of scientific method, these studies should prepare young persons to know and respond to the laws and processes, but also the gifts and splendors of their physical existence. Through these studies the school must challenge the learner to understand, to appreciate, to use, and to extend the treasures of nature in harmony with its ways, in service to man, and in stewardship to God.

Social Sciences. In these studies man's societal life and environment in all their diversity and complexity are examined. They present man's needs and tensions in his many relationships, organizations, and institutions, all understood as man's *shared* life within ordinary society. These studies challenge the young person, through both empirical observations and moral judgments, to understand, appreciate, and participate in man's interrelations within society in appreciation of his fellow men and in obedience to God.

History Studies. These studies present man in his historical existence. They present man, who lives in nature and society, as living also in a vertical environment, in a chain of relationships that not only unites past, present, and future, but also discloses meanings and understandings essential to knowing contemporary life. Through imaginative reconstruction of the past by means of appropriate historical inquiry, these studies emphasize that man lives inescapably within a flow of time, but also within once-for-all situations in which goals must be set and decisions must be made. Presenting man's failures and tragedies, as well as his successes and achievements, history studies must make clear to young persons that of them, too, are required unrepeatable personal choices within the structures of nature and society, but also within a flow of time that requires openness to God's purposes both in and beyond history.

Literature and the Arts. The studies in this group present man in his creative perceptions and responses as he lives within nature, society, and history. Through a wide variety of artistic and literary forms, they present man as the fashioner and sharer of an inner vision. In addition to the knowledge, pleasure, and appreciations these studies foster, literature and the arts can help a young person to prize his own personal identity and that of others, to find and love his neighbor in authentic human relationships, and in these ways also to discover how truth and compassion revealed in the manner appropriate to art can enrich his religious growth.

Religious Studies. In these studies God's special revelation to man is presented. Centering in the redemptive love of Jesus Christ, they present man as engaged by God and as commanded to respond to God from within his natural, social, historical life—to respond, moreover, as both a unique person and as a contributing member of the Christian community. The perspective of these studies enriches and illumines all other studies, and with special directness challenges young persons to know and hear and respond to God from within the fullness of their own expanding life and world.

Of course, the various dimensions of life and the world distinguished in these curriculum groups do not represent separate domains of man's existence; they are all interrelated, and in a Christian school especially, man's relation to God will be stressed in all studies. But these groups of studies do present *conceptually* distinguishable areas of life and the world, and also distinguishable modes of inquiry by which life and the world may be known. Such a conceptual cataloguing of both content and modes of inquiry can alert teachers, when they fuse or integrate various studies— history and social studies, say, or literature and reading—not to obscure the essential content or discipline of any of the combined studies.

Regardless of how subject matter is rearranged for teaching and learning, the school ought to let curriculum groupings like those above function as reminders of what curriculum ought to do and be in Christian education and function also, therefore, as a prod and a guide in the school's periodic self-examination.

If a Christian school seeks by means of both its major learning goals and its priority curriculum commitments to bring about whole education—whole with respect to the learner's intellectual, moral, and creative endowments and whole with respect to the range and complexity of the world around him; and if such educational closure is sought under the control of the school's religious aim, the result could be superior Christian education.

Some Cautions and Clarifications

Before the school's major learning goals are examined in greater detail, the remainder of this chapter presents some additional general comments about the recommendations presented in the foregoing.

1. It should be stressed that if a school judges learning goals and curriculum pattern to be first-order concerns it should not therein find license to ignore or even postpone solutions to other problems. A school's problems are all interrelated. Specific problems in other areas not discussed here range from investigations into how children learn to decisions about playground supervision. They have to do with testing programs, types of report cards, ability grouping, teaching machines, audio-visual media, ungraded classes, guidance programs, remedial instruction, "new" mathematics and science, classroom discipline, PTA programs, in-service teacher education, and much more. Solving first-order problems will not solve these problems. What a school should believe, however, is that clarity on the basic aims and strategy of Christian education must guide teachers, wherever possible, also in these other problem areas.

2. A Christian school's designation of priority learning goals and curriculum pattern does not entail a doctrinaire indifference to other kinds of developmental goals and other kinds of subject matter. In addition to the major learning goals designated above, indeed, in support of and as a culmination of those goals, the school should also foster a young person's normal social and psychological development. So too, in addition to its basic curriculum commitment the school should offer a variety of elective choices, including so-called practical courses in typing, in office practice, perhaps in domestic and manual arts, perhaps even in automotive repair and hair-styling. What a doctrine of priorities does entail is that in its philosophy of education a Christian school make conceptual distinctions between learning goals and subject matter that are *more* directly produc-

tive and those that are *less* directly productive of the intellectual insight and understanding, the moral awareness and choice, and the creative disposition and freedom that are essential to social and psychological development on the one hand, and to vocational dignity and competence on the other. A Christian school should adopt a doctrine not of either-or exclusions but of priority educational emphases.

3. Rejecting the notion that its priority education is an aristocratic education suitable only to the most able and talented, a Christian school should provide such education for all normal young persons. The slow-learning, the late-blooming, or the practical-minded young Christian is not a second-class person to be shunted off into all sorts of substitute courses, to be fed a low-grade educational diet from junior high school on. A Christian school should shun the easy way of solving the problem of the unusual student, the way typical of some contemporary education, and should rather give him the special attention he needs and deserves. Encouraging him with suitable practical courses, it should nevertheless all along the line educate him also interiorly, for understanding, commitment, self-acceptance, and creative participation in ordinary life, particularly if high school graduation will likely end his formal education. To meet the needs of this kind of student for basic Christian education, the school should make all sorts of special provisions: selected ability grouping, the best teachers, the most effective audio-visual aids, the most ideal pupil-teacher ratio, and the like. It should do this as religious obligation, out of regard for all the human persons in its charge, as well as to meet the needs of the whole Christian community it serves.

4. Whether students need special motivation or are mainly self-propelled, success in achieving major learning goals through a disciplining curriculum requires careful selection and focus. Mere fact-gathering and inert knowledge can stifle young minds. Learning must be related to learning; it must be cumulative and generative. Not all sorts of things need to be learned; rather, patterns of learning should be aimed at. Manageable, attainable goals should be set, goals suitable to readiness and ability level and related to both previous and later learning. If, for example, the date of King David at c. 1000 B.C. is to be stressed, it should be when time sequences have begun to mean something to the learner, but it should also be related to, say, Abraham at c. 2000 B.C. and to Daniel at c. 400 B.C.— to provide some sense of time-span and sequence so essential to understanding the Old Testament. Or if the great length of the Amazon River is to be stressed, the river should be related to human life along its shores and to traffic on it and should also be compared with, say, a river of the learner's direct acquaintance. By themselves dates and lengths of rivers are inert and

meaningless.

5. So, too, a balance must be struck between regard for the experience and readiness of learners and regard for the inherent structures of the subjects studied. Learning must be related to life, but the pupil's life must be constantly enlarged and enriched through new and disciplining subject matter. Such subject matter can be poorly or competently introduced. It will be competently introduced if, on the one hand, it is presented as much as possible within its structural context, and if, on the other hand, it is related to the life and experience of the learner. Thus, if the Reformation is studied by ninth graders, its historical significance and contexts should be clarified, but it should also be related to the contemporary realities of a vernacular liturgy, marrying priests, Catholic-Protestant union services, and the like. So, too, with fifth grade astronomy and current moon-shots; with eleventh grade English and a Bob Dylan lyric; with seventh grade Civil War studies and Black Power. In each case some aspect of an educationally important discipline is put into range of the learner, and in each case the learner, in his life situation, is put into range of the subject matter. Christian teachers should aim at such closure between subject matter and experience as a first law of good teaching.

6. Teachers should ensure that, wherever possible, whole learning takes place—intellectual, moral, and creative, and not just one of these. They should also try to adjust such learning to student interests or aptitudes. Thus unrelieved intellectual demands could in some young persons snuff out other dreams or passions: to be a nurse, a farmer, a heating expert; or to play an instrument, write poems, or design model airports. Even though all young persons need intellectual development, in the case of some, the way to it may need to be less direct, through creative exploration, perhaps. But the subject studied may also require more than one kind of learning emphasis. Thus, intellectual mastery in a given subject could be poor teaching if it did not lead to significant moral growth. Teaching only *about* slavery, or the New Deal's response to the depression, or starvation in India, or contemporary poverty, or environmental pollution, or history's religious wars, without involving young Christians in the great moral issues they represent, would be truncated Christian education. So, too, a failure in whole education would result if in teaching a poem, a painting, or a novel the teacher emphasized mainly its historical background, its philosophical assumptions, its esthetic theory, even its moral impact—and failed to let the poem or painting or novel bear in on young persons as an artistic encounter, with its own speech and impact. And, of course, the other way would also be miseducative: when either moral judgments or programs of action are offered, by teachers or students,

without the rational controls that understanding and insight must bring. Learning must be cumulative in a Christian school and must be learning by whole persons, in all, not part, of their endowments and capacities.

7. A major concern of the school should be that learning be also *discovery*. Important for intellectual growth, it is no less important for moral and creative growth. Discovery entails active learning such that it gradually becomes self-propelling. In science studies, for example, or in history studies, the way of inquiry and discovery not only fastens down what is learned but also generates new inquiries and discoveries. The student learns to learn. Of course, he needs to be told, shown, taught many things. He must be led and guided into the complexities of mathematical processes, of historical relationships, of Christian doctrine. But in response to such *teaching,* the pupil must periodically get caught up with the magic of *discovery,* with the power of searching things out by himself, with the rewards of struggling through a problem into the light of understanding. Especially in schools that tend to be authority-oriented and system-oriented, as Christian schools are, such learning should be fostered.

8. Although the products of the multi-media revolution should not replace books in the education of human beings, Christian schools should recognize that important learning growth can be marvelously stimulated by means of audio and visual aids. Interest and motivation, as well as awareness and understanding, can be directly fostered through informational and dramatic films, recorded poetry readings or musical productions, colored slides of art objects, filmed or taped panel discussions. Whether the subject be the geography and customs of biblical Palestine, the evolution of contemporary music, the discovery of penicillin, hunger in America, or the dramatic crusades of the Middle Ages, audio-visual media can directly enrich the learning of young persons. They can do this for all the persons in a classroom, but for the slow learner, the under-motivated, the late-bloomer, the use of such media may well make the difference between a truncated and diminished education and a vital share in the growth all young Christians need and deserve.

Because Christian calling in the world is not simple but complex, education for response to that calling must go beyond what is sometimes called simple covenant nurture. God's appointment of man to the earth is an appointment to a complex life of commitment and discipleship. Such a life requires use by man of all his unique endowments as image of God; it requires, moreover, that with those endowments he interact with life and the world around him—with people, institutions, events, crises, opportunities, needs, challenges.

This chapter has emphasized that in order to prepare young Christians to live such a complex life and to live it obediently before the face of God, a Christian school should carefully select its major learning goals and priority curriculum. Refusing to take sides in what was earlier called the great debate, the school should believe that only in educational closure between the two sides of education can whole education take place. If such closure and such whole education, from earliest grades on, is bound into the service of its Christian world and life view, the school will be doing its part, next to Christian homes and churches, to prepare young Christians, not only for the complexities of the Christian life, but also for the loyalty and commitment such a life requires.

Cornelius Jaarsma:
Editor Introduction

Of all the recent Reformed educators, Cornelius Jaarsma was the most prolific in publishing his views. During his time as Professor of Education at Calvin College, he wrote not only extensive syllabi for his courses, but also regularly disseminated his views through popular periodicals like *The Banner* and *Christian Home and School*. He also addressed fellow scholars in the *Calvin Forum* and *Evangelical Quarterly*. Over seventy-five articles poured from his pen over a forty year period. In addition, he was editor of, and contributor to, a set of readings, *Fundamentals of Christian Education* in 1953. His major work appeared in 1961, entitled *Human Development, Learning and Teaching*. At the time of his death in 1966, he was in retirement preparing a full length book to represent his most mature thought.

The excerpts which follow attempt to reflect his major contributions. He was the popularizer of the "whole child" term, which for him captured his understanding of what both the Bible and child psychology revealed about human beings. He placed his views over against traditional education in both goals and methodology, as well as the anthropology in which these are grounded. The following excerpts are drawn from various published works in anthropology, goals of education, curriculum, and methodology.

It is in the relentless combining of all of these into a unified view that marks Jaarsma as one of this century's significant Reformed educators.

A Christian Theory of the Person

by Cornelius Jaarsma

The Bible seems to give us three groups of references that direct us to an understanding of the person. One group deals with man's creation, another with the term "heart," and a third points to a varied use of concepts to designate the person.

Creation

The first group, dealing with man's creation, includes the following:

> And God said, "Let us make man in our image, after our likeness, and let them have dominion over the fish of the sea, and over the birds of the heavens, and over all the earth, and over every creeping thing that creeps upon the earth." So God created man in his own image, in the image of God created he them; male and female he created them (Gen. 1:26-27, RSV).

> ...then the Lord God formed man of the dust of the ground, and breathed into his nostrils the breath of life; and man became a living being (Gen. 2:7, RSV).

For similar passages, see also: Job 33:4; Job 27:3; Psalm 104:29a; Psalm 8:4-8; Hebrews 2:7; and I Corinthians 15:27.

Five truths about man as a person are revealed in these passages:
1. God fashioned man from the substance of creation that preceded him.
2. Man's life-giving essence is the breath of God, or spirit.
3. He became a living being, an organic unity.
4. He is made in God's likeness.
5. He was made lord of creation.

Let us take a closer look at each of these important truths about man.

Excerpt from *Human Development, Learning and Teaching*, pp. 40-51, 1961.

(1) God took of the materials of the natural world of creation that preceded man and shaped or formed him. These materials need not have been only the things we call matter, though the Bible uses the expression "dust of the ground." Vegetative life and animal life, structure and function, preceded man. There is soul life in the animal world. But even if materials must refer to matter, the very nature of matter is under scientific scrutiny today. And we are told that ninety percent of the human body consists of oxygen, carbon, nitrogen, and hydrogen.

(2) We learn further that God took the human form so constructed by his hand and breathed into him the breath of life. God, not himself being a human form, cannot exhale carbon dioxide or even oxygen and breathe it into man. No, we recognize that we have here an anthropormorphic expression (a truth set forth in language perceptible to man). God's "breathing into" has reference to his creative act of making the human form a living being in whom the spirit (breath of God) is the life-giving essence, the life principle. Human life is the living spirit. Man is of vertical origin, from God. He is spirit. Horizontally he is linked to creation in the form he takes from creation about him. God infuses spirit in man's earthly form so that he becomes an organic whole.

(3) Because man is an organic whole, it is incorrect to teach that soul and body, or spirit, soul, and body are separate parts of man. The Bible uses all these terms, but in such a way that they are distinguished (not separated) as different functioning structures in the organic unity we call a person. The Bible clearly indicates the unity of man.[1]

Let us develop this concept of organic unity a bit further. We have said that, on the basis of Scripture, we must think of the person as an organic unity in whom the ego, self, or I is the life principle. Every function, both mental and physical—to use a common distinction among functions—is an activity of the self. The light waves upon the retina, the sound waves upon the ear drum, etc. set up a physiological activity in the nervous system. These are experienced by the person as a part of himself and are translated into personal experience. In the activity of seeing, I identify a house as my residence. As a person I call it my home. All that home stands for, love, security, rest, good food, etc. enters into the total activity of the person. The whole person is involved in the process from the first stimuli to the final self-conscious act of identification and acceptance.

We have become accustomed to grouping the functions of a person as mental and physical. The distinction is helpful as long as we do not sharply differentiate the two. We do not know where the one ends and the other begins. The morning grapefruit has a bitter taste about it which one has come to like. Because of the taste, the grapefruit has acquired personal value as a breakfast food. When the season for good grapefruit is past, mother inspects the grapefruit at the market carefully, knowing that at this time they can be nearly tasteless. Mother's act of selecting grapefruit with careful discrimination is based upon the experience of tasting and valuing grapefruit according to the symptoms that suggest their taste. Psychic functions and body functions interact, flow into one another, but one cannot point out the point of transition. What common factor have they to give rise to the unity of experience as mother selects her grapefruit? It is very evident that mental function is based on physiological structure and function. Without the sense of taste no such selective experience could take place. A blind person must find suitable sensory substitutes to function meaningfully in his mental life. Cerebral activity is necessary for thinking. But the cerebrum is not the thinker. *I* think. William James said thoughts are our thinkers. No, thoughts are mental, psychic functions. The person is the thinker. The center of activity, whether it be tasting or thinking, is the I or self. The very spirit, breath of God, is the explanation of all function, psychic and physiological. The life of man is the life of the spirit.

Once we see the limitations of talking about "parts" of an organic unity, we should also recognize that because man is a **complex** unity we cannot begin to understand him without **some** sort of analysis or "breaking-up." The following diagram is an attempt to reveal both the complexity and the unity of the person *(see figure 1)*. Recalling our previous discussion (Chapter I) of the self and the person, we proceed to signify the self or ego with the Greek term *pneuma,* meaning breath, standing for the self-conscious center of all experience. The mental processes and functions, such as thinking, feeling, willing, and perceiving, we designate by the Greek term *psyche,* meaning soul. The Greek word *soma* is conveniently used for body structure and function. All of these words are also used in Scripture with approximately these meanings.

The center circle represents the pneuma. The lines extending from it to the periphery indicate the life-giving and directing activity, the infusion of the pneuma into the psyche and soma. It penetrates the entire organism as the life-giving spirit. Human life is the life of the spirit. The psyche or soul life is represented by a very irregular line indicating the difficulty with which we distinguish between mental and physical activity in human behavior. Where does the conscious feeling of a toothache begin and nerve action leave off? I feel, not the nerves. Feeling is the soul action of the person. The soma, or physi-

Person and Personality

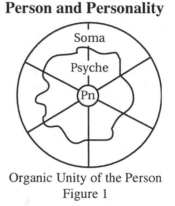

Organic Unity of the Person
Figure 1

ological structure and function, is represented by the outer area. These are three facets of the unity of a person. The actual unity in the spirit eludes our grasp. We cannot describe the interrelationship of these three facets other than to say that they constitute an organic unity.

(4) Man is made in God's likeness. In a sense this is true of the whole creation, because it displays the power and wisdom of God. But man is uniquely the image of God because he is a spirit. Only of man is it said that God's breathing into him made him a living being.

What, precisely, does it mean to have the image of God? From their classes in Christian doctrine students learn that there are at least two answers to this question. One is principally Roman Catholic, though some Protestants also hold it; the other is Protestant, or more specifically, Reformed. Because this theological disagreement has implications for psychology and education as well, we will discuss it here.

According to the Roman Catholic view, the image of God is something added to human nature. Man is a unity composed of an immortal soul and a mortal body which together constitute the whole of his humanity. By nature man has mental and physical powers by which he lives harmoniously with himself and the world, but which by themselves do not make him religious. The image of God on the other hand, is an added gift *(donum superadditum)* given to man over and above his natural gifts; this is a gift of grace by which man becomes godlike and hence religious. Having the image of God, therefore, is not essential to being a human being; according to the Roman Catholic, man is not **intrinsically** a religious being.

The Reformed view, in contrast, holds that the image of God is essential to man's humanity. Man is a religious being in very essence. He is of God, a son of God. He can never cease to be a son of God. But as son of God he can turn from God. In the fellowship of God he has knowledge, righteousness, and holiness. Apart from God, he is still image of God, he is still a religious being, but without knowledge, righteousness, and holiness. Man is either a worshipper of the true God or an idolater. And this is because man is a religious being. This conception of the person as religious being will keep recurring in our study.

The disagreement between Roman Catholic and Reformed theology at this point is relevant to our study in at least two ways: in the first place, according to the Roman Catholic view it is possible to describe human nature and its processes apart from any reference to man's religious nature, so long as we restrict ourselves to the "natural level." This thesis is contrary to the approach we have adopted in this book. In the second place our Scripture passages, our immediate self-consciousness, and the best insights of modern psychology alike testify that there is a basic unity in human experience which is hard to reconcile with the Roman Catholic scheme of body-soul-*donum superadditum.*

We should say more about the image of God in man since it is foundational to our thinking in psychology and education. The following may prove helpful to see the relationship of this truth to our study.

a. In the primary sense, man is the image of God **collectively.** That is, the whole human race with all its potentials and expressions manifests the personal being of God, just as creation as a whole manifests the wisdom and power of God.

b. How, then, can we say that a single individual is the image of God? Because he partakes of the qualities of the human race. The human race is an organic unity; hence each man has the image of God, and hence, too each man has Adam's sin imputed to him.

c. Because the individual partakes of the image of God, he has certain native capabilities and tendencies which express his godlikeness. In particular, every man has an urge toward **unity** and **freedom**—two important concepts in psychology and education. Unity and freedom, to the degree that they are achieved by the individual or the race, are possible because God has made them possible. They are not merely products of development, but are progressively realized in learning and development.

d. Man is free, not to be something else than man, but as man to give expression to God's likeness or not to do so. Man cannot change his being. Metaphysically, as we say in philosophy, he is man. This is his created being. But in his humanity he can choose to give expression to the image of God which he is in essence or can choose not to do so. He is given dominion over all creation beneath him, but he can neglect or violate his created right and become a victim to and slave of the forces he was destined to control.

e. As a free being man is responsible to God as his Creator to realize the purpose for which God created him. As a religious being made in the image of God, he is obliged to fulfill, express, and realize this being. In this setting the modern concepts of self-realization, self-expression, and self-fulfillment state the goal of all education.

(5) Man was made lord of creation. He was created to have dominion, to be viceroy of God's handiwork. He is appointed to be nature's master, under God, to order and develop it to God's glory. What a task! Notice, not adjustment, the term of modern psychology and education, but dominion is the charge given man by his Creator. No praise is returned to God by a mute creation. Only a person can bring God genuine praise, for he can do so consciously and voluntarily. Man was created to be the mediator of nature's praise to God. And he was created to mediate the work of God in nature. As the acme of God's creation he is called upon to mediate between God and nature as the one who is given dominion over all things.

The Heart

A second group of Scripture passages, this time dealing with the "heart," gives us another clue to the nature of the person. Among the many possible instances we cite the following: [2]

Heart as center of feeling: Ex. 4:14; Lev. 26:36; Ps. 4:7; Ps. 119:11; Luke 24:32; John 14:1; Rom. 9:2.

Heart as seat of willing: Ex. 25:2; Ex. 35:5: Jos. 24:23; II Cron. 19:3; Is. 29:13; Luke 21:14; Acts 11:23.

Heart as the seat of thinking or memory: Gen. 6:5; Deut. 29:4; Ps. 19:14; Prov. 2:2; Is. 6:10; Matt. 9:4; Matt. 15:19; Luke 2:19; Rom. 10:6.

Heart as the seat of sin: Gen. 6:5; Ps. 95:10; Luke 6:45; Deut. 15:7; Prov. 28:14; Eph. 4:17,18.

Heart as the seat of the regenerated life: Deut. 30:6; Ps. 51:10; Ezek. 11:19-20; Acts 16:14; Rom. 2:28, 29.

Heart as the seat of processes that involve man's spiritual renewal, faith, and the practice of Christian virtues: Ps. 28:7; Luke 8:12; Acts 15:9; Eph. 3:17; II Thess. 3:5; I Peter 1:22; Matt. 18:35; Jas. 4:8.

What do all these passages indicate to us? They help us to answer the question, what, according to Scripture, is the primary or directing center in man. The Greeks thought it to be the intellect. Medieval and early modern philosophy and psychology thought it to be mind or soul, some non-physical entity or force. The Bible says the heart. But what can the Bible mean by heart? Surely, we should relate all these and similar passages to the passages we quoted from Genesis which tell us that man is an organic unity in whom the spirit is the life principle and that in the organic unity of the race man individually and collectively is the image of God.

Variety of Biblical Concepts

Not only does the Bible ascribe properties of soul life to the heart, but to other parts of the body as well:

Attributes of soul life are ascribed to the blood: Ps.94:21; Is. 59:7; Luke 22:20; Rom. 3:25; Ps. 20:9.

We read of "eyes of the heart": Eph. 1:18.

In I Cor. 3:17 we read, "Ye are the temple of God"; and in I Cor. 6:19, "...your body is the temple of the Holy Spirit."

Body is used to represent all the faculties of man in Romans 12:1.

We are to love God with heart, soul, and mind. Matt. 22:7; Deut. 6:5.

From these Bible passages we may, it seems, infer some important truths concerning the human person.

1. Every man has something of the miraculous in him.[3] The Scriptures recognize that we inherit certain aptitudes, powers, potentialities, and dispositions from our ancestors, but over and above these, they point to a kernel or essence that is new in each person.

   This kernel or essence is the life principle in man, the directive center of his total being. It infuses the whole. It gives the whole organic unity. According to Kuypers, it is this center (in psychological terms, the self or ego) that the Scriptures speak of as breath of God, spirit, and heart. It is this center, moreover, that is said to live, die, and put on immortality.[4]

2. The Bible clearly indicates the unity of the person. He is a living being of whom the Bible speaks as heart, soul, mind, body, blood, and the like. In each concept the whole is represented. These are not technical terms to label parts in an analytic fashion, as we do in science. Each points to the whole in its functional relationship. The organic unity of the person is clearly established in Scriptures. The Bible does not confront us with man in his component parts, nor with a comparison of human existence over against that of animals. Rather, it gives us the compelling aspect of man's existence in his relationship to God.

3. The Scriptures clearly distinguish between the essence of man which lives, dies, and puts on immortality and the functions in man as represented in his soul life and body life. In the language of A. Kuypers it is the distinction between the moral and the functional, man in the essence of being and his mental and physical activities. Since modern psychology regards the totality of man's functions to exhaust his being, this distinction in Scripture is especially significant for us as we face our study.

4. The Bible clearly teaches a functional neutrality.[5] Functional neutrality means two things: (a) there is no hierarchy of function in man, and (b) no function is the seat of evil. One function cannot be thought to be superior to another. Under Greek influence human reason or the intellect has for a long time been regarded as supreme in man. We read much of the supremacy of the intellect, and, in the nineteenth century, as reaction to a one-sided emphasis, of the supremacy of desire or will. We have seen that the Bible points to the very core of man, the essence of his being of which intellect, desire, will, etc. are functions. Any optimism or supremacy of the intellect is excluded.

    Neither is any function the seat of evil. Evil proceeds not from man's functions, according to the Scriptures, but from the center of his being, the I, the self. Functions are good in themselves. Every gift of God is good.

5. The Scriptures present man as a religious being. The image of God as we have been trying to understand it, is of the very essence of man. It is infused in the totality of man's person. The Scriptures do not present man as an organism who attains to religious values among other values of life. "Religious" describes his very being. This too is important in our approach to psychology and learning. Motivation in man is

basically religious and all human seeking is to be interpreted accordingly. So is learning. So is teaching.

6. The Scriptures instructed us in the unconscious life of man long before psychology turned to it for scientific exploration. The psalmist, wearied of self-examination and feeling that the depths of his soul life have not been reached, opens himself to God in the words of Psalm 139:23,24, "Search me, O God, and know my heart, try me and know my thought, and see if there be any wicked way in me, and lead me in the way everlasting." Psalms 16 and 26 likewise point to a depth in the soul life which wields a mighty power in the behavior of a person. Nowhere, however, do the Scriptures assign indigenous motivation to the unconscious. It too is a manifestation of the self, the ego, the I. It is inherent in the organic unity of which the I is the essence or life principle.

7. The Bible also teaches us that man is adapted to the natural world about him. He needs interaction with the natural world for self-realization and self-fulfillment in body life and soul life. And the natural world is amenable to his powers. Man has dominion over a world whose resources he needs for the full realization of what he is, the image of God.

Personality Theory

The student will recall from Chapter 1 that personality is that unique group of characteristics which describes the individual in relation to other people. Hence infants, for example, can hardly be said to have personality even though they are clearly persons. They are persons by creation; each is an organic unity of spirit, soul life, and body life. But they must **become** personalities: they must acquire and develop those traits which identify them as individuals in the social sense.

Obviously this distinction is tied very closely to the Christian view of the person. Hence we should not be surprised to discover that secular psychologies obliterate it. The three psychologies discussed earlier, for instance, view man as originally a biological (not a spiritual) entity who **becomes** a person (or personality). Everything distinctively human about a person is acquired, not innate. Hence these psychologies have no real basis for distinguishing person from personality.

The Dimensions of Personality
When we describe personality we describe how a person affects others.

When we describe how a person affects others we characterize, so to speak, extensions of that person into his community. Assuming a posture or facial expression in public is, for instance, to "extend one's person into the community"; so is being irritable, or congenial, or uncomprehending.

Dimensions of Reality

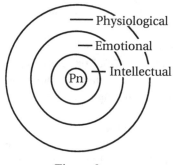

Figure 2

It is convenient to classify these extensions of oneself into four "dimensions" of personality. They are the physiological, the emotional, the social, and the intellectual. Of course these are not separate entities; as dimensions of a single personality they are always involved in one another. Take a hearty laugh for instance; this is physiological, but its concomitants are understanding the joke (intellectual), being pleased (emotional), and joining in the festivities of the party (social). The qualities that constitute one's personality are like a constellation or cluster that reflect a larger whole.

In Figure 2 the unity of personality as integrated in the pneuma or spirit is diagrammed analogously to the unity of the person in Figure 1. The student will notice that the social and emotional dimensions have been conjoined, for reasons which are intuitively evident.

The Whole-Person-In-Life

Personality is obviously the most **inclusive** concept that we can apply to an individual. Within its scope fall not only what we have called pneuma, psyche, and soma, but also the various dimensions of the person's social expression. Personality is also the most **concrete** concept we have used so far; it applies to the individual as we actually observe him living his life. Personality traits are not theoretical abstractions, but revelations of the person in action. Therefore it is useful at this point to introduce a term that suggests this concreteness and inclusiveness: the "whole-person-in-life."

There is a competitive term, the "whole-person-in-**action**," which is used by some psychologists operating within the secular perspective. These psychologists reason this way: We begin with an organism in an environment. Events occur in the environment, called stimuli; other events occur within the organism, called experience. The events within and outside the organism form patterns of response and action in the organism. The elements of these patterns we call personality traits, and their aggregate we call personality. The essence of personality, then, is to engage in **actions**.

The implications of this view of personality for education are not easily overstated. As a matter of fact they are among the determining factors in educational theories today. Our further studies should disclose to the student what this means for education. Just this much for the present. It is held that as a biological organism man is in constant tension with his environment. Events from within and events from without must find equilibrium, balance to relieve the tension. In the interaction the organism develops modes of adjustment in which conflicting events are brought into balance. The various patterns of adjustment constitute the acquired traits of behavior. It is the sum of these traits that constitute personality. When well-integrated for effective adjustment, they constitute a positive, wholesome, balanced personality. When poorly integrated, they constitute a maladjusted personality.

But this is unacceptable from the Christian point of view. The person is not the personality, and personality is not identical with actions. Activity is derived from **life** and that life is not merely biological but spiritual. Therefore when we contrast the term "whole-person-in-life" with "whole-person-in-action" we mean to point out that personality as a concrete unity has its ultimate genesis in the divinely-created life principle, the ego or spirit. The person is the ego operative in psychosomatic functioning. The person, in turn, expresses himself in life through his three dimensions of personality.

When a person communicates in the dimensions of life according to consciously accepted ends, he is a personality. When ends and the direction of communication of a person fail to constitute a field of related activity, he is without personality. An infant, comparatively speaking, is without personality. Likewise a person has lost contact with his in-life relationship when ends and relationship fail to constitute a field of meaning. The latter is true of extreme forms of abnormality in the mentally ill. Personality is strong when the in-life relationship is well established, weak when it lacks adequate field relationship. Personality is bad when the in-life relationship of the dimensions of life violate standards of righteousness, good when they are valued as right. A person communicates in the dimensions of life, and it is in the in-life relationship that these dimensions are formed according to consciously chosen direction of the person. We speak, therefore, of the whole-person-in-life.

Notes

1. A. Kuypers, *Inleiding in de Zielkunde* ("Introduction to Psychology") (Kampen, the Netherlands: J. H. Kok, 1953), p. 24.

2. The word "heart" is in every instance a translation either of the Hebrew *lebh* or *lebhabh,* or of the Greek *kardia.* This fact, along with the Scripture references here cited, derive from an (unpublished) study by the author's colleague, Dr. A. A. Hoekema, Professor of Systematic Theology at Calvin Seminary.

3. Kuypers, *op. cit.,* pp. 24-25.

4. *Ibid.,* p.7.

5. *Ibid.,* pp. 24-25.

How to View Learning

By Cornelius Jaarsma, excerpted from *Human Development and Teaching*. pp. 161-173, 1961

Two Learning Situations

We are visiting a first grade in an elementary school located in a large metropolis. The school is surrounded by business establishments, apartments, and tenement houses. Most children in this community never look beyond the large city buildings that surround them. Their playground is the hard-surfaced schoolgrounds and the busy streets. Their homes are the crowded tenement houses of the community.

"What did you have for breakfast this morning?" asks the teacher of the entire class.

All hands go up. "Jackie, will you tell us?"

"I had orange juice, milk, whole-wheat cereal, and toast."

"That was a good breakfast," continues the teacher.

Many other children report a similar breakfast. Nearly all had milk.

"I am glad you all had milk. Milk is good for boys and girls. For older people too, but especially for children. Why should all children drink milk, Mary?"

"It makes them grow," replies Mary.

"How many of you boys and girls think Mary is right?"

All hands go up.

"I think so too," agrees the teacher. "Do you know where the milk you had for breakfast comes from?"

Some hands go up. Some hesitate. Another group, then another, until nearly all hands are up. Some very vigorously seek the floor.

"Bennie, you tell us," says the teacher with a broad smile, for Bennie was on his feet by this time.

"From the milkman," replies Bennie with all the self-assurance he has.

169

"He brings it in bottles, and my mom puts it in the refrigerator. It is cold...and good too."

"Where do you suppose the milkman gets the milk?" continues the teacher.

Several hands go up, but most of the children look perplexed.

"Henry, you tell us."

"My daddy says it is brought in by big tank trucks."

"What is a tank truck?"

Few pupils seem to know.

"John, will you tell us?"

"That's a truck that has a big (he stretches his arms to full length in opposite directions) tank on it."

"Now I am going to ask a question that may be a little harder for us. You are right when you say that milk is brought to us by tank trucks, the kind of trucks John described to us. This is the question. You think about it. Where does the driver of the truck get the milk?"

One hand goes up; another; but few try to answer the question. The answers that are given do not even approximate the right one.

Learning as Verbalizing

"Well, that is a hard question, isn't it? Then I shall tell you, if you listen carefully. Ralph, are you listening? will you remember where the trucker gets the milk, after I tell you, Joe? This is the answer. The truck driver goes to the country, outside of the city and fills the tank truck from large cans on the farm. The farmer fills the cans after milking his cows. When the tank truck is full, the truck driver brings the milk into a large milkhouse. Here the milkman heats the milk to kill all germs. When the milk is cooled, the milkman puts it in bottles. Now the milkman brings as many bottles to each house as the people want."

The children look at the teacher with a feeling of strangeness.

"Do you think you can tell us now where milk comes from, Wallace?"

Wallace tries: Henry tries; but each seems to be repeating words without getting a connected story.

"Let us make a story about milk on the board."

The teacher writes and reads while she writes:

The farmer milks the_____.

"Cow," quickly responds Louise.

The teacher continues on the board.

The farmer sells the milk to _____.

He brings the milk to town by _____.

When the milk is brought in he heats it to _____.

Then he lets it cool and puts it in _____.

Jackie fills in the right words in all the spaces. He gets an A. He knows where milk comes from. Mary misses two spaces. She gets a C. But does Jackie know milk? He can tell us all *about* milk.

Later it happens that Jackie has the first opportunity in his life to visit a dairy farm at some distance from the city. As one filled with curiosity about the strange environment in which he suddenly finds himself, he walks around in utter bewilderment. As he walks into the barn he sees a farmer milking a cow, a strange sight for a city-bred boy who was *told* *about* milk.

"What are you doing to the cow?" asks Jackie of the farmer.

"Milking, my boy, milking," replies the farmer. "We have to do this every morning and evening."

"Milking?" asks Jackie in amazement at what he sees. "Milking?" he continues. The word seems to register with him, though he does not at once recall the connection with what he learned about milk. "Do you get milk by pulling on the cow like that?" and he goes through the motions.

"Yes, my boy," the farmer went on, "this is milk." When he says this he holds the bucket of milk with foam on it toward Jackie so he can see it. But Jackie backs away as he takes a look at the milk. "Do you want some? It is good for you. All boys and girls should drink milk if they want to grow."

Where had Jackie heard that before? He reflected for a moment.

"You mean...you mean..that there, that you pulled out of that cow? Is that milk?'

"Yes, it is. But perhaps you don't like it warm from the cow. Come with me to the milk cooler. You may have some cold milk if you like."

Jackie follows with a mixed feeling of misgiving and curiosity. But he goes. At the cooler the farmer offers Jackie cool milk in a dipper. Jackie looks, comparing it with the milk he saw the farmer draw from the cow.

"Is that the same as what you just pulled out of the cow?" asks Jackie looking up to the farmer.

"Yes, try it. You drink milk, don't you?" asks the farmer.

"Yes, but my mommy gets it from a big bottle," says Jackie.

"Well, this is the same," retorts the farmer.

But Jackie pulls back. "No," he says at last, "I don't think I'll like it."

Does Jackie know milk? We have defined knowledge as the apprehension by a person of the object presented. We distinguished knowledge by acquaintance and knowledge by acceptance. To know is to be informed of the truth pertaining to the object of knowledge. Genuine knowledge, however, is apprehending the object in its reality and integrating it in life for what it really is. Has Jackie accepted milk in his life for what it truly is?

Jackie accepted milk as it came from the cold bottle in the refrigerator. Everything else he had heard about milk left him unaffected. It did not change him inside. Milk fresh from the cow was repulsive to him. Jackie saw no connection between the milk coming out of a cow and the milk he learned about in school as coming from the farm. He had learned milk in the artificial context of a refrigerator. What he learned of milk beyond that consisted of words about milk.

Is this learning? Three centuries ago Comenius, the Moravian educator, spoke of the schooling of his day as words, words, words. A century later Pestalozzi, the Swiss educator, repeated this description of the schools of his day. Apparently very little change had taken place. And how much do we rely today upon mere words for effective learning? Jackie too had learned about milk in words. He had repeated the words of the teacher and received high approval for it. When he faced milk in its real context he was unable to accept it. He failed to recognize milk for what it truly is, and appraise and accept it accordingly.

Isaiah, the great prophet of God to Israel, complained of something similar in his day. The Lord says of His people,"...their fear of me is a commandment of men learned by rote." (Isa. 29;13). They excused themselves from knowing the law by saying that the book of the law was closed to them or that they could not read. But the Lord tells them that the law for them consists of repetition of words.

We call this kind of learning (if it may be called learning) *verbalization*. The perceptual field that gives the words meaning is lacking. Hence, the words used do not represent understanding of the relationship involved. Words are merely sounds that are repeated. Farmer, feeding, milking, grazing, warm milk from the cow, and the like are words for Jackie that lack a perceptual field. They do not constitute a unity in experience. Likewise for the people of Israel the law consisted of ritual or forms to be memorized and repeated, but life remained unaffected by it.

Words, words, words. But words alone do not constitute language. Language is the articulation of human needs for communication. The needs grow out of understanding. One may have something to communicate to another, to make known. He does so when the occasion arises, that is, when the need is felt. He then communicates in articulations which signify certain perceptual experiences. The language will be understood by others when they have similar experiences for which the language is an articulation of felt needs. If I want to communicate the serious illness of another I may say, "Henry is sick unto death." When the other person understands that sickness and death stand in cause and effect relationship to each other, I am communicating. Otherwise I am merely sounding forth words. Sounding forth words and repeating the words sounded forth are often mistaken for learning.

Verbalizing, therefore, cannot constitute learning, for it is not based on understanding. Without understanding there is no communication.

Learning as Experiencing Truth

Suppose that the first grade teacher is well aware of the fallacy of verbalization in learning. She knows that a child brought up in a metropolitan community who hardly sees a blade of grass lacks a perceptual field for meaningful communication about milk. She knows too that merely telling the boys and girls in her class about milk will not provide them the perceptual field needed.

But why should Jackie know that milk is a product of cows raised and milked for the purpose of feeding people? Because this great truth understood by Jackie will form his personality. He will come to accept the farm, the farmer, the cow, and dairying as a valuable phase of his life and that of others. He will be formed in the physiological dimension of his personality as he drinks milk with appreciation of its food value. In the social-emotional dimension he will be formed by his attitudes to farming and farmer. In his knowing dimensions he will be formed by the knowledge of milk in its broad context of farm products and food.

However, these outcomes follow from understanding and communication, not from repeating words. Words, words, words, cannot form personality. Neither can mere facts, but only truths disclosed by these facts.

How, then, does the teacher who understands learning proceed? Rather than saying, "I shall tell you" when she reaches the point at which children begin to wonder where milk comes from, she continues with something like this:

"How many of you would like to follow the tank truck to the place where the driver picks up the milk?"

All hands go up.

"Where will the truck take us, Joan?"

"To the country," answers Joan.

"To the farm," remarks Howard.

"All right, we'll all go to the country and to the farm."

To accomplish her purpose the teacher takes her class on an imaginary journey by picture and story, the closest possible substitute for living on a farm. To know the farm one must live on the farm. But not all people can live on the farm. Instead of a concrete experience of living on the farm and engaging in farming chores, a city-bred youngster can experience the farm and farming vicariously. At any rate farming and farm life must have perceptual content for a child to know milk. The class visits Uncle Bill's farm where the tank truck picks up milk to bring it to the city. They see and hear the animals on the farm. They visit the barns. They observe the feeding of the animals, milking, and other farm activities. In school the farm and farm life begin to live in their experience. In the course of their visit the children begin to feel dependent upon farming and the farmer. They begin to respect the farmer as a valuable worker that provides food for many people. Among the many indispensable contributions of the farm is the milk that they drink so lustily for breakfast, dinner, and supper. And the cow provides us the milk. How hard the farmer works to feed the cows! What a valuable animal the cow really is! These, and many like impressions, develop new understandings and attitudes in the children.

Following the study of the farm, Jackie returns to his breakfast and drinks his milk with a new understanding of and feeling for the farmer and farming, and a feeling of gratitude for Uncle Bill and his hard work on the farm. He says his morning prayer with a new appreciation and emphasis as he thanks the Lord for Uncle Bill and his farm.

In contrast with learning as verbalization, the latter process is learning as experiencing of truth. Words are essential, for we communicate truth largely through words. But words are articulations of truth only when they are meaningful.

Some General Observations about the Learning Process

Learning Proceeds from Within

Children are not mere animals, and therefore we may expect that their learning is fundamentally different from that of animals. At least one such difference arises from the fact that human beings are spiritual selves, subjects, created in the image of God. The child has the capability of self-direction (subject always, of course, to God) and cannot be treated simply as a passive object. Rather, he should be treated as one who is self-active, who calls to order his own way of life according to the truth. He can be forced to do things, but he cannot be made to understand, will, and accept or reject the object of knowledge.

Moreover, learning is a religious act because the person who learns is a religious being. As religious being the person is rational, moral, social, aesthetic, free, and responsible. Learning by the person as religious being, therefore, involves the understanding, appraising and accepting or rejecting of truth. Truth understood and appraised with reference to one's own relation to it forms the personality, for truth understood and accepted or rejected by the person becomes the directing power of the person as he orders his way of life in the dimensions of personality. In learning a child taps the resources of his thinking, feeling, and willing with reference to the truth.

Learning is Primarily Development, not Growth

The reader will recall that we defined growth as maturation of structure, and development as maturation of function. This distinction applies as well to the psychical as to the physiological aspects of the person.

There is a psychic structure as well as a physiological structure. The relation of sensory experience to the perceptual, of perceptual to recall and thinking, of thinking to generalization in concepts and ideas, and the like, are structural in the same sense as relationship of the digestive process to glandular secretions. And of course there is psychic development, as when a child acquires greater thinking capacity, perfect skill, or gains insight into problems. Sometimes the meanings overlap, as when we speak of a growing insight into a perplexing situation and of developing better insight. The former refers largely to maturing structure; the latter to more effective use of function.

It is important that we keep these ideas as distinct as possible because we are subject to great confusion at this point as we study current psychology and education. If man is only a biological organism as assumed by modern psychologies, then function is a qualitative change based on biological or physiological structure. All function must be referred to physiological structure for its explanation. On this basis growth and development are practically synonymous terms referring to a progressed adjustment of an organism to the environment in which it is to operate.

Man, however, is not merely a biological organism but an organic unity (which includes the biological and the psychic) based on the spirit. Maturation, interaction, learning, and forming are the fruit of a developmental urge of the spirit organically united in the psycho-physiological structure. Hence we are not going to confuse growth and development as terms descriptive of a maturing person, though the two terms of necessity overlap.

Learning, then, is a form of development, not merely of growth. A child can learn to speak when physiological organs involved in a speech have grown to sufficient maturity to articulate communicatively, that is , in a way that others understand. Speech and speaking are developments in the personality. Learning is development in the whole person. Nothing is learned in isolation. Nor can any structure function in isolation with reference to learning. Development is a three-dimensional process in the person. The whole personality is involved in our teaching whether we recognize it or not. Learning is a personal activity.

Learning Defined

What is learning? We find a curious reluctance on the part of psychologists to offer a definition of learning, according to Bugelski. [1] He refers to learning psychologists telling us more frequently what learning is not than what it is. In 1945 Guthrie, a student of learning, said that a scientific theory of learning has yet to be agreed upon and Bugelski writing in 1956 tells us that this is even truer today. [2]

We cannot wait for the psychologists to reach some agreement on a scientific definition of learning. Anyway, suggests Bugelski, we would not want psychologists to teach our children. "We don't even ask psychologists to train our bird dogs," says Bugelski, "We go instead to a bird-dog man. How much further are we [he refers to learning psychologists] from telling our kindergarten teachers how to teach our children?" [3]

Shall we conclude that psychological studies have nothing of value to contribute to our understanding of how a child learns? This is not what Bugelski means to say. He is rightly interpreted in the context of his writing, it seems, when we take heed lest we think psychology can give us as teachers a complete and final description of what takes place in learning.

Bugeslski himself ventures a definition after several preliminary considerations. Says he, "Learning is the process of the formation of relatively permanent neural circuits through the simultaneous activity of the elements of the circuits-to-be; such activity is of the nature of change in cell structures through growth in such a manner as to facilitate the arousal of the entire circuit when a component element is aroused or activated." [4]

This definition might pass for an answer to the question as to what happens in the nervous system of a person when associations are made in experience. There are other answers, but this is one of several in keeping with recent laboratory studies in learning based chiefly on animal experimentation. And this kind of experimentation and description has its place.

But what benefits accrue to a teacher, especially a Christian teacher, from such a definition of learning? The Christian teacher who views the learner as religious being looks elsewhere for an account of the nature of learning. He will not discard the suggestions projected, but he will look for a more adequate and comprehensive description.

We come a little closer to the true nature of learning when we see it defined as a change of behavior resulting from experience. If one's response to a given situation is different this week from last week, one is said to have learned.

Since the word experience is used here in connection with learning, it is well that we have a clear understanding of how it is used in connection with learning and teaching.

In everyday language we make a distinction between hearing or reading about something and having experienced it. The difference is that between Jackie hearing about milking and farming and Jackie coming concretely into contact with these activities and even participating in them—or between the Jackie who heard his daddy's sermon and the adult in the pew who had a personal encounter with God in choosing for a sanctified life of service. Another illustration: Two people read about getting ready for spring gardening. One is a city man who has never come into personal contact with soil and growing plants, having grown up in a city apartment. The other is a suburban city worker who regularly cultivates his yard for luxurious plant growth. What will the first man learn from his reading?

We must distinguish between two kinds of experience, experience which is concrete and in first-hand contact with the object, and vicarious experience, substitute-contacts. For example, the teacher could not take her pupils to a farm, but sought to reproduce the farms by picture, action, story, perhaps interviews with others, etc. Pupils vicariously lived on the farm. The city dweller might page through a picture volume of gardening, or actually watch a gardener at work without engaging in the activity himself. Sometimes we can hardly experience vicariously what others experience in the concrete. This is being written when Hungarian refugees are arriving in America after their awful experiences in conflict with the Communist regime. We see pictures in *Life* magazine, read of their crossing into Austria, etc. But have we experienced in any sense the deprivation and anxiety these people were subjected to? Insofar as all humans experience suffering, to a greater or less degree we can enter into the lives of the afflicted Hungarians. But how abstract and academic this still is, compared to the reality!

Now the definition of learning as a change of behavior resulting from experience takes on some meaning. Experience has reference to the interaction of a subject and an object in which the subject undergoes a change such that a new relationship is established between the two. In the case of a person this means that his personality has undergone a change. For example, he likes olives now but he did not when he first tried them some time ago. He speaks French now, but he did not understand a word when he first came to France.

To be sure, learning involves a change of personality as a result of experience. Ones's behavior is an overt expression of one's personality. Momentary behavior, however, may indicate merely what one has learned to do under given conditions. When some responses occur with increased frequency in a repeated situation, there is still more evidence of real learning. One is beginning to give evidence of having accepted in his heart certain standards of conduct. Now it is not merely his behavior that shows his learning, but his very act disclosing what kind of person he has become.

When one has come to accept truth for self-discipline, one has truly learned. There may be momentary slips into deviations, but they represent what one has learned to do under certain conditions. The evidence of heart acceptance is not in the isolated doing, but in the consistency of integrated action.

It should become increasingly evident how understanding and a feeling of security are related to learning. These constitute the keys to acceptance. As religious beings we are relentless security-seekers, and we find security only through understanding. We commit ourselves only to that which we understand or discloses meaning to us. "Learning is the quest for meaning, and meaning is the link between learning and life." [5]

We ask again, what is learning? We venture at this point a tentative, working definition. It must be explored further as we continue. *Learning, we might say at this juncture, is the activity of a person as he focuses his attention upon an object for understanding and acceptance of it in its true nature.*

Critique of Current Views of Learning

When we say views of learning, we do not mean *theories* of learning. Let us restrict the term "views" to over-all accounts, i.e., to interpreted descriptions of the learning process as a whole, and use the term "theories" to mean accounts of the learning process that are based explicitly on experimental evidence. In terms of this distinction a view will be primarily a reflection of philosophical perspective rather than the inductive result of factual research. The first view of learning which we reject is what may be known as the biological view. This view says essentially that learning is the process of transforming mass action of a biological organism into well-defined, organized responses. A child is a biological organism with propensities for becoming human, in the same sense as a little runabout pig is a biological organism with propensities for becoming a mature pig. For example, vocalization of unrelated sounds becomes organized speech; throwing hands and feet at the sight of a red ball develops into catching and pitching with precision in a ball game; scribbling on a large sheet of paper becomes the recording of premeditated ideas in an article on philosophy or politics or business.

Now we do not deny that these organizations of mass action do take place. Body organs grow structurally so that they can function in complex activities such as speaking, walking, writing, thinking, and composing. But these refinements of mass action do not constitute learning, though they are involved in learning and even constitute a part of the process. Learning cannot be defined wholly in terms of these refinements, for a child is not merely a biological organism. He is a person who as a phase of his organic unity has biological life. So we reject the view, not the fact of biological structure and function.

The second view we reject may be called the social or cultural view. This view says that learning is the process of stimulating innate, inherent capacity to its greatest possible self-fulfillment by environmental activity in an ever-changing culture. For example: All children vocalize, but some have the capacity for developing the language arts with creative genius, others develop a reading and speaking ability for daily communication only. Furthermore, a child in the United States develops facility in the use of the English language in an American context. Learning is the process of self-fulfillment in a social and cultural context.

Again, we do not deny that innate capacity is developed in a given milieu, and that the opportunities provided either limit or facilitate the development of capacity. And the social and cultural structure will have much to do with the direction this development takes. A child does take on forms of life style of his community as he interacts with them. But learning is not essentially a matter of self-fulfillment in a given milieu. It is more than making temporary or more permanent adjustments. Learning is essentially the understanding, appraising, and accepting or rejecting of the milieu as one comes to understand and accept oneself.

The Setting for the Learning Process

As a story has a setting and as a drama has a stage, so the learning process may be thought of as having a setting or stage. We may think of the setting as being threefold. There is, first, the self-active learner, a person-with-a-history; there is also a goal which qualifies all goals made perceptible to the learner; and there is the medium in which perceptible goals as direction-process goals are being realized.

The Self-Active Learner

A child comes to school as an immature person with his own life style. His present life style may prove an asset or a liability to him as he sets out to learn in school. It generally is both in several ways, but he lives, moves, and has his being in it. He cannot be reached for educational purposes apart from his life style. He must feel that he is accepted in it before he can tolerate changing it. He may feel ever so insecure in it, but it is his present world which enables him to function with a measure of integration. He is a learning unit in his life style. His learning potential, what he can come to understand and accept as the moment, depends upon the unity of his person in his present community. He is motivated and must be motivated from within the twofold unity of his life if he is to learn. This phase of the setting may be thought of as the developmental urge, or the inner drive or positive forward impetus to maturity, of a child at a given level of development.

Perceptible Goals

The second phase of the setting may be called the developmental goal. It is the goal which qualifies goals made perceptible to the learner. We shall see in our further study that a learner is motivated to focus his attention upon an object for understanding by goals perceptible to him. When Jackie was in church with his mother all he heard was words, words, words, except for the word "house" which referred to the church, for that is what daddy and mother called the church, namely God's house, and "zeal," which had something to do with those seals mother read about. But zeal for the house of God sounded frightening to him in the context of "eaten me up." Such an adult goal as zeal for the house of God can, therefore, never constitute a constructive goal for Jackie. No, he needs the kind of goal the teacher provides when she takes the class on a visit to a farm. That kind of goal, originating in his perceptual field, can be formulated into meaningful words or concepts that will activate needs in Jackie to felt needs and thus motivate him to constructive action.

But today's perceptible goals must be realized in order to make larger goals perceptible. So we go on from lesser goals to greater goals. End-lessly? No. We have seen that there is a final goal for the religious being. His personality must be formed to give expression to what he really is, a son of God, created in God's image. This is the single, all-inclusive developmental goal. It is the goal perceptible to the teacher, who is a mature person. The perceptible adult goal must be translated into percep-tible goals according to the level and life style, according to the develop-mental urge of a child. We may call the perceptible goals of the learner *directional process goals*. That is, they give direction to the learning process as goals. And the directional process goals get their direction in the thinking of the teacher from the ultimate goal.

The Medium

In addition to a learner and a goal, learning involves a medium, a something through which a learner reaches a goal. For our purpose this medium is the organized program of the school as we know it today. The program of the school is the medium in which perceptible goals as directional process goals are being realized. We may think of the organi-zation of the school as a series of developmental tasks. Organizing the program and executing it consists of executing developmental tasks. Developmental tasks are defined by Havighurst as follows:

> A developmental task is a task which arises at or about a certain period in the life of the individual, successful achievement of which leads to his happiness and to success with later tasks, while failure leads to unhappiness in the individual, disapproval by society, and difficulty with later tasks. (6)

Learning to read, for example: when a child is ready for it and experience calls for it, it is a developmental task the school is equipped to carry out. The place of the school is in this setting.

Endnotes

1. Bugelski, *The Psychology of Learning*, p. 5.
2. *Ibid.*, p.3.
3. *Ibid.*, p.9.
4. *Ibid.*, p.120.
5. Mursell, *Psychology for Modern Education*, p. 321.
6. R.J. Havighurst, *Human Development and Education*, pp. 1-5.

The Christian View of the School Curriculum

By Cornelius Jaarsma, excerpted from
Fundamentals of Christian Education
pp. 229-41, 1953

When we speak of the curriculum with reference to the schools, we are thinking of areas or fields of subject matter as learning areas, however they may be organized. Throughout the centuries we have taken the cultural product of the human race and organized and adapted it to learning areas appropriate for learners at various levels of maturity. So we have thought that the coming generation must have some systematic knowledge of the past in order to have a conscious link with historical continuity and to enter understandingly into the issues of the present. Hence, we have included history in some form among the learning areas in the schoolroom. In order to graduate the learning materials of history according to the learning readiness of the learner we have tried to ascertain whether a biographical approach, or a logical approach, or a problem approach, etc., was psychologically and sociologically most sound. Thus the various areas of learning have taken shape more or less scientifically and now constitute the curricula of our schools.

The question for our discussion now is whether there is a distinctively Christian view of the curriculum. Can we say amidst all the controversy in the field of education that Christianity lays down certain basic principles with reference to the nature and meaning of the curriculum?

What determines the Christian view of anything? What determines the Christian view of government, of the economic life, of war and peace, etc.? One might reply the Bible, for it is our only infallible rule of faith and life. In a general sense this is true. But the question of what is the Christian view of this or that is not so easily or naively answered. Genuine honesty, for example, is required of every Christian. The Bible is crystal-clear on this requirement for Christian living. But in our complicated culture it is not always clear what is the honest thing to do. And sometimes the choice is between two evils rather than the good and the evil.

I think with reference to education this may be said. The end which education is made to serve determines whether it is Christian, when we consider that this end is present at the very beginning and judges the process throughout.

Let me attempt to make my point clear. Our cultural activity we have in common with all men. We build bridges, sell products of our farms and factories, engage in laboratory research, etc. All of this activity, however, needs an end or destiny for its justification. From the Greek-Roman classical world we have received two ends or destinies. One is the natural, the end or destiny that finds the justification of all human activity in the fulfilment of man's natural propensities. It is a naturalism, to be distinguished from a materialism. The other is the ideal, the end or destiny that finds the justification of all human activity in the realization of an ideal life of reason. It is an idealism. The Hebrew-Christian tradition confronts us with the rule of God centered in the heart of man, the center of his very personality as a created being. It finds the justification of all human activity in the glory of the Creator. There is a third end or destiny for all cultural activity of man which recognizes no final purpose anywhere. It finds the justification of human activity in meeting human needs as human only. It is the Renaissance-modern interpretation of life and its meaning and purpose.

Bringing this over into the field of education, we have this qualification of it as Christian. Education is distinctively Christian when the authority of Christ and the realization of his authority in the lives of men is the justification of all educational activity. This is very definitely according to the Hebrew-Christian tradition.

It is our responsibility to indicate how this concept of Christian education can be implemented in the construction of curricula. To do this we should try to answer three questions: 1. What are the views of the nature of curricula? 2. How do we appraise these views in the light of the above concept of Christian education? 3. How can we make curricula distinctively Christian?

Views of the Nature of Curriculum

In the history of education we discern four major curriculum concepts.

By this I mean that instructional materials or learning areas have been organized and adapted for learning purposes with one of four major purposes in mind. They are: the information or knowledge-getting concept, the disciplinary concept, the social concept, and the creative concept.

In the first or knowledge-getting concept the factual material of subject matter is organized for mastery. The gradation of subject matter is based on a quantitative increase of amount and complexity from level to level. Finally one's education is measured in terms of the amount of information he has stored up during the years. The human mind is viewed as a sort of container into which one pours content at will, with the exception that it has the capacity to organize and recall, also at will, any combination of previously acquired information. The emphasis is on memorization or recall.

The disciplinary concept looks upon subject matter as a means of forming the learner in his mental powers. It is generally based on some form of faculty psychology. The mind is in possession of certain powers or faculties which are exercised and molded in the process of mastering essentials of subject matter. What is learned is not as important as the sustained effort involved in its mastery. Then too, there is an external mold or pattern according to which the learner is to be formed. In the process of learning he begins to take on this form of things.

The two curriculum concepts referred to thus far have come down to us from ancient times. Early schools and those of the Middle Ages were entirely dominated by them. Only occasionally were they called in question. It was not till the modern period that other concepts began to prevail.

The social concept is more of a utilitarian nature. From a survey of the needs of the individual with reference to his successfully functioning in society it is determined what learning activities and materials must be included in the curriculum. Our modern industrial society in which the worker rightly makes his just claims and which operates in the framework of the democratic ideal provides the pattern for curriculum construction in our time. The question, which is paramount, is what does the learner need to know and to do in order to participate in this kind of society for the welfare of all concerned? What kind of mathematics will he be called upon to know and use? How much history must he know and how is it to be organized and interpreted that he may be able to enter intelligently into the issues of the day? Knowledge-getting in itself is meaningless apart from the social structure in which it must function. As a discipline education must take account of the relationship of the individual to the social whole.

The fourth concept we mentioned turns to the individual in his psychological make-up for its basis of the curriculum. It recognizes in man a creative capacity which, though varying in degree among individuals, is the primary goal in education. The development of man as a creator is the primary concern of a society that seeks not merely its self-preservation but that seeks social progress. Learning activities are organized to call forth the creative expression of learners. Learning is a cooperative activity in which the learners launch on an exploratory tour. Self-expression, self-appraisal, motivation, self-activity, and the like are the key words in learning as a great enterprise. The curriculum consists of activities which vary according to pupil needs. In some quarters it is known as the experience curriculum.

Here we have the four common views of the curriculum. They should not be thought of as chronologically following each other. The first two, as we said, are of ancient date. They survive today, however, in several ways. Tests and examinations frequently give evidence of the knowledge-getting emphasis when they are almost exclusively factual in character. When the classroom recitation is but a "giving back" what the teacher said or what was read in the textbook, the knowledge-getting or information concept is supreme. Arithmetic and higher mathematics textbooks still contain problems of mental gymnastics, and lecture notes are still reminiscent of memory exercises for their own sake. The social concept is used by some as the basis of a curriculum for social and political regimentation, and by others more democratically as the social orientation of the individual. It is obvious that the creative concept of education is compatible only with a social order which commits itself to the potential integrity of the individual.

What shall we say about each of these concepts when viewed in the light of the Scriptural teaching of man and his place in this world?

Appraisal of Curriculum Concepts from the Christian View

We must base our appraisal on certain essential teachings of the Scriptures with reference to man and his place in this world, for it is with these that education as a process is primarily concerned.

As to the nature of man and his needs, let us note first that education is concerned with man as a whole. He never functions mentally apart from his emotions. Never can we seek his mental development without affecting him spiritually. His social growth is involved in the mental and emotional.

And his physical progress affects his emotional adjustment. It is comparatively recent that we learned that an infant needs emotional satisfaction as much as food. As a matter of fact the feeding problem of children is as much emotional as it is physical. Hospitals are adjusting maternity wards to this fact. Let it be remembered likewise that the whole child goes to school, and the whole child is involved in every learning activity.

Furthermore, it should be noted that the whole person in all his resources, physically, emotionally, socially, mentally, and spiritually was created to be patterned after the excellences of the Creator. This is what we understand by the Scriptural teaching that God created man in his image. In all his resources he is responsive to his world about him that being activated by it he can be formed and form himself after the nature of it, above all after the nature of God himself. This is man's supreme prerogative among God's creatures. This means that education is a process of man-making, not merely a training of the intellect or stuffing the mind or adjusting the human organism, etc.

We must follow this observation immediately with the fact, however, that the perfection of which man was capable in all his resources by creation has been lost by the disastrous consequences of sin. By voluntary act of disobedience man deprived himself of the one source according to which he was to pattern himself that in his response to the world about him he might cultivate the perfections of which he was capable. This source is God himself. Having thus deprived himself, he did not cease to be a responsive being, but continued to function thus and according to the natural inclinations of a heart inclined toward self and its indulgence rather than the fulfilment of his original nature according to creation. The natural man of sin is involved in the tragedy of history, unable to extricate himself. In all his resources he is perverted and unable to respond according to his created nature. It is particularly in his mental and spiritual resources that distortions have been so damaging. Because he is mental and spiritual he is a creative being, rational and moral. He has created a culture made to serve himself according to his perverted heart. The final culmination will be the full realization of his own perversion, unrestrained by influences in his world reminiscent of his origin. What a tragedy! Education which fails to recognize this awful reality is not true education, but mal-education.

Thanks be to God that we can follow this tragedy of tragedies by the glorious truth that God is in Christ reconciling men and the world unto himself. There is hope! There is salvation! There is redemption! Man can again be made responsive to God and thereby responsive to the truth of his world in all his resources. He can again be formed, patterned after the excellences of his Creator. This is the gospel of the risen Christ. Education to be true must now be redemptive. It must cultivate the individual in all his resources in keeping with the awful reality of sin and all its tragic consequences and the saving grace of God in Christ Jesus that delivers him from the human tragedy to be made responsive to the truth and to be formed or patterned after it.

Now, what are man's primary needs in view of these teachings of the Scriptures? First, that before he is conscious of the truth about himself and about his world he be surrounded by influences which take into full account this truth. Though the child is unresponsive to the truth by natural inclination of the heart, Christian parents have the promise of God himself, "Bring up a child in the way he should go and when he is old he will not depart from it." The Holy Spirit alone can transform hearts, but he promises to accompany the word of truth and make hearts responsive. Second, we must continue this influence according to the needs of our time by soliciting the growing consciousness of the learner in the understanding and mastery of the truth and the commitment to the truth to be disciplined by it. The latter is the special task of the school on its various levels. Surely, the home, the church, and the community play a large part in this task, but in our modern society it is the formal schooling of the youth which officially assumes this responsibility. Education which fails to meet this basic need is mal-education and will fail of its most cherished goals.

There is another criterion by which we must judge the curriculum concepts which we listed. We must ask the question, What is man's place in this world? In the language of Christ himself this is described as being *in* the world but not *of* it. The meaning of this should become clear later. But we should ask of each of these concepts whether it will give us a curriculum which will help us function *in* this world *as not of* it or whether it will cause us to function *as of* it. For Christianity this is of utmost importance. To live in this world as of it is to be worldly. To live in this world as not in is world-flight. To live in this world as not of it is to fulfil one's Christian task or God-given calling. This is education's task in our world.

Now we must return to each of the curriculum concepts briefly to appraise each in the light of the criteria presented.

The information or knowledge-getting concept is right when it asserts that there is objective, preexistent truth to be apprehended. There can be no true education without understanding it and mastering it for recognition and recall, at least to a degree. There is need for logical organization of the materials of knowledge that it may tend to form the learner's thinking.

But a curriculum organized on the basis of knowledge-getting fails to take account of the whole man. It leaves all resources other than the mental resource of man, and even some aspects of the mental, a sort of accidental in education. Little thought is given to them and no phase of the curriculum aim specifically at their activation and forming. Benefits may accrue to the cultivation of other resources, such as the emotional, but they will be quite incidental. On the other hand there is a great danger that erudition may be achieved at the expense of the emotional or the social. And on the religious side we know that in formational knowledge about God is not synonymous with knowing God unto salvation.

The discipline concept is right when it calls attention to the fact that the mental resources of the individual are strengthened by their exercise and that they must undergo a forming according to the pattern of real being. There are basic laws of logic which must mold our intellect. There are basic principles underlying effective memorization for retention and recall.

A curriculum organized essentially in terms of this concept, however, fills textbooks and learning activities in mental gymnastics with little regard for the value subject matter in itself. Mental acuity may by achieved at the expense of desirable emotional and social growth. It can produce debaters and arguers, but will make only incidentally lovers of the truth, if at all. To make lovers of wisdom requires more than either a storehouse of information or a well-disciplined mind.

The social concept is right when it emphasizes the social resources of the individual. Man is a social being. Cooperative activity in the interest of a great cause is difficult for one who has not matured socially. Maturation socially is no more an automatic process than is intellectual maturation. Education must be directed at certain essential social qualities as well as at necessary basic knowledge and intellectual skills.

When the social concept of education makes social adjustment the end and criterion for all educative activity, we respond by saying that the fulfilment of man's deepest needs transcends the social milieu. Society needs an end or destiny beyond itself for justification. A curriculum organized on the basis of the social concept will fall short of developing basic knowledges and understandings, and will neglect the forming of the intellect according to patterns of truth. It will either regiment forcefully or propagandize the individual to the end that he conform to the social context of his time.

The creative concept is right when it calls attention to one of the greatest capacities of the human personality, namely, through insight to reorganize past experience that relatively new patterns of thought and action are produced. This originality is not limited to the few geniuses who write poetry, sculpture human forms, invent machines, etc. It is an integral part of the whole learning process. From the kindergarten through the university we encourage originality. To repress it is to squelch essential motivating drives toward growth.

A curriculum organized on this concept, however, will neglect the forming of the individual according to preexistent patterns of thought and action. Emphasis will fall on expression with little to express. Norms for judging the quality of expression will be lacking. The individual becomes a law unto himself. All systematic learning ceases. Education as a process is aimless, lawless, and capricious. The individual learner determines the curriculum.

Let us summarize our appraisal. All the curriculum concepts we discussed have elements or aspects of truth, according to the criteria we secure from the Scriptures. There is preexistent truth to be understood and mastered. Our mental resources gain power through their exercise in knowledge-getting. Our social resources are responsive and must be cultivated. And finally, we are creative beings, and our capacity for originality must be given opportunity for expression.

We should add immediately that all four concepts are found wanting on essential counts in the light of the same criteria. Every one fails to take account of the individual in all his resources. Especially the social and creative concepts fail to recognize a preexistent order of truth to be understood and take no account of the great tragedy of human history and its dire consequences. Likewise they find no need for a process of redemption outside and independent of man's own efforts.

A combination of these concepts in eclectic fashion will not do for a Christian view of the school curriculum. They are all essentially rooted in a view of man and his world contrary to the teachings of the Scriptures. And, let it be said that any view of anything to be Christian must take its departure from the basic tenets of the Scriptures. I say, its basic departure. By this I mean that the Scriptures as the revelation of God, in which God has spoken, are for us the corrective, the one true orientation of ourselves and our world because it re-orients us to God.

The Christian View

The basic criteria for appraisal of those discussed before send us in another direction for educational concepts. In keeping with these criteria we must ask three questions: (1) What materials are available to us for educational purposes? (2) What end or destiny must they serve? (3) How shall we select curriculum materials?

First, then, what materials have we available? Here we generally think of areas of subject matter such as history, geography, language, etc. And this is correct. But to appraise them as educational media, we must look a little deeper than to view them as organized bodies of knowledge.

What is subject matter? It embodies in organized form the cultural and spiritual products of man. These products are the fruit of cultural and spiritual activity through the ages. Let me try to make these statements clear by illustration. There is a given in the world of nature outside of man which constitutes his environment. There is the sunshine and the rain. According to the alternation of these in a given geographic area man develops an agricultural practice and technique which produces the necessary victuals for his consumption. A system of exchange is developed to profit from each other's enterprise. In a similar way communication, transportation, manufacture, construction, etc., are the products of man's use of the naturally given to create for himself the means for life and its enrichment. This activity we call man's cultural activity, using the word culture in its broadest sense.

It is this cultural activity and the cultural product which have constituted the media for the education of the growing generation throughout the ages. In the course of history the cultural product was organized into systematic bodies of knowledge or information. These bodies of knowledge variously organized became the curricula of the schools. They constitute our subject matter today.

But we cannot stop at this point to find the ground for subject matter. There is another given that is presented to man. It does not come to us in the form of nature, as nature is generally understood, that is the world of creation. This given is God himself as he comes to us in his word, in Jesus Christ the Word made flesh and in the inscripturated word, and in the Holy Spirit as he accompanies that word in our consciousness. Man's response to this given is man's spiritual activity, in distinction from his cultural activity.

Now it is peculiar to the Christian that he engages in both. He is in this world and as such is involved in the activities related to this world. But he is not of this world. And it is precisely his spiritual activity that gives direction to his cultural activity. His citizenship is in heaven.

Here we could at length enter into the discussion of the tension this creates in the Christian's life. How can the Christian cultivate his spiritual activity in a mixed culture? How can his heart be set aglow with love for

Christ in a world so full of enmity to Christ? This tension is reflected in the Christian view of the curriculum as we shall see.

It should be said that man's spiritual and cultural activities find their justification in a common end, that the authority of Christ may be realized and manifest. This is our citizenship. Hence, the Christian says with Paul, "to be with Christ is far better." He cannot rest until the Christ within him has come to full expression. He longs to be delivered. But with Paul, too, he finds himself in a dilemma. He would fill his place in this world in keeping with God's will for him and abide God's time for his deliverance. In this cultural activity he will struggle to make the claim of Christ upon his life effective. In his spiritual activity he will cultivate a personal fellowship with God in Christ which gives direction to his cultural activity. The Christian's end or destiny is his heavenly citizenship. All his spiritual and cultural activity finds its justification in this end. And it is from the spiritual and cultural products that we have our curriculum or media for education.

What concept do we need to select curriculum materials from our spiritual and cultural products to the end that "the man of God may be perfect and thoroughly equipped to every good work," which is the same as saying that one may exercise his heavenly citizenship? We have found the four concepts that have prevailed in the history of education inadequate. I trust this is even clearer now after the discussion of the Christian's spiritual and cultural activities and their destiny. But can we find a comparable concept that will serve our purpose?

We are concerned with men as creatures of God who have fallen from their God-given state and who, in the face of the tragedy of a perverted heart and world, are called to turn to Christ in whom God is reconciling man and the world unto himself. We are concerned with the whole man, the individual in all his resources. We recognize man's primary need to be his personal restoration of fellowship with God. He must be saved. We recognize too that the media at our disposal must be employed to realize the meaning of a saved life for this world and the world to come. The best concept I know is that of the Scriptures, citizenship of heaven. We may also call it citizenship of the kingdom of God when this kingdom is placed over against the kingdom of darkness or the devil. To be subjects of Christ in this world, this is our citizenship. Our curriculum materials must be selected to cultivate this citizenship.

What we want, then are curriculum materials taken from the spiritual product and cultural product that will energize, direct, and form the learner on his level unto citizenship of heaven. This is Christian education's task. Without the cultural product it cannot be education. Without consideration of level it cannot take into account the whole man. Such is our curriculum problem.

The Curriculum Itself

We can divide the areas of subject matter into seven major groups: religion, language arts, philosophy, historical sciences, social sciences, natural sciences, and creative arts. What can each of these areas contribute to the energizing, the directing, and the forming of the individual in all his resources as a citizen of heaven?

The primary task of Christian education in each of these areas is to cause the learner to face God. In every area he should encounter the demands of God upon his life in an attitude of submissiveness to that demand. Heart attitude is our primary objective. The very center of the human personality must be inclined to the divine order and the patterning of the individual in keeping with that order. This is the essence of a heavenly citizenship.

Our first criterion, therefore, in the selection of areas and of subject matter within these areas is, can the learner on his level be directed to face God and God's demands upon his life that he may come consciously to submit to this demand? Let me illustrate this criterion on two levels. First on the primary level, the first level of formal schooling; and then on the level of what we call secondary education, especially the senior level, which are grades ten to twelve.

On the primary level the child, of seven or eight says, hears and reads Bible stories, first largely centered in great Bible characters and later in the form of narration of events. He joins the teacher and the class in prayer, in the singing of sacred songs, and in devotional reading of the word of God. He comes face to face with God in his direct dealings with men in the history of the people of God. He faces God as he joins in group devotions in which he takes an active part. Throughout these activities the demands of God upon his life enter his consciousness.

In the language arts he learns to interpret the printed page and to express himself orally and in writing. His reading material deals with real life as he lives it in a Christian community, including its hazards, its joys, and its responsibilities. Speaking and writing is gauged by the standard of our companionship in which Christ is the unseen guest on every occasion.

The historical, social, and natural sciences at this level come in the form of readings, stories, and individual and group projects aiming at an initial understanding of our world through the world closest to our present interests. This may be our immediate community or it may be the children and their way of life in other lands. Let it be, for example, the Eskimo children. How are they living without the Christ? What is being done to bring the Christ? What is our obligation who know the Christ to them who know him not?

The creative arts take the form of construction, coloring, cutting, etc. Some pupils may begin to show talent in composing prose or poetry, or in color, or in mechanical arts, etc. What are we doing with the special talents God has given us? How well do we cooperate with others in the use of tools, etc.? Can we make or do something to make others happy?

Now an illustration of how this criterion applies to the secondary level. Through a study of the Bible and its doctrines and through the study of the history of the Christian church through the ages since the New Testament days, the learner enters more rationally and intelligently into the religious life. He is confronted with the claim of God upon his intellectual life as well as his moral and devotional life. Class devotions in which all participate take on a more mature character of intercesary prayer and personal consecration. Exchange of religious experiences can be productive of energizing and directing one another if wisely guided by a spiritually mature and tactful teacher.

In the language arts young people are stimulated to read and express themselves. A more mature study of language in its structure and function becomes necessary. Here too we remember that language is our means of communication. The fellowship we keep will determine largely the kind of language we use. When Jesus is our constant companion in all the company we keep, our language will be qualified accordingly. What language is appropriate to this company? What language is in keeping with the citizenship we cultivate?

Of the sciences, I shall refer to the historical only. We meet with God in his inscrutable wisdom and purpose when we note that he permitted the devout Huguenots to perish when the Pilgrims were saved in their journey over Holland to America. We meet God when we see the Christian church going down in times of cultural productivity but standing firm when shorn of this opportunity and bitterly persecuted. The learner faces the claim of God upon his life when he begins to ascertain his position in this kind of world.

Thus without sermonizing, moralizing, or preaching, the claim of God upon each individual life enters the consciousness of the learner. It is the primary criterion for the selection of curriculum materials. Curriculum materials are selected and organized with this primary end in view.

I shall have to confine myself to the brief mention of two other criteria. A citizen of heaven in this world faces the tension, as we say, of keeping himself unspotted from the evils of the world while trying to make his citizenship of heaven effective in the mixed cultural activity of our time. Curriculum materials must be selected to make victory over the evil in our cultural activity the freely chosen pursuit of the learner. The areas of subject matter are to be explored that the learner on his level is cultivated in all his resources according to their respective functions in the life of the individual to discern among cultural products and in his cultural activity. As a member of a productive unit in industry he must understand his position as a citizen of heaven. As participant in governmental affairs he must discern in what he is involved.

I think a third criterion with reference to the selection of curriculum materials should be mentioned. As citizens of heaven in this world we are called upon to be workers. Curriculum materials are to be selected and organized in view of the various callings of life. In this rapidly changing and uncertain socio-economic order the call upon one's life for service presents a most perplexing problem to the Christian. The curriculum materials of the various areas of subject matter present opportunities for guidance with reference to this problem. Curriculum makers are to take this problem into account.

In selecting and organizing curriculum materials, therefore, for any level of Christian education, we ask three important questions. First, what is needed on this level to have the learner face God and God's claim upon his life? Second, what is needed to have the learner discern the cultural product and cultural activity of man with reference to his heavenly citizenship? Third, what is needed to have the learner face the call of service as a worker?

I have endeavored to place before you the basic principles involved in the Christian view of the school curriculum. I believe these principles are universally applicable in whatever community Christian education is taken seriously.

Permit me to recapitulate. The curriculum for Christian education is selected and organized from the areas of subject matter embodying the spiritual and cultural products available to us. These areas of subject matter constitute the media for energizing, directing, and forming the individual in all his resources unto his heavenly citizenship. Curriculum materials are selected and organized for the various levels, according to the basic criteria as stated before.

It is obvious that only a Christian school wholly committed to the concept of Christian education included in this discussion can prepare the curriculum according to the principles set forth here. No half-way measure is possible. In no sense can a school be called Christian which fails to make the citizenship of heaven its destiny. In no way can a school be a school which fails to employ the cultural product meaningfully toward a destiny or purpose. The Christian school is the answer to the confusion of the educational scene.

Calvin College Curriculum Committee: Editor Introduction

College professors, whether as literature or as science specialists, have felt moved to write on Christian schools as individuals. Philosophers like Harry Jellema of the previous generation and Nicholas Wolterstorff of this one have shared with the Reformed community their concerns in both individual journal articles and chapters of books. English professors, like Zylstra and Tiemersma have done the same. And Cornelius Jaarsma and Lambert Flokstra as professors of education have added their insights. All have claimed to impart a Reformed vision of Christian education, however different their interpretations might be.

The following excerpt from *Christian Liberal Arts Education* published by Calvin College and Eerdmans Publishing Company in 1970 represents the efforts of a committee of scholars to capture their vision of Reformed general education for Calvin College. Since college professors both instruct prospective teachers and also have beliefs about Christian education, the excerpt following, while specific to the college level, is instructive for all those committed to Christian education with a Reformed perspective.

If their views have a certain ambiguity and their curricular alternatives a familiar ring, it is likely that the committee itself reflected the variations that the Calvin faculty have expressed in personal publications. The committee acknowledged the validity of two notions of a liberal arts curriculum, and proposed as superior a third. Debated in the sixties by the Calvin faculty, it was voted upon and constituted for a decade the blueprint for Calvin's new core curriculum. Now out of print, the curricular recommendations are rarely referred to and the vision has not been reaffirmed in any published form.

The excerpts which follow represent the best of collective scholarly wisdom about general education at the college level, and deserve a hearing by successive generations.

Christian Liberal Arts Education

Calvin College Curriculum Committee

Our discussion thus far pertains to Christian education in general. We must now narrow our scope, and focus on Christian liberal arts education that is, on a Christian higher education which is non-professional and nonvocational in its orientation.

We are conscious that there are current in the Reformed Christian community and in the evangelical Christian community generally, certain views, alternative to our own, of what a Christian liberal arts education should be. Before we amplify and defend our own view, we wish to examine what we regard as the two most significant of these alternative views. Perhaps no one would fully accept the alternative views as we state them. That is always a difficulty when one tries to discern form in the thoughts and practices of men. Yet we are convinced that the contours of these views, as we sketch them, will be readily recognizable. By thus elaborating what we regard as the major options to our own view, we hope to bring into prominence some of the issues which must be faced and settled if a coherent program of Christian liberal arts education is to be developed. For to say that a Christian liberal arts education is a nonvocational education whose aim is to train students to live the life of faith in contemporary society, is not yet to say enough for a satisfactory address to the problems of curriculum. We must also discuss what ought to be the primary focus of such an education. To that task we now turn.

It should be emphasized that we regard the two alternative views which we discuss as basically Christian views of liberal arts education. Each view holds that the aim of Christian education is to equip the student to become a citizen of the Christian community in contemporary society; and each holds that education must always be conducted within the framework of the Christian religion. In these fundamental ways both are Christian views. So our ground for discarding them is not that on these fundamental matters they are non-Christian, but rather that they are incomplete, and wrongly focused, and do not achieve as well as possible the agreed-on ultimate aim.

Pragmatist View of Christian Liberal Arts Education

One view of the proper focus of a Christian liberal arts education may, with some license, be called the *pragmatist* view. According to this view, the primary principle to bear in mind in setting up a program for such an education is that the acquisiton of knowledge is to be justified primarily in terms of its utility for the solution of concrete practical problems in contemporary life. It is the problems which human beings face in real life, not the abstract problems which theoreticians invent and discover, that are the proper concern of the Christian. The alternative to this principle, the proponents of the pragmatist view insist, is the view that knowledge is desirable for its own sake, that disinterested learning is an end in itself; and this, they claim, is redolent of Greek intellectualism.

As sometimes developed, this pragmatist view calls into question the very existence of liberal arts education as we have defined it—namely, as non-vocational and non-professional education. For it is held that since the graduates of our college will all have to enter one or another vocation or profession, what we teach them must be of some direct use in their future occupations. No one will become just a Christian man; be will become a banker, or plumber, or editor, or minister, or what have you; and it is held that to put out of mind the specific occupations which our students will some day hold down is to waste their time and to act as if we were educating for a leisured aristocracy. It is felt that whether or not there was ever a time in which it was justified for Christians to educate cultured men of leisure, that time is no more.

The same pragmatic view of education, however, can be, and frequently has been, developed in such a way that a liberal arts education still has a justification.For,it is said,the utility which must be kept in mind need not be utility for solving the problems faced in some specific occupation, but rather utility for the solution of those practical problems which face men in general, or at least large numbers of men. The skills and knowledge requisite for holding down some specific occupation can be acquired on the job or in some technical or professional course. But there are also problems which face men in general, arising both in their occupations and outside of them; and it is with these that liberal arts education must be concerned. Some of these may be relatively limited in scope, such as, How can one most economically shop for groceries? But others may be problems which face the entire Christian community (Should political parties be organized along religious lines, and if so, how is this to be accomplished?), or our entire nation (How must the menace of an aggressive world power be handled?), or all mankind, perennially (How can we most effectively prevent crime?).

When liberal arts education is given this sort of focus, then a natural and frequently drawn conclusion is that any curriculum which consists primarily of the disinterested exploration of the various aspects of reality must be abolished; human learning must be structured in terms of the contributions it can make to the solution of the practical problems facing contemporary men. Normally, this will mean that the traditional divisions among the disciplines will be ignored with, so it is said, the eminently desirable result that human knowledge will be integrated and will no longer be split up artificially into watertight compartments.

This view, that a curriculum ought to be structured in terms of the practical problems facing contemporary men, has drawn support in the twentieth century from the psychological claim that if learning is to be effective and efficient it must be organized around the problems and interests of the student. Knowledge, when developed and presented as the disinterested consideration of some subject matter, is said to be sterile, lifeless, and useless; to have relevance and vitality it must be organized around the problems of the learner, both the problems he already faces and the problems which he will face when he takes his place as a member of society. Hence a psychologically sound curriculum, so it is said, will be organized around a series of real problems faced by a learner—problems to him; and whatever knowledge and skills are available in the logically organizedpackagesofferedbytheseveraldisciplinesmustbe unpackaged, reorganized, and brought to bear on the solution of significant life problems.

In the past, an education structured in terms of the disinterested investigation of various aspects of reality has sometimes been defended on the ground that it disciplines and exercises the mind, thereby making the mind more fit for the performance of all tasks. But this too would be questioned by the defenders of the pragmatist view on the ground that contemporary learning theory has shown that the notion of mental discipline must be rejected. The mind, so it is said, is not made up of faculties which can be strengthened by exercise and then applied to all sorts of tasks. Mental skills, though real, are not transferable; the parsing of Latin sentences in no way trains one to become an insurance adjuster. Thus the notion that the traditional disciplines have some inherent qualities which make the study of them exceptionally useful in strengthening mental faculties must be scrapped. If we want our students, upon graduation, to bring a Christian intelligence to bear on the problems which will face them in life, we must, in our education, consider those problems.

Education, then, it is said, must focus on the problems, present and future, of the student. Only such an education is justified for Christians, and only such an education will be pedagogically successful.

But how, in a Christian college, is this to be done? Do the advocates of this view intend that we should merely present problems as neutrally as possible and let the student pick among the possible answers? Not at all. In a Christian college we must aim at developing persons conformed to the image of Christ, mature Christians, capable of living a Christian life both in and out of some vocation or profession. The problems considered, the manner of considering them, and the answers recommended, must all be determined by this primary goal. The Christian must exercise and manifest his faith in all his day-to-day activities, not just in some special acts of worship and meditation; and so the Christian college must see to it, as far as possible, that it is indeed a Christian faith which will be exercised and manifested in the future activities of its students.

In short, a Christian liberal arts education, in this pragmatic view, must focus on exploring the practical problems of contemporary life so as to develop mature Christians. And all curricular content will be selected by reference to this question: What is the most effective medium for developing mature Christians, capable of coping in a Christian manner with the concrete problems which some day will face them?

There are a number of elements in this view which deserve our assent; but we find that, *as a whole,* we cannot accept it. Here we shall select just a few points for comment; our estimate of other points will become clear later in our discussion.

Fundamental to the whole pragmatist view is the contention that, for a Christian, the acquisition of knowledge is legitimate only if it clearly will be of some use in the solution of practical, concrete, contemporary problems. Now we do indeed insist that the acquisition of knowledge on the part of a Christian must be part of his service of God; we do not hold that knowledge is to be acquired because we believe that man's highest good lies in theoretical contemplation. But it does not follow, we believe, that a Christian may seek knowledge only if he thinks it will serve some concrete, practical end. On the contrary, we hold that the disinterested pursuit of theoretical knowledge is a legitimate, and even mandatory, occupation of the Christian community. Of course, it is not mandatory that *every member* of the community undertake this pursuit. But then, it must not be expected that a Christian liberal arts education be of *direct* service to every individual person, but rather that it be of service to the Christian community as a whole. The individual must not be considered apart from the community; for it is in the community, the city of God, that he must find his place. For it he must render his service.

We also hold that the psychological claims used to bolster this view are far from being established. It is a truism that students should, ideally, take an interest in their education, that it should not be put down them by force. But it has certainly not been established that only a few aberrant geniuses have and can have any interest in the methods and results of disinterested learning. A course oriented toward the disinterested exploration of some aspect of reality can be taught so as to prevent or kill all student interest; but so can a course oriented toward the practical problems of contemporary man. A course in pure mathematics is no more doomed to psychological ineffectiveness than is a course in applied mathematics.

Furthermore, we believe that one of the arguments in favor of liberal arts education is that the knowledge thus acquired will be of some use in solving practical problems; but we believe that the student himself, to a great extent, can and will bring the knowledge acquired in the disinterested exploration of reality to bear on the solution of practical problems. This need not all be done for him. We hold, in fact, that a disinterested exploration of reality is the only solid basis on which technical understanding can be built. To orient an education toward a consideration of concrete problems is to run the risk that such problems will have disappeared when the student graduates, leaving him then without any sound and systematic structure for his own thoughts and actions. Sound practice can never be divorced from a sound and systematic understanding of God, man, and the world.

Classicist View of Liberal Arts Education

Another view of the proper focus of a Christian liberal arts education may be called, again with some license, the *classicist* view. According to those who hold this view, such an education should, in the first place, aim at developing the man in each individual the whole man, the moral side of him, the intellectual, the aesthetic, and the rest. The ideal is that all these sides in a man's existence should be integrated and should exist in harmony and balance. However, such a development is not to be achieved merely by cultivating student interests; rather, the student is to be patterned and disciplined by objective reality, by all of it, not just by physical reality. The aim is the development of a wise and cultured man.

Furthermore, a liberal arts education, says the classicist, should not aim at producing specialists. It should renounce the notion that wisdom lies in specialization. It should abhor learned provincialism. It should aim to avoid those distortions in personal life which arise from being learned in one field and ignorant in all others, and that disintegration in society which threatens when men are so caught up in their specialties that they no longer have any thorough understanding of each other, and so are neither intelligent leaders nor intelligent followers. It should stress the importance of men living in community. It follows that a liberal arts education should always in some sense be general education, designed to give the student a conspectus of the main features of human culture. The classicist would emphasize, though, that a general education, in the sense desired, will not be achieved by grouping together a number of specialist courses in different areas. What must be aimed at is not details, not research methods, not technical discussions, but rather the broad patterns and structures to be found in the subject matter under consideration. It must be kept in mind that the problems to be dealt with, though often theoretical, must still be problems which are or ought to be of concern to intelligent men in general. Along the same line, the classicist would hold that, though there may be some justification for allowing specialization in college, such specialization must always be kept firmly in check, and made thoroughly subordinate to the program of general education.

The classicist would hold, further, that we must not be content merely to instill in the student some notion of the broad features of *contemporary* culture; for such an education is still parochial, *historically* parochial. We must, in addition, give the student some sense of the whole cultural heritage of man. In this way he will be able to see beyond the transitory features of contemporary civilization to the more permanent features of human existence. What is even more important, in this way he will be able to contrast the contemporary mode of thought with alternative modes of thought, the contemporary mind with alternative minds. For that whole complex of attitudes, feelings, goals, beliefs, and assumptions, with which men approach the problems confronting them, differs from age to age; and we must not, by our practice, sink into the assumption that the contemporary mind is the only one, or that it is naturally the best. The student must be made to realize that contemporary natural and social science is itself a cultural product of the modern world, and that there are other, not necessarily worse, ways of approaching the same problems. Further, the choice of a certain mind with which to do one's thinking is ultimately a religious choice; and only by having his historical perspective expanded will the student gain an understanding of how various religious options can be manifested in men's cultural activities, and how his own religion can best be manifested. So a major aim of liberal arts education should be to inquire into the various minds with which men think; any consideration of details and methods ought to be subservient to this.

Finally, though this is implicit in what we have already presented of the classicist view, the world of nature has its laws and patterns, but so does the world of culture; and a knowledge of the latter is far more important to us than of the former. Thus natural science, too, ought to be regarded chiefly as a cultural product, related to the concerns of men. It is perhaps not wholly worthless to talk scientifically about nature and man; it is very much more worthwhile, however, to talk about the science of nature and man.

It might be thought that an inescapable consequence of this view is that the humanities would be assigned a very dominant role in education and the natural sciences a very minor role; and often, indeed, this is the result. This does not seem, though, to be an essential part of the view. If it were, this would immediately give us ground for objecting to the view. For the natural sciences bulk much too large in contemporary culture to be admitted grudgingly into an educational program. Furthermore, the humanities themselves can be taught in a non-humane manner, and the sciences, conversely, in a humane manner. What the view rather leads up to is this: All liberal arts education ought fundamentally to be intellectual and cultural history, aimed at discovering the various minds behind men' s cultural activities and subjecting them to a religious critique, to the end that the student may become more aware of the implications of his own faith.

If, finally, it is asked what is to be done with such an education, the answer is: Anything at all. A student thus educated is ready for anything whatsoever.

We find this view of Christian liberal arts education enormously attractive, in many ways a corrective to the former view, and, as will become clear later, possessing many emphases which we wish to adopt as our own. Yet we feel that we cannot accept it *as a whole* either.

What disturbs us above all is the passivity of such an approach to education. The emphasis is all on understanding and judging culture, not on contributing to it; whereas we are convinced that the great and continuing task of the Christian community on earth is to build a culture. This means, in part, that, guided and enlightened by our Christian faith, we must ourselves *develop* the various disciplines; and, as a corollary, that we must educate new generations for productive and creative work in the various disciplines. This insistence, on our part, that the Christian community must work creatively at the various disciplines does not at all mean that we wish to play down the importance of transmitting and evaluating what men have already done; it means rather that our task includes this as part of something larger.

Perhaps the classicist's most cogent reply to the objection just raised is that in thus developing the various disciplines we are succumbing to the contemporary mind. For if we work at physics, we will of course be working at contemporary physics and doing physics in the contemporary manner; and similarly, if we prepare a student for work in physics it will be for work in contemporary physics. But surely it remains to be demonstrated that a Christian cannot do physics in the modern mathematical manner. There will be all sorts of differences between a Christian's working at physics and a non-Christian's. Yet we see no reason to suppose that a person thinking with a Christian mind cannot engage in mathematical physics. The contemporary non-Christian man sets physics in the wrong perspective; but this is not to say that the Christian cannot engage at all in contemporary physics.

Furthermore, we too are inclined to think that the world of culture is, on balance, more important and significant for man than the world of nature. Yet we also think it very important that natural science somewhere be explored as a cultural phenomenon. It seems to us that the Christian community is, except in unusual circumstances, as much under injunction to explore physical nature itself as the history of physics, biological nature as literature, mathematical laws as philosophy. In nature, too, God is revealed. We cannot accept the view that Christian liberal arts education ought to consist almost entirely of intellectual and cultural history. On the other hand, the sense of the importance of history which underlies the classicist view is a healthy corrective to the "presentism" of the pragmatist view.

Another issue on which we agree is that our goal ought to be not only to educate for the learned professions but to give an education which is relevant to the lives of intelligent men no matter what occupations they choose. One way in which a liberal arts education is relevant is this: When an economic or artistic or political issue arises in the community at large, our graduates can give the community some competent guidance on these matters. But if liberal arts education ought to be relevant in this way, then, in our opinion,we have a justification for a good deal of concentration.The various disciplines are now so complex that the average person with a *purely* general education will not have much competence in any given area at all. Not only this; it also seems to us that the peculiar skill or knack essential to making good judgments, say, on music is by no means always accompanied by an equal skill or knack for making good judgments, say, on politics. And further, if a student never digs deeply into one area, he never realizes the manifold and subtle ways in which details and generalities blend in the make-up of a discipline. We do not think that we can any longerlookformenwhoarewiseonallmatters;wecanonlylook for a wise community. We do, indeed, accept the reasons offered for the importance of a general education. What we want to insist on, however, is that general education be balanced with a more thorough and concentrated education in some particular area. We should not apologize for allowing students to concentrate. We should demand it.

Disciplinary View of Liberal Arts Education

With this sketch of two views, alternative to ours, concerning the proper focus of a Christian liberal arts education as a background, let us now develop our own view. This may be stated in summary form thus: The primary focus of a Christian liberal arts education should be on teachers and students together engaging in the various scholarly disciplines, directed and enlightened in their inquiries by the Word of God. Let us call this view, though not very felicitously, the *disciplinary* view. As the first step in developing the view, let us explain what we have in mind when we speak of disciplines, and how we think the major divisions among the disciplines should be determined.

The Nature and Divisions of the Disciplines

What is a Discipline: When we speak of the *disciplines,* what is it that we have in mind? As a general formula, to be clarified as we proceed, let us say this: A discipline is the scientific (theoretical) study of some aspect or segment of reality. Examples of disciplines, as we conceive them, are sociology, mathematics, and music criticism.

To engage in the disciplines is to engage in *scientific* or *theoretical* thought. A person, through out his ordinary life, learns and applies concepts, draws conclusions, and justifies those conclusions; thus, he thinks. He tries to balance his checking account, to find the cause of the rumble in his record player, to organize a Community Fund Campaign, to get the Democrats and the Republicans to agree on a tax-reform program; and each of these demands a good deal of thought. But this is not the sort of thinking which is characteristic of the disciplines. It is not scientific thought. Rather it is, as some would call it, pre-scientific or non-theoretical thought. It should not be supposed, however, that there is some sharp line between theoretical and non-theoretical thought. On the contrary, nontheoretical thought often merges *without* break into theoretical thought.

One may *engage* in some discipline i.e., in the theoretical study of some aspect of reality either in order to solve some concrete practical problem, or simply in order to discover how things are and why they are as they are. Thus one may engage in geometry in order to improve land-surveys, or simply to uncover the truth about certain sorts of shapes; in a study of the stock market in order to manipulate it, or simply to find out its workings; in a study of the chemistry of paint in order to improve the anti-blistering qualities of the paint of some particular paint company, or simply to find out the answer to some questions about the nature of paint; in the study of a certain topic in theology in order to prepare a sermon, or simply to discover the truth on the matter. Again, there is no sharp line between interested and disinterested theoretical thought; the one motivation shades without break into the other.

This distinction between interested and disinterested thought is, however, important because the structure we give to a discipline and to the results of a discipline, the topics we are led to discuss and the research we are led to perform, will be quite different if our thought is oriented toward the achievement of some concrete practical aim from what it will be if it is not so oriented. A history of Russia conducted in order to find out whether the Russians can be relied on to keep their treaties, and so to give light on whether or not a proposed treaty should be signed, will be quite different from a history conducted simply in order to uncover the pattern of Russian history. There may be considerable overlap in the results, and both studies may clearly be cases of theoretical thought; yet the results as a whole will, in all likelihood, be quite different—they will be structured differently and topics assigned major importance in the one will not even appear in the other.

We have already argued in our discussion of the pragmatist view that in a liberal arts education, when teachers and students together engage in a discipline, they ought to do so for disinterested reasons. They ought not to bend their discussions and investigations to restrictively practical problems.

This is by no means to say that no practical results can be expected from other engaging in the disciplines, that the knowledge acquired in a disinterested exploration of reality can never be bent to practical ends. Certainly it often can be. Nor is it to say that learning ought to be isolated from life, nor that there is some ultimate value in knowledge *per se*. It is just to say that other engagement in the disciplines should not be primarily slanted toward the achievement of restrictively practical aims.

Henceforth, when we speak of a discipline, we shall mean the disinter-*ested* theoretical study of some aspect or segment of reality.

What Differentiates the Disciplines: What makes one academic discipline distinct from another? How are they to be differentiated? Primarily, they are to be differentiated in terms of their subject matter. Sociology differs from physics because its subject matter is different. There is an abundance of different systems of sociology and theology; what makes them all systems of sociology or theology is the subject matter with which they deal.

Two disciplines, furthermore, may be distinct either because they deal with different aspects of entities, or with different sorts of entities, or both. Suppose, for example, that we explain fine arts criticism as the study of works of visual art. This would be inadequate. For a work of visual art is always a physical object, and thus comes under the purview of the physicist and the chemist as well as of the art critic; physical and chemical laws hold for paintings as well as for other sorts of physical objects. In addition, the painting may be of interest to the historian as illustrating or supporting some thesis in cultural history; and it may be of interest to the psychologist as illustrating some psychological law. In short, works of visual art belong to the subject matter of many different disciplines. What differentiates these disciplines is that each is concerned with a different aspect of the entities which fall under their joint purview.

It seems likely, however, that sometimes two disciplines can be differentiated from each other only by reference to different *sorts* of entities. Suppose, for instance, that we could distinguish the aesthetic aspect of entities from all the other aspects that entities may possess. Then we could say that music criticism differs from literary criticism by virtue of each being concerned with the aesthetic aspect of different sorts of entities. Similarly, one could scarcely explain what geology is without making reference to a specific entity, the earth.

The disciplines, then, differ from each other in being concerned with different aspects or segments of reality.

The lines between the various disciplines are often not very sharp. Operas belong to the subject matter of both music criticism and literary criticism; and, more important perhaps, the aesthetic aspect of things shades almost imperceptibly into the moral, the psychological, the physical. Similarly, if one tries to differentiate biology from other disciplines by saying, in part, that it deals with what is alive, one must be prepared to confess that it is not always clear whether a certain thing is or is not alive.

The Aim of the Disciplines: In the study of one or another aspect or segment of reality, what is it that we want to discover? What are the results that we seek?

Sometimes the desired result of the scientist's investigations is a knowledge of some specific property of some specific entity. The historian, for example, is often concerned to find out what a specific man did at a certain time on a certain day; the music critic is often concerned to uncover the structure of a specific musical composition; and the geologist is concerned to discover various features of the earth. Perhaps this concern to uncover specific properties of specific entities is missing in some sciences, such as physics, but there is no doubt that it plays a large part in others. At other times, the scientist is concerned to discover some property of all entities of a certain sort, or to discern the behavior of some specific entity under all or most circumstances of a certain sort. He is concerned to establish laws and principles and generalizations; he aims, that is, to discover structure in the subject matter. This goal is probably much more striking in physics than it is, say, in history and art criticism; yet even in these latter, generalizations are clearly an important part of the desired results of the discipline.

In our study of at least certain subject matters there is something else we can aim at—namely, discovering whether an entity in the aspect under consideration is good or bad and whether all entities of a certain sort, in the aspect under consideration, are good or bad. We can, in other words, try to arrive at correct evaluations, both particular and general, of the moral aspects of entities and situations, the aesthetic aspects, the economic aspects, the political aspects. There is, as is well-known, much dispute in the contemporary world as to whether it is or is not the proper business of the historian, the economist, the art critic, the sociologist to make evaluations. It is our conviction that in a Christian view of the disciplines a proper aim of our scientific endeavors is to determine which things are good and which bad in various respects. Indeed, in many cases such evaluations are subtly but inextricably intertwined with the other results of our scientific endeavors. Of course, judgments as to better and worse aspects of the subject matter will not be a part of every discipline. There are, for instance, no such evaluations of subject matter to be made in physics. One atom or electron is neither better nor worse than another.

Finally, in those disciplines in which we study the institutions and creations and activities of men, what we as Christians also aim to uncover and discern is the religious perspective, the mind, behind all those cultural products. This, indeed, is one of the most important results we are looking for in such disciplines. For a fact of great significance about a man's cultural endeavors is that they are the expression of his religious allegiance and dogmas . What eminently deserves investigation, then, in other consideration of human products—whether these be economic institutions, political arrangements, works of art, philosophical systems, liturgical practices—is the spiritual kingdoms which inform and pervade those products.

In summary, we expect the disciplines to yield, though in differing degrees, a knowledge of specific properties of specific entities, a knowledge of the structure of the subject matter under consideration, a knowledge of which specific products and which sorts of products are good and which bad in respect to the aspect of reality under consideration, and a knowledge of the religious allegiances which inform and animate the products being studied.

Concepts and Methods: In order to formulate these results, and to state the problems or questions to which the results are the answers, a scholar working in a discipline needs a conceptual framework, a body of more or less inter-connected concepts. To some extent these will be ordinary concepts put to new and rarefied uses; but in great measure they will be new, technical concepts, introduced deliberately in order to carry out some scientific investigation. The logician, for instance, introduces the concepts of entailment and necessary truth; the art critic introduces the concepts of form and style and meaning, the physicist introduces the concepts of electron and proton and gamma ray. Since it is in terms of a conceptual framework for a certain discipline that the questions are asked and the answers formulated, an understanding of the problems and results of a certain discipline presupposes an understanding of the conceptual framework in terms of which these problems and results are expressed. One could not understand the formulation of certain of the laws of logic without having the concept of entailment, though one could have the concept of entailment without knowing any, or very many, of those laws of logic.

There is also in every discipline a certain methodology—that is, a certain body of methods, techniques, and procedures taken to be appropriate for arriving at the right answers to questions asked. Some of these procedures will be ordinary ones, or at least rather obvious elaborations of ordinary ones. For example, the procedure by which the literary critic arrives at his conclusions is only a subtle elaboration of a procedure which we all use in reading newspapers and magazines. Other procedures will be more recondite and complicated; witness the procedures by which physicists and mathematicians arrive at their conclusions. Either way, we will normally not be able to reduce the methodology of a certain discipline to a catalog of rules; learning the methodology of a certain discipline amounts to picking up a skill or acquiring a knack. Still, one condition of something's being a method is that it be at least somewhat decisive; a method which consistently yields conflicting results, even for skilled practitioners, is no method.

The conceptual framework of a discipline in large part determines its methodology; given the conceptual frame work of modern physics, the methodology of medieval physics is for the most part thoroughly irrelevant. It must not be supposed, though, that to each conceptual framework there corresponds just one method for answering the questions set within that framework. All depends on the specific question asked. Even for questions asked within a given conceptual framework there may be methods for answering those questions which are significantly different from each other. It is also the case that different disciplines, with significantly different conceptual frameworks, may contain methods which are strikingly similar to each other. This is true for the method of controlled experiment to be found both in modern chemistry and modern physics.

The conceptual framework and methodology in terms of which it is thought appropriate to study a given aspect of reality varies from age to age. Even at a given period in history there are often competing methodologies and conceptual frameworks within the same discipline. In fact, divergences in conceptual framework and methodology are an important feature of the contemporary intellectual scene in all fields but the natural sciences and mathematics. Even there they are by no means completely absent.

These divergences are usually not trivial. A great deal hangs on whether one adopts the conceptual framework of Freud or that of stimulusresponse behaviorism for one's study of human psychology, and whether one adopts the conceptual framework of traditional grammar or that of transformational linguistics for one's study of language.

Divergences in conceptual frameworks throughout history, and within a given historical period, are to be traced to a number of factors. For one thing, they are often connected with divergent convictions concerning the facts and with advances in knowledge. Usually, significant advances in knowledge both require and lead to the introduction of new concepts. Just as often such divergences reflect religious and philosophical differences. The behaviorist refuses to adopt Freudian concepts because in using them he would be committing himself to the existence of entites which he abhors, such as The Unconscious. The Christian rejects a Marxist framework of historical analysis because in using it he commits himself to a nonChristian view of man. Ernst Mach rejected the framework of modem physics because he felt that in using it he was committing himself to the existence of entities which he thought non-existent such as electrons and atoms. Mersenne, a member of Descartes' circle in Paris, argued for the adoption of mechanistic concepts in physics on the ground that it would enable men to form a much more noble view of God's manner of working in the universe. And the conflict among Tillichian, Barthian, and Thomistic approaches to theology obviously reflects deep differences in religious outlook.

Earlier we said that the disciplines were to be distinguished from each other by reference to their subject matter. What we must now add is that a person is led to see the subject matter of a discipline, its scope and terrain, differently depending on the conceptual framework which he adopts. The behaviorist takes the subject matter of psychology to be something different from what the Freudian takes it to be, and as a result he sees its relationship to, say, physiology, differently. A modern chemist's explanation of the subject matter of his discipline, and of its difference from physics and biology, would differ from that of an eighteenth-century chemist. Similarly, if we asked the logical positivist to explain to us the scope of philosophy, we would get a different answer from that of a phenomenologist. Of course, we do feel that both the Freudian and the behaviorist are doing psychology, that both the eighteenth-century and the twentieth-century men are doing chemistry, and that both the positivist and the phenomenologist are doing philosophy. We do feel, and to some extent we could perhaps explain this feeling, that in each of these cases they are dealing with the same subject matter. Yet if we try to go beyond this vague feeling and state clearly what we take to be the subject matter of the discipline, the differences in conceptual framework become crucial. For the point is not just that in each case the language used to explain the scope of the discipline varies; rather, the scope of the discipline as explained in these different manners turns out to be different. The behaviorist denies the existence of what the Freudian says that he wants to study, The Unconscious; the modern chemist denies the existence of the phlogiston which the eighteenth century chemist took as his major concern; and what the Thomist says that he wants to study by reason, namely God, the Barthian says cannot be the object of thought at all.

Thus the alliances and differences we see among the disciplines, the differences in subject matter which we take to be significant, the large boundary lines which we claim to perceive, will be divergent just as our conceptual schemes are divergent, and will reflect differences of equal importance. The terrain of the disciplines will look different depending on the state of our knowledge and on our religious and philosophical convictions.

Integration and Division: How then do we decide where the main joints between the disciplines are? How do we determine which are the most significant divisions within the whole realm of scientific knowledge? How do we find out which are the major disciplines? These are key questions in any attempt to develop a curriculum.

No doubt one can classify the disciplines in many different ways. The dominant contemporary classification is probably into natural sciences, social sciences, and humanities. When this scheme is adopted, philosophy is usually classified with music as one of the humanities . Presumably, then, philosophy is thought to bear more significant relations to music than, say, to psychology, which is typically classified as a social science. Perhaps it does; but if so, what are those relations? This question usually goes unanswered. Similarly, the disciplines have on occasion been classified into those which deal with nature, those which deal with man and his creations and institutions, and those which deal with God. Presumably economics and music criticism would both be put into the second of these classes. But has one pointed out any significant unity between these two disciplines by observing that both deal with the creations of men? And presumably biology would be put into the first of these classes. But does not biology also deal with men?

It seems natural to group botany and zoology together into the more comprehensive discipline of biology. Might one just as appropriately group biology and chemistry into some new and more comprehensive discipline of which these are two major divisions? What other divisions would there be in this new discipline? Physics? Or ought we to go in the other direction and recognize that botany and zoology each have the same status in the scheme of the disciplines that chemistry has? Or is there indeed, as we vaguely sense. a more significant break between biology and chemistry than between botany and zoology? Again, it seems natural to group geometry and arithmetic and algebra together as branches of the larger discipline of mathematics. Would it be just as appropriate to go one step further and regard mathematics and physics as branches of a more comprehensive discipline? Or is it mathematics and philosophy that should be regarded as branches of some more comprehensive discipline? Or all three? Or do geometry and algebra and arithmetic each have the same status in the scheme of the disciplines as physics and philosophy; are the divisions among these five all equally natural and significant? We naturally regard symphonic criticism and string quartet criticism as species of music criticism, and sonnet criticism and epic criticism as species of literary criticism. Is it arbitrary not to follow through and regard literary and music criticism as branches of art criticism? Is there, in any significant sense, a discipline of art criticism in general?

Or are all divisions among the disciplines equally arbitrary and unnatural, as some contemporary thinkers have suggested? Is scientific knowledge such a fine, unbroken web that no rational distinctions can be made?

We suggest that the most important relationship which two disciplines can bear to each other is this: They can share in common a significant body of concepts with whose application they are jointly concerned. Normally, if they do share a significant body of concepts with whose application they are jointly concerned, there will also be a significant number of principles or laws, expressed by means of those concepts, with whose validation they are jointly concerned. When this is the case—when two disciplines share, in the way indicated, a significant number of concepts and principles— then the subject matters of the two disciplines are unified in the important sense that they provide us with different applications of the *same* concepts and with different instantiations of the *same* principles and laws. This, we suggest, is the most important unity which one discipline can have with another. This is the most significant kind of integration to be found in the disciplines. Integration is not something which we must accomplish by rearranging courses and trying our best to integrate, but something which is inherent in the discipline. Thus the major divisions among the disciplines should be seen as running between those disciplines which share no significant body of concepts and laws in common . The more significant the body of concepts and principles shared between two disciplines, the more they are, in fact, unified.

It should be noted, however, that there are two different sorts of concepts with whose application two disciplines can be jointly concerned.

Certain concepts are such that all disciplines are concerned with their application—concepts such as identity, truth, property, and thing. And there are certain other concepts, mathematical concepts—such as function, set, and curve with whose application a wide range of different disciplines are concerned, by virtue of their all speaking the language of mathematics. Concepts of both these sorts might be called formal concepts. When we speak of two disciplines being jointly concerned with the application of a significant body of concepts, we mean to exclude from consideration such formal concepts. The fact that two disciplines are jointly concerned with the application of such concepts gives them no significant unity.

So is there, in any significant sense, a discipline of art criticism in general? Critics of all the arts use such words *as form, symbol, meaning.* If it is established that they are using the same concept when they use these words, and not just analogous concepts; and if there are more such concepts which have application in all the arts jointly; and if further there are a good number of principles which hold for all the arts jointly; then the line of division between music criticism and literary criticism is not as significant and fundamental as that between, say, art criticism in general and history. But if the various forms of art criticism share little more in common than that they all deal with an aesthetic aspect of things, this is not enoughtopreventourseeingamajordivisionamongthem;and to put them together into one course would not be to achieve any significant sort of integration. Similarly, if there is an important body of concepts and principles whose application and validation is the common concern of both botany and zoology, then the division between these two disciplines is not as fundamental as that between biology and chemistry; to a considerable extent we have in them merely applications of the same concepts and instantiations of the same laws in different subject matters. But if botany and zoology have little more in common than that they both deal with living things, this is not enough to lead us to regard biology as one of the major disciplines; botany and zoology in that case would be major disciplines.

Of course, to say that two disciplines share, in the way indicated, no significant body of concepts and principles is not to say that their subject matters have no inherent or intrinsic relations to each other. There are important intrinsic connections between the subject matter of physics, chemistry, and biology; and between that of psychology, sociology, and cultural anthropology; and these all deserve to be emphasized. But the fact that there are such connections does not by itself establish that these disciplines can, in any significant way, be treated as parts of a larger and more comprehensive discipline.

In conclusion, it should be remarked that one discipline *sharing* with another a significant body of concepts whose application is the concern of both and a significant body of principles whose validation is the concern of both, is different from one discipline *presupposing* the concepts and principles of another. One concept presupposes another if it is defined or explained in terms of the other; and one principle presupposes another if it could not be true unless the other were true. It may be that certain concepts of chemistry can ultimately be explained only by reference to certain concepts of physics, and that certain laws of chemistry could not be true unless certain laws of physics were true. Yet it might be that chemistry is not itself concerned with the application of those concepts but only with concepts presupposing them; nor with the validation of those laws, but only with the validation of laws presupposing them.

Faith and Learning

The Christian scholar will engage in the disciplines as an exercise of his Christian faith, and will strive to see reality in the perspective of the biblical revelation. In sociology as well as theology, in literary criticism as well as philosophy, in all the disciplines, he will try to see reality in the biblical perspective. He can do nought else. For his faith in Christ is the fundamental fact of his life. The biblical perspective on reality is for him authoritative. He aims to make it his, to be directed and enlightened by it. His vocation, as that of every other Christian, is to be a manifestation of faith; it is to be penetrated and suffused by God's Word to man.

The Christian scholar is convinced that Scripture does not speak only of supernatural mysteries, leaving him to his own devices in unraveling nature. He knows that it does not speak only of the sacred, allowing him to treat the secular as he will. It speaks of *m(m*—his nature, his destiny, his inclinations, his proper relation to other men, to nature, to God; it speaks of God—his character, his relation to man, to the world; it speaks of the world—its origin, its relation to man, its proper use. It provides him with a basic framework of convictions. Of course, the Bible is not a philosophical and scientific textbook, a systematic and disinterested discourse on the nature of reality. Any Christian scholar who wants things easy, and looks for that, is bound to be disappointed. The aim of the Bible is to reveal the way of salvation in its universal and total significance for human life, thus inducing in man a religious commitment which opens up a comprehensive perspective on reality. The Christian scholar, by virtue of being a Christian, will, in his appropriation of reality, try to see reality in that perspective. To do anything else is to defect.

The proper object of study for the Christian scholar is *reality,* that which confronts him. The sciences cannot be erected by deduction from the Bible. The Bible, once again, is not a handbook on physics, or chemistry, or mathematics, or literary criticism, or even philosophy. It does, however, provide us with a framework and a structure for our thought. It is our duty and privilege as Christian scholars to roof and side the posts and beams. It provides us with a perspective on reality. It is our duty and privilege to study reality in that perspective. The Christian religion is not an irrational bias which we intend to hold on to at all costs, ignoring the facts. It is not an astigmatism which we resolve never to get corrected. On the contrary. It is the spectacles with which we are enabled to see the facts aright. But look at the facts we must.

Further, the biblical framework of conviction is more elaborate in some areas than in others. No doubt the scriptures speak more immediately and richly to theology, philosophy, and the sciences which deal with man, his cultural endeavors and products, than they do to those sciences which deal with physical nature and mathematics. Yet even here the biblical message is not silent and irrelevant.

Of course, reality is not hidden from the man whose perspective is alien to that of the Scriptures. The man of sin is not blind to reality. Rather, his perspective yields distortion. The nature and degree of distortion will vary greatly. Positivism is all in all perhaps a more severe distortion than Platonism; materialism, than Kantianism. And distortions in the field of the natural sciences will typically be less severe and pervasive than those in the area of the humanities. But the elimination of fundamental distortions—this is the conviction of the Christian—cannot occur until we adopt the perspective on reality, the framework of convictions, of the Scriptures.

Somehow a sizable part of the contemporary world has come to be of the belief that one must choose between science and religion, between a scientific approach to reality and Christianity. The fault here lies on both sides. Christians have often been perverse in their refusal to consider evidence, and even in their rejection of learning generally. But nonChristians, too, have often distorted and gone beyond the evidence, and have developed and interpreted the sciences in such a way as to make them hostile to the Christian religion. In that case, they have incorporated and presupposed another perspective, one as little capable of proof as that of the Christian.

In the contemporary Christian world, however, the prevailing view no doubt is not that Christianity is incompatible with scientific investigations but that the two are independent. On this view, Christian education consists of capping an ordinary curriculum with chapel services and studies in theology. For example, in the statement of Aims and Objectives of one well known American Protestant college, we find these words: 'The College takes the position that men and women are called by God to faith and service. Accordingly, it provides the opportunity for worship and seeks to graduate students who are morally sensitive and theologically literate." And later, "As a college of the_____ Church,_____, committed to a principle of wholeness in education which means that the study of theology is an integral part of a liberating academic experience. For this reason students are required to complete courses in the Department of Religion. In addition to this the College provides time, facilities and personnel to sustain the worshipping community in its life and growth." We see here how the impact of the Christian religion on the educational program is limited to the study of theology and to engaging in worship. Nothing is said of the need to have all disciplines developed on Christian foundations. The assumption is, presumably, that these are neutral.

Surely the testimony of history, as well as the biblical teaching, is all to the opposite. The medieval scholastics already were convinced that, except for theology, all the disciplines should be founded solely on human reason. If men but used the natural light of reason they could come to agreement on all but supernatural mysteries; and errors, it was held, were all *demonstrably* errors. After the ebb and flow of centuries of philosophical systems, is this view still plausible? Were all the philosophers irrational? Were they all ignoring the natural light of reason? If so, where are the proofs? And are the special sciences *really* impervious to larger philosophical issues and to changes in philosophical perspectives? Why then should the Logical Positivists, in spite of their admiration for the sciences, still have made it a part of their program to reform them on positivist foundations?

Only if theoretical inquiry is conducted under the guidance of the biblical revelation is there the possibility of overcoming our distorted perceptions of God, man, and the world and of attaining a full and correct understanding of reality. We must "lay Christ in the bottom, as the only foundation of all sound knowledge and learning."

But how? All this is abstract and unenlightened by example. In what ways can our Christian perspective have an impact on our scientific endeavors? In what ways can alien perspectives yield distortion? To answer these questions is of course the business of the college. Full and satisfactory answers cannot possibly be given here. Perhaps it will be of benefit, however, to give a skeletal summary of typical ways in which the biblical revelation may give structure and direction to our work in the disciplines.

For one thing, the biblical revelation can inform our view of the place of disinterested theoretical inquiry in human life—its limitations, its proper aims. The twentieth century has seen natural science adulated, with the hope expressed in Positivism, Marxism, and Pragmatism that this science will eventually solve all our ills if we but trust it to do so. In classical times, Aristotle saw in theoretical contemplation man's highest good. For a Christian, disinterested inquiry is important. Yet it does not constitute man's ultimate hope.

Secondly, the biblical revelation often speaks to the conceptual schemes, methodologies, and presuppositions which we employ in our work in a discipline, as well as to what we do or do not accept as fact, particular or general. The sociology text pervaded by the thesis that the source of evil in human affairs is defective conditioning on the part of society is thereby pervaded by a dogma alien to the Christian. The determinism of behaviorists and Marxists makes history and psychology and theology quite different when developed by them from what they are when developed by scholars committed to the idea of freedom embodied in classical Liberalism, and also quite different from what they are when developed by scholars committed to the Christian religion. The areas of concern in each case are roughly the same, but the results are different.

Again, the biblical revelation speaks to our interpretation of the results of disinterested inquiry and our choice of a larger philosophical perspective in which to place those results. Bertrand Russell in his famous essay, "A Free Man's Worship,'t takes the results of contemporary physical science and gives to them an interpretation which is profoundly antithetical to Christianity; various thinkers have done the same with the results of contemporary biological science. And in the eighteenth century Immanuel Kant developed a profound and comprehensive interpretation of Newtonian science which is opposed in fundamentals to the Christian religion.

Further, the biblical revelation speaks to our view of the place of each discipline in the scheme of the disciplines, of the limits of a particular discipline, and of its bearings on other disciplines. The Pythagoreans thought that mathematics was the only discipline. Descartes thought that all disciplines ought to be reformed on the model of mathematics. Hume thought that psychological anthropology was the fundamental discipline in that it was presupposed by all the others. The post-Hegelians thought that history was the fundamental discipline if not the only one. The positivists wished that they could reduce everything to physics. And recently, extravagant claims have been made on behalf of linguistics and communication theory. When the assumptions underlying these views are uncovered, it becomes clear that the biblical revelation is vitally relevant to this tendency, manifested throughout history, to single out one facet of reality as the clue to all the others.

Again, the biblical revelation can inform the direction of our investigations, the emphases we give, and the theses we try to establish. The Enlightenment historians clearly *set out* to establish that the Middle Ages were dark, and that this darkness was due to the baleful influence of the Christian church; they did not arrive at this conclusion after scrupulous historical investigations. The Catholic historian of philosophy often sets out to prove that after St. Thomas, all was regrettable decline. And the Freudian literary critic tries to show that the main clue to the understanding of a poem is to be found in the workings of the author's and the reader's Unconscious.

Further, in those disciplines in which one can properly make evaluations of the subject matter, the biblical revelation can go to shape and form these evaluations. Our estimate of the laissez faire economy and the Communist economy, of democracy and monarchy, of the devotional verse of the metaphysicals and "The Yellow Christ" of Gaugin—all these are matters on which our faith can be formative.

Finally, the biblical revelation speaks to what we do with our theoretical knowledge, for what purposes or ends we use it. It speaks to the use to which we put our knowledge of sociology in the handling of social problems, our knowledge of economics in the handling of economic problems, our knowledge of political theory in the handling of political problems.

All this is still only a skeleton. The primary and unending business of our academic community is to put flesh on these bones by discovering and communicating, concretely and in detail, the direction and enlightenment which the Word of God gives for our work in each of the disciplines. The task calls, of course, for personal Christian faith and commitment; no less obviously it calls for scientific competence, continuous study, creative reflection, intellectual initiative, courage, and imagination. Such qualities are indispensable if we are to avoid the ever-present temptation to replace the impact of a vital Christian faith with a sterile and mummified system of propositions labeled *Christian*. From this one can, as occasion demands, extract a proposition and bring it into external contact with the subject matter under discussion, allowing living, dynamic Christian faith to be increasingly relegated to a sphere of its own.

Intensive and Extensive Study of Disciplines

We ought to be more specific, finally, about the sort of study of the disciplines which we are recommending for our students.

We believe that in a complete liberal arts education the student should be introduced to the disciplines on two different levels. In the first place, he should acquire a *general* or *extensive* education by following a rationally determined pattern of required and optional courses in the various major disciplines, the fundamental unifying element in this pattern being the Christian perspective within which everything is presented.

What do we hope for as the outcome of the student's general or extensive education in the disciplines? One thing we hope for is that he shall acquire some knowledge of the more significant features of the subject matter under consideration. In our study of human creations and institutions, such knowledge will include a knowledge of whether the things under consideration are good or bad in the respects being considered and, just as importantly, of the religious perspectives or minds out of which those creations and institutions have developed. We hope, in other words, that the student shall acquire a knowledge of the more significant *results* of the various disciplines.

We hope for more than this. In the study of human products, we hope that the student will *himself* learn to make evaluations and that he will *himself* learn to discern and judge the religious allegiances which animate and infuse those products. We do not think it sufficient for the student to learn the teacher's views only on these matters. The student will have to learn not just the results of those disciplines but, to some extent, their *methodologies* as well; he will have to become, on a more or less amateur level, a practitioner of those disciplines. This we hold is an achievable aim in most disciplines in which human products are considered—disciplines such as theology and literary criticism and economics. It is also an important aim; for the student, when he takes his place in society, will be *forced to* make such evaluations and will be forced to discern and judge religious perspectives. But even in those disciplines in which one cannot make evaluations on the subject matter, nor discern and judge religious perspectives in it, we believe that the student should not only be presented

with the current results of the disciplines but that he should also acquire some insight into their *workings;* that is, an acquaintance with the methodologies by which their results are obtained. The aim of this cannot be to make all students amateur practitioners of such disciplines; this can scarcely be hoped for in the case, say, of physics, nor do we see any reason why it should be. Its aim is rather to give the student an understanding of
    the nature of the discipline itself. The scholarly disciplines, after all, are among the most significant of all man's cultural products.

A final outcome for the student of his general or extensive study of the disciplines should be this: Whenever possible and illuminating, in his study of a certain discipline, he should become acquainted with alternative approaches to the same subject matter.He should learn how contemporary men, of different religious and philosophical convictions from his own, approach the same subject matter and, to overcome historical parochialism, he should also learn how men of other ages approached the same subject matter. In this way he will gain a richer understanding of the various spiritual kingdoms of mankind and also a better understanding of the full significance of his own membership in the City of God.

Secondly, we believe that, in addition to such a general or extensive education, each student should also be required to concentrate in some particular discipline and thus to supplement his extensive study of the disciplines with an intensive study of some one discipline. This intensive study will have fundamentally the same aims as those we have given for the extensive study . In this field of concentration, however, the student can achieve these same aims more fully, more intensively, with more detail.

Defense of the Disciplinary View

We have explained what we take to be the proper focus of a Christian liberal arts education. But we have not justified our view beyond raising certain objections to alternative views . It is to this justification that we must now turn. We must show the utility of this sort of education for the Christian community. Before we do so, however, it may be well to address ourselves directly to the objection, raised throughout the course of Christian history, that disinterested inquiry is not even a legitimate project for Christians.

Disinterested Learning as a Faith-Task of the Christian Community:
The New Testament, it is sometimes said, tells the Christian to turn the other cheek, to give water to the thirsty, to give clothes to the naked, and above all, to tell the world of the revelation which has come in Jesus Christ;

nowhere does it enjoin the Christian to study philosophy, pure mathematics, or literature. Indeed, the study of such topics, it is said, is not merely idle, but dangerous and insidious. The aim of any education ought to be to lead men into a closer personal relationship with Christ; and it is said to be more likely that a course in projective geometry or Platonic philosophy will lead a person away from this than toward it. True, to convert one's enemy one must know what he is thinking, and to minister to men one must have *some* knowledge; *some* higher learning can be justified on these grounds. But apart from this, we know all we should or need to know when we believe the Scriptures. In short, the claim is that disinterested theoretical inquiry is an illegitimate project for Christians. An especially vivid statement of this line of though can be found in Tertullian's *Prescription against Heretics.*

Many themes in the Scriptures can be developed so as to lead to the conclusion, not just that disinterested inquiry is legitimate for Christians, but that it is in fact one of the faith-tasks of the community. There is, for example~ the pervading theme that man' s vocation is to know and serve God, and that God is knowable in His creation as well as in His Word. But let us here select for development only a certain facet of the biblical doctrine of creation. In the first chapter of Genesis, after the creation of everything but man has been narrated, we find this passage: "And God said, let us make man in our image, after our likeness: and let them have dominion over the fish of the sea, and over the fowl of the air, and over the cattle, and over all the earth, and over every creeping thing that creeps upon the earth." In Psalm 8 the same line of thought is expressed when the Psalmist says of man, "Thou madest him to have dominion over the works of thy hand; thou hast put all tbings under his feet."In these passages man's unique place in creation is stressed. Man' s condition is that of a creature of God. In this he resembles all other contingent beings. But along with His resolve to create man, God also assigns man a special *task:* He is to have dominion over all other creatures, putting all of them at his own service. This task, assigned to him by God, man can either carry out or fail to carry out. What is equally important, be can carry it out in the right or the wrong way. For just as man is commanded to put all creation in subjection and make it obedient to him, so he is commanded to put himself at God's service, as is clear from the whole Bible, already from Genesis 2. This then is the second general command given to man at his creation, and the two are bound together. It might be thought that to subdue and to have dominionamountstoverylittlemorethanfarmingorfishing.Butmanhaswider capabilities than the performance of such practical tasks. He also has the capacity to create works of art and to erect systems of theoretical knowledge. These capabilities were present in man's creation. They are not the result of sin but are rather one of the good features of God's creation; it would be a mark of complaint against God to decry their use. Further, it is clear from the following chapters in Genesis, in which there are related certain incidents from the building of early cultures, that the writer of Genesis had more in mind than the performance of those practical tasks essential to continued existence. In short, what we have in Genesis is, what has sometimes been called in Protestant theology a *cultural mandate,* a command to man to build a culture and thus a command to produce art and science as well as to hunt and fish and farm.

After the ingression of sin into human life, though man does indeed still work at culture and thus fulfill the cultural mandate, he no longer does it in order to serve and praise God. His works of science and art are produced out of the wrong motives and often reveal those motives. It is man's redemption in Christ which again puts things straight. Now again there is the possibility of putting all things in subjection to God. The themes of creation and sin are in this way bound up with the theme of redemption, and the life of the redeemed, as we have already seen, is a life of serving God in our cultural tasks. Redemption is the restoration of God' s creation to its intended ends. The Christian man is now once again in a position to put all things in subjection to himself *in the right way.*

Thus those people who hold that the sole tasks permitted a Christian, beyond those necessary for continued existence, are the proclamation of the Gospel and the performance of acts of mercy, are mistaken. St. Paul often speaks of the peculiar interim status of the Christian's existence and the burning urgency of proclaiming the Gospel which follows from this status. But he does not hold that every individual Christian must spend his whole life preaching the Gospel. Rather, the Christian community, through certain of its members, must see that the Gospel is proclaimed. The task of the Christian community in this world is to build a Christian culture, different members of the community specializing in the performance of different aspects of this whole task. This cultural task will include the development of the various disciplines. Scholarship, like any other cultural activity, should be part of man's service of God. It is enjoined, not indeed on each and every individual Christian, but certainly on the Christian community as a whole.

The Benefits of Christian Liberal Arts Education: To turn now to the final issue; what benefit may the Christian community expect to receive from its support of Christian liberal arts education as we have explained it?

What benefits can we cite in urging young Christians to acquire such an education? These become especially pressing questions when one renounces, as we have renounced, the Greek and Catholic-Christian view that man's end is theoretical contemplation, and adopts the Reformers' view that man's end is the service of God in his daily work. The student, when he graduates, will have to occupy some specific positttion in the Christian community, some specific task. It is in his vocation as well as outside it that he is to exercise his allegiance to God. Yet we are not only proposing a non-vocational and non-professional education, one not slanted toward preparing a student to hold down some particular sort of job; we are also proposing that such an education consists mainly of disinterested theoretical inquiry. Can we claim that such a liberal arts education is of any importance for the Christian community? Of course, it is indispensable for the important and ongoing task of Christian scholarship. But is that all? Is it only a program for training scholars and conducting research?

This question is also acute because of the state of knowledge in the twentieth century. It can no longer be argued, as possibly it once could be, that in a liberal arts education a student becomes acquainted with all significant knowledge and is thus prepared to hold down any job whatsoever. It is becoming more and more apparent that the Renaissance and Enlightenment educational goal of developing the capacities of the student in such a way as to make him a well-rounded, fully-developed man is becoming impossible of attainment. So, can a liberal arts education as we have conceived it be justified for people other than future scholars?

The most obvious answer to these questions is that a great many occupations today are such that if one is to work in them successfully he must acquire a more or less thorough knowledge of the various disciplines. Traditionally this was true of those occupations known as the learned professions—law, medicine, diplomacy, the ministry. But nowadays a liberal arts education at the college level is regarded as an indispensable requirement for successful work in many more occupations, and we can expect of a Christian liberal arts education, as indeed of any other, that it will provide the necessary theoretical background for competent work in these occupations. Technical and professional training courses are more and more being offered to students *after* they have completed a liberal arts education rather than as an alternative to such an education.

ButthejustificationofaliberalartseducationintheChristian community does not rest solely on these immediate and practical considerations, important as they are; nor should the liberal arts education of a student be slanted primarily toward his future occupation and toward the practical use to which he expects to put his theoretical learning. A liberal arts education, as we conceive it, plays a role in the Christian community which is broader than that of giving the training necessary for holding down specific vocations and professions. As we see it, the fundamental justification for maintaining a program of Christian liberal arts education is that it enables the Christian community in American society better to perform its task of bringing all its cultural endeavors into captivity to Christ.

For one thing, we hold that a liberal arts education, better than anything else, will instill in students, and thus in the community, those habits of reasoning and attitudes of mind which constitute intellectual competence. It will develop the student's capacities to think logically and clearly, to attack a problem correctly, to assemble relevant facts, to organize thoughts, and to present them with clarity and force; it will develop the student's imagination, broaden his horizons, and enlarge his perspective; it will give him balance, and prevent the distortions and narrowness of concern which are so often induced by the extreme specialization of tasks in modern society; in general, it will teach him to use his intelligence to best effect no matter what matter he is dealing with.

Secondly, we hold that a Christian liberal arts education, better than anything else, can train the student to become a leader or a perceptive follower in the task of molding society according to Christian standards and promoting Christian culture. This it does by helping him to understand the society and the culture in which he will find himself, by training him to make informed Christian evaluations and to pass solid judgments on this society and culture, and by giving him some general understanding of what the Christian should aim at in his own social and cultural endeavors. We look especially for these benefits among the ultimate outcomes of requiring our students to study those disciplines dealing with the cultural products of mankind.

Further, the results of theoretical thought are now so deeply woven into every aspect of human life that it is imperative for as many people in the community as possible to understand these results. The Christian community, if it is to be an integral part of society, does not have the option of letting or not letting his thought and actions be influenced by the results of scientific learning. Its only choice is to see to it that the members of the community understand these results on as many different levels as possible, are able to discern whether or not they are inimical to Christianity, and are able to apply them intelligently. Unless it does this, the community will be victimized by its ignorance and by those whose religious faith it does not share. But most important of all, through a study of the various disciplines the student will be enabled to discern more clearly than otherwise possible the various spiritual kingdoms of men and their cultural manifestations, thus making it clear to him

> that all things human are religious, that human culture, while inevitable, is not in itself enough, in that it requires religious justification. And it is so that the Christian student will be taught and confirmed in his conviction that the religion of Christianity is the only adequate religion. . .It is so easy in the name of Christianity to turn one's back to art, to science, to politics, to social problems, to historical tensions and pressures, in one word, to culture, if you will. But once the conviction seizes on you that these all, precisely because they are cultural realities, exhibit a religious allegiance and an ultimate loyalty, that none of them is neutral but rather that all of them are faith-founded, all laid on an altar, all dedicated to a god, then you realize that they are at the very least important. Then you realize, too, that the true discernment of the God behind the culture, the assumption underlying the thought, the dogma beneath the action, the soul in the body of the thing, are precisely what it is the business of our schools as schools to disclose and to judge. In that lies the strengthening of the moral sinews of our young Christians. It is so that their choice for Christ and God can become a meaningful human choice.[1]

Finally, a liberal arts education can be recommended on the ground that it will form and deepen our appreciation of man's and God's artistic creations. The function of art in human life is, in part, to give joy and delight; we can expect of a liberal arts education that it will form and deepen the student's appreciation of works of art. But God too is a creator, indeed, the prime creator; and, as Calvin says, He has placed us among the splendors of his creation for our enjoyment. As a result of his studies we may expect the student, and through his influence the community, to gain a deepened appreciation of God's works.

In summary, it is by developing Christian intelligence, decision, discernment, and appreciation in its students that a Christian liberal arts education, in the form we are recommending, can be of service to the Christian community in the performance of its task of making Christ lord in all spheres of human life.

A few words should also be said in defense of our view that our students ought to acquire both a general and an intensive education.

One reason for insisting that our students should all acquire a *general* education is that a community of understanding can thereby be developed both among the educated members of the Christian community and among educated men generally. The Christian community cannot be a genuine community unless there is understanding among its members at various levels of insight. And though a society can exist without a common religious outlook, it too cannot exist without mutual understanding among its members at various levels of insight. And though a society can exist without a common religious outlook, it too cannot exist without mutual understanding at various levels of sophistication. If we allowed each student to concentrate on whatever narrow branch of knowledge struck his fancy, the bonds of understanding in community and society would obviously be threatened.

Further, the branches of knowledge cannot themselves be adequately understood in isolation. The philosopher's investigations have import for literary criticism; the theologian' s, for psychology; and the physicist' s, for biology. The field of knowledge is a web. Each compartment has strands relating it to others. To be ignorant of these is to run great danger of distortion, or of error.

There are also solid grounds for demanding that each student concentrate in some discipline or combination of disciplines. Given the present structure of graduate schools, if a student intends to study a certain discipline on the graduate level he will have to concentrate in that discipline already in college. Or if a student concentrates in a certain discipline and then enters an occupation in which he puts his knowledge of that discipline to direct use— if he concentrates in economics and then goes into business, for example— he benefits of concentration are again obvious.

But it certainly cannot be guaranteed that every student will find an occupation in which he can put to direct use the knowledge acquired in his field of concentration. Suppose, for example, that a person, when he graduates from the educational program we are projecting becomes a bank clerk. It might happen that this person's field of concentration in college was not economics but rather, say, English literature. In such a case, when the knowledge acquired in a student's concentration could not be put to direct use in his occupation, was there really any reason for having him concentrate? Or should we require everyone to concentrate simply on the ground that it is impossible to know in advance who will and who will not enter an occupation for which a particular concentration is a prerequisite?

We think there are other grounds than this . For one thing, it is important that the student get beyond the generalities which inevitably constitute the major part of extensive education in the disciplines, so that he can see in detail how a discipline is built up, how theory is intertwined with fact, and how generalization is supported with evidence. Not only will this increase the student's understanding of the nature of a discipline; it will also counter-act those habits of hasty generalization which a *purely* general education is likely to produce.

But further, even when the knowledge of a certain subject matter which the student builds up by concentration in a certain discipline is not of direct use in his future occupation, it still can be of importance to his future life. For a man' s service to the community is not exhausted by what he does in his occupation. There are other uses to which his special knowledge can be put. The Christian community is constantly being pressed for its judgment on new works of literature, on how to respond to the menace of Communism, on new developments in medicine, on how to vote, it is constantly under challenge to make its own positive contributions to the fields of literature, foreign affairs, medicine, and politics. If the community as a whole is to respond intelligently to the issues in these fields, and is to make its own contributions to them, it needs men who are educated in these areas. What we should expect of the bank clerk who graduated from college as an English major is that for the community as a whole he will be especially competent to make some intelligent Christian assessment of the literature which comes its way, and that he will be of special service in encouraging the development of Christian literature. Similarly, of the man who majored in economics we have a right to expect that he can make some especially competent assessment, say, of the American farm problem, and that he will be of special service in aiding the development of a Christianly informed solution to the problem. By this diversity of contribution the Christian community as a whole can gain wisdom in its judgments and decisions.

In short, we hold that a Christian liberal arts education as we have explained it—an extensive and intensive engagement in the disciplines, defined and enlightened by God' s Word—is the best way to prepare a wide range of young people for living the Christian life in contemporary society. The maintenance of such an educational program is indispensable if the Christian community is to perform its tasks in the present-day world. The Calvinistic tradition has always emphasized the importance of an educated laity for the spiritual health and vigor of God' s subjects. We are convinced that that emphasis is still justified.

Notes

' Henry Zylstra, "Christian Education," in *Testament of Vision* (Grand Rapids, 1958), pp. 147-148.

Louis Berkhof:
Editor Introduction

Louis Berkhof was first and foremost a systematic theologian, and published multiple volumes on what he called "Reformed Dogmatics". He was also capable of providing a condensed version, for use in high school and college classes, in *Manual of Reformed Doctrine* (1933). Professor of Theology of Calvin Seminary during much of the first half of the twentieth century, he also used his talents to advance the cause of Christian education. Both of the following were published (in *Fundamentals In Christian Education*, C. Jaarsma, ed., 1953) speeches given at conferences of Christian educators in the early thirties.

While heavy going for some readers, they give a glimpse into how at least one theologian thought Reformed theology and world view not only validated the need for Christian schools, but also shaped its early contours.

Later generations of teachers, both prospective and practicing, should benefit from capturing from the past this case for the usefulness of the doctrine of the covenant and the enthusiasm for being Reformed in education.

Being Reformed in Our Attitude Toward the Christian School

by Louis Berkhof from *Fundamentals in Christian Education* C. Jaarsma, editor, 1953

As the years roll by and conditions change, the conviction is growing on us that we need the Christian school and need it very much. The free Christian school has been a source of inestimable blessings for the Reformed people of the Netherlands and for the nation of which they are an important constituent. It has also been a boon for the Reformed circles in our land and may by the grace of God help us to contribute something worth while to the life of our nation. Experience taught us to appreciate this school. Outsiders have frequently congratulated us on its possession, described it as one of the mainstays of our churches, and exhorted us to guard, to continue, and to develop it. And however much many may decry it as inimical to the unity of our national life, it certainly points the way to the solution of a problem that is now weighing heavily on our public school system.

It is just because we regard the Christian school as a real blessing that we are so solicitous about it. We have been willing to finance it, even though we also had to pay our share for the maintenance of the public school. We resent the expression of opinions in our circles which might dampen the ardour for the Christian school and put it in jeopardy. We are anxious to see this school continue and to bless us with its fruits in the future as it has done in the past.

If our Christian school is to continue in the future, it is absolutely essential that we be thoroughly Reformed in our attitude to that school. This means that we must have a firm grasp of the fundamental principles that are basic to our school system. It means that we must be positively convinced of the necessity of these schools of our children. It means that we must not be half-hearted in praying and giving and working for the maintenance and the improvement of those schools. It means, too, that we must convince the coming generation of the absolute necessity of our Christian schools, and must persuade them to sacrifice and to labor for their continued existence.

Let us begin by asking ourselves the question, What should determine our attitude to the Christian school, if we are truly Reformed? Shall we say that the spirit of nationalism in education, which asserted itself in many lands in the previous century, and which calls for "tax-supported, publicly controlled and directed, and non-sectarian common schools," ought to be the determining factor? If we are of that opinion we shall reason somewhat as follows: The state is supremely interested in welding its citizenry into a unity, in developing a national spirit, a national character, a national sense of justice, etc. Its future welfare, inner strength, and prestige among the nations of the world depend on this. The development of such a truly national spirit can only be accomplished by the establishment and main-tenance of a national school system, a system of free schools, offering equal opportunity to the rich and the poor, and patronized by all the people. The establishment and maintenance of such schools requires taxation, and their efficiency will be commensurate with the measure in which the people are compelled to send their children to them. Only the state with its sovereign power can tax the people and can make education compulsory. Hence it follows that only the state can establish and maintain an effective free school system. Our public schools, which are schools for the state, are necessarily also schools by the state. They do not lose sight of the interests of the individual or of society in general, but they are primarily interested in the welfare of the organized community, i.e., of the state, in the training of American citizens. And as loyal citizens of the state we ought to appreciate those schools, improve the opportunity they offer for our children, and zealously oppose all partisan schools, because they make for division rather than unity.

Now it will hardly be said that this is a characteristically Reformed attitude. It clearly implies the adoption of a species of utilitarianism. It proceeds on the assumption that a general education of the people permeated with a strong spirit of nationalism, is of paramount value for the state because it contributes to its unity, greatness and strength, and to the happiness of the greatest number of its citizens. It takes for granted that this is true even when the education given is divorced from religion. And because this is so, it is held that every citizen should seek this education for his children. But right at this point a good many questions clamor for answer. Is it true that a strong spirit of nationalism pure and simple is the greatest boon of the state? Is there not a great deal even in the present demand for an international consciousness that is more in harmony with the supreme religious and ethical ideal of humanity? Will not a nationalism permeated with the spirit of true religion prove to be the greatest blessing for the state and contribute most to the happiness of the people? Shall we say that the preferences of the state ought to determine our attitude? Would we act on that principle if the state should decide to introduce a state religion ? We leave these questions for your consideration and pass on to another idea.

Shall we say with modern evolutionary pedagogy that the child is the standard and measure of all things in education, and that a study of the child ought to determine the requisite education and should also be the determining factor in our attitude towards any school that makes a bid for the education of the child ? If so, then the possibility is given that we shall reason somewhat along the following lines: The child reveals great similarity with the higher brutes and is clearly a product of evolution. The brute origin of the mental make up of the child ought to be carefully considered, for this will point the way in its further education. There are many imperfections in the life of the child, but these do not constitute sin. They are merely manifestations of the lower animal propensities which are struggling for the mastery. The child is fundamentally good, however, and under proper conditions and wise guidance will naturally develop in the right direction. It is of the utmost importance that palatial school buildings be erected, surrounded by spacious and attractive playgrounds, that the halls be adorned with masterpieces of art, and that the classrooms be cheery and well ventilated. In any attempt to teach and guide the child, its needs, its desires, its will, and its rights should be carefully considered. It should not be taught that it is utterly corrupt and cannot in any case attain the ideal, but ought to be made conscious of the natural urge within it to soar to the loftiest ethical heights, and of the inherent power to overcome evil and to rise to a state of moral perfection. It should never be constrained to learn things which are beyond its comprehension, such as religious mysteries and profound theological truths, but only what it can fully understand and assimilate. Above all, it should be left free to develop its own religion in harmony with the teachings of science, and should not be urged to accept the myths of the Bible, however beautiful they may be, nor to believe the Hebrew conception of creation and providence, of angels and devils, of sin and atonement, of heaven and hell.

Now if we adopt that position and reason along those lines, we shall hardly be enthusiastic supporters of our Christian schools. But again we remind ourselves of the fact that it is not Reformed to say that psychology, that the study of the child, must ultimately determine our attitude to the school in which the child is educated. Moreover, the study of the child does not necessarily lead to the view indicated in the preceding, however common this may be in the present day. And even if it did, it would only represent the result to which man with his darkened understanding, subject to the power of error and deception, came in reading God's general revelation, a revelation which, while it is sufficient to leave man without excuse, is yet obscured by sin and ceased to be a perfect reflection of the truth. It is only in the light of Scripture that man can give a true interpretation of God's revelation in nature, and it is therefore to the Bible that he must turn for guidance.

If we are truly Reformed, we shall say that the will of God should determine our attitude to the Christian school, and that this will is revealed to us in his general, but above all in his special revelation.

God has made known to us whom He regards as the responsible educators of the child. He has indicated this in his general revelation in nature in the ordinances which He has established. In the animal world He shows us how the old provide for their young; how they protect them and train them. We see the eagle fluttering over her young, exciting them to fly, hovering over them for protection, and carrying them when they are wearied; we see the hen gathering her brood under her wings. Jeremiah even holds up the jackal as an example for Israel, when he says: "Even the jackals draw out the breast, they give suck to their young ones: the daughter of my people is become cruel, like the ostriches in the wilderness" (Lam. 4:3). The gentile world hit upon the idea of parental obligation in the work of education. It is true that Plato wanted the state to take charge of this work, but his ideal state existed only on paper. Athens placed the responsibility for the work of education squarely on the family; all its schools were private schools. And of the five rights of the Roman citizens, that of the father over his children was the very first. He took great personal interest in the education of his sons. The home rather than the school was the center of the educational system. And even with respect to the school Pliny the younger expressed the opinion that the principle, the school belongs to the parents, was the only sound principle. It should not surprise us that even heathen people without the light of special revelation saw that the parents were the proper responsible educators of their children, for nature itself points the way. The children are born of the parents and therefore belong to them first of all. The parents have them under their care until they set up for themselves and are prompted by their parental love to provide for their physical, mental, moral and spiritual needs; to guide them, to protect them, and to promote their best interests. There is no one that is interested in their welfare as much as the parents are. Hence it is but natural that the parents should be the responsible educators and that, if the parents should feel constrained to call in the help of others, these others should feel that they stand in loco parentis.

God's special revelation teaches us the same truth with even greater clearness. Negatively, it may be said that the Bible in speaking of the duties of the state never mentions the work of educating the children of the nation (cf. Ex. 18:22-26; Deut. 1:16, 17; Matt. 22:17-21; Rom. 13:1-7; I Pet. 2:13-15). It is a striking fact that even the Old Testament, in which we find God dealing with the nation of Israel rather than with the individuals that belong to it and consequently speaking primarily in national terms, always refers to or addresses the parents as the responsible educators of the children. The book of Deuteronomy, the book of Proverbs, and the 78th Psalm are very instructive in this respect. In the New Testament it is clearly indicated that the government must guard the interests of all those that belong to its realm, must judge between a man and his neighbor, must preserve order by punishing evil-doers, and must levy taxes for the support of its work (Rom. 13:1-7). But when it speaks of the education of the children, it turns to the parents in the words: "Ye fathers, provoke not your children to wrath: but nurture them in the chastening and admonition of the Lord" (Eph. 6:4).

The Word of God also indicates very explicitly that the education which the parents are in duty bound to provide for their children must be fundamentally religious. In fact, its emphasis is so exclusively on religious training that it almost seems as if it regarded this as the whole of education. This finds its explanation in the fact that it deals primarily with the religious and moral needs of man, that it regards religion as the most fundamental, the most basic thing in the life of man, and that it would not consider any education as sound and satisfactory that was not permeated with the spirit of religion. Let us notice a few passages that bear on this point. In Gen. 18:19 we find God saying with respect to Abraham: 'For I have known him, to the end that he may command his children and his household after him, that they may keep the way of Jehovah to the end that Jehovah may bring upon Abraham that which He has spoken of him." In these words we are informed respecting the reason why God decided to give Abraham an insight into his counsel touching the coming destruction of the cities of the plain. Abraham was chosen by God to be the father of a mighty nation and a blessing for all the nations of the world. But in order that the promises to Abraham might be fulfilled and the Lord might really bring upon him the promised blessings, Abraham would have to teach his descendants "to keep the way of Jehovah, to do righteousness and justice." And in order that he might be a truly effective teacher of the great lesson that the blessings of Jehovah are enjoyed only in the way of obedience, and that the way of disobedience spells death, it had to be revealed to him that the cities of the plain were about to be destroyed for want of justice and righteousness. The book of Deuteronomy is shot through with exhortations to the Israelites to be diligent in reminding their children of the wonderful way in which God had led the nation in the past in order that these children might serve Jehovah with willing hearts. And we hear what may be regarded as the jubilant answer of the pious Israelite to all these exhortations in the words of the poet:

I will open my mouth in a parable:
I will utter dark sayings of old,
Which we have heard and known,
And our fathers have told us.
We will not hide them from their children,
Telling to the generation to come the praises of Jehovah,
And His strength, and His wondrous works that He hath done.
For He established a testimony in Jacob
And appointed a law in Israel,
Which He commanded our fathers,
That they should make them known to their children
That the generation to come might know them, even the children that
should be born;
Who should arise and tell them to their children,
That they might set their hope in God,
And not forget the works of God,
But keep his commandments (Ps. 78:2-7).

It is that type of education that is pregnant with the promise of real blessings. If Abraham diligently teaches his children the way of the Lord, then the Lord will bring upon Abraham and his descendants the things which He has promised them. Listen to the words of divine wisdom: "Train up a child in the way he should go"—mark well, not "in the way he would go," but "in the way he should go," and this, according to teachings of Scripture, is the way of the covenant —"and even when he is old he will not depart from it" (Prov. 22)

It is no wonder, therefore, that the New speaks in the same vein as the

Old, exhorting the parents to educate their children religiously: "Ye fathers, provoke not your children to wrath; but nurture them in the chastening and admonition of the Lord" (Eph. 6:4).

This emphasis on religious education is exactly what we would expect in view of what the Bible reveals respecting the essential nature of the child. It is often said that man is incurably religious. Moreover, missionaries and students of comparative religion inform us that never a tribe was found without religion. The import of this is that the idea of God cannot be eradicated from the human soul. And this is impossible because man is God's offspring, the image-bearer of the Most High, everywhere and always. To separate the image of God from man is to rob him of his humanity. The image of God is the most fundamental thing in man, and consequently also in the child. And that which is most essential in the child cannot be ignored in its education without doing an injustice to both the child and its Creator and without turning its education into perversion. It is true that man by sin lost those moral and spiritual qualities that constitute the image of God in the more restricted sense, but this does not mean that he has ceased to be the image-bearer of God. He is still a rational and moral being, able to distinguish between good and evil; he still shows a certain appreciation of what is true and good and beautiful; and he still has a certain sense of the divine and an urge within him to engage in religious exercises. Moreover, we must bear in mind that the Spirit of God is operative in covenant children—I do not say, in every covenant child—and is restoring the image of God that was lost by sin. Therefore, Christian parents have an added reason to look upon their children as image-bearers of God.

Now sound psychology and pedagogy teaches us that we must take that which is most fundamental in the life of the child into consideration in the whole of its education. There is a strong tendency in present day psychology to emphasize the fact that the soul of man is a unit, acts as a unit, and consequently also reacts as a unit to all external influences, though it may manifest its action in a variety of ways. The old doctrine of the separate powers of the soul is not popular today. We are constantly reminded of the fact that it is the whole man that perceives and thinks, that desires and wills. Consequently, his education should also be regarded as a unitary process. It is utter folly to think that you can inform the intellect without giving direction to the will, that you store the head with knowledge without affecting the emotions, the inclinations, the desires, and the aspirations of the heart. The training of the head and of the heart go together, and in both the fundamental fact that the child is the image-hearer of God must be a determining factor. Again, in view of the fact that education is and should be a unitary process, we understand the absolute absurdity of saying that the school is concerned only with the head and should limit itself to secular education, while the home and the church make provision for the heart by adding religious education. We should never forget that the education which the child receives in the school, though divorced from religion, is nevertheless an education of the entire child and is bound to make a deep impression on the heart.

These considerations naturally lead us on to another point that deserves emphasis. The soul is a unit and education is a unitary process, aiming at the development of man's essential nature into a harmonious life, full and rich and beautiful. But this end can never be attained, if the home and the church on the one hand, and the school on the other hand do not have the same conception of the essential nature of the child, and do not agree in the fundamentals of their teachings. How can an education that proceeds in part on the assumption that the child is the image-bearer of God and in part on the supposition that it bears the image of the brute, an education that is partly religious and partly irreligious, i.e., anti-religious, ever result in a life that is truly unified? It can only lead to one thing, and that is a divided life so strongly condemned by our Saviour (Matt. 6:21, 22), a life with scattered energies and dissipated powers, swayed and torn by conflicting opinions, wanting in singleness of purpose, in stability and strength, and in that true joy that fills the soul which is consciously moving in the right direction. We are in perfect agreement with the Modernists on this point, the only difference being that, while we maintain that in the training of Christian children the education of the schools should fundamentally conform to the religious education of the home and of the church, they strenuously assert that the religious education of the home and of the church must be in conformity with the scientific teachings of the schools. To the oft-repeated complaint that many young people suffer shipwreck religiously in our colleges and universities and even seminaries, they simply answer that the Christian home and the Christian church are to blame, because they have not prepared their children and young people for the advanced views in religion that are now taught in the schools.

The Reformed man, who believes that the child is the image-bearer of God, naturally proceeds on the assumption that that most fundamental truth may not be ignored in any part of its education, and especially not in its school education. This fact may well be stressed in our day. In view of the fact that the influence of the Christian home is waning, and that the church can devote only a couple of hours a week to the religious training of its youth, the school is easily the most important educational agency of the present. Is it not the height of folly even from a purely educational point of view to let the most important agency in education ignore that which is most essential and most fundamental in the life of the child? And can Christian parents reasonably expect their children to be imbued with a spirit of true religion if they persist in sending them to a school where for twenty-four hours a week they are taught in a spirit that is fundamentally irreligious, if not positively anti-Christian? The answer can only be a decided negative. And experience will bear out the correctness of this answer. America is today reaping in its churches what it has sown in its schools. It has sown through the secularized schools, and it is reaping a purely naturalistic religion.

In view of all that has been said, it ought not to be so difficult to determine what is a truly Reformed attitude to our Christian schools. We may begin by saying that a person who is really Reformed, i. e., who makes the will of God the law of his life, and who is guided in all the relations which he assumes and in all the activities in which he participates by Reformed principles, cannot possibly assume an attitude of hostility to the Christian school without compromising his religious connections. It is true that we sometimes witness the strange phenomenon that persons who profess to be truly Reformed reveal a decided opposition to the Christian school. And if we inquire into the reasons for this hostility, these persons frequently resent the query and leave it for us to surmise the truth. Sometimes, however, they will answer, and then point to one of the three following reasons or to all three combined. They tell us that public opinion is down on the Christian school, and that it is foolhardy to go contrary to the prevailing ideas of the day. Public opinion is after all, as President Wilson said, "the mistress of the world." Chances are that they who speak after that fashion are more concerned about their popularity than about their religion. Very often they create the impression that the great expense entailed in the maintenance of separate schools constitutes their great objection to the Christian school, though they are generally loath to give expression to this sentiment. Their love of money plays a great part in their opposition. They seem to rate the material things higher than the spiritual. Again, we find them pleading their Americanism as a ground for their hostility to private schools. The public school is the school of the nation and every loyal American should send his children there for their education. By taking this stand they stigmatize as disloyal citizens the thousands and millions of Roman Catholics and Lutherans who maintain their own parochial schools, and also that large number of wealthy Americans who prefer and establish private schools for their children; and that in spite of the fact that the nation and the states do not require that all children shall attend the public school and have never officially taken the stand that the establishment and maintenance of parochial and private schools conflicts with true Americanism. Those who advance this argument would evidently revise the statement of Jesus respecting the necessity of seeking first the kingdom of God, and make it read: "Seek ye first America, and all other things will be added unto it." And if there were alongside of the many free churches in our land also an established church, they would undoubtedly feel conscience-bound to join the latter, irrespective of its fundamental tenets. Now, surely, such considerations as these do not warrant Christian people in opposing schools that make it their business to educate children in the fear of the Lord. It is hard to see how any child of God can make himself believe that in waging war against schools for Christian instruction he is fighting the battle of the Lord.

But let us consider a slightly different attitude. Many Christian people who send their own children to the public school grant us at once that they would not be justified in taking a hostile attitude to the Christian school. They want to be tolerant. While they prefer the state supported schools for their own children, they have no objection to those who insist on having their children educated in private schools. Sometimes they are even willing to contribute to the cause of the Christian school. They seem to regard it somewhat as a matter of indifference, whether they send their children to the Christian or to the public school. This is not altogether the case, however. Their attitude reflects the idea that one ought to send his children to the public school but may send them to the Christian school. Now this is certainly not a Reformed position. The standard of duty on which this proceeds is certainly not that of the Word of God, but simply some utilitarian consideration, centering on the individual, or on society, or on the state. Before we assume any such attitude as that, we ought to prove that the Bible, which is our ultimate standard of life and practice, explicitly or by implication favors state education for our children, whereas it also permits, but merely permits, the parents to assume the direct responsibility for the education of their children by establishing and maintaining their own private schools. We should be in a position to maintain that the Bible deems it best that the religious element be excluded from the greater part of the education of our children, though it also allows, but merely allows, that their school education should also be permeated with religion. Now I do not think that any Reformed Christian would be very keen on trying to prove either one of those propositions. No one who regards the Bible as the ultimate standards of faith and duty can proceed on the assumption that the Christian school is a matter of indifference. Much less can he entertain the notion that the secularized school, the school that is divorced from religion, deserves the preference.

But granted that all this is true, is it not possible to assume a compromising attitude? There are Reformed Christians who evidently proceed on the assumption that the education which their children receive in the schools may not be divorced from religion and need not necessarily be irreligious in the public school. They maintain that it is possible and permissible to include the religious element in the instruction that is given in the tax supported schools of the state. Consequently, they do not regard the Christian school as an absolute necessity, except in localities in which the last vestige of religion is excluded from the public school. We readily see that in taking that position they assume the right to yield their parental prerogative in the education of their children, to pass their responsibilities on to the state, and to leave it to the state to determine how much and what kind of religious training their children shall receive. This is certainly not in harmony with the Reformed principle that the parents are the responsible educators of their children, and consequently have the right to determine and the duty to control the religious spirit in which their children are educated.

Some are inclined, however, to waive the principle that the school belongs to the parents provided the parents can rest assured that their children will be educated religiously. Did not the government of the Netherlands in the post-Reformation period establish and maintain the schools where the children of the nation were educated? Did not the great Synod of Dort recognize and honor the government as having authority in educational matters ? And then too, have we not been told repeatedly that there would have been no school struggle in the Netherlands if it had not been for the secularization of the national school ? All these questions may be answered in the affirmative. But the facts implied certainly do not prove that the principle that the parents are the responsible educators of the children and should therefore be able to control the spirit of the education that is given in the schools, is not thoroughly Scriptural and Reformed. A great deal might be said in explanation of the fact that this principle did not always control the educational praxis of our Reformed forebears.

But suppose that we leave it out of consideration for the present and face the question whether the public school can give the children the religious training on which Reformed parents must insist. A priori, it would seem to be entirely out of the question that a state which has no established religion but which hrieantees equality and religious freedom to all its citizens, a state which claims absolute neutrality in religious matters, should teach any particular religion in its educational institutions. It would even seem that such a state could consistently do only one thing, i. e., exclude all religious instruction from its schools. This is exactly the condition that obtains in France, where, according to Payne (Contributions to the Science of Education, p. 207), "The French Revolution made appear for the first time, in all its definiteness, the conception of the lay state, of the state neutral among all creeds, independent of all ecclesiastical authorities, and free from all theological bias." Our government has been moving in the same general direction though it has not yet shaken off all vestiges of religion. Its Puritan traditions still make themselves felt, and in virtue of these some insist on calling the United States Christian. It is perfectly evident, however that the term so applied is shorn of its real significance. Batten correctly remarks that "a state does not become Christian when it incorporates the name of Christ in its constitution or opens the sessions of Congress with prayer; neither is a state Christian when certain theological ideas are embodied in its legislation and certain ecclesiastical functionaries dictate the policy of cabinets. In any real sense a state is Christian when it possesses the spirit of Christ and seeks certain great Christian ends in and through its life and service." (The Christian State, p. 408). Because of this difference between the United States and France, the public school of our nation is not yet everywhere neutral in the sense and to the degree that the French public school is neutral. In some localities the public school has retained something of a religious chraracter. At the same time authorities, when speaking of it in general terms, do not hesitate to speak of it as the secularized school.

But just how much religious teaching will be tolerated in the public school? Draper says in his work on American Education that religion is not barred from the schools, but sectarianism is, and this is a distinction that is met with repeatedly. The line is generally drawn at sectarianism or denominationalism. But, of course, even this is a rather uncertain line, since even the Bible has repeatedly been declared to be a sectarian book in official decisions and opinions. Payne expresses the opinion that "the genius of our institutions seems to require that our public school should be purely a lay institution, i. e., an institution divorced from religion." He quotes the authoritative work of Judge Cooley on Constitutional Limitations to the effect that "compulsory support, by taxation or otherwise, of religious instruction" is one of "those things which are not lawful under any of the American constitutions"; and that "not only is no one denomination to be favored at the expense of the rest, but all support of religious instruction must be entirely voluntary." From this Professor Payne concludes that "the American public school should not only be unsectarian, but should be absolutely neutral as to religious bias." (Contributions to the Science of Education, p. 213 f.). Our own Michigan School Law says: "Sectarian instruction is abolished from all public schools; and, while the reading of the Bible may properly become a part of the daily program of the public school, the comment thereon by the teacher should be of such a character that pupils and parents of all religious faiths may not detect the slightest traces of sectarian prejudice."

In view of what has been said we may be sure that in the public school the teaching of the doctrine of election, of the total depravity of man, of his absolute dependence on the grace of God for salvation, of the limited nature of the atonement in Christ, etc., doctrines which are specifically Reformed, is altogether out of the question. More than that, it is impossible to teach the doctrines of the Trinity, the deity of Christ, redemption by his atoning blood, the necessity of conversion, etc. Still further, it would not even be permissible to teach that Jesus is the Christ, the Messiah promised by the prophets, and that Christianity is the only true religion. In other words, the very heart must be taken out of religious instruction before it can be permitted in the public school. And surely it ought to be out of the question for any Reformed Christian to compromise on such a basis.

But perhaps some will say that they have been able to make the public school in their locality thoroughly Christian and even Reformed. I am not able to control this contention. There may have been, and there may be today cases in which this is actually done, though I doubt it very much. In connection with this point I will only make the following remarks: (1) The laws of the land, even where they permit or even require Bible reading in the public school, forbid that sectarian or denominational teaching should be given there. (2) The decisions handed down by the courts of several states and the opinions expressed by attorneys-general are all in harmony with the fundamental position that sectarian instruction must be absolutely excluded. I have yet to see the first verdict or opinion to the contrary. (3) According to Judge Cooley, certainly no mean authority, it is unlawful under any of the American constitutions to use the money that is raised by taxation for sectarian instruction. (4) In cases in which the school-board of some country district succeeds in evading the law by introducing sectarian instruction, the complaint of a single individual will prove sufficient to put an end to its doubtful practice. And it would undoubtedly be rather embarrassing for a Christian school board to be called to time by one who is perhaps an unbeliever. (5) We may be sure that the opportunity for such an evasion of the law will also decrease in the measure in which the district school is replaced by the town school. And the tendency at present is rather strongly in that direction. In view of all this it appears that the practice of introducing sectarian instruction into the public school is very questionable, both from a legal and from a moral point of view. They who engage in it are using money, raised by taxation, for sectarian purposes, and this is contrary to the law. They introduce denominational teachings into the public school in spite of the fact that this is explicitly forbidden. They surreptitiously employ a state institution for the dissemination of specific religious doctrines. Surely, the foundation on which they are building is a questionable and a precarious one. It is a foundation that may crumble at any moment, a foundation that is "sinking sand." And one who is truly Reformed cannot consistently build on such a foundation in the important task of the religious education of his children.

Shall we then say that the home, the catechism class and the Sunday school can take care of the religious training of the child, and that the school need not be burdened with this in any way? This position has been taken by many in the past, but the fallacy of it is becoming ever increasingly apparent. Educational reformers are proclaiming from the house tops that our educational system has not provided sufficiently for the religious training of our youth. Psychologists are reminding us of the fact that education is a unitary process. And if this is so, it is sheer folly that the most important educational agency of the present should neglect the most fundamental element in education; and also that the education of the school should be diametrically opposed in spirit to that of the Christian home, because this is bound to result in a divided life. Moreover, the many plans that are devised for the injection of a larger amount of religious education into the training of youth such as the North Dakota plan, the Colorado plan, the Gary plan, etc., all testify to the insufficiency of the religious education of the last half century. And, unfortunately, they themselves are only half-way measures, which do not help us to escape from the dualism that now exists between the education of the public school and that of the Christian home.

If we allow ourselves to he controlled by the will of our God and by thoroughly Reformed principles in providing for the education of our children, we shall seek wherever this is at all possible, to establish and maintain schools which will consider it a sacred duty to educate our children in the spirit in which we solemnly promised to have them educated. And if we find such schools already in existence, we will thank our God for them, we will love them, we will send our children to them. We will pray for them, work for them, and be ready to sacrifice for them. If in that spirit we and our children continue to labor for the cause of Christian instruction, we shall have the satisfaction of an approving conscience; shall confer an inestimable boon upon our children, keeping them from the curse of the divided life and instilling into their hearts and minds ideas and ideals that are truly Christian; shall make an important contribution to the spiritual welfare of our community and nation by depositing a seed that may yield thirty-, sixty-, and even a hundred-fold; and shall above all reap the blessings of our covenant God, who has promised that "our sons shall be as plants grown up in their youth, and our daughters as cornerstones hewn after the fashion of a palace."

The Covenant of Grace and Its Significance for Christian Education

by Louis Berkhof from *Fundamentals in Christian Education,* C. Jaarsma, editor, 1953.

Advocates of Christian education have always maintained that the Christian school is an outgrowth of the covenant idea, and is absolutely necessary in order to enable the child to appreciate its covenant privileges and to understand the solemn significance of its baptism in the name of the triune God. They are convinced that the Christian school, as well as infant baptism, finds its main support in the doctrine of the covenant, and are therefore unalterably opposed to the tendency of some to slight this doctrine and to relegate it to the background.

In the American ecclesiastical world the doctrine of the covenant is almost entirely unknown. You can take up one work on systematic theology after another without finding a single chapter devoted to it. Such works as those of the Hodges, Thornwell, and Dabney form exceptions to the rule. Moreover, it is quite evident that in most of the churches of our land, even in those who theoretically subscribe to the doctrine of the covenant, this doctrine has no grasp on the life and the conscience of the people in general, and fails utterly to have a determining influence on the education of their children.

In the present controversy between the Modernists and the Fundamentalists the hearts of all serious-minded Christians naturally go out to the latter, because they take their stand on the infallible Word of God; but unfortunately they are nearly all Premillennialists, who drive a wedge in between the Old and the New Testament, claim that the covenant made with Abraham and sealed by circumcision includes only the natural descendants of the patriarch, and therefore deny that we and our children have any part in it and that this is sealed to us by baptism. Experience has already taught us that they who come under the spell of Premillennialism finally lose their covenant conception and turn to the position of the Baptists.

Occasionally some well-meaning persons in our circles express the fear that we speak too much about the covenant and are in danger of making people averse to it. Now there may have been a time when this fear was warranted, but in our opinion it is quite unnecessary at present. There is more point to the oft repeated complaint that in our day the doctrine of the covenant is not stressed as it ought to be. And even if the fear expressed were perfectly justified, that would he no reason why we should refrain from discussing this subject. It is a striking fact that, while the advocates of Christian education always insisted on the close relation between the covenant idea and the Christian school, I have not been able to lay my hand on a single book or pamphlet, either in the Holland or in the English language, devoted to a discussion of the subject in question.

The fact is that in our struggle for Christian schools the doctrine of the covenant was always the great presupposition. The relation in which the covenant idea stands to the Christian school may have been discussed time and again in sermons and lectures that did not appear in print. On the printed page we find an occasional reference to the fact that the children of Christian parents should be religiously educated in view of the fact that they are covenant children, and that, when they were brought to baptism, their parents promised to provide such an education for them. But nowhere do we find this idea worked out. Hence it can hardly be regarded as superfluous that a paper be devoted to the relation of the covenant idea and the Christian education which we desire for our children. Even so the presentation of it can hardly be commensurate with its great importance.

For a proper understanding of the covenant of grace it is quite essential that we have some conception of the covenant idea in general. It can hardly escape the attention of Bible students that, while the essential elements of the covenant of grace are already present in the Protevangelium, its formal establishment is introduced comparatively late in the history of revelation. It was nearly twenty centuries after the creation of the world that God formally entered into covenant relationship with Abraham and his seed. And there was a perfectly good reason for this delay in the general method of divine relation, in which the natural precedes the spiritual and spiritual realities are presented in forms derived from the natural world. Under the providence of God the various forms of life, of the interactions of the social groups, and of the associations among men, were first brought to development in the natural life of men, and were then used by God as the vehicles of his special revelation.

Thus people had to grow accustomed to the idea of covenant agreements first, before God could utilize such an idea in the revelation of the eternal verities of the covenant of grace. And then He employed it, first of all, in the revelation of the so-called covenant of nature with Noah, and only after that in revealing the covenant of grace with believers and their seed.

The necessity of entering into covenant agreements was felt first of all by individuals and tribes that were brought into close relation with each other and had no authority above them to secure their mutual rights and privileges. They sought the coveted security by entering into a voluntary agreement in which the mutual obligations and rights of both parties were clearly set forth and fully secured. A covenant so made, and often ratified by drinking sacrificial blood, eating a sacrificial meal, or eating salt together, was held to be most sacred and binding. It was not, as a rule, an expression of that self-seeking spirit that is so characteristic of modern international covenants or agreements, but generally resulted from a genuine desire for closer union, more intimate relationship, lasting friendship and mutual devotion.

But though the covenant idea first found expression in the natural life of man, and was only after that embodied in the divine revelation, it should not be thought that the human covenants were the original and real covenants, and that the covenant of God with believers and their seed is only a copy of these, or that this idea is merely a figure used to express the close relation between God and his people. If we turn this right around, we are nearer to the truth. God's covenant is the divine original, and all covenants among men are but faint reflections of it; it is not a mere figure of speech but a blessed reality rich in promises and full of heavenly comfort.

If we reflect for a moment on the covenants that were so frequently established among men, especially in the early patriarchal times, we cannot but notice that they are marked by certain definite characteristics. There are always two parties in such a covenant (in fact, a covenant of one party would be a contradiction in terms), and these parties are of such a kind that they can meet on a footing of equality. There are also two parts in every covenant; each party solemnly pledges himself to the performance of certain duties and in turn is assured of the fulfillment of certain promises. And the guarantee that the covenant requirements will be met and that the covenant promises will be fulfilled does not lie in any superior power that can and will force the parties to meet their mutual obligations, if need be, but only in the sacred character of the agreement and in the honor and faithfulness of the covenanting parties.

Now let us take a closer view of the covenant of grace. We do not intend—and in fact, it would be quite impossible—to discuss this in all its details, but will only stress the points that need elucidation in an intelligent discussion of this subject. We generally speak of the covenant of grace as being that gracious compact or agreement between the offended God and the offending sinner, in which God promises salvation through faith in Christ and the sinner accepts this believingly. It may be well to use an illustration that will serve to bring out just what the covenant of grace involves, before we stress some of the more important particulars of the covenant relation. We should bear in mind, however, that the illustration conveys to us only an imperfect approximation of the truth.

Let us imagine a rich and beneficent slave-holder with a thousand slaves, who are in duty bound to labor faithfully for their master, without any claim to reward, it is true, but with the assurance that, after a period of faithful labor, they will obtain their freedom. After a period of scrupulous attention to duty the slaves gradually grow restive under the yoke, begin plotting against their master, vent their dissatisfaction in murmurings and grumbling and muttered curses, which like the distant thunder announce the coming storm, and finally break into an open revolt in which they seek to shake off their fetters and to overthrow once for all the regime of their landlord. But the latter is well disposed toward his mutinous bond-servants and is anxious to raise them to a higher level. So he himself opens the way to a full and free pardon, though it involves a great deal of self-sacrifice, and resorts to all possible means to insure their future obedience. He even condescends to come down to their level and to deal with them as on a footing of equality. He makes a compact with them, in which he promises to pardon their insurrection, to adopt them and their children into his own family with the full rights and privileges of children, and to make them and their descendants heirs of his extensive possessions; and they, in turn, accept his pardon on the stipulated conditions, vow obedience to him as their lord, and pledge themselves to his service. Naturally they, as bond-servants, were in duty bound to accept whatever arrangement their master might make, and after the compact was closed they are doubly obliged to honor its provisions. Moreover, it was in their interest that they should live up to the terms of the agreement, Since it opened up the brightest prospects for them and their children, and brought to them what they could in no way hope to merit by their labors—a congenial home, the precious gift of liberty, untold riches, the pleasure of life, and a choice society in which to move.

Now if we reflect on this covenant arrangement which may, at least in a measure, serve to illustrate the agreement between God and the sinner in the covenant of grace, we shall notice that, while it certainly has all the essential characteristics of a covenant, it is yet marked by certain peculiarities. There are in this, as in every other covenant, two parties; but the parties are not of such a nature that they can meet on a footing of equality. This is something unusual. We do not ordinarily find a slave-holder making a covenant with his slaves. In his estimation they have no rights that would entitle them to such consideration. He simply issues his commands, and expects them to obey.

Thus our attention is directed at once to a very important feature of the covenant of grace. The distance between God and man is infinitely greater than that between a landlord and his slave, for the latter does not transcend the measure of the purely human. However different their social standing may be, the master and the bond-servants are all men and in so far equals, and even the latter have certain rights which the former may not disregard. But God is far greater than man; He gives no account of his doings; He is not under obligation to any of his creatures. To the sorely afflicted Job, crushed and perplexed, who had shown an inclination to question the doings of the Almighty, He says: "Who then is he that can stand before me ? Who hath first given unto me, that I should repay him? Whatsoever is under the whole heaven is mine" (Job 41:10, 11). Man has absolutely no rights in relation to God. God has but to command, and man is in duty bound to obey. And not only that, but sinful man has actually forfeited his life, and forfeited whatever rights he might have had in virtue of an original divine grant.

In the covenant of grace, therefore, we find two very unequal parties: the infinite God, the Creator of the universe, "glorious in holiness; fearful in praises, doing wonders," and finite man, a transient creature of the dust, sinful and polluted. The one is the rich possessor of all things, man included, and the other merely a steward of treasures entrusted to his care; the one has rightful claims on the life, the possessions, the time, and the service of his creatures, and is under no obligation to them, and the other is in duty bound to render all to God and yet obtains no claim to any reward; the one can offer riches and honor and joys beyond compare, and the other can offer nothing, not even the bankrupt life which he sometimes calls his own.

In view of this fact it is no wonder that some theologians do not regard what we usually call "the covenant of grace" as a covenant at all, but prefer to speak of it simply as a divine arrangement, a gracious disposition, or a testament, thus stressing the one-sided character of the transaction. And undoubtedly, in its origin and in its effective operation, the covenant is one-sided. At the same time it is clearly represented as a covenant in Scripture, and being essentially a covenant, it is necessarily of the nature of an agreement between two parties. God condescended to come down to the level of man in the covenant of works, and promised to reward a temporary obedience with life eternal. Again, He condescended to come down to the level of *sinful* man in Christ, and now in the covenant of grace offers eternal life to all that accept Christ by faith. The gracious element that was present even in the first covenant is far more pronounced in the second. What condescending love in God to enter into covenant relationship with sinners in Christ ! Well may we be grateful for the dignity thus bestowed upon us, sinful creatures.

In the illustration used I pointed out that it involved a great deal of self-sacrifice on the part of the landlord to enter into covenant relation with his bond-servants. The same thing applies where God enters into a covenant of grace with sinners. He could not simply come down to the level of wilful transgressors and make a covenant with them without maintaining his justice and safeguarding his holiness. He could deal with sinners only in the person of someone who undertook it voluntarily to be their surety and who guaranteed that the demands of justice would be met both objectively and subjectively, i.e., that the inflexible justice of God would be satisfied by a sacrificial death, that the original demand of the law would be met by a life of obedience, and that they who would share in the blessings of forgiveness would also consecrate their lives to God. Now there is nothing peculiar in the fact that there should be a surety in the covenant of grace. This is a rather common occurrence in covenants. The moral or financial standing of one of the parties to a transaction may be of a rather dubious character thus making a surety or guarantor quite essential. In our day great companies exist for the purpose of supplying the necessary bonds. But in the covenant of grace the striking thing is this, that the party known to be absolutely reliable itself supplies a surety for the bankrupt party with which it is dealing. God gives His only-begotten Son, and the Son voluntarily takes it upon Himself to become a Surety for lost and helpless sinners. Here too the gracious nature of the covenant shines forth.

And the promises, all the promises, as many promises as there are and that are yea and amen in Christ Jesus,are for us *and for our children.* That is the glad assurance we have in the covenant of grace. Hence Christian parents who take their baptismal vows seriously may always plead these promises for their offspring.

But now it is time to remind ourselves once more of the fact that there are two elements in the covenant, promises and requirements. This is all the more necessary because there are some really pious people who are inclined to deny that there are any requirements in the covenant of grace. They regard this denial necessary in order to avoid the errors of Pelagianism and of Arminianism. They are anxious to maintain the position that the work of salvation is a work of the grace of God from the beginning to the end, and that man contributes absolutely nothing to it. Hence they are averse to the idea that the covenant of grace is in any sense conditional. Let us consider this question for a moment. Is the covenant of grace conditional or is it not? This question cannot be answered by a simple negative or affirmative, but must be answered with careful discrimination.

If we consider the foundation of the covenant, we find it to be just as conditional as the covenant of works. Just as the covenant of works was conditioned on the obedience of Adam, so the covenant of grace is conditioned on the suffering and obedience, in short, on the merits of Jesus Christ. It is only on the basis of his atoning work that we can share in the blessings of the covenant of grace. But since all are agreed here, it is quite evident that this is not the exact point at issue. The real question is whether there is any condition with which man must comply, in order to enter the covenant and to obtain the covenant blessings and the covenant end for himself and for his children.

Now it is implied in the very idea of a covenant that there should be conditions; if there were none, there would be no covenant. Moreover, the Bible clearly teaches us that there are certain conditions. But the word conditions is not always used in the same sense, and it is possible to use it in a sense which does not apply in the covenant of grace. There is no condition attached to the covenant of grace which includes the idea of merit on the part of man. Because Christ has merited all the blessings of the covenant, the idea that man should merit anything is absolutely excluded. Moreover, there is no condition which man must fulfill in his own strength. He is constantly reminded of the fact that he needs strength from above in order that he may answer to the requirements of the covenant. Bearing these things in mind, however, we undoubtedly can speak of certain prerequisites for entering the covenant, for sharing the life of the covenant, and for obtaining the full covenant blessings.

Men enter the covenant relationship either by birth from Christian parents, or, if they are not born within the pale of the Church, by a profession of faith in Christ. They become conscious partakers of the covenant life only by a saving faith in Jesus Christ that is wrought in their hearts by the Holy Spirit, a faith by which they merit nothing but simply appropriate Christ as the fountain of all spiritual blessings. And they obtain the full possession and enjoyment of the covenant blessings and of the glorious covenant inheritance only by faith and sanctification, by separation from the world in consecration to God, and by a life of childlike and loving obedience. In the case of Christian parents this naturally involves the duty that they be diligent in training their children in the fear and admonition of the Lord, in order that these children, when they come to maturity, may willingly take upon themselves their covenant obligations and may, with their parents, enjoy the rich covenant blessings.

In this connection it is highly necessary to bear in mind that living in the covenant relationship is something more than living under the Gospel, under the free offer of salvation. There is here something more than an offer, something more than a promise; there is an agreement. The covenant is an *established covenant*, a *covenant agreed to,* agreed to by parents *also for their children.* When they sought the seal of baptism for their offspring, they promised, as Joshua did in the days of old: "as for me *and my house, we will serve Jehovah.*" This means that, for the children of the covenant, the covenant is not merely an offer which they can accept or reject, but an agreement which they entered; and that, if they do not live up to the terms of the agreement, they are covenant-breakers. Even as creatures of God they were already in duty bound to accept whatever arrangement He made for them. But in virtue of the agreement entered by their parents also in their behalf, they have an added responsibility. They are now doubly obliged to honor the covenant, to live into it, and to meet its requirements with a grateful heart.

It may be said that when Christian parents make such a promise they promise more than they can accomplish, for they cannot impart the new life to their children, cannot create within them the spirit of obedience. Now it is perfectly true that the parents cannot guarantee spiritual renewal; nor does God expect or require it of them. They make their promise entirely on the strength of the promises of God. If the promise to intercede for their children, to educate them in the fear of the Lord, and to set them an example of true Christian piety, they simply promise to utilize the means which God has ordained for the realization of the covenant life in their children; and they have the blessed assurance that God will enable them to meet these covenant requirements. And if they promise that they with their children will fear the Lord, they do it in trustful reliance on the never failing promises of God that He will work in those children and create within them a clean heart and a willing spirit.

Occasionally we meet with people who consider it reprehensible that parents make such a promise for their children. They claim that the parents have absolutely no right to enter into such an agreement for their offspring. The children should be allowed to choose for themselves when they come to maturity. But suppose that some beneficent capitalist offered poor parents untold riches, and offered to extend his munificence also to their children provided the parents would educate them into a right appreciation and a grateful acceptance of that wealth and the children would show themselves worthy of it by a good moral conduct—and suppose that the parents accepted the offer and entered the agreement for themselves and for their children, promising to do all that lay in their power to meet the conditions, could that rightly be considered as an injustice to the children? And would it not be utter folly on the part of the children to break the agreement? Children of Christian parents have every reason to be thankful that, along with their parents, they stand in a blessed covenant relation.

Now the question arises, How does the covenant relationship furnish a basis for Christian education ? Our form of baptism clearly implies that there is a close connection between the two. Only three questions are put to the parents, and of these three one concerns itself entirely with the matter of Christian education. The first question seeks recognition of the fact that, though our children are born in sin and therefore subject to condemnation, they are nevertheless sanctified in Christ and as such entitled to baptism. The second requires a renewed confession of the parents that the doctrine contained in Scripture and taught in our church is the true and perfect doctrine of salvation. And the third exacts of them the promise that they will be faithful and diligent in teaching their children that glorious saving truth. The first is expressive of the title which the children of Christian parents have to baptism: the second, of the parents' right to seek baptism for their children; and the third, of the obligation that is involved in the privilege.

It is deserving of notice that the promise is a very comprehensive one. The parents publicly assume the responsibility of instructing their children in the "aforesaid doctrine"; and this is not merely the doctrine of the covenant, as some have asserted, but the doctrine contained in the Old and New Testament, the whole round of Christian truth with its broad sweep, touching every realm, every sphere, and every relation of Christian life. Thus we have a very clear indication of the spirit that ought to permeate the instruction of covenant children.

And now we repeat the question: In what way does the covenant relation involve the duty to give the children of the covenant a truly Christian education? There are especially three lines of thought that suggest themselves here. Let us consider these for a few moments.

In the *first* place this necessity is involved in the fact that the children of Christian parents are, with their parents, adopted into the family of God. Think for a moment of the illustration that was used at the beginning of our discussion. The generous landlord adopted his bondservants and their children into his family. But in doing this he at once encountered the problem of their education. The privilege which he bestowed upon them made it incumbent on them to live on a higher cultural level, to move about in refined company from day to day, and to reflect their high station in life in their habits and customs and general manner of living; all of which would be quite impossible for them unless they were educated and trained for that new life of culture and refinement. It would be but natural, therefore, that the landlord should make provision for the necessary education of his bond-servants and should make arrangements which would insure a corresponding education for their children. He naturally could not permit them to degrade, but would want them to be an honor to his name.

Now the children of the covenant are adopted into a family that is infinitely higher than the family of any man of rank or nobility. They are adopted into the family of the covenant God Himself. Even while on earth they are privileged to join the company of the redeemed, the saints of God. They take their place in the Church of Jesus Christ, which is the heavenly Jerusalem. Moreover, they are destined to live and move about eternally in the company of just men made perfect, of the innumerable hosts of the angels of God, and of Jesus Christ, the King all-glorious. Perfect life in the most intimate communion with the triune God is their grand ideal; heaven with all its glories is their eternal home. Can we at all doubt whether this calls for Christian education? Can we really suggest in all seriousness that in a world such as we are living in Christian education in the home, in the Church, and in the Sunday-School is quite adequate? Ought we not rather to ask: Is the best religious education we can give our children, no matter how comprehensive and how thorough, really commensurate with the high dignity to which our children are called? Should we not bend all our efforts to make it richer and fuller, and to bring it more into harmony with their high calling and their exalted duties? Would we want our children to be a dishonor to the household of God? Let us ever be mindful of the fact that the King's children must have a royal education.

The necessity of Christian education follows, in the *second* place, also from the fact that the children of Christian parents fall heir to the covenant promises. The master making a covenant with his slaves pardoned their insurrection, endowed them with material riches, and made them co-heirs with his own children. This is the very thing that God does in the covenant of grace. Now suppose that our children had been robbing some wealthy land-owner and were caught in the act, and that this land-owner did not prosecute them, but instead heaped coals of fire upon their head by making them the heirs of untold riches. Would not this at once suggest a new duty to us, the duty to impress upon our children their utter unworthiness and the munificence of him whom they sought to deprive of his possessions, and to make them fully conscious of the immense wealth so magnanimously bestowed upon them and of the responsibility which it involved? It is quite evident that this would appear desirable for more than one reason. We would naturally feel it incumbent on us to engender in our children a spirit of true gratitude, to promote their happiness by helping them to obtain a proper realization of their great riches, and teach them the right use of their sudden wealth.

Children of Christian parents, in spite of their unworthiness, fall heir to the blessed promises of the covenant, and these promises cover the whole range of life, natural and spiritual, temporal and eternal, and as such guarantee them all the riches of grace and glory that are in Christ Jesus. These bounties naturally call for gratitude. God expects his covenant children to praise Him with thankful hearts. The unthankful are classed with the notoriously wicked (II Tim. 3 :2). After Moses had reminded the children of Israel of their covenant privileges and had pointed to the blessings which they were about to receive in Palestine, he said unto them, "And thou shalt eat and be full, and thou shalt bless Jehovah thy God for the good land which He hath given thee" (Deut. 8:10). Our children too must bring their thank-offerings to the Lord. But how can they be adequately thankful unless they are taught to see how much they have received? They should be brought to a realization of the fact that never ending thanks are due and that even the best they can bring to the Lord is but an inadequate expression of the gratefulness they owe their covenant God. If the question of the poet finds an echo in their heart:

What shall I render to the Lord
For all His benefits to me?
How shall my soul by grace restored
Give worthy thanks, O Lord, to Thee?

–then Christian education must help them to find an appropriate answer.

It may be shown also from another angle that the rich promises of the covenant naturally call for Christian education. If the promises of God, which constitute the true riches of all the children of God, are to promote the real happiness and blessedness of their recipients, these must learn to understand the wide bearing of these promises and to know what treasures they include. Let us remember that, subjectively, we are no richer than our comprehension of what we possess, and that it is the true appreciation of our wealth which determines the measure of enjoyment derived from it. New Testament believers are more blessed than those of the Old Testament because they have a clearer conception of their covenanted riches. Jesus said to his disciples "Blessed are your eyes, for they see; and your ears, for they hear. For verily I say unto you, that many prophets and righteous men desired to see the things which ye see, and saw them not, and to hear the things which ye hear, and heard them not" (Matt. 13 :16, 17). Many children of God are even today living in spiritual poverty, though they are rich in Christ and heirs of the world, because they have not been taught to see the greatness and splendor of their spiritual heritage. If we do not want our children to live as paupers in spiritual penury and want while untold riches of grace and mercy are at their disposal, we must employ all the means at our command to unfold before their very eyes the treasures of divine grace of which they are heirs in Christ Jesus.

Once again, the promises of the covenant necessitate Christian education, because they inevitably impose upon our children a heavy responsibility. If all other things are equal, the affluent man has a far greater responsibility than the man of small means. He may not squander his wealth; on the contrary, he must invest it to the best advantage. And if he is not a born financier, he will need careful training for the proper administration of his wealth. Inherited riches often become a curse for the recipient because he has not been trained in the proper administration and use of money. Through lack of training the whole inheritance is sometimes lost. And may we not say of our children, to whom God entrusts great wealth in his covenant promises, that they are not all born stewards in the household of God? Yet stewards they must be, for God has enriched them with spiritual treasures in order that they should administer this wealth for the honor of His name and for the extension of His kingdom. Are we warranted in assuming that they will naturally be faithful to their trust and will make the best possible use of their God-given possessions? Are there no reasons to fear, in view of the natural tendencies of their hearts and of their lack of spiritual discernment and spiritual understanding, that like the unprofitable servant they will hide their "pound" and let it lie idle, that they will apply their wealth in the wrong direction, or that they will squander it, unless they are taught to see their responsibility and are carefully taught the proper use of the wealth which God has placed at their disposal? Surely, we cannot be too careful nor too diligent in training our children for their responsible duties in life.

This idea very naturally leads on to our *third* consideration. The necessity of Christian education also follows from the requirements of the covenant. God requires of covenant children that they believe in Jesus Christ unto salvation and that they turn from sin to holiness, i. e., follow the highway of sanctification through life. It is a very comprehensive requirement, the nature of which ought to be well understood. Hence the need of Christian education.

Faith is required in the children of the covenant. Faith, first of all, as a receptive organ by which they lay hold on Christ and all the blessings of salvation. This faith may not be a bare intellectual assent to the claims of Christ nor a mere stirring of the emotions resulting from an impassioned plea nor, finally, a momentary impulsive choice under high psychological pressure. It must be the deliberate response of a heart that is deeply conscious of sin to the glorious offer of salvation in Christ; the "amen" of the soul, elicited by the Holy Spirit, to all the blessed promises of the Gospel; the hearty and unqualified acceptance of all the covenant obligations. It is not something of a momentary or evanescent character, but an abiding attitude of the soul in which it recognizes its own sinfulness and lost condition and ever anew embraces the righteousness of Jesus Christ. But the faith that is required of covenant children is not merely passive, is not only a receptive organ; it is also active as the principle of a new obedience. From this faith must spring love to God, to Jesus Christ, and to the people of God. And all the thoughts and words and actions of covenant children must be motivated by that divinely wrought love. Then only will their lives be well pleasing to God.

But this already points to the second requirement of the covenant. Faith is the only condition for *entrance* into the life of the covenant; but for the *full realization* of that relation of friendship between God and man for which the covenant stands, faith must be complemented by a life of sanctification. The covenant child belongs to a peculiar people, a people that is separated from the world in consecration to God; separated, not like Israel of old by towering mountains, vast waters, and arid deserts, but by a far more effective line of cleavage wrought by the Spirit of God. And what does the Lord require in that capacity? With Micah we may say, "to do justly and to love kindness, and to walk humbly with thy God"; or with Paul that, "denying ungodliness and worldly lusts," they should "live soberly and righteously and godly in this present world." The life of the covenant child should ever increasingly become a true reflection of the life of Christ that is born within the heart. Nothing short of the perfect life is its grand ideal.

Now surely it needs no argument that children of whom such great, such spiritual, such heavenly things are required must be educated in the fear of the Lord. Christian education is one of the means which God is pleased to use for working faith in the heart of the child, for calling an incipient faith into action, and for guiding the first faltering steps of faith. It teaches the child to flee from sin and to strive after holiness, without which no one will see the Lord. It takes the child by the hand, and leads it step by step on the highway of sanctification to the city of the eternal King. What a blessed task, this task of Christian educators; but also, what a responsible duty! Oh, for hearts aflame with the love of God, for men and women filled with the Spirit of Christ, for teachers that speak with the tongues of angels, to perform the well-nigh staggering task of helping to qualify covenant children for their covenant responsibilities !

We sought to give an answer to the important question how the covenant of grace naturally calls for Christian education. In answer to the query why Christian parents are in duty bound to give their covenant children a specifically Christian education, we are usually referred to their baptismal promise. And rightly so. But this answer is apt to lead a reflective mind on to the further question, Why does the form of baptism insist on it, as it does, that covenant children be given such an education ? We have made an attempt to point out that the covenant relation itself naturally and necessarily calls for this. May our feeble efforts contribute something to a better understanding of this important subject. May our eyes be opened ever increasingly to the glorious heritage that is ours and our children's in the covenant of grace. And may the interest in our schools grow apace, for we have in them the most effective agency to train our children for their high dignity as members of the household of God, to teach them a due appreciation and the right use of the covenant blessings, and to qualify them for their covenant responsibilities. Then God will receive all the honor; we and our children will sing unending praises to his glorious name.

Christian Scholar's Review:
Editor Introduction

This scholarly journal, begun in 1971, has given serious attention to numerous intellectual, ecclesiastical, and moral questions. These have been addressed by a wide spectrum of evangelical scholars, and representing various disciplines.

Essays on education have appeared less frequently than other topics but the two following are representative of scholarly interest in Christian schools, and specifically from Reformed thinkers. The first and longer treatment is by educational historian Peter P. De Boer and educational philosopher Donald Oppewal, both of the Education Department of Calvin College. It gives a picture of both the intellectual roots of the Calvinist school movement and some projections for the future as they saw it in 1984.

The second inclusion is by Paul Scotchmer, a pastor who has observed some of the cross currents of thought about Christian schooling in America. Using H. Richard Niebuhr's schema of Christ and culture options he contrasts an Anabaptist and a Reformed view. He argues that the transformation view is the better justification for the existence of Christian schools.

Together these documents, reprinted with permission, reflect the larger intellectual movements within which the Reformed perspective has come to expression in the United States.

American Calvinist Day Schools

By Peter De Boer and Donald Oppewal
from *Christian Scholar's Review,* XIII:2,
1984, pp. 120–140

The term "Calvinist" is used to distinguish the schools described below
from Catholic, Lutheran, Anglican, Baptist, and other Protestant denominational or independent church educational efforts. Calvinists in North
America do not commonly refer to their schools as Calvinist schools.
Instead they call them "Christian schools," a practice begun in the
Netherlands in the nineteenth century. Calvinist Christian schools arose in
the United States in the middle to late nineteenth century. Since 1920 these
schools have been organized as the National Union of Christian Schools,
which in 1979 became Christian Schools International (CSI). With head-
quarters in Grand Rapids, Michigan, CSI has nearly 400 schools as
members, employs over 3700 full-time teachers, and enrolls over 72,000
students.*

This essay describes and analyzes briefly some ethnic or cultural
influences on these American Calvinist schools, especially their roots in
The Netherlands; the ecclesiastical or denominational affiliation of the
schools, especially with the Christian Reformed Church in North America;
the biblical or theological grounding of the schools, including some
consequences for educational theory; and finally, some problems and
prospects for the future.

---

*Recent statistics (92-93 CSI *Directory*) show 424 schools, 5,017
teachers, and 92,878 students, a modest but persistent growth, in the last
decade-Editor.

Cultural Roots: The Netherlands

While the roots of the Calvinist day schools in America reach back to The Netherlands, their common soil is the religio-philosophical system called Calvinism. Founded by John Calvin in sixteenth-century Geneva, Calvinism played a crucial role in the spread of the Protestant Reformation to France, The Netherlands, England, Scotland, and America. Although it has assumed different roles in each of these countries, in none of them has it operated simply as a set of specifically doctrinal or liturgical beliefs; it has always found cultural expression and produced an effect upon economics, politics, and education, although not to the same degree in all countries. The fundamental principle upon which the Calvinist system rests is the sovereignty of God in the totality of life.[2] Education being one of the crucial issues in life, it is not surprising that a standard reference work notes that "one of the ... most permanent influences of Calvinists in Geneva, France, Holland, Scotland, England, and America was their contribution to education."[3]

In Holland, for example, under the influence of Calvinist Geneva, the universities of Leiden (1575), Groningen (1614), Amsterdam (1630), Utrecht (1636), and others were founded and enjoyed an international reputation. Moreover, popular education was decreed by the church and maintained by the state. The Calvinist Synod of Dort (1618-19) resolved that

> Schools in which the young shall be properly instructed in piety and fundamentals of Christian doctrine shall be instituted not only in cities, but also in towns and country places... The Christian magistry shall be requested that honorable stipends be provided for teachers, and that well-qualified persons may be employed and enabled to devote themselves to that function; and especially that the children of the poor may be gratuitously instructed by them and not be excluded from the benefits of the schools.[4]

Thus, during the sixteenth and seventeenth centuries, during the height of Calvinist influence, the Dutch founded noted universities and made state-supported "Christian" elementary education available to the poor as well as the rich.

The Dutch Republic, founded in 1579, ended in 1795 when the Dutch came under French control. Twenty years later, when the Dutch established a kingdom called The Netherlands under William I, historic Calvinist creeds were officially recognized, these being the Heidelberg

Catechism, the Belgic Confession, and the Canons of Dort. Calvinism was in effect the national religion, and the Reformed Church (now called the Hervormde Kerk) the state church.

However, under new rules for church government adopted under the monarchy, pastors in the churches and professors in the universities were permitted to interpret these confessions rather freely.[5] Orthodox Calvinists protested the changes in church doctrine, liturgy, and polity. Some of those who wanted to be faithful to the historic creeds labored to restore the Reformed Church to its original purity; others began a movement which culminated in their secession from the state church in 1834.

The Secession of 1834. The Secession of 1834 had been preceded by an evangelical revival begun in Geneva, but one which spread to the Netherlands under the leadership of Bilderdijk, Da Costa, and Groen Van Prinsterer, upper-class laymen opposed to the liberal theology espoused by the state church, in favor of reform of the church from within.[6]

Others were less patient.[7] In 1834 Hendrick De Cock—trained in liberal theology at Groningen but converted during his early ministry and convicted of the need for regeneration and the fact of total depravity—withdrew from the state church with 144 members of his congregation and began a new denomination: the Old Netherlands Reformed Church. Subsequent secessions in other provinces, led by a handful of sympathetic pastors (including A. C. Van Raalte, who was ordained in 1836 at the first synod of the new church, and H. Scholte), augmented the new denomination so that within a half year it numbered sixteen congregations.

The Seceders sought government approval to exercise freedom of religion, but were denied the right of assembly. Refusing to obey the prohibition, the Seceders were persecuted by arrests, fines, imprisonments, and other forms of harassment. Though persecution largely ceased in 1840 with the abdication of William I, discrimination continued, and the worsened economic situation— high taxes, a potato blight, high unemployment—soon led many Seceders to contemplate emigration.[8] Though they considered such possibilities as Indonesia and South Africa, they eventually opted for America. In 1847 Van Raalte led one group to western Michigan, while H. Scholte led another to Iowa.

One of the reasons for the Secession was the conviction that the schools under the supervision of the state were becoming neutral in matters of religion. The Seceders objected to the educational policies instituted during the period of French influence, policies which remained in effect after the restoration of Dutch in dependence. These regulations designated only certain portions of the Bible as suitable for classroom use; they also eliminated from the curriculum the teaching of denominational doctrines, specifically the teaching of the Heidelberg Catechism.[9] Further, efforts by the Seceders to achieve state approval so they could establish their own parochial schools were repeatedly frustrated by the civil authorities.

What had been one of the chief reasons for the Secession of 1834—the issue of Christian education—became one of several reasons for emigration to the United States. As pastors Brummelkamp and Van Raalte expressed it,

> Especially we would desire, that they, settling [in the U.S.] in the same villages and neighborhoods, may enjoy the privilege of seeing their little ones educated in a Christian school—a privilege of which we are here [in the Netherlands] entirely deprived, as the instruction given in the state's schools may be called but a mere general moral one, offensive to neither Jew nor Roman Catholic...[11]

Thus the ideal of the Christian school was carried to America by both the relatively poor groups of immigrants who in The Netherlands had frequently kept their children from attendance at the state schools and who had repeatedly failed to achieve approval for their own church schools,[12] and also by their university-educated leader, A. C. Van Raalte, who looked forward with great anticipation to establishing schools.[13] Given the immigrants' need literally to hack out of the heavily-forested wilderness of western Michigan a form of civilized life which, over time, only approximated life in The Netherlands, one should not be surprised to discover compromises with the ideal of a church-controlled school, especially with the district (public) school offering its attractions as an alternative, nor surprised with the disappointments of Van Raalte. [14]

The Kuyperian Revival of the 1870s. The Calvinist day school movement in America was enriched by the Calvinist revival in The Netherlands begun in the 1870s under the leadership of Abraham Kuyper.[15] For fifty years in The Netherlands Kuyperian Calvinism "addressed every facet of national life . . . and wrote much of its political and cultural agenda."[16]

Fully as orthodox as the Seceders, and as fervent in piety, Kuyper believed that Calvinism was not limited to matters of religion narrowly defined, but included politics, economics, science, and the like—or in Kuyper's favorite phrase, "every sphere of life." On the occasion of the founding of the Free University of Amsterdam in 1880, Kuyper enunciated a principle later called "sphere sovereignty," whereby he maintained that the basic spheres of life—such as family, state, church, art, agriculture, science, education—have their own nature or character and are subject to their own laws, laws established by God in the creation itself. Each sphere is subject to the all-encompassing sovereignty of God. The spheres are interrelated, yet no sphere has the right to interfere with the sovereignty, under God, of any of the other spheres. Thus, for example, the sphere of academic science, schooling, or education, being a sovereign sphere, has to develop the task assigned to it by God while free of interference from both the state and the church.[17]

Kuyperian Calvinists, unlike the Seceders, did not denounce certain fields of activity (politics, scholarship, art) as inherently "worldly"; rather, the faithful were called to address such areas as legitimate human concerns and to restore them to something of their original perfection rather than turn their backs on them.[18] With such impetus, these Calvinists established, besides the Free University, a nationwide network of Christian elementary and secondary schools which were free of both the state and the church.

Many immigrants settled in the new world fully aware of, though not always in agreement with, the "world and life view" of Kuyperian Calvinism.[19] The presence in America of newly-arrived pastors, professional educators, and influential laypersons on fire with Kuyperian Calvinist ideas brought interest and enthusiasm not only for Christian education, but for Christian schools administratively independent of churches. The schools became officially controlled by societies of laypersons, especially parents, rather than by churches through their councils or consistories.[20]

Thus the Calvinist day schools in America find their ethnic and cultural roots in The Netherlands. The soil of Dutch Calvinism in the nineteenth century produced two roots: the Secession of 1834, and Kuyperian Calvinism of the 1870s and beyond. The Seceder root branched into an overwhelming concern for purity of doctrine, a pietism which often took on an anti-cultural color, and a desire to establish Christian schools controlled by the churches, which would guarantee the survival of the churches and safeguard the faith of the true believer. The Kuyperian Calvinist root branched into a persistent concern for cultural engagement, testing the spirits to see whether they be of God, and seeking to establish the lordship of Jesus Christ in all areas of life. The Kuyperians established schools controlled by parents and interested laypersons, convinced that neither church nor state controlled education. How these two roots and their branches, with their opposing views on education, became fruitfully fused over time within the shifting and ambiguous relationship that existed for years between the Christian Reformed Church and the Calvinist school system, will be addressed in the next section.

Ecclesiastical Roots: The Christian Reformed Church

The Calvinist day school, transplanted to America from The Nether-lands, grew slowly and made little progress between 1850 and 1890. The American version was begun by A. C. Van Raalte, who led the Seceders of 1834 to western Michigan in 1847 and settled at Holland. Other immigrants settled nearby at Zeeland, Graafschap, Vriesland, Overisel, and Drenthe, or in the already established cities of Grand Rapids, Kalamazoo, and Grand Haven. Joined together to form a church union called Classis Holland, the entire classis in 1850 joined the Dutch Re-formed Church, whose roots in America went back to the seventeenth century.

The union of Classis Holland with the Dutch Reformed Church helped Van Raalte realize part of his educational ideal. For with gifts from people largely in the eastern sector of the church, Van Raalte was able to establish an academy in 1851. Soon named Holland Academy, the school came under the control of the General Synod of the Dutch Reformed Church and reached collegiate status in 1866 with the founding of Hope College.[21]

Van Raalte's larger vision included Christian primary schools. His concept of the "task God has laid in our hands" included "the matter of education and the establishment of a Christian Society." He judged that only education could "deliver this people and their confessions from irrelevance."[22] Yet his followers were so poor that, in 1850, they tempo-rarily refused to tax themselves to support even the public school in Holland. Classis Holland, in 1855, did recommend to the Board of Education of the Dutch Reformed Church the need for financial support to erect a church school in Kalamazoo, and a year later Classis Holland did the same for the Second Reformed Church in Grand Rapids. Van Raalte, soon convinced that the local public school was inappropriate for Chris-tians, proposed to his own consistory the organization of a parochial school where the Bible could be used as a textbook, where instruction could be given in the Heidelberg Catechism, and where the Dutch language could be included as one of the subjects of study. But the school, by 1862, died for lack of interest and support.[23]

Thus, except for Holland Academy (later Hope College) in Holland, Michigan, and parochial schools in Kalamazoo and Grand Rapids, the Seceders associated with Van Raalte in the western wing of the Dutch Reformed Church showed little zeal for the Calvinist school idea. How-ever, that ideal did survive within the True Dutch Reformed Church (later

called the Christian Reformed Church), born in 1857 when four congregations in western Michigan seceded from the Dutch Reformed Church.
Ironically, the little parochial school begun in 1856 in Grand Rapids by the
Second Reformed Church became the first of an eventually flourishing
line of Christian schools when that congregation, by secession in 1857,
became the First Christian Reformed Church of Grand Rapids.

Beginning of the Christian Reformed School Movement.

The secession of 1857, which gave birth to the Christian Reformed
Church, "was made in the same tradition and spirit as the Secession of 1834
in the Netherlands"[24] and thus had a similar impact on education. With
Dutch as the language of instruction, the few secessionist schools were all
church-controlled; they aimed mainly to nurture true faith and sound
doctrine among the youth to help preserve a small and struggling denomination.

Though for years the Christian Reformed have enjoyed the reputation
of being advocates of Christian schools, the early growth of the church far
outran the growth of the Christian schools. Consider this: When the
Christian Reformed Church was born, there was but one little Dutch
parochial school in a denomination numbering four congregations. In
fifteen years the denomination had grown to twenty-five congregations
served by thirteen ministers; yet there was still only this one school in
Grand Rapids, Michigan. By 1880 the church had grown to thirty-eight
congregations; in that year there were only four "little Dutch schools," two
of them in Grand Rapids. By 1900 the denomination had grown to 144
churches served by 101 ministers; yet there were still only about fourteen
Christian schools, seven of them in Grand Rapids with its eleven Christian
Reformed churches.[25]

Several factors explain the slow growth of the Christian Reformed
school movement. Many of the immigrants and their descendents were
poor. This, in the absence of effective compulsory attendance legislation,
meant that children went to work while still young.[26] Second, the public
schools in the United States were still tolerable, especially those in rural
communities where boards of education could employ Christian teachers
and permit Bible reading and devotions. Third, many parents judged that
the existing Christian schools suffered from glaring weaknesses. Their
aim was overly narrow and their teachers were often untrained, inept, very
young, and inclined to leave their posts after a few years.[27]

For its justification of such schools, the Christian Reformed Church in this era referred to Article 21 of the Church Order of the Synod of Dort which, prior to its revision in 1914, read in part, "Consistories shall see to it that there are good schoolmasters ..." Part of the Heidelberg Catechism, until revised, read "that the ministry of the gospel and the schools be maintained."[28] On these foundations the church insisted it "had a warrant ... to establish and maintain day schools to insure her continued existence and vitality."[29] But late in the century Kuyperian Calvinists challenged such justification for parochial schools, with some intriguing results.

The Kuyperian Calvinist Challenge.

During the last decade of the nineteenth century, the Kuyperian notion that Christian schools should be free from control of both state and church gained ascendancy in the Christian Reformed Church. The pressure came especially from Christian school principals and pastors educated in The Netherlands, who desired to transplant Kuyper's concept of sphere sovereignty to the American scene.[30] Acceptance of the concept entailed at the least a significant shift in the locus of control from the church to parents and other interested supporters. But beyond that, the leaders of this new Kuyperian educational movement hoped that by giving Christian education "a roof of its own" instead of existing by the grace of the church, students from churches other than the Christian Reformed would be welcome; that "Reformed symbols" such as the Heidelberg Catechism would not be formally taught (though there would be adherence to "undiluted Reformed principles"); and that English would become the language of instruction in the schools.[31] Underneath all this lay the hope that freedom from the church meant freedom for the schools to prosper.

In 1892 the Christian Reformed Synod adopted a resolution encouraging the organization of a national society to promote Christian education.[32] Within weeks a Society for Christian Education on a Reformed Basis was organized,[33] committed to stimulating the establishment of more schools and the expansion of those already existing, as well as the training of young people to be "Reformed teachers" for the schools.[34]

But what can be read as a victory for Kuyperian Calvinism and, theoretically at least, a significant separation of the schools from the control and influence of the church, ought not to be so understood. Consider that the newly born Society, in Article One of its constitution, found its basis in "the Holy Scriptures as expressed in the Formulas of Unity of the Reformed Church."[35] Hence there was no open break with a long tradition linking Christian education with church creeds. Neither did the individual schools quickly move to shed their ecclesiastical controls.[36]

Nor were Kuyperian principles rigidly argued by the leadership of the Society. The man who softened the impact of such principles more than any other person was Klaas Kuiper, a pastor in the Christian Reformed Church and the Society's first president. In favor of the Kuyperian ideal of society-controlled education, K. Kuiper refused to raise his opinion to the level of inviolable principle that would make church ownership of schools illegitimate.[37] Further, the Society did not engage in a campaign opposing church involvement in education. Instead, the Society reminded all pastors in the church of their obligation to support Christian education and urged them to organize local chapters of the national Society within their congregations. The Society even went as far as to allow church consistories operating schools to join the Society as corporate bodies.[38]

Thus Kuyperian Calvinism, transplanted to America, did lead to society–or parentally-controlled schools. But the constitution of the national Society, the justification offered by the Society for the separation of the schools from the churches, and the membership practices of the Society were such as to create, already at the outset, a highly ambiguous relationship between the schools and the Christian Reformed Church. In theory the Calvinist schools were free to develop their own life sphere; in fact then and for many years after the Calvinist schools were virtually parochial, perceived as an arm of the church and essential to her life.[39]

This close relationship of the schools to the Christian Reformed Church "has lent a definite denominational coloring to a school system that is not in principle to be limited to that denomination,"[40] and helps to explain the character and some of the tensions associated with two vital aspects of the life of the schools: teacher education, and Christian Schools International.

Teacher Education Efforts.

Since 1900 Calvin College in Grand Rapids, owned and operated by the Christian Reformed Church, has been the major supplier of teachers for the Calvinist day schools, owned and operated by societies of parents and other supporters. For fifty years Calvin had almost no competition in teacher education.[41] Why, one might ask, didn't teacher education for the Calvinist schools lodge with a society rather than the church?

Calvin College and Seminary began in 1876 as a theological school to train young men for the ministry. Its curriculum consisted of four years of studies in a Literary Department followed by three years of professional training in a Theological Department. In 1894 the Society for Christian Education on a Reformed Basis requested of the Synod its moral support

274 Voices From the Past: Reformed Educators

and encouragement for a normal school that would originate with the Society and be under its direct control. The Synod refused to comply.[42] In the same year there were at Synod several requests, including one from the Theological School's Board of Trustees, to separate the Literary Department from the Theological School. Instead, the Synod expanded the potential clientele of the school by declaring that the Theological School would now admit "also those who do not look forward to the ministry...."[43] The Society then made an effort to organize teacher training on an apprentice model,[44] but with little success. Formal teacher education had to wait until 1900, when the Literary Department of the Theological School was finally expanded into an academy or preparatory school. Here, at the secondary level, under denominational auspices, Christian school teachers were educated in what slowly developed into a fairly distinctive four-year curricular track: the teachers' course. For nearly twenty years, the faculty cited this teachers' course (second only to the pre-seminary course) as a reason for the existence of Calvin.[45]

A serious shortage of teachers for the Calvinist schools developed during World War I and immediately afterward. To meet that need, several institutions developed within the Christian Reformed Church which threatened Calvin's hegemony in teacher preparation.

One source of competition was Christian secondary schools. Until about 1915 Calvin's preparatory school was the only secondary school in existence within the Christian Reformed Church. But almost overnight Christian secondary schools sprang up in Michigan, Illinois, Iowa, New Jersey, and elsewhere. With or without a special teachers' course, many of the graduates became teachers in Christian elementary schools.

Another was the rise in 1916 of the Christian Reformed College of Grundy Center, Iowa. At first controlled by Classis East Friesland (a predominately German-speaking subdivision of the church), Grundy College became a society controlled school in 1920.[46] As preparatory school and two-year college, Grundy offered teacher education courses until its demise in the early 1930s during the Depression .

An even greater potential source of competition for Calvin arose within the city of Grand Rapids itself. In 1918 about three hundred supporters began the Society for Christian Normal Instruction, its birth partly the result of long-standing criticism by Christian school teachers and principals that Calvin's teachers' course was not sufficiently practical.[47] Reflecting the upgrading taking place in normal training in Michigan, this Christian Normal School, begun in 1919, sought mainly to enroll high school graduates to teach in Christian elementary schools. Unfortunately for the school, few students enrolled. Operations were suspended after only two years.[48]

Meanwhile, responding to the argument that a church-controlled college should not operate a preparatory school, Calvin began in 1920 to dismantle its preparatory school while concurrently Grand Rapids Christian High School came into existence. Intending to enlarge its offerings in secondary teacher education, Calvin, by the spring of 1921, also approved plans for a two-year normal program for training elementary school teachers. Within a year Calvin had graduated six secondary education students who qualified for the state certificate.[49] Concurrent with the phasing out of seniors in the preparatory school teachers' course, Calvin College in 1922 phased in its new two-year normal course for elementary teachers with the advice and consent of the National Union of Christian Schools, begun in 1920.[50]

The subsequent history of teacher education within the Christian Reformed Church and the Calvinist day schools is largely one of cooperative interaction and continued upgrading. By 1930 most of the Christian high schools had ceased their teacher education programs.[51] By 1924 Calvin had four-year programs in elementary and secondary teacher education; yet until the middle fifties the college maintained a little publicized two-year elementary teacher educationprogram as a favor to some of the Christian schools who could not afford to employ four-year graduates. Partly at the request of the National Union, the college offered a full slate of summer courses, mainly aimed at teacher preparation, from the 1950s onward. Much of the theoretical work on behalf of Christian education was developed by the college faculty. In the seventies Calvin began a graduate program leading to the Master of Arts in Teaching degree, fulfilling a desire of the National Union for a Christian graduate level program in teacher education. Thereby graduates from similar Christian colleges can, if they choose, continue their education at Calvin.

Presently Calvin counts four schools as "sister" colleges: Dordt, in Sioux Center, Iowa; Trinity Christian, in Palos Heights, Illinois; King's, in Edmonton, Alberta; and Redeemer, in Hamilton, Ontario. Unlike Calvin, which is owned and operated by the Christian Reformed Church, these schools are all controlled by societies. Thus far only Dordt and Trinity engage in teacher education.

Dordt College, begun in 1955, was a direct response on the part of members of the Christian Reformed Church in the Midwest to a profound teacher shortage. For nearly a decade Dordt graduated teachers from its two-year program, though some of the graduates interested in teaching transferred to Calvin to finish their programs. Beginning in 1964 Dordt established four-year programs, including one in teacher education, which then matched the upgrading that Calvin had earlier achieved.

Trinity Christian, begun in 1959, operated as a two-year college until 1970. Until then, many of the graduates of Trinity transferred to Calvin to complete their teacher education. After 1970 most of the students remained at Trinity.

Thus, even though the Calvinist day schools and the sister Christian colleges are controlled by societies while Calvin College has remained church-owned and operated, there has been fruitful interaction and close cooperation both between Calvin and the schools united into a National Union and between Calvin and her sister colleges. This harmony has reinforced the ties of the denomination to the Calvinist schools.

Service Organizations.

When in 1892 the Society For the Promotion of Christian Education on a Reformed Basis came into being, with the endorsement of the Christian Reformed Synod, it found itself with only a dozen schools and the abstract cause of society-controlled education to promote. The administrative break between the denominational system and the existing schools left the schools with no formal budgetary support, no national network of communication, and no appointed spokesmen for the cause.

The Society was not a viable alternative to the denominational structure it was to replace. Local school boards and their societies wrestled alone with the details of adequate finances, adequately trained teachers, and acceptable locations for instruction. As each local society struggled with these details, as well as with the goal of providing teacher training and teaching materials, they soon saw that collective efforts were necessary if any progress was to be made. No single school board could hope to provide leadership in these areas in addition to raising funds, staff, and buildings for local school operation. A grass-roots movement for bringing Calvinist school societies together into some kind of collective cooperation began as early as 1900 and grew as the number of schools increased.

Alliances.

These cooperative efforts were called Alliances, and were formed into the Michigan, the Chicago, the Western, and the Eastern Alliances.[52] The same logic which led to the forming of geographically local alliances soon persuaded them that only a national organization could adequately cope with common problems. It was the Chicago Alliance which took the initiative to form a national organization to serve all the struggling schools across the United States. It called the first meeting, to which thirty-seven local school associations sent representatives. By 1920 organizational problems had been overcome and a National Union of Christian Schools was born. With its birth the alliances maintained their identity by eventually becoming constitutive parts of a national organization, and are now called Districts.

National Union.

When the Union was organized it became apparent that there were two schools of thought about its purpose. Some looked upon it as an authoritative body which would unite the various local school associations and establish policy for all schools. Others held that the Union should offer its services, whether these be pension plans or materials for teachers, but that the local school was free to adopt or not to adopt any of them. This latter perception prevailed, leaving school societies with large amounts of local autonomy.

It is significant that the Union was a union of lay-member school boards, not church officials. It took from 1892 to 1920 to replace a denominational structure with a non-ecclesiastical national structure. The reverberations of this action have been many, not all of which can be given in this brief summary. Suffice it to say that they have all stemmed from the attempt to maintain a Calvinist-oriented school system which is neither administratively, nor in funding, nor in its goals a parochial school system. It produced on the American educational scene a citizen and parent-controlled conception of day school education. It remains today as almost unique in American religious schooling, a system with religious orientation but not administered by any denominational structure. This has freed the Calvinist schools to be ecumenical in ways not open to the various parochial schools.

The intent to broaden the base of support for the National Union has over the years caused changes in the "Basis Article" of its Bylaws. Each change was an attempt to identify more clearly the requirements for voting membership. The changes signal that the principles are both biblical and educational, and that the biblical grounding is in educationally relevant elements.[53]

At its inception the National Union had numerous goals.[54] One was the ambitious goal of establishing a Christian normal school for the training of teachers. Unable to agree on whether teacher training was a national or local responsibility, it soon became apparent that the National Union could not achieve this goal.

The Union then turned toward cooperation with Calvin College, which is owned and operated by the Christian Reformed Church. It contributed to the expense of preparing a Christian school principal to serve as Director of the Normal Department at Calvin College. For many years it has also provided scholarships and grants to prospective teachers who attend Calvin or the several other Reformed Colleges established since 1955.

In 1922, only two years after its founding, the Union succeeded in translating another of its purposes into reality. That, as Article 4 of its Bylaws expressed it, was "establishing and maintaining of a teachers' and School Boards' Magazine." First called *Christian School Magazine,* it soon became more popular and less professional in its content and was named *Christian Home and School.* While for some years it attempted to speak to both parent and professional educator concerns with various special departments variously called "Teacher's Exchange" and "The Teacher's Bookshelf," it was chiefly a monthly periodical for the parent and school board member.

The National Union took seriously its initial goal of assisting the classroom teacher in being professional and in implementing the distinctive features of the Calvinist school. It did so in at least three areas: professional organizations, a professional journal, and the publication of textbooks and teaching materials. Each of these merits a brief description.

First, the National Union, acting in concert with the Calvin College Education Department, provided personnel and some funding for meetings to help teachers organize as a professional group. While slow to organize, teacher associations, with more or less activity, have now come to number thirty-two in the national directory. While plans have been made for a national Calvinist teacher organization, none has yet appeared. In encouraging such associations the Union was motivated by a desire for professional growth of its teachers.

Second, recognizing that its own *Christian Home and School* was chiefly a board member and parent magazine, the Union gave both personnel and funding for a professional educator's magazine. Acting in concert with Calvin College it subsidized and founded in 1961 the quarterly *Christian Educators Journal,* and appointed a member of the Calvin Education Department as its first editor. The Midwest Christian Teacher's Association soon joined, and presently a dozen teacher associations, Christian colleges, and other service organizations are official members. While for many years the masthead of the journal declared it to be a medium for the Calvinist school movement, it later expressed an ecumenical outreach by changing the key word to "Protestant." The statement of purpose now speaks of being a channel of communication for educators committed to the idea of evangelical Christian schools.

Third, the Union has taken seriously that provision in an early version of its Constitution which called for "encouraging the publication of literature of a pedagogic nature."[55] While it has also published promotional materials and studies of the philosophy of Christian education, the Union has expended considerable amounts of its budget on classroom materials such as textbooks, curriculum guides, and resource units. Early interest in Bible materials and hymnbooks for classroom use soon expanded into history textbooks, civics and social studies texts, and literature anthologies.

Since 1967 the Union has had a full-time administrator of a Curriculum Department, plus a number of part-time consultants who work on a contract basis to produce teaching materials in science, music, language arts, physical education, and other areas. These materials reflect a determined effort to integrate religious outlook with a given curriculum area. Working with a lower budget than commercial publishing houses, it has not yet produced materials for all grade levels or in all curricular areas. Efforts so far have shown a commitment to counter the secularizing effect in commercial texts with a Christian view of life and learning. Such extensive concern with production of Christian materials has been one of the early distinctive features of the Calvinist school movement, a concern which was matched only recently by other Christian groups sponsoring schools.

Christian Schools International.[56]

In the early 1950s waves of Reformed immigrants from The Netherlands came to Canada. Wherever there were sufficient numbers they established local Christian schools, based on their experience in The Netherlands. While many schools joined the National Union, the geographic and political differences between the United States and Canada made it difficult for the National Union to meet their needs. Foundations for fund raising for Christian textbooks had to be separately chartered, and teaching materials, particularly in social studies, had to be constructed before Canadian concerns could be fully recognized. In 1979 the name was changed to Christian Schools International, and it reflected changes in everything from Board of Trustees representation to Canadian teaching materials. Although these efforts to incorporate Canadian concerns produced some strains, both ideological and otherwise, the commonalities appear to be greater than the differences, and the Canadian contingent is rapidly being assimilated into the CSI system.

The movement promises to become even more international in the future, with affiliations being made with Reformed groups in places as far apart as Australia and Ireland. In Australia the National Union of Associations for Christian Parent Controlled Schools, as an affiliate member representing twenty-three schools across that continent, seems to be the most significant on the international horizon.

Biblical And Theological Grounding

Though Calvinist schools are today less strongly influenced by their ethnic and denominational roots, their grounding in Calvinist biblical-theological principles has persisted unchanged for 130 years. The leaders and spokesmen of the movement have over the years forged a web of interrelated doctrines which provide its religious foundations and which have endured through its trials, both economic and ideological.

The case for the Calvinist school does not rest on any presumed or real deficiencies in isolated practices of the American public school, such as the teaching of evolution in a given school system or an unacceptable "values education" course in another. It does not reside simply in an immigrant mentality or a desire for social isolation. The Calvinist school is a protest movement only in the sense that its theology provides it with educational positions on key questions that make the very conception of a religiously neutral, government-sponsored educational system pedagogically problematic if not impermissible.

At least three interrelated educational positions are undergirded by Calvinist theology. The first is that the locus of educational authority is neither in the church nor the state but resides in the family. This has led to the founding and propagation of schools owned and operated by societies of like-minded parents and citizens. The second is that education should be neither neutral toward all religions nor devoted simply to indoctrination in one religion, but rather that a religious worldview should be integrated into all curriculum content. This has led to serious attempts to produce textbooks and other teaching materials in numerous curriculum areas which incorporated this religious outlook. Finally, the aim of such education is not evangelization for church membership, nor is it value-free information-giving. Rather, it should prepare the learner for living a Christian life style in contemporary society.

We now turn to five theological concepts which support these educational positions.

The Sovereignty of God.

The most pervasive, but also most abstract, is the doctrine of the sovereignty of God.[57] Perhaps it is the tap root among other roots. Whatever else this doctrine has meant for soteriology, for education and the schools it has meant that schools express not merely a secular concern. Calvinists see politics, business, and also education as embraced in the Christian's calling to apply this understanding to all areas of life. Thus educational policy and practice are derived from this worldview, in which the sovereignty of God is the fundamental principle.

Sphere Sovereignty.

A second doctrine, derived from this tap root and more directly decisive in shaping educational policy, is sphere sovereignty.[58] According to this view numerous social spheres or institutions operate within their own areas, with what are called creation ordinances governing each. None is subordinate to others, or under their control. For our purposes here it is important to note that academics or schools are in one of the spheres, and this renders both the parochial, church-owned school and the public, state-owned school a violation of sphere sovereignty. Although often viewed by others as parochial schools because of their past ties with the Christian Reformed Church, Calvinist schools are in fact owned and operated by groups of citizen-parents. Thus the locus of educational authority is neither the state nor the church, but the parent community. This doctrine has been influential in affecting both the aims of education and the curriculum, but it has done so by determining the question of ownership and control.

Covenant.

Another doctrine especially relevant to parental control of schools is that of the covenant.[59] While this doctrine, the terminology of which at least is unique to Calvinism, has many ramifications, the effect of it on the conception of schooling is that God uses the institution of the family to carry forward the Kingdom of God.[60] "Family" here refers not to the biological family but to the total spiritual community of adults who provide funds and support for education.

General and Special Revelation.

Another peculiarly Calvinist doctrine is that of commitment to *both* general revelation and special revelation. This "two book" theory of the sources of knowledge identifies the Bible as one book and the book of nature or creation as the other. The two are held to be in tension and interpenetration with each other, with no basic dichotomy between the sacred and the secular, between Scripture and nature as sources of truth.[61] Both emanating from one sovereign God, both are trustworthy sources of truth.

Given this distinction, areas of cooperation and specialization can be mapped out between the church and the Christian day school. The church as institution is the expert in interpreting special revelation, while the school offers its leadership in interpreting general revelation. The school, through Christian teachers trained in the investigations of history, science, and psychology, among others, aims at cultural involvement and transformation, not mastery of church doctrine or evangelization. This legitimizes a liberal arts curriculum for the school as a means for discovering creation-ordinances, with the aid and direction of the Bible. The goal has more to do with community membership than with church membership. In the curriculum, Bible study becomes one among many academic areas for exploration, with biblical insights related to each area but occupying neither a higher nor a lower status in the curriculum than other areas of investigation to discover God's truth.

Cultural Mandate.

The foregoing considerations are enhanced by the related concept of cultural mandate. Rooted in the Genesis command to till the soil, exercise dominion over creation, and to shape society, the cultural mandate gives the school an aim which distinguishes it from the merely secular goals of the public school and the denominational goals of parochial schools. This aim is to be a Christian citizen, a worker in the world of politics, business, and art, or— as in a more recent statement—to live the Christian life in contemporary society.[62]

This school task of helping young Christians to exercise cultural dominion, rather than seeking cultural isolation, has important consequences for the curriculum, and the Calvinist school movement has followed through on its rhetoric about goals by translating them into textbooks and other teaching materials.[63] These materials reveal a serious attempt to integrate, rather than keep separate, a religious outlook with curricular raw material.

Such integration has taken two forms. One form consists of adding to descriptive material, whether in science or civics, some interpretation or evaluation as seen in religious or biblical perspective. In a civics text for junior high, for example, the description of alternative forms of government (e.g. monarchy, oligarchy, etc.) is followed by evaluation and assessment of democracy in the light of biblical principles and passages.[64] Another and more recent form of integration is that of reorganizing curricular materials so that they cut across the disciplines, integrating them in new ways so as to focus on some area charged with values where the Calvinist faith has a bearing. Two such areas are health education and technology.[65] The first of these correlates aspects of biology, physical education, and biblical materials, with a focus on human sexuality broadly considered. The second, on technology, correlates health and science materials with a focus on responsible Christian stewardship of resources.

These are but brief examples of how the Calvinist doctrines of cultural mandate, and of general and special revelation, have given theological direction to curriculum, and have distinguished publishing efforts from other Protestant groups also involved in publishing Christian teaching materials.

Theoreticians of the Calvinist schools have not always articulated these connections between the network of peculiarly Calvinist doctrines given above and educational policy, nor have they limited themselves to the above doctrines. Treatises on goals of education, for example, have drawn on some of the above, but also have developed a holistic Christian anthropology, as well as used empirical research to articulate what the literature has come to call intellectual, moral (or decisional), and creative learning goals that should characterize Calvinist schools.[66] Others have focused on curriculum and given various justifications.[67]

The Future: Prospects And Problems

No movement, either in its past or present form, is as simple or unidirectional as our description might have indicated. There are always cross-currents of thought and practice which serve to blur the outlines. To the scholar these cross-currents are valuable to note chiefly for historical accuracy, but also for predicting future directions. Here we shall highlight just a few of the problematics of the past which will carry forward into the future.

Relation with the Christian Reformed Church.

Some observers have warned of the dangers of parochialism.[68] Most in the school movement have accepted the moral and financial support of the denomination gratefully while guarding jealously the autonomy of the lay-member school board and professional staff.

Disassociation from a denomination, but not from a religious tradition, has opened up new possibilities of educational ecumenism in at least two areas. One is the very practical area of student recruitment and enrollment. Denominational schools, whether Catholic or Protestant, most strongly attract parents affiliated with that denomination, and their goals and curriculum reflect such sectarianism. The Calvinist school, in theory, can attract support across denominational lines. Its distinctive features are not so much the peculiarities of an ethnic group or a social class, of a creed or a denomination, as they are generic features of a Christian view of life and learning. The student population of these schools in the last ten years has changed from a predominantly Dutch, white, middle class and Christian Reformed population to one that is much more diversified, both denominationally and racially. The urban, and particularly inner-city, schools reflect this much more than the rural schools.

There is evidence that this ecumenical outreach is more than a desperate effort to keep schools alive and growing in the face of a declining birth rate. There is serious concern to face the theoretical consequences of this diversity in student population.

A problem arises from this ecumenical outreach when parents of religious affiliation other than Christian Reformed apply for voting membership in the school society. The Basis article (often Article II) of the Constitution of such societies typically states the criteria for membership in terms of a set of Christian beliefs about man, society, and education. Debate over what these touchstone beliefs ought to be has focused on whether these are simply the Christian Reformed ecclesiastical creeds or some more generic beliefs, particularly those that identify the school's educationally distinctive features.[69]

In the early 1970s Christian Schools International altered its Basis and Principles article, dropping specific reference to denominational creeds and referring instead to "Reformed creedal standards."[70] Both before this change and since, debate over this action has continued in both periodicals and at CSI annual conventions.[71] In the early eighties a special task force was appointed to draw up a more comprehensive statement of beliefs which involves not only a policy of student admission and society membership qualifications, but also the criteria for selecting teaching and administrative staff. Clarification of these issues remains a challenge for the future.

Public Funding.

Like all nonpublic schools, Calvinist schools have always had a problem with access to public funding. Acting in concert with other religiously oriented schools, the Calvinist school movement has in the last two decades aggressively participated in both legislative and litigation efforts to secure its share of the tax dollar allocated to education. These political alliances have succeeded in small ways, like bus rides and loan of textbooks, but failed in efforts to get more than miniscule amounts of tax support. They have been defeated in their efforts by both public referendums and by Supreme Court rulings on legislation.

Efforts for the future are directed at both tax credit mechanisms and the voucher idea. Both promise to be on the agenda of the Calvinist school movement of the future and have received significant treatment in its literature.[72]

Curriculum Integration.

A third area of problem and prospect lies in curriculum. The seventies have produced a massive effort to publish distinctive textbooks and teaching materials. Integrating faith and learning into textbooks has proceeded vigorously and rigorously through the efforts of the Curriculum Department of Christian Schools International. What remains to be worked out from theory to practice is the meaning of integration which goes beyond inserting Christian evaluations and interpretations into academic areas. What has emerged in the literature is the concept of cross-disciplinary curriculum-making with focus on personal-social problems as the integrating force. The translating of this vision into textbooks remains as an agenda item.[73]

Ecumenical Influence.

Within evangelical Protestantism the Calvinist school system has the potential for educational ecumenism, for being both influenced by and influencing others. A growing number of evangelical Protestant groups have come to see the importance of the trinity of home, school, and church in rearing youth in the fear of the Lord. Lacking a tradition of both educational thought and practice, they run the risk of finding their educational rationale more in their objections to specific public school practices than in biblical perspectives. Such small struggling groups may seek an identity without the benefit of experience in dealing with the complexity of a school's relationship to the state on the one hand and the church on the other. Some may, for lack of a wider vision, become simply weekday Sunday Schools, or pockets of isolation in a culture seen as hostile to Christian beliefs.

Calvinist schools have much to learn from them, but also much to give. Educational ecumenism, without merging institutional identities, promises to help all participating schools move toward a clearer vision of Christian education that is relevant to American society without being imitative of the public school. Calvinist schools, with over twenty years of experience publishing a professional journal *(Christian Educators Journal)* and over fifty years of experience embedded in a service organization (Christian Schools International) have something to contribute to the dialogue. Beyond goals and ideals, the dialogue should get down to the practical expressions of Christian principles in curriculum, textbooks, and teacher resources. If the Calvinists could combine efforts with other evangelical groups, perhaps by a convention held every five years, the witness of both could be the stronger.

Notes

[1]*Directory 1982-83*, (Grand Rapids, Mich.: Christian Schools International, 1982), p. 44. For comparative purposes, the Lutherans, Seventh Day Adventists and Baptists are much larger; such Protestant school systems as the Eastern Orthodox, Episcopal, Friends, Jewish, Methodist, Presbyterian, and Mennonite are smaller than the Calvinist schools—if Canada is added to the U.S. figures. See U.S. Department of Education, *Private Schools in American Education* (Washington, D.C.: National Center for Education Statistics, 1981), p. 17.

[2]H. Henry Meeter, *Calvinism: An Interpretation of Its Basic Ideas* (Grand Rapids, Mich.: Zondervan, 1939), p. 37. See also Robert D. Knudsen, "Calvinism as a Cultural Force" in *John Calvin: His Influence in the Western World,* ed.W. Stanford Reid (Grand Rapids, Mich.: Zondervan, 1982), pp 13-29.

[3]*Cyclopedia of Education,* ed. Paul Monroe (New York: Macmillan, 1911), s.v. "Calvinists and Education" by Herbert D. Foster, 1:491.

[4]Foster, pp 494, 495.

[5]Albert Hyma, *Albertus C. Van Raalte and His Dutch Settlements in the United States* (Grand Rapids, Mich.: Eerdmans, 1947), pp. 13-18. See also Gordon J. Spykman, *Pioneer Preacher: Albertus Christian Van Raalte* (Grand Rapids, Mich. Calvin College and Seminary Library, 1976), pp. 13, 121

[6]George Stob, *The Christian Reformed Church and Her Schools* (Ann Arbor, Mich.: University Microfilms, 1974), pp. 23-24.

[7]John H. Bratt, "Dutch Calvinism in America," in Reid, *op.cit.,.* pp. 297-98. See also John H. Bratt, "The Christian Reformed Church in American Culture," *Reformed Journal* 3 (Jan. 1963): 4.

[8]One reason for the poverty of the Seceders was the complete lack of government financial aid for ministers' salaries, for the building of churches, or for the needs of the poor—since the "separated ones" had cut themselves off from state church support. See Marian M. Schoolland, *Die Kolonie* (Grand Rapids, Mich.: Christian Reformed Church, 1974), pp. 89-93 for these and other forms of harassment.

[9]Herbert J. Brinks, "The Origins of Christian Education in the Christian Reformed Church" (unpublished paper, Heritage Hall, Calvin College, n.d.) pp. 2-3.

[10]A. Brummelkamp and A. C. Van Raalte, "Appeal to the Faithful in the United States in North America May 25, 1846,— in Henry S. Lucas, *Dutch Immigrant Memoirs and Related Writings* (Assen, Netherlands: Koninklijke Van Gorcum, 1955), 1:17. See also Stob, p. 26. Brinks notes that in the Netherlands not until the

1850s were the Seceders able to establish Christian schools as an alternative to the "neutral" state schools. See p. 3.

[11]Brummelkamp and Van Raalte, p. 17.

[12]Stob, p. 32. The precise economic status of those who settled in or near Holland, Michigan, between 1847 and 1850 is difficult to assess. For insights into these and other considerations, see Robert P. Swierenga and Harry S. Stout, "Dutch Immigration in the Nineteenth Century, 1820-1877: A Quantitative Overview," *Indiana Social Studies Quarterly* 28 (Autumn 1975): 7-34.

[13]See a letter from A. C. Van Raalte to G. Groen Van Prinsterer, Sept. 21, 1946. Regarding incentives for emigration, Van Raalte wrote: "And the needs of my family and especially the need of school instruction give me, besides other urgent reasons, keen incentive for this." In Lucas, *Dutch Immigrant Memoirs* 1:22.

[14]Stob, pp. 37, 38.

[15]Kuyper was for forty years head of the Anti-Revolutionary political party, a member of the national legislature, and for four years prime minister of the Netherlands; author of works in theology, politics, education, science, philosophy; editor of a political daily and religious weekly newspaper; cofounder of and professor at the Free University in Amsterdam; advocate of Christian elementary schools and the Christian labor movement, and much more. See James D. Bratt, *Dutch Calvinism in Modern America: The History of a Conservative Subculture* (Ann Arbor, Mich.: University Microfilms, 1978), pp. 27-71. See also Frank Vanden Berg, *Abraham Kuyper* (Grand Rapids, Mich.: Eerdmans, 1960).

[16]James Bratt, p. 27.

[17]A. Kuyper, *Souvereinitiet in Eigen Kring* (Amsterdam: J. H. Kruyt, 1880), as cited in Stob, pp. 117-18.

[18]James Bratt, p. 33. See also Kuyper, *Souvereinitiet, p.* 35: ". . . there is not a single inch on the whole terrain of our human existence over which Christ . . . does not exclaim, 'Mine'!" as cited in James Bratt, p. 33.

[19]James Bratt, p. 27.

[20]Donald Oppewal, *The Roots* of *the Calvinistic Day School Movement* (Grand Rapids, Mich.: Calvin College Monograph Series, 1963), p. 13. See also Henry S. Lucas, *Netherlanders in America* (Ann Arbor, Mich.: University of Michigan Press, 1955), p. 602: "Kuyper's influence was powerful . . . especially in the Christian Reformed Church... The Dutch immigrant's ... 'Christian schools' ... may be regarded as his most striking contribution to the field of education."

[21]Stob, pp. 65-66: "[Van Raalte] conceived the idea of a Christian academy . . . laid it as a challenge on ... his people, and begged the [Dutch Reformed Church] for assistance ... Van Raalte was the chief donor of the grounds...of the academy, and the financial agent for... soliciting... funds . . . and . . . construction of its buildings. This is more remarkable [since] Van Raalte obtained little encouragement" from his own people in western Michigan.

[22]Stob, p. 35.

[23]Stob, pp. 45-49.

[24]Oppewal, p. 16.

[25]Stob, pp. 97, 129. See also *Yearbook of the Christian Reformed Church, 1900.*

[26]*Encyclopedia of Education* (New York: Macmillan and Free Press, 1971), s.v. "Compulsory Attendance" by Peter P. DeBoer, 22:375-80.

[27]Stob, pp. 72-76. In the school of the First Christian Reformed Church in Grand Rapids the curriculum consisted of reading, writing, arithmetic and Psalm singing. The language of instruction was Dutch. The children attended until eight or nine years of age. Thereafter they attended the "English" schools (i.e. public schools). Some of the children who went directly to the public schools went to the First Church school for language instruction during the summer vacation. Neither the first teacher nor his successor was professionally trained. When the first teacher resigned in 1862 to take up farming, his successor was the church janitor who resigned three years later because of inadequate pay.

[28]Stob, p. 116.

[29]Oppewal, p. 17.

[30]Stob, p. 117.

[31]See P.R. Holtman in *De Wachter* (Grand Rapids, Mich.), June 22, 1892; July 4, 1894, as cited by Stob, pp. 119, 121-122.

[32]*Acts of Synod*, 1892, Art. 23, as cited by Stob, p. 120.

[33]See *De Wachter*, July 13, 1892, as cited by Stob, p. 120.

[34]Stob, p. 120.

[35]I.e., the official creeds uniting the Christian Reformed Churches: the Belgic Confession, Heidelberg Catechism, and Canons of Dort.

[36]Though the national Society was formed already in 1892, by 1905 only nine schools out of twenty were society controlled. Three years later, however, out of twenty-seven schools only four were church controlled. See *Yearbook of the Christian Reformed Church (Grand Rapids, Mich.), 1905, 1908.* One school (Kelloggsville) organized as late as 1912 as a church-controlled school became society-controlled in 1924. See Stob, p. 143.

[37]He argued that the church as such was not called to own and operate educational institutions; yet if a congregation thought it in the best interest of the children to maintain a school, such an undertaking would manifest the fellowship of the saints. See Henry Zwaanstra, *Reformed Thought and Experience in the New World* (Kampen, The Netherlands: J. H. Kok, 1973), p. 139.

[38]Zwaanstra, p. 141.

[39]Thought all supporters would not agree with his assessment, George Stob concludes that though the schools have been good for the church, the obverse is not necessarily true. See Stob, p. 461.

[40]Oppewal, p. 25.

[41]In 1955 a society of persons whose church membership is limited to the Christian Reformed Church began Dordt College in northwest Iowa; in 1959 a society of persons whose church membership is not limited to the Christian Reformed Church began Trinity Christian College just outside Chicago.

[42]*De Wachter*, Sept. 19, 1894. Synod's rejection likely reflected, in large measure, the practical consideration that the Theological School was having

sufficient difficulty financially not to risk further diffusion of education effort.

[43]Acts of Synod, 1894, Art. 48. Some who promoted the separation argued, Kuyperian fashion, that it was not the church's calling to operate a liberal arts school; others simply argued that it was unfair to burden the whole church with the cost of educating somebody else's children. See also Stob, p. 223.

[44]Zwaanstra, p. 142; *De Wachter,* Sept. 19, 1894.

[45]Jacob Vanden Bosch, professor of English, noted that the teachers' course at Calvin was the "principal source whence our free Christian schools from the Atlantic to the Pacific do derive their teachers." See *The Banner,* Aug. 24, 1911.

[46]*The Banner* (Grand Rapids, Mich.), Dec. 23, 1920.

[47]See, for example, J. L. Zandstra, "Is Calvin College Sufficient for the Training of Teachers? If Not, What Must be Done?" in *De Calvinist* (Grand Rapids, Mich.), Feb. 28, 1918.

[48]*Minutes, Board of Trustees,* June 9, 1921, Arts. 25, 27, as cited by Stob, p. 140.

[49]Calvin College *Yearbook,* 1922-23, p. 66.

[50]*Banner,* April 19, 1923.

[51]Western Christian High School at Hull, Iowa, was an exception. It continued the practice until 1955 when Dordt College in Sioux Center, Iowa began as a two year college.

[52]Henry Kuiper, "A National Union of Christian Schools is Born," *Christian Home and School,* April, May, and June, 1954.

[53]For a full discussion of the debates over the writing of such an educational creed see the entire issue of *Christian Educators Journal,* April, 1971.

[54]See the entire issue of the March, 1970 fiftieth anniversary issue of *Christian Home and School* for the details.

[55]*Christian Home and School,* March, 1970, p. 7.

[56]Christian Schools International should not be confused with the Association of Christian Schools International (ACSI), a California based organization founded in 1978, and created to bring together a wide variety of Protestants interested in Christian schools.

[57]H. Henry Meeter, *The Basic Ideas of Calvinism* (5th ed.; Grand Rapids, Mich.: Baker, 1975), pp. 32ff. See also the same claim in H. Henry Meeter, *American Calvinism: A Survey* (Grand Rapids, Mich.: Baker, 1956), p. 6.

[58]*Meeter, The Basic Ideas of Calvinism,* ch. 15, "The Sovereignty of the Social Spheres." For a more theological and historical treatment see Gordon Spykman, "Sphere-Sovereignty in Calvin and the Calvinist Tradition," in *Exploring The Heritage of John Calvin* ed. by David Holwerda (Grand Rapids, Mich.: Baker, 1976), pp. 163-208. For application of this view to a rejection of a statist view of educational control, see Rockne McCarthy, and others, *Society State and Schools: A Case For Structural and Confessional Pluralism* (Grand Rapids, Mich.: Eerdmans, 1981).

[59]For one statement of the necessary connection between the doctrine of the covenant and belief in Christian schools see Louis Berkhof, "Covenant of Grace

290   *Voices From the Past: Reformed Educators*

and Christian Education," in *Fundamentals of Christian Education,* ed. by C. Jaarsma (Grand Rapids, Mich.: Eerdmans, 1953), pp. 20-38. See also N. Henry Beversluis, *Toward a Theology of Education* (Grand Rapids, Mich.: Calvin College Occasional Papers, Vol. 1, No. 1, February, 1981), pp. 20ff.

⁶⁰For biblical evidence and the organizational chart see "The Organization of the Parental Christian School", a publication of Christian Schools International, 3350 E. Paris Avenue, S.E., Grand Rapids, Michigan 49508.

⁶¹Louis Berkhof, *Manual of Reformed Doctrine* (Grand Rapids, Mich.: Eerdmans, 1933), pp. 26-27. See especially p. 31 for the idea of mutual interdependence of the two revelations. See also Donald Oppewal, "Toward a Distinctive Curriculum for Christian Education," *Reformed Journal* 7 (Sept. 1957) p. 21ff. for a treatment of the role of general revelation.

⁶²Nicholas Wolterstorff, *Curriculum: By What Standard?* (Grand Rapids, Mich.: Christian Schools International, 1966), p. 14ff.

⁶³For a complete listing of such textbooks and teaching materials see CSI *Publications Catalog* 1982-83, a publication of the Curriculum Department of Christian Schools International, P.O. Box 8709, Grand Rapids, Mich. 49508.

⁶⁴The civics text is *Under God,* by William Hendricks (Grand Rapids, Mich.: National Union of Christian Schools and Eerdmans, 1976), pp. 16-17. For the theological explanation of instances such as these see "Culture in the Christian Life", a section in N. H. Beversluis's *Toward A Theology of Education.*

⁶⁵For health education texts and teaching materials published by CSI see *Respecting God's Temples,* by Henry Triezenberg *et al.,* 1977; *Toward Christian Maturity-K-6: A Curriculum Guide for Teaching Human Sexuality,* by William Hendricks, 1978; *God's Temples* (junior high) by William Hendricks, revised 1982. For technology as a curriculum area see *Using God's World* (grades 4-6) by Theodore De Jong, Gerald Laverman *et al,* 1977. Canadian Calvinists at the Curriculum Development Centre, 229 College Street, Toronto, Canada M5T IR4 have also made a contribution to interdisciplinary teaching materials. Its *Joy in Learning: An Integrated Curriculum for the Elementary School* by Arnold De Graaff and Jean Olthuis, revised in 1975, is an instance, and it has published others under the rubric of Transportation.

⁶⁶Two noteworthy examples of articulation of Calvinist goals are N. Henry Beversluis, *Christian Philosophy of Education* (Grand Rapids, Mich.: National Union of Christian Schools, 1971) and Nicholas Wolterstorff, *Educating for Responsible Action* (Grand Rapids, Mich.: Christian Schools International and Eerdmans, 1981).

⁶⁷Geraldine Steensma and Harro Van Brummelen (eds.), *Shaping School Curriculum: A Biblical View* (Terre Haute, Ind.: Signal, 1977), which stresses integrated curriculum, and Henry Triezenberg *et al, Principles to Practice* (Grand Rapids, Mich.: Christian Schools International, revised 1979), written by teams of curriculum consultants for numerous curriculum areas.

⁶⁸Donald Oppewal, "Parochialism in Christian Schools: Its Perils," *Reformed Journal* 20 (September, 1970): pp. 12-14.

[69]For one instance of the debate see the entire April, 1971 issue of *Christian Educators Journal* in which arguments for an educational creed are presented.

[70]*See Christian Educators Journal,* April, 1971, pp. 20-21 which gives an explanation of the change as well as the complete Basis article.

[71]The 1982 CSI Convention contained a spirited debate over the kind of beliefs undergirding the Calvinist school. A CSI Task Force has distributed widely a document which seeks to identify the present Calvinist consensus, and called "In Their Father's House: A Handbook of Christian Educational Philosophy" (March, 1982).

[72]Donald Oppewal, "Education Vouchers: The Emerging Coalition," *The Reformed Journal, 31* (February, 1981): 18-20. For a more elaborate treatment of funding problems and proposed actions see Rockne McCarthy *et al., Society, State, and Schools.*

[73]While a number of sources allude to this new meaning of integration, one which treats it most consistently is Van Brummelen and Steensma (eds.), *Shaping School Curriculum.* See also Jay Adams, *Back to the Blackboard* (Phillipsburg, N.J.: Presbyterian and Reformed, 1982).

Christian Schools: Anabaptist or Reformist?

By Paul F. Scotchmer from *Christian
Scholar's Review*, Vol. 15, No. 4, 1986.

Several years ago an acquaintance, who teaches ethics and hails from a Plymouth Brethren background, raised the question whether anyone in the Reformed tradition could push Christian schools and remain consistent with the picture of Christ as Transformer of Culture.[1] Having long since shed the social aloofness characteristic of his childhood church, he asked if abandoning public schools was not a dereliction of one's responsibilities to help transform the world.

My friend is right, of course, about the Reformed commitment to the world beyond one's pew; a world not merely of individuals, but also of social institutions in need of Christian concern. Indeed, it might even be shown that the publicness of our public schools has its origins in the Reformation tradition, not least because of the success of the Common-wealth Party, in Tudor times, in securing public support for an enterprise previously run by the church. My friend is also right to acknowledge implicitly that the commitment to be fully within the world, transforming as one can what lies beyond one's own Christian community, is not a mark of every Protestant tradition. Anabaptists, in particular, are noted for their portrayal of Christ Against Culture.

What cannot be assumed, however, is that public education is still viable as an institutional agent of social transformation, or is still itself subject to transformation, along Christian lines. Nor, on the other hand, should it be supposed that all Christian schools are incapable of serving as agents of social reform within contemporary society. These two assumptions lie at the heart of this essay.

To satisfy my ethicist friend, it must simply be shown that Christian schools can be justified from a Reformed perspective. But I propose to up the ante. I wish to explore whether there is any alternative to Christian schools, from a Reformed perspective; and if not, what type of Christian schools should they be? I begin by proposing that Christian education in the Protestant tradition can be traced to two basic models. Both were launched in the sixteenth century, one by the Anabaptists, the other by what I have subsumed under the term Reformists. In the pages which follow, the educational aims of each will be brought to bear upon three questions: (1) What does each of these models of nascent Protestantism say about the idea of Christian schools? (2) What are the implications for contemporary public schools? And (3) What does historic Protestantism suggest about the necessity and nature of Christian schools today? Under each question consideration will be given to the constituents, the curriculum, and school control .

Parenthetically, two observations must be made about terms used in this essay. First, the term "Christian schools" has come to be associated with Protestant Fundamentalism. The likely reason is the proliferation of schools founded by fundamentalist groups and churches, often with no denominational ties. These schools cannot be called Catholic, Lutheran, Reformed, etc., so they are simply called Christian. For present purposes, however, the term Christian schools will be understood more broadly. Included are all schools—old and new, Protestant and Catholic, independent and affiliated—which have been established and are currently operated with the intent to provide Christian education.

Secondly, the terms Anabaptist and Reformist, when applied to contemporary groups, have less to do with ecclesiastical lineage than with opposing attitudes toward the relationship between Christianity and culture. As our myriad denominations have unfolded since the Reformation, theological lines of demarcation have become blurred. Nonetheless, both separatist and transformationist tendencies seen at the time of the Reformation remain very much alive.

The Reformation and the Idea of Christian Schools

Sixteenth-century Anabaptists were not especially enamored of the idea of school at all; but insofar as they did support schools, they most certainly favored Christian schools. Like other Anabaptist social ideas, their educational ideas revert back to the doctrine of separation *(Absonderung)*. As worded by the Schleitheim Confession (1526), "all creatures are in but two classes, good and bad, believing and unbelieving, darkness and light, the world and those who [have come] out of the world, God's temple and idols, Christ and Belial; and *none can have part with the other.*[2] Among the things to be avoided were "all popish and antipopish works and church services, meetings and church attendance [in the established churches], drinking houses, civic affairs," holding public office, soldiering, and swearing oaths (for legal or other purposes).[3] In brief, separatism was the touchstone of Anabaptist social thought. There was a palpable sense of "over-againstness" toward the rest of society. Theirs was a society set apart. Communion with other religious groups was impossible; subjection to civil authorities was unnecessary.

Educationally, the Anabaptist principle of separation took three forms. The first and most obvious is that youngsters from homes of true believers were to be kept separate from other children. The importance of this conviction is seen in the catechism of Martin Czechowic (1575), a pastor of the Polish Brethren. In accordance with the community's pacifism, children were enjoined against going onto a battlefield or striking a blow. But the instruction went beyond pacifism. When the catechumen asked if it is also wrong to go onto a battlefield when commanded by the king, even if one does not strike others, the answer was clear: that, too, is wrong. The reason given: one may not be yoked together with unbelievers (2 Cor. 6:14).[4] The transparent lesson to be drawn from this example and the general doctrine of separation is that anything but a Christian school, limited to like-minded pupils, was out of the question.

Not so for the Reformists. We include under this term all Protestants who sought reformation of the old social and theological order, rather than separation. Lutherans and Calvinists are both included, later to be joined by the Dutch Reformed, French Huguenots, English and American Puritans, and Scotch Presbyterians. Sometimes called "magisterial reformers," the early leaders favored a cooperative relationship between church and state. And nowhere, perhaps, is this spirit of cooperation more apparent than in their approach to education.

Martin Luther, whose views on education are prototypical of the entire Reformist tradition, agreed with the Anabaptists in one respect, but only one. He agreed that religion must be at the center. "See to it, that you cause your children first to be instructed in spiritual things—that you point them first to God, and, after that, to the world," he admonished. "In these days, this order, sad to say, is inverted." These words were directed toward parents, but the same priorities were applied to teachers, who act as surrogate parents: "'We had hoped that schoolmasters would remedy this evil," lamented the Reformer, "that in school, at least, children would learn something good, and there have the fear of God implanted in their hearts. But this hope, too, has come to nought." And the cost of failure is great: "This is one reason why Christianity is fallen. For all its hopes and strength and potency are ever commited to the generation that is neglected in its youth, it fares with Christianity as with a garden that is neglected in the springtime."[5]

It was not until several years after these words that the Peasants' Revolt drove a wedge between Luther and the Anabaptists. But even before this event, we descry a crucial difference between the two. "Point them first to God," said Luther, "and, after that, to the world." The Anabaptists left off the second half. They did so in practice by segregating their children from those who remained in the world. Luther, as we see in this broadside against monastic education, rejected the hothouse environment favored by monks and Anabaptists alike:

> Solomon was a right royal schoolmaster. He does not forbid children from mingling with the world, or from enjoying themselves, as the monks do their scholars; for they will thus become mere clods and blockheads, as Anselm likewise perceived. Said this one: "A young man, thus hedged about and cut off from society, is like a young tree, whose nature it is to grow and bear fruit, planted in a small and narrow pot." For the monks have imprisoned the youth whom they have had in their charge, as men put birds in dark cages, so that they could neither see nor converse with any one. But it is dangerous for youth to be thus alone, thus debarred from social intercourse. Wherefore, we ought to permit young people to see, and hear, and know what is taking place around them in the world... [6]

A second type of separation applies to the substance of Anabaptist education. The aim was almost entirely salvific, the subject matter substantially religious. If a child could read and write, had been instructed in the standards of the faith (the Ten Commandments, the Twelve Articles, and the catechism), and had acquired a practical skill (farming or sewing, usually), that was enough. Instruction in the arts and letters, and of course all higher education, was unnecessary; indeed, it was dangerous. If religious guidance beyond Scripture was required, it was to come from the Holy Spirit, not from scholars corrupted by pagan literature. In political matters, the Sermon on the Mount was deemed no less sufficient for a community of true believers than for the individual Christian. Further instruction was superfluous. In short, religious subject matter was separated from the larger world of learning, the former to be mastered at an early age, the latter to be spurned by all.

Luther, on the other hand, spurned nothing as a possible source of wisdom, save the Anabaptists. Luther was no Humanist, but he was every bit as committed to the Renaissance tools as the best of the Humanists. He especially valued the study of languages; not for their own sake, but for the sake of the Gospel. Indeed, "we will not long preserve the gospel without the languages," wrote the Reformer in a letter to the councilmen of the German cities. "The languages are the sheath in which this sword of the Spirit [Eph. 6:17] is contained, they are the casket in which this jewel is enshrined; they are the vessel in which this wine is held; they are the larder in which this food is stored...."[7] Alongside Greek, Hebrew, and Latin, Luther would include in his ideal curriculum: Aesop's Fables, selected Latin literature and plays, rhetoric, dialectics, mathematics, astronomy, ethics, theology, and history.[8] The aim of all such studies he reduced to a single phrase: "A happy Christian social order in respect to both body and soul . "[9]

Calvin, no less than Luther, affirmed the universality of knowledge regarding earthly things; namely, those things which "have some connection with the present life, and are in a manner confined within its boundaries." Included are matters of public policy and economics, the mechanical arts, and liberal studies. Man is by nature a social animal, says Calvin, in good Aristotelian fashion. He is disposed by nature to cherish and preserve society. Likewise, the writings of the ancients on mathematics, medicine, rhetoric, and natural philosophy deserve our highest admiration. "If we reflect that the Spirit of God is the only fountain of truth, we will be careful, as we would avoid offering insult to him, not to reject or contemn truth wherever it appears. In despising the gifts, we insult the Creator. "[10]

The third type of separation found in Anabaptist communities was of parents and children. Nowhere was this more extreme than among the Hutterites. From birth, everything possible was done to underscore the priority of community over family. Women in labor were put into a common room; newly born babies were cared for by widows in another room; and children were placed in boarding schools from the age of two or three. Even such things are gifts for children and visits between parents and their children were subject to strict regulations.[11]

The important point to be observed about this third type of separation is the attempt to protect the community of true believers at all costs. Not every Anabaptist fellowship went to such lengths as the Hutterites, but all were agreed on the sacred status of the community of saints. The way into the community, for those willing to consent to its discipline, was the sign of baptism. The way out, for those guilty of heinous or obstinate violations of community rules, was the ban. The hope was that the sinner would repent of his worldly ways.

Luther also felt justified in circumscribing the rights of the family in respect to education. No more than the Separatists was he willing to allow the individual family to jeopardize the welfare of the wider circle. The difference lies in the radius of that circle. *For the Anabaptists, education was directed toward the preservation of Christian community, narrowly defined; for Luther, education was directed toward the reformation of Christian culture.*

It was on behalf of Christian culture that Luther felt obliged in 1527 to ask the Elector of Saxony to organize ecclesiastical visitations in his territory. During the next two years, Luther joined other pastors in making a survey of church and school conditions. He was shocked by the widespread ignorance and outraged by the indifference of parents toward the educational needs of civil government and the Christian church. It was shortly thereafter, in 1529, that he penned his shorter and larger cat- echisms, for use as textbooks by all children and ignorant adults. But that was just the first step toward educational reform.

In 1530, Luther wrote a powerful treatise on education. It came in the form of a sermon on the duty of sending children to school.[12] Like an encyclical, the sermon was sent to pastors, for delivery to the people. Its purpose was to redress an abuse which had arisen out of the Reformation itself. People had stopped sending their children to school, assuming that Christians were sufficiently enlightened by the Scriptures. But it was the Devil, not God, who promoted this idea, charged the Reformer. For it was in the Devil's interest to produce a nation of irrational brutes. Christian culture requires educated leaders in both the spiritual and temporal realms.

Luther reminded his fledgling church that civil government is a divine ordinance. And it is a service rendered to God to maintain this ordinance by nurturing wise and judicious leaders. "A pious jurist and true scholar can be called, in the worldly kingdom of the emperor, a prophet, priest, angel, and savior." As a result of their work, "you have peace and tranquility for your wife, daughter, son, house and home, servants, money, property, lands, and everything that you have. For all of this is compre- hended in, encompassed by, and hedged about with law. What a great thing this is can never be fully told in any book; for who can adequately describe what an unspeakable blessing peace is, and how much it both gives and saves even in a single year?"[13]

To counteract parental neglect of their children's education, Luther maintained that "it is the duty of the temporal authority to compel its subjects to keep their children in school.... For it is truly the duty of government to maintain the offices and estates that have been mentioned, so that there will always be preachers, jurists, pastors, writers, physicians, schoolmasters, and the like, for we cannot do without them." [14]

The instrument used to ensure that children got properly educated was the school ordinance *(Schulordnung)*. This was usually embodied within the church ordinances *(Kirchenordnungen)* drafted for individual towns or principalities subsequent to the ecclesiastical visitations. With this measure, the state became formally involved, alongside the church, in the education of German youth.

It was not long thereafter that the same basic model was applied in Strasbourg under the leadership of Bucer and Sturm; in Geneva, under Calvin and Beza; and in Tudor England, under the impetus of the Commonwealth Party during the reigns of Edward VI and Elizabeth I. In each case, Reformist preachers obtained the support of civil government for the establishment of new schools. The aim was everywhere the same: to provide Christian learning for the mutual benefit of all members of society. [15]

The Reformation and the Public School

As we look back on the educational ideas of the early Reformers, we discover the origins of several features of modern public education. First, unlike Anabaptist and monastic schools, the schools founded by the "magisterial reformers" were common schools. That is, they were open for all members of society, not just for those with a religious calling or for members of a community of saints. The Reformers believed that a Christian education was needed by all. At the very least, this meant literacy for all, so that the catechism could be mastered and the Scriptures studied. But it also meant giving every child a chance to display his talents, so that these could be cultivated for the benefit of all members of the nation or commonwealth.

Secondly, it was understood that one's talents were best cultivated through a liberal education. The Reformist curriculum rests squarely upon Luther's doctrine of vocation. "Every occupation has its own honor before God, as well as its own requirements and duties," wrote Luther in his Sermon on Keeping Children in School. [16] From there, he went on to show the spiritual and social value of several callings. Whereas Anabaptist education assumed an agrarian lifestyle within a confined community, the Reformers assumed a diversity of callings within an increasingly urban and complex society. Physicians, scholars, jurists, teachers, preachers—all had their place in "a happy Christian social order." And all must be equipped with the accumulated wisdom of the ages.

A third feature of Reformist education shared by modern public schools is involvement by the state. As previously indicated, Luther's justification was that civil government, as an institution ordained by God, had the responsibility to compensate for parental unwillingness or inability to meet their children's educational needs.

Having noted these areas of agreement between early Protestant and contemporary public education, it is equally important to note their differences. Only then will we be able to consider the need for Christian schools today, from a Reformation perspective.

On the matter of school control, Protestantism represents a *via media* between the virtual monopolization of education by the medieval church and the eventual monopolization of education by the modern state. A *via media,* not a bridge. Certainly it was never intended by the Reformers or their like-minded successors that education should be taken over by the state. What the Reformists started, and managed to preserve for a very long time, was a cooperative relationship with the state. Their intent was really quite in line with medieval political theory, whereby temporal authorities would supply the physical means to implement the spiritual ideals defined by the church. Accordingly, the reformed state was empowered to do what it could to ensure that the educational experience outlined by the Reformers was made universal. This basic model was maintained in America until the middle of the nineteenth century. It was at this time, starting in Massachusetts and New York, that individual states began to restrict tax monies to government-run schools.[17]

The demise of religious control was not immediately followed by the dismissal of religion from the public school curriculum. Although advertised as "nonsectarian," the public schools of the Nationalist Era were by no means religiously neutral.[18] Catholic Americans, knowing this all too well, were forced to maintain their own schools. The alternative was to lose their ethnic and religious identity.

Over the decades since that time, the "public theology" of American culture has changed; and with it, the ideological thrust of the public school curriculum.[19] The moralistic "Protestantism" of McGuffey, which prevailed in the nineteenth century, was eclipsed in the twentieth by the philosophical pragmatism of Dewey. When the Supreme Court issued its controversial prayer decisions in the early 1960s, it was no more than the detritus of past Protestantism that was removed from the public schools.[20] It is in this light that the recrudescence of Christian schools, now privately supported, must be seen.

In both the Anabaptist and Reformist traditions, the record is plain that the home, the school, and the church must work hand-in-hand toward the cultivation of Christian souls. And this raises a serious challenge to the viability of public education today. To defend contemporary public education before a Protestant tribunal, it would be necessary, at the very least, to include it among those things categorized by Luther and Calvin as *adiaphora*—indifferent things. More precisely, it would have to be demonstrated that public education is (a) religiously neutral and (b) an enterprise which in no way jeopardizes the aims of the Christian home and Christian church. If this cannot be done, the necessity of Christian schools is beyond question. And even this test would not satisfy the Anabaptists, who refused to be yoked under any circumstances with the children of Belial.

A proper comparison of the educational aims of contemporary public schools and historic Protestantism would be too much of a detour for inclusion here. The best that can be offered presently is a few questions about religious neutrality. First, if it is contended that public education is religiously neutral, what definition of religion underlies the contention? The notion of religious neutrality rests upon the assumption that religion is made up entirely of such externalities as cultus and clergy, which operate between the devotee and God. By this view, schools are religiously neutral if they avoid all clerical presence and cultic practices, such as school prayer, devotional readings of Scriptures, religious songs (excepting perhaps Christmas carols because of their "cultural significance"), and all textbooks and other reading materials adulterated by revealed truths.

This familiar definition of religious neutrality is seriously flawed by its failure to address the possibility of religion disguised as mere rationality. This raises a second question: If it is argued that public education is religiously neutral, on what basis are its aims and priorities determined? Many fundamentalist Protestants have a ready answer to this question: "secular humanism." But the term is an endorsement of the secularist's assumption that the "secular" can be distinguished from the "sacred." Realistically, can educational aims and priorities be determined without being grounded in some set of "ultimate concerns" (Tillich), or protected by a "sacred canopy" (Berger), or conformed to a "paradigm" (Kuhn), or patterned after a "symbol system" (Geertz)? If not, is the secularist's approach to determining educational aims and priorities any less religious, all appearances aside, than the approach taken by religions such as Christianity that wear no disguise?

Finally, if the apologist for public education argues that there is no basis for determining educational aims and priorities, what safeguard is there against educational relativism—an educational system without any philosophical point of reference whatsoever? If there are safeguards (a point of reference), it would seem that we are dealing with something other than religious and philosophical neutrality. If there are no safeguards, then neutrality must be synonymous with relativism. In either case, there is a fundamental incompatibility between the educational principles of historic Protestantism and the *modus operandi* of the public schools. In short, from the perspective of historic Protestantism, whether Anabaptist or Reformist, public schools are not viable and the need for Christian schools is imperative.

The Reformation and Today's Christian Schools

As for the nature of Christian schools, there will no doubt remain differences akin to those found in the sixteenth century. And even though we label them Anabaptist or Reformist, the staying power of these different approaches to Christian education can be attributed to the even more ancient and perpetual tensions within the Christian Church regarding relations with the world at large. Very briefly, let us return to the three focal points of our inquiry: the clients, the curriculum, and school control.

Some Christian schools insist upon a religious purity of clients redolent of sixteenth-century Anabaptism. This is most likely to be seen in schools run by more fundamentalist groups. Even when there is no overt religious discrimination, there are generally no efforts to welcome youngsters from outside the fundamentalist subculture. In contrast, schools consciously affiliated with the Reformist tradition must actively welcome all comers, regardless of religious orientation of pupils and their families. Here, school is not so much a shelter from the winds of secularism as a nursery for the cultivation of Christian citizens.

An outstanding example of a school fitting the Reformist description is Risen Christ Lutheran School in Brooklyn; or more precisely, in Brownsville, a once fashionable but now forsaken neighborhood in the bowels of Brooklyn. As poverty, ruin, and despair go, the community is now rivalled only by the infamous South Bronx. But amidst the rubble, there is a bright spot of hope. It is a school that works, despite the sociologists' axiom that schools have not learned how to overcome the disadvantages of a child's home life. Somehow, the staff at Risen Christ (on a salary of substantially less than $10,000 a year) have learned to beat the odds. While public school in District 23 are among the worst in the City of New York, with reading and math scores well below the national average, the vast majority of pupils at Risen Christ are performing on grade level. Nor is there any selection procedure used to ensure results. In fact, parents usually enroll their children at the school because they are failing in public schools. Most of the pupils who transfer in are two or three years behind. By the end of their first year, most transfer pupils are at grade level.

Unlike the vast majority of urban parochial schools, Risen Christ is not a relic of better times (before the blacks and Puerto Ricans moved in), now forced to make the best of things or join the exodus of white ethnic groups. Risen Christ was begun after the exodus, precisely to help meet the obvious needs of that neighborhood. It was begun with the convictions that Christ does His greatest work where the needs are greatest.

Secondly, some Christian schools are demonstrably afraid of liberal learning. Out of fear, they are unwilling to introduce their young charges to ideas that run the risk of being inconsistent with Christian faith. Oftentimes the standards of selection are superficial. Books with crude language or depictions of immoral behavior are banned, regardless of the author's intent and the value of the work. Portions of the Bible itself must be disallowed by this standard, along with innumerable scientific materials excluded because they are at odds with a hyperliteralistic interpretation of the biblical account of Creation. Ironically, this same parochialism rules out much of the latest scientific research on quantum mechanics and the "Big Bang" theory, which are now causing physicists to reconsider the scientific community's own parochialism in opposition to Creation.

In contrast, Christians within the Reformist tradition must bring their faith into dialogue with a free market of ideas from every quarter. Anything less is inconsistent with what Catholics know as natural law and what Calvinists call "common grace." Such openness does not rule out the need to make sensitive choices among the countless materials competing for our children's time. Nor does it rule out sensitivity toward the timing of a child's exposure to one thing or another. Nonetheless, to insist that materials be of, by, and for the members of one's own tribe is a kind of spiritual blindness, which fails to see the preservative hand of God at work in His world today.

Thirdly, some Christian schools insist upon total control by the church or by families who maintain the school. The American Law Association, whose attorneys have defended numerous fundamentalist schools, argues that Christian schools must be as free from government regulation as the church.[21] Even fire, health, and safety codes which exceed those applied to churches are rejected; and certainly all educational requirements, however minimal. In contrast, the Reformist educator will acknowledge the state's legitimate interest in the educational welfare of children and young people. Generally, there is simply an insistence that the state also respect the church's legitimate interests. Among these interests is the right not to be harassed by unreasonable regulations which offer no real benefits for the schoolchildren themselves. Another is the right to a share of tax revenues collected by the state for educational purposes.

Many fundamentalists oppose government aid, fearing that it would be attended by government control of their schools. This is consistent with the Anabaptist tradition, provided that the rejection of aid is strictly voluntary. What is not consistent with the Anabaptist tradition is opposition to government aid, even for those who desire it, on alleged Constitutional grounds. This tack is taken, for example, by the Baptist Joint Committee on Public Affairs. It has nothing in common with the reasoning of Menno Simons, Roger Williams, and other spokesmen for the Anabaptist tradition. Anabaptist separation from wider society is strictly voluntary, a tenet of their faith. The idea that Christian schools should be denied public aid on grounds of "church-state separation" is a tenet of secularism .

Educators within the Reformist tradition have every reason to expect government support for patrons of their schools, equal to what is enjoyed by public schools. Obviously, modern educators, unlike Luther and Calvin, must operate within the strictures of a pluralistic society. Accordingly, they can no longer expect the state to provide benefits not extended to other religious groups, whether Anabaptist or secularist. But in a society which bans piety from the classroom, yet prides itself on religious tolerance, those in the tradition of sixteenth-century Reformists have every reason to expect government support of their schools. There is nothing in the nature of pluralism, nothing in a strict reading of the Constitution, and nothing in the Reformist tradition which justifies discrimination against those who prefer Christian schools to public schools.

We return now to the question asked by the ethicist who opened this discussion. The question was whether anyone in the Reformed tradition could push Christian schools and remain consistent with the picture of Christ as Transformer of Culture. The answer is that Christian schools are the only real hope, so far as formal education is concerned, for transforming society along Christian lines. But it is essential that these schools be committed to the idea of reform. They must be open to the general population, embrace the idea of liberal learning, and be willing to work cooperatively with the state toward minimal educational standards and an equitable structure of school finance. Objection to such guidelines indicates an unwillingness to be engaged with one's culture in the area of education.

This line of argument might still be resisted on grounds that Christian schools, no matter what their intentions, are pockets of isolation within a much more diverse society, and that only by participation in public education can we truly be engaged with our culture. There are at least two problems with this objection. One is the implicit suggestion that the only worthwhile engagement with our culture takes place between individuals. Thus we have the picture of little Johnnie Christian going into his local school like Daniel into the lion's den. If that is what we mean by engagement, we might as well be talking about the nearest shopping mall or the remotest Gulag. The whole idea of schools is that the institution might have some positive effect upon the individual.

Besides the implicit individualism of this objection, there is also an all too facile acceptance of the status quo. Christian schools do not need to be isolated pockets. They can be, and in some cases are, as diverse as the population at large. And at present, there is probably nothing that discourages broader public interest in Christian schools so much as the existing structure of school finance. Who but the "true believers"—or those repelled by conditions in their local public schools—have the incentive to purchase a private education after paying taxes for public schools?

Obviously, the charge that Christian schools are too isolated from society to help transform it takes us beyond the reach of Reformation ideas. We are brought up against the hard realities of American politics, past and present. For it is politics, fully as much as religion, that has established the character of today's Christian schools. As a result, the prospect of transforming society through Christian schools is contingent upon the achievement of educational choice through the political process.

Notes

[1]H. Richard Niebuhr includes the Reformed tradition in his chapter on"Christ the Transformer of Culture"; see *Christ and Culture* (New York: Harper & Row, 1951).

[2]Schleitheim Confession, Article 4; emphasis mine.

[3]Ibid.

[4]G.H. Williams, *The Radical Reformation* (Philadelphia: Westminster Press, 1962), p. 747f.

[5]Frederick Eby, *Early Protestant Educators* (New York and London: McGraw-Hill, 1931), p. 24f.; original in Georg Walch, *Luther's samtlich Schriften*, vol. 3, pp. 1817-1825).

[6]Ibid., p. 21.

[7]*Luther's Works*, Jaroslav Pelikan and Helmut T. Lehmann, eds., 55 vols.; vol. 45: *The Christian in Society*, Walter Brandt, ed. (Philadelphia: Muhlenberg Press, 1962), p. 360.

[8]Eby, *Early Protestant Educators*, p. 162f.

[9]Letter to Councilmen, in Eby, *Early Protestant Educators*, p. 79.

[10]Calvin, *Institutes*, Book II, ch. 2, sections 12-17; Beveridge trans.

[11]Clause-Peter Clasen, *Anabaptism: A Social History, 1525-1618* (Ithaca: Cornell University Press, 1972), pp. 266-271.

[12]*Luther's Works*, eds. Pelikan and Lehmann, v. 46, pp. 207-258.

[13]Ibid., p. 240. In our own day, the beneficent side of government has been expatiated by George Will, *Statecraft as Soulcraft* (New York: Simon and Schuster, 1983).

[14]*Luther's Works*, eds. Pelikan and Lehmann, eds., v. 46, p. 256.

[15]See Miriam Usher Chrisman, *Strasbourg and the Reform* (New Haven: Yale, 1967); Ernst-Wilhelm Kahls, *Die Schule bei Martin Bucer in ihrem Verhältnis zu Kirche und Obrigkeit* (Heidelberg, 1963); Charles Borgeaud, *Histoire de l'Universite de Geneve* (Geneva, 1900); and Joan Simon, *Education and Society in Tudor England* (Cambridge: The University Press, 1966).

The educational impact or English Puritans has been statistically documented by W. K. Jordan. Comparing the seven decades before and after 1550, when Puritanism emerged as a political and ecclesiastical force in England, we find a fivefold increase in charitable contributions for grammar schools, mostly from the pockets of Puritan mer-chants. By the time of the Restoration, there were approximately 500 grammar schools in the ten counties studied by Jordan, compared to 34 in 1480. This is but a small fragment of the story unfolded by Jordan's remarkable research; see *Philanthropy in England, 1480-1660* (New York: Russell Sage Foundation, 1964).

[16]*Luther's Works*, Pelikan and Lehmann, eds., v. 46, p. 246.

[17]See Diane Ravitch, *The Great School Wars* (New York: Basic Books, 1974).

[18]See Paul F. Scotchmer, "The Aims of American Education: A Review from Colonial Times to the Present," *Christian Scholar's Review* XIII:2 (1984): 99-119.

[19]Ibid.

[20]*Engel v. Vitale*, 370 US 421 (1962) disallowed use of a prayer composed by the New York Board of Regents; *Abington School District v. Schempp*, 374 US 203 (1963) ruled that devotional Bible reading and recitation of the Lord's Prayer were unconstitutional.

[21]See the news story by Tom Minnery, "Does David Gibbs Practice Law as well as He Preaches Church-State Separation?", *Christianity Today* (April 10, 1981): 48-51.

Donald Oppewal:
Editor Introduction

Donald Oppewal retired in 1991 from the Education Department at Calvin College. For thirty years he taught in both undergraduate and graduate programs in philosophy of education and in curriculum theory. During this career he was for twelve years Managing Editor of the *Christian Educators Journal,* which he helped found in 1964. He published extensively both editorials and articles in it, as well as several in the *Reformed Journal.* He contributed chapters in books on religious schooling in America, one of which is reprinted in this volume, called "American Calvinist Day Schools" as it appeared in *Christian Scholars Review.*

Two major separate publications were part of the Calvin Monograph Series. His first in 1963 was *Roots of the Calvinistic Day School Movement,* an intellectual and cultural history of Reformed schooling.

The following is his most recent (1985), and represents his most significant contribution to a theory of knowing that entails a curriculum and teaching methodology appropriate to Reformed schooling. Having just gone out of print, it is included here to represent recent and continuing growth in the body of literature on Christian schools available to those interested

Biblical Knowing and Teaching

by Donald Oppewal, a Calvin College
Monograph, 1985

Introduction

This monograph addresses professional educators who wish consciously to relate educational decisions to a biblical world view. It is not
a survey of all of the linkages that could be made between Christian belief
and educational policy. It will focus mainly on two matters: a theory of
knowing and a classroom methodology which is compatible with it. A
general conception of how one comes to know anything, called by
technical philosophy an epistemological method, will be linked with a
general strategy for classroom teaching, called methodology, one which is
a single generic strategy rather than a set of pedagogical moves suggested
by 'methods of teaching'.

The treatment of epistemology will not be as extensive or thorough as
philosophers might wish, since it is not addressed to philosophers. The
treatment of classroom method is not as detailed as some educators might
wish because it will result in a theory of methodology rather than a set of
specific methods of instruction. It should, however, enable the classroom
teacher to select from a vast repertoire of 'methods' those which are most
congruent with the generic methodology offered.

Since not all epistemological topics or questions are directly related to
classroom instructional methods, the method of acquiring knowledge will
be emphasized, and this discussion will deal less with how philosophers
determine the validity of given beliefs than with constructing a biblically
grounded understanding of how we come to know anything (a rock, a
person, God), and its instructional counterpart.

For fully fifty years Reformed thinkers, such as educational philosophers and others, ably assisted by biblical scholars, have developed a

rationale for the existence of the Calvinist school movement. They have turned to various facets of theology for help in providing directions for the Christian educational enterprise, for lower, secondary, and higher education.

Biblical doctrines like covenant, cultural mandate, and Kingdom, to name just a few, have sprinkled the pages of many a popular article and serious essay. While these have been helpful in supporting the need for distinctly Reformed education, they have only weakly spelled out what specific policies and programs characterize such schools. For example, the doctrine of the covenant, peculiar in language at least to Reformed thinking, has been used chiefly to establish the case that in the biblical view the parent community, and not the institutionalized church or the political state, is the proper locus of educational authority. This has led those committed to such beliefs to reject the public school governance model as well as the parochial school model. Such schools are then distinctive because they turn the direction of the educational enterprise over to a citizen-parent group rather than to the church or civil government.

However, this use of the covenant doctrine does not yet speak to distinctiveness in the goals of such schools, or in their curriculum, and much less in their teaching method or classroom management models. Some attempts to use the doctrine to identify goals have given some help in identifying the goal as one that includes the affirmation of culture.[1]

In addition to the biblical doctrines noted above, one that has helped shape more specific directions for educational distinctiveness is the doctrine of human nature, a biblical anthropology. Numerous writers have argued that the biblical vision of the human being is that of holism. While this is not the only view present among Reformed thinkers,[2] most educators have adopted a holistic view for their educational thinking.[3]

This literature on education developed particularly in the last decade is replete with evidence that the Bible reflects a view of man which opposes all dualisms, particularly when such dualisms identify higher and lower elements, with the location of the image of God in one element but not in the other. An early proponent of this holistic view is Cornelius Jaarsma, who adopted the term "organic unity" to capture his view. By it he meant that the image of God resides in man by virtue of his being, unlike all other creatures, a "self-conscious center of all experience."[4] He held that the self, while able to be analyzed into functions or components (like mental and physical or psychic and physiological), could not be dealt with in schools through any one component without destroying such organic unity.

A group of scholars and theologians, supported with careful biblical exegesis, have articulated what they call "a holistic view of man." As they see it:

Man is one, a centered unity dependent upon God and responsible to Him. The basic terms for man used in Scriptures do not indicate parts of man, the sum of which is man as a total creature. Rather each of the basic terms refers to the whole of man from a specific point of view. The difference is of far-reaching impact: between man as a whole functioning in various relations and man as composite of different elements in which the lower "bodily" parts are related to the higher rational-moral or "soul" parts.[5]

Other sources contain more tentative judgments. A cautious view speaks in the language of not-only-but-also. N. Wolterstorff, as an example, puts it thus:

> The Christian life is not the life of a pure spiritual soul which happens, for some God-alone-known reason, to be attached to a body. It is not the life of a mind, a rational-moral principle, which happens to be imprisoned in a chunk of flesh. Rather it is the life of a creature who is soul and body, inner man and outer man, a conscious personal being and a biological being.[6]

Attributing the rejected view to residual Platonism in Christian thought, he holds such view to be "at almost every juncture, an anti-Biblical conception," and offers instead to underscore the difference, that "We are, on the contrary, physical and biological creatures who are at the same time conscious, personal creatures."[7]

The sources given above explicitly reject the notion of a hierarchy of functions within the person, and hold that the totality must be redeemed. All conclude that it is the whole man which must be educated. Each gives its own version of the Biblical case for such a position. Numerous other sources indicate that this is a widely argued position on anthropology and its implication for Reformed schooling.[8]

Reformed literature contains little that carries this anthropology into the arena of epistemology and knowing. Even less has been written about teaching methodology as it might relate to such a view of knowing. This has left classroom methodology as an independent variable in the beliefs about the school, and has encouraged the perception that methodology is but a grab bag of motivational devices and techniques for teaching specific kinds of lessons.

This monograph attempts an answer to the question: How do persons, conceived as whole beings, come to know anything, whether it be God, an idea, or an object? It presupposes that the case for holism in human nature is sufficiently treated by Reformed thinkers, and focuses on the biblical and theological evidence for holistic knowing as that which should shape

Christian thinking about teaching methodology. It will give some attention to the implications for achieving distinctive goals and an integrated curriculum.

Holistic Epistemology

Descriptions of how the human being comes to know are as numerous as positions in anthropology, metaphysics, and ethics. The philosophical literature abounds with disputes between schools of epistemology, and new ones are always being formed and refined.

Were education not the enterprise in which adults teach the young both what knowledge is and how to separate it from superstition and error educators could well leave such disputes to professional philosophers. Unlike shoe salesmen or engineers, teachers and the education profession have usually claimed to impart knowledge, and not shoes or bridges, to their clients or pupils. And the claim is that educators deliver not only a product (knowledge) but teach a process (method of acquiring knowledge). In popular language it is the claim that in schools a society teaches the young not only *what* to think but *how* to think. Schools transmit, in textbooks and lectures, a body of accepted knowledge, but also model by way of teaching method, a way to acquire knowledge.

Thus textbooks in philosophy of education typically include attention to epistemology, identify the various schools of philosophy, like idealism, realism, and pragmatism, and show their respective implications for goals, curriculum and teaching method.

If a Christian educational vision is to permeate the whole educational enterprise, educators must attempt to articulate a model classroom methodology which comports well with its goals and curriculum, as well as with a biblical anthropology. The case for a holistic theory of knowing will now be made, followed by its implication for classroom instruction.

Spectator and Respondent Theories

Many models of knowing exhibit what may be called a spectator theory of knowing. In it the knower is depicted as examining some evidence (whether with the senses or by the mind) and noting the degree of correspondence between such evidence and objective reality. The outcome of such a process is beliefs which are taken to be true reports of how things are. This view can be called a spectator theory of knowing because the verification process is mental, a seeing with the mind, although assisted by the senses. The method does not require any action upon such objective reality to confirm or repudiate beliefs.

Another variation on the spectator view is that of coherence as the test of truth. It holds that knowledge is reliable in the degree to which a given truth is internally consistent with others and that all are derived by rational deduction from self-evident truths.[9] One example of this latter view may be given to show that epistemology has educational consequences. It is in the school subject called geometry, and the point will be to show that in teaching the subject matter a method of acquiring knowledge is simultaneously taught.

Geometry typically begins with certain axioms or postulates, like "If equals be added to equals the sums are equal" and "Parallel lines never intersect." From these all other propositions about lines and shapes are 'proved' or found to be true, because they have been derived from the basic axioms as self-evident truths and from other theorems. Believers in this method applied to all of life, and not just to lines and shapes, are inclined to view mathematics in general as the model method of getting truth. Students who ask why they should study geometry and other forms of higher mathematics are told that it teaches them how to think clearly, even if they never become engineers or consciously use these proofs anywhere else.

The mathematical mode of knowing, when it is taken to be superior to other forms of knowing, is a claim that best fits the coherence theory of knowledge, a variation on what is here a spectator theory of knowing. A similar case could be made that when teaching the content of science, a paradigm of knowing, namely the scientific method is also taught. This would comport with a correspondence view. Proponents of this method assume, for example, that creationist accounts of the origin and age of the earth can be verified by only the scientific method.

What shall the educator wishing to think biblically do with such curricular content, and its implied epistemological method? Is reasoning from self-evident truths to their deductive conclusions the paradigm method for all knowing for a Christian? Is a Christian version of coherentism compatible with the Biblical way of knowing? Or is a version of correspondence theory what the Bible reflects?

A number of Reformed philosophers and theologians have rather recently argued that correspondence or coherence epistemologies are flawed.[10] Some have argued that they do not comport well with the biblical perspective on knowing.[11] From these arguments it is clear that thinking about epistemology is in ferment among Reformed thinkers. In ferment is not only *what* an appropriately Christian method of acquiring knowledge would look like, but also *how* it is to be defended, how a plausible case for its Christian character can be made. In theological language, this is the area of apologetics, that is, defense of the faith.

One standard technique, in Christian philosophical circles, is to defend Christian beliefs by turning attacks against them back against the critics, showing that the criteria used to find Christian beliefs wanting would also show the attacker's beliefs to be lacking in reliability.

Belief in the existence of God, for example, has been challenged by positivists as having not reliable grounds. A Christian defense often proceeds by showing that the tests of truth posed by opponents would also render belief in the existence of persons untenable. Success at this maneuver in Christian apologetics makes Christian beliefs no less respectable or reliable than those held by opponents. Destroying the opposition's criteria thus renders their rejection of Christian belief self-referentially incoherent. This attacking of the attacks is a basic strategy in establishing an affirmative answer to the question "Is Belief in God Rational?"[12]

This approach, however, leaves unanswered the question of just what are the methods to which a Christian epistemology is committed? By what method are Christian beliefs justified, or at least permissible?

In the ongoing dialogue among professional philosophers about religious knowledge, many tactics are possible. In trying to establish the philosophic respectability of theism as an alternative to other schools of philosophy, the tactics may be different from those which seek to give aid and comfort to believers in theism, although both sets of tactics attempt in scholarly fashion to show that there is no inherent contradiction between faith and reason. Dialogues with both those outside the faith and those within the faith must go on, for the Christian faith is surely under assault from all sides; professional philosophers as well as the layman wonder about religion's continued viability, so much so that this is being called a post-Christian age.

Since this monograph is addressed to those within the Christian faith it need not use the philosopher's analytic tools either to attack opposing ideologies or to attempt to find common ground arguments which defend the faith. It can instead use the tactic of Scriptural evidence that Christianity, as a belief system, does have grounds for its beliefs; it does have an epistemological method, however different that may be from the reigning epistemological models. This essay for Christian educators attempts to provide such reassurance.

It would seem that a plausible approach should be to discover in Scripture itself patterns which indicate that it does exhibit, but of course not offer a case for, a theory of knowing. Scripture is no more a textbook on epistemology than a textbook on science. It is a record of those who experienced God, and who acted in obedience or disobedience to God. We shall have to infer from Scripture what theory of knowing biblical writers reflected, and whether it reflects a spectator or respondent theory of knowing. The case will be made that it reflects the latter.

The Interactive Model

A promising approach, and one rich with implications for teaching methodology, is one which we call a respondent or interactive theory of knowing. Briefly put, it is that knowing is a process of thinking and doing, of mental and physical acts. To know a rock is thus not only to engage in mental acts about its nature in the scheme of things, but also to push or pull it, to act upon it to discover its nature or know the truth of it. Similarly, to know God is to engage in constructing mental acts about Him (rooted in revelation) but also to know Him by responding to Him, by what Scripture calls obedience or disobedience.

While the above seems to describe two separate acts, separated in time and even place, such is not the intent. It is rather that mental action is only one aspect and physical action the other, both constituting together the act of knowing. Put in the technical language of one Bible scholar:

> The perceiving subject exists in an active relationship with that which he perceives, not in the "tabula rasa" relationship of passive observer. Thus the perceiver and the perceived exist as poles of a dynamic continuum, rather than as dichotomized, static entities[13]

Scriptural instances of the use of the term "know" in this sense of a "dynamic continuum" abound. When Abraham knew Sarah and she conceived and bore a son, it is not merely a euphemism for sexual intercourse, but a Biblical paradigm of all knowing. It captures the concept of interaction as that which constitutes knowing, in this case a person. It is in the give and take, in the mental acts of classifying Sarah as female and wife and the physical act of sex, that he knew her. Without the act of intercourse (itself a term from Latin suggesting two-way action) the knowing is that of spectator, not participant.

When Job says "I know that my Redeemer liveth" (Job 19:25) he is not uttering this, spectator-like, as a process of rational induction or deduction, but out of holistic engagement with God, undergoing and responding, of perceiving God as having such and such qualities, and of living with poverty, illness, and despair. It is uttered as a conclusion to both his mental constructs and his doing.

When in I Samuel 3:7 it is said that "Samuel did not yet know the Lord," it is not that he had no mental constructs of God, since we assume that he had been told such by Eli the priest since being brought as a child to the temple by his mother Hannah. It is that he had not yet interacted with (obeyed) God, and thus did not know Him. The calls in the night constituted information, not knowing, until Samuel could say "Here am I, Lord."

Christ also spoke in this manner when referring to truth and knowledge. He spoke of "doing the truth", "living in the truth," "abiding in" and thus "being in the truth.'"[14] Knowing the truth in such a setting consists not simply of mental acts of accepting propositions about Christ, but of doing what Christ did, and thus knowing Him who said, "I am the way, the truth, and the life."

If the foregoing are not to be disposed of as merely poetic utterances or isolated word studies, they suggest that Scripture indeed consistently speaks a special language when it comes to epistemology and a description of knowing. It excludes forms of thinking in which only propositions are regarded as relevant to knowing, and in which belief is defined as a product of certain mental acts following accepted rules of logic.

Scripture distinguishes between 'believe in' and 'believe that', where the latter refers to propositions or assertions, such as belief *that* Christ arose from the dead. Scripture instead says to believe in the Lord Jesus Christ, and you shall be saved, implying a different conception of knowing. As the book of James has it (James 2:14-20) mere belief *that* God exists is what devils possess. Belief in God includes the response of discipleship, not just intellectual perception that some such being exists. When James says that "faith without works is dead" (vs. 26) its epistemological significance is that head knowing is incomplete knowledge without deeds. James notes of Abraham: "You see that his faith and his actions were working together, and his faith was made complete by what he did" (vs. 22).

Philosophers may try to pull apart thinking and doing, allowing only the thinking to produce knowledge, with deeds or doing being a separate act of applying such knowledge. Scripture does not talk that way. It talks instead, as the passage above indicates, of "working together" and of faith being "made complete" by doing. James even notes a parallel between a holistic view of man and a holistic view of knowing when he concludes: "As the body without the spirit is dead, so faith without deeds is dead" (vs. 26).

The distinction between belief *in* and belief *that is* one that is susceptible of many interpretations in ordinary language.[15] The point being made here is that the first is not merely a linguistic oddity, and is not simply reducible to the second.

The Apostle's Creed, that great ecumenical creed of Christendom, uses believe *in* consistently, as in "I believe in God, the Father"... "and in Jesus Christ," and continuing with "I believe in the Holy Spirit." These all suggest the holistic view of knowing in which there is commitment to a way of life out of which these propositions arise. They are not uttered as intellectual assent as the result of reasoning from first principles to these conclusions.

Thus, both Scripture and creeds speak a different language when it comes to a model way of knowing. Some Reformed thinkers have caught this vision when faith (knowing) is declared not to be assent to propositions, rationally derived. The Biblical alternative is sharply stated in the following extensive quote:

> How, then, ought we to think of faith? I suggest that the model we must have in mind is not that of believing propositions, but rather that of believing in a person. You all know, from your own experience, what it is to believe in a person. It is to trust him, to be loyal to him, to serve him, to give him one's allegiance, to be willing to work for him, to place one's confidence in him.[16]

While the context of the above quote indicates that the paradigm of knowing is knowing God as person, it is here offered as a model for all knowing. Thus knowing an idea or an object has the same components. While it may seem strange to talk of being 'loyal' to a rock, it would be redolent of Scripture to do so. Knowing God's creation does not follow an utterly different model from knowing Him who created it, and who exists in it. To know a rock is then to have both mental and physical acts relating to it. To know its nature is not simply to perceive it in the mind as belonging to a given class of objects, but also to act upon it, break it, stack it, sit on it, etc. In a word it is to be in interaction with it, in the best etymological sense of that word. Knowing is an action between (which is what inter means in Latin) the knower and the known. To pull the two apart is to reduce knowing to a mental proposition-making act. To do physical action alone, without the associated mental acts, is the other side of such reductionism, doing as blind stimulus-response behavior. Neither is the full Scriptural meaning of the act of knowing.

The more authentically biblical model of knowing as an interaction between the knower and the known is named by some theologians as co-relation, in which the knower is in the Truth, participating in it and walking in it.[17] Others have called it a *praxis* theory of knowing, stressing its action, or practice, component as a necessary supplement to thinking.[18] All have given extensive documentation and scriptural exegesis too elaborate to be given here.

Revelation's Role

Revelation is a key term in theological talk concerning epistemology. It refers to the topic of Christian belief about both the nature and source of truth or knowledge. Reformed thinkers have distinguished between two sources of revelation: general and special. The latter refers to scripture and the former refers to the physical creation and history.[19] What has not been treated sufficiently is the question of whether the two sources of knowledge call for commitment to two methods. The thrust of this section on holistic knowing is that a single generic method of knowing is compatible with the biblical message and will lead to a single generic classroom teaching method that is most appropriate for teaching the young how to know in an identifiably Christian way.

Revelation, as a theological term for the acquiring of knowledge, has been treated by numerous theologians. Archbishop Temple, for example, in a discussion of "Revelation and its Mode," puts it this way:

> ...there is no imparting of truth as the intellect approaches truth, but there is event and appreciation; and in the coincidence of these the revelation consists.[20]

Thus Temple asserts that perception of the existence of some objective reality is not yet revelation. It occurs if and only if there is "appreciation" or response.

All creation and not just Scripture is revelational. For, according to the psalmist, the heavens declare the glory of God and the firmament shows his handiwork (Psalm 19: 1-6). And according to Romans 1:18-21 such revelation is available to all men. But some "suppress the truth by their wickedness" even though "what may be known about God is plain to them" (vs. 18 & 19). Note in the above that it is not lack of intellectual insight which prevents some from knowing God, but wickedness, i.e., an improper response. Thus revelation occurs only in the coming together of objective event and appropriate response. As one interpreter says it:

> As we respond in unbelief...our discernment is clouded and our decision making is perverted. Only as we respond in faith... can we discern clearly and decide rightly.[21]

Stated even more bluntly is the following:

Because man is a religious being, all knowing necessarily involves obedience to the Word of God. Knowledge is not a matter of (cognitive) facts plus (attitudinal) values. All knowledge involves analytical distinction, but no more than it involves commitment to obedient action: we can only really speak of 'knowledge' when an integral subjection to the norms for human acting is involved.[22]

From none of the above description of this interactive model of knowing is there any implication that there is no place for intellectual operations in acquiring knowledge or receiving revelation. Intellectual insight is an integral part of knowing. But belief statements arise out of interaction, out of encounter, rather than being the end of knowing. They are derivative, not ultimate; they are a means and not an end. When Job asserted, "I know that my Redeemer liveth" it was within the fact of encounter; when Paul said, "And we know that in all things God works for the good of those who love Him... (Romans 8:28), it was not rational deduction but interaction. Neither is there any implication that truth or revelation is not also objective, existing independently of the knower. Denial of such objectivity would make man the maker of truth and knowledge. The interactive, encounter model set forth above holds that such objective reality (the revelation) and the human responder are two foci of a single process, with the responder discovering or uncovering what is by what is done to it. This model is a rejection of the spectator views discussed earlier in which the knower perceives objective reality with the mind rather than out of encounter. It is also far from the pragmatic model of knowing in which the knower creates truth by testing its consequences.

The following extensive quote is instructive in noting how Scripture speaks in a language quite unlike that of a Greek mode of knowing which has so pervasively affected Christian thinking on this matter:

The understanding that present day Christian have of "know" and "Knowing" is often unrelated to the meaning of these words as revealed in scripture...(it) has been influenced by philosophical inquiry, especially as it came from the Greeks. For them "to know" was to be involved in objective investigation apart from context, ... apart from one's immediate experience. "Knowledge" for the Greeks was a fixed possession. It sought the essence of things, not the relationship of the person to that which could be known. This "knowledge" was outside the person; it contained no personal significance nor did it require personal commitment.[23]

In summary it has been argued that the method of knowing that is most compatible with the biblical revelation is one in which the usual dualisms of thinking and doing, cognition and action, are rejected in favor of a single generic mode incorporating both. Knowing propositions, whether facts of history, theorems in geometry or noting that a rock is hard and heavy are all partial or incomplete forms of knowing. They are subsumed under the interactive method of knowing, one in which the action on the known by the knower completes the act of knowing.

Explication and elaboration of this holistic view have been necessary before we examine its implication for teaching method done Christianly. Looking ahead to the next section it should be already clear that what we seek is a generic classroom instructional model which can incorporate the various phases of knowing into one methodology.

Holistic Classroom Methodology

Crucial to a search for a method of knowing which is generic enough to embrace all knowing is the distinction between methods and methodology. The former is plural, the latter singular; the former is a series of discrete teacher maneuvers which can be used in varying combinations as the situation demands; the latter is a single generic and normative flow which allows various methods but endorses some more than others. The plea here is that what Christian educators should have is a methodology which is anchored in the Judeo-Christian epistemological tradition.

Classroom teaching methods are often portrayed as little more than techniques for effecting learning, each having a different configuration of teacher and student behaviors. Thus there is the lecture method, the simulation method, the audiovisual method, the demonstration method, the inquiry method, the Socratic method, the activity method, just to name a few. The general impression is given that the successful teacher is the one whose repertoire of such different strategies is extensive, and that the selection of each is made in the light of the peculiarities of the learners or the material to be learned.

Some treatments of teaching method assume that the nature of the subject matter dictates the strategy. Teacher training institutions and some state certification codes lend support to this impression by requiring methods courses in each of the several teaching areas or subjects. Thus, if one curriculum area is called science, it follows that a course will teach the peculiarities of the methods of teaching science. The same would be true for art methods, reading methods, language arts methods, and so forth. Such courses may in fact have much overlap, with only minor differences in terminology, as when science methods may highlight something called the demonstration method, and social studies highlight the lecture method. The different terminology masks the similarity, as both will feature a teacher talking with some visual aid or realia giving assistance. What is common to all such discrete methods courses is the assumption that the peculiarities of each kind of material somehow dictate how data are to be learned or known.

At a higher level of generality teaching method is sometimes conceived of as strategies which cut across all subjects in the curriculum. The terminology then suggests that all lessons should have such strategies as set induction, stimulus variation, planned repetition, and closure, for example. These are more generic teaching skills, and are presumably appropriate to any lesson, whatever the raw material or subject being taught. Whether the material is linguistic, mathematical, artistic, or literary, the elements of the lesson are the same, with only minor variations in emphasis.

What the above conceptions of classroom method lack is any generalized conception of knowing. While each of the two types has implicit assumptions about how learning best occurs, their defense is usually stated in terms of their respective motivational value or retention value. Psychology is taken to be the discipline which vindicates the methods, individually and severally. Little attempt is made to find an epistemological grounding for selection from among them, or a framework into which to fit them.

Secular philosophers of education have proposed a classroom methodology, a series of classroom events, whose flow is peculiar to their philosophical commitment to a way of knowing. It typically contains phases or elements in a sequence which will culminate in knowledge, not just information or discrete learnings. Plato, for example, both conceived such a methodology and exhibited it in his various dialogues, the *Republic* and others. It is called the Socratic method after his teacher Socrates. It contains a flow of question and dialogue that is not merely random discussion but knowledge seeking. When the dialogue is ended the pupil has knowledge, as platonic idealism conceives it.

Other philosophers of education have proposed a quite different methodology as a better way of acquiring knowledge, a better way of getting in touch with reality, as their philosophical allegiances dictate. John Dewey wrote voluminously on various aspects of education, including the proposal of a generic methodology, usually called problem solving. It has five phases or "constituent elements." While the phases could subsume under them various methods, such as the lecture method and the discussion method, they each fitted into the larger flow of movement from ignorance to knowledge. Called the "complete act of thought" it induced not only learning some content, but learning to think, as conceived from an instrumentalist philosophy of knowing.

What is a Christian educator, wishing to be true to Scripture, to make of such options? One conclusion, as the previous examples have shown, is that a teaching methodology is no more philosophically neutral than an epistemology. Also, individual strategies like the lecture method may find their place within several methodologies, although even these are accorded a different status in the various methodologies. While individual methods and strategies may be neutral, surely less so is a methodology, particularly if it is the classroom equivalent of the preferred epistemological method of knowing reality reliably.

The second thing Christian educators can learn from the presence of competing methodologies is that one can be adopted only if the epistemological counterpart of the classroom method is congruent with a biblical mode of knowing. The adoption of a classroom methodology proposed by others, whether it arises out of Platonic idealism, Deweyan pragmatism, or realism, is fraught with the danger of inviting the Trojan horse into the City of God. That is not to say that such philosophical parentage automatically discredits such teaching methodologies. Because of common grace, all thinkers have some vision of the created world and each has some possibility of proposing a methodology congruent with the biblical view of knowing and teaching. Elsewhere I have argued that the binding marriage of a given methodology with secular philosophy is often made in the heaven of academia but is not automatically binding on the earth of the classroom. Compatibility with a biblical vision, is the test of legitimacy of any methodology[24] and not its possible secular parentage.

What can be said with confidence is that acceptance or rejection of any overall classroom strategy for teaching children how to think and know Christianly must be congruent with the biblical view of knowing. One has been outlined in the previous section of this essay, and we shall shortly see what this classroom methodology might look like. To do less than to derive our own is to run the risk of behaving secularly. To adopt only methods, without framework of methodology, is to reduce teaching and learning to the level of psychological devices for retaining bits and pieces of subject matter. It is to ignore the potentiality in methodology for deliberately inculcating in the youth a process, a mode of thinking for lifelong acquiring of knowledge in biblical perspective.

Christian educators could then go beyond paying lip service to the claim that in Christian education we teach pupils how to think, and not merely indoctrinate in what to think. They could model in the classroom how a Christian comes to know God and His created world, and not just transmit answers. They could, in a word, redeem methodology from irrelevance to Christian thinking and redeem it from being merely imitative of secular philosophies.

Stemming from the description of the biblical model of knowing, classroom methodology is, I believe, characterized by an interactive flow between the learner and some data, a give and take between the knower and the to-be-known.

Before describing the phases or elements we should note that the outcome will be truth, but not final truth. It will always be a truth relative to and appropriate to the age level of the student, and will be a more general truth for the advanced learner in high school than for the elementary pupil, even though the phases will be the same. For example, a learner hopefully progresses through something like the following in a perception of the "truth" about Santa Claus:

— He is an actual person who lives at the North Pole, and who comes down my chimney with presents.
— He is a name for my parents and relatives who give me gifts.
— He is the spirit of goodwill that comes at Christmas in the form of gift giving.
— He is the secular substitute for the Christ child, who is the embodiment of good and God's giving of Himself.

All the above are successive approximations to the truth, and it is teachers who will decide at what grade level each would be most appropriate. The point is that classroom teachers deal always with truth and knowledge which is conditioned by the level of maturity of the learner, and usually do not deal, as epistemologists might, with final truth. In a biblical mode of knowing the truth about Santa Claus will be "complete" when the intellectual perception is joined with action appropriate to that age level.

Phases of Methodology

The methodology could be divided roughly into three phases, which will be called the consider, choose, and commit phases. While the sequence is not arbitrary, neither is it rigid and inflexible. Movement back and forth among them is permissible and desirable. Also, within each a variety of methods can be used. These could include lecture, discussion, field trip, or reading.

In the *consider* phase the learner is confronted with the new material.

Exploratory definitions and distinctions are made, and attention is focused on the various dimensions of the material. Such initial exposure must be selected so as to be related to the learner's life experience or previous learnings, so that it can truly be encountered and not perceived, spectator-like, as from a distance and without chance of more than belief that some such entities exist. Whether the raw material is a mathematical concept, like place value, or a phenomenon like dew on the grass on some mornings, the consider phase begins the interaction by having the teacher relate it to the learner.

The material may not even carry a science, art, or history label (except in the mind of the teacher) but will be labeled with an aspect of the life of the learner as the pupil has experienced it. This initial phase will more powerfully provoke the second phase if it carries with it some problematic, some unresolved elements which do not by themselves make sense, but which call for resolution. If the biblical model of believing in such material is to prevail, then the initial phase must introduce each cycle of learning in a context which not only relates to present life, but stretches the learner beyond the now to both the past and the future. It must have the potential for differing responses, different value judgments about its worth, different ways to react to it, always assuming such different ways are not simply intellectual classification, such as that a cow is a four-footed animal with a split hoof. In a word this initial phase must have some dissonance in it, where perplexity is not merely intellectual incompleteness, but an unresolved tension that is felt.

Without the careful selection of the curricular material to meet the above criteria the movement to the second phase is difficult if not impossible.

The second phase is the *choose* phase. Here the options for response are clarified and their implications better understood. Here the moral tensions are sharpened and the principles which govern the options are studied in more detail. It is in this phase that biblical data and directives are most explicitly brought into play, again by any number of specific techniques.

If the first phase dramatizes what it *is* that the learner faces, the second phase highlights whatever ought are involved, these often but not always being biblical oughts. The movement from is to ought will enhance the likelihood that the interactive model of knowing will occur because now the biblical mandates are part of the learning situation and they call for obedient response. The biblical data function as perspective giving, and not just as more facts or pieces of information. Also in this phase not only moral considerations arise, but also aesthetic, legal, scientific, and other principles relevant to the subject matter. This phase of the methodology may occupy the longest time of the three phases, because deepening understanding, as well as exposing alternative points of view, is time consuming. It is here also that multiple methods of instruction can be subsumed. The lecture method, the discussion method, the explication of readings, the simulation method, and even field trips take their place in the flow of the three C phases. It is in this phase of the total methodology that acceptance or rejection takes place, and prepares for the final phase.

The third phase is the *commit* phase. It moves beyond intellectual understanding, beyond exposure of the moral and other considerations, and toward commitment to act on both the is and the ought. It highlights the response part of the total methodology, with response identified as both verbal and behavioral. While not all school situations allow actual action, the commitment to a form of action is the absolute minimum. Without this phase the knowing consists of knowing *that* many possibilities exist in the abstract, of head knowledge which is the beginning but not the end of knowing. This phase may be the briefest of the three in terms of classroom time if the preceding two phases have been thoroughly done. Should the action response be possible within the classroom or even outside the school setting, then the time involvement may be greater.

A brief example of how this methodology would handle a given piece of curriculum content may be helpful to the classroom teacher. Although examples run the risk of being criticized or rejected on various grounds, the following is offered as that which reflects the spirit, if not the letter, of the proposed holistic methodology of the three C's.

The topic is the person of Abraham Lincoln as president, and it is imagined as part of a larger unit on "Authority: Its Power and Problems."

1. *Consider phase*

In this phase the student is presented with the facts of presidential action in the Civil War, with the focus on economic, political, and military aspects of that conflict. What is slowly brought to the fore for special scrutiny is the problem of slavery in the conflict between North and South. It ends with the reasons for issuing the Emancipation Proclamation. Lectures, readings, films, and pictures are used to bring to life whatever were the factors in the situation.

2. *Choose phase*

In this phase the discussion method is used prominently to sharpen the choices a president had, and the political and moral dimensions of each. Then the simulation method could be used to make the historical question a personal moral question: Should he have begun the effort to free the slaves? What norms for society does the biblical vision exhibit for both peace and justice in any society, then and now?

Here the new content added is whatever biblical episodes or passages are relevant to the racial question, and the debate method can be used to highlight the possible biblical positions.

3. *Commit phase*

In this phase each student is asked to apply the principles in the choose phase to his/her own position on social questions like equal opportunity among the races, intermarriage among the races, and racial integration in schools. Decisions on what action one would follow, individually or collectively, in each would end the lesson.

The lesson is by no means teachable as outlined, particularly because the crucial factor of the age or grade level is not specified. It is given to show only the flow of the holistic methodology. The flow is intended to reveal the necessary interaction of thought and action, thinking and doing, which were contained in the previous discussion of epistemology.

Method and Goals

The three phases are integrally related to goals of Christian education as they have been articulated in Reformed thinking about schooling. For example, Christian Schools International has identified three distinct but interacting goals: intellectual, decisional, and creative. Each is an identifiable dimension of the single aim of preparing the student to live the Christian life. They can in summary be distinguished as follows:

1. Intellectual dimension, focusing on achieving a grasp of states of affairs, what is.

2. Decisional dimension, focusing on achieving decisions where choice can be made based on relevant norms or standards, on what ought to be.[25]

3. Creative dimension, focusing on achieving life responses to both what is and what ought to be.

Much thought by curriculum writers has gone into how these may be achieved in the various subjects in the curriculum. Sometimes these goals are perceived as achieved separately, in different areas of the curriculum, with math perhaps featuring the first in clearest form, religion the second, and physical education the third. Such perceptions wrench apart what should be kept whole, if the holistic nature of the learner and of knowing is to be honored. All subject matter, if taught Christianly, should achieve all three, if not simultaneously at least sequentially. And it is here that the proposed methodology of the three C's makes its contribution.

The proposed holistic methodology, if followed, would keep all three goals together, with each phase of the methodology making its unique contribution. The first phase, the consider phase, lends itself best to the intellectual dimension, the choose phase lends itself to the decisional dimension, while the culmination in the commit phase lends itself to the creative dimension of learning goals.

What holds together the various curricular materials, then, are the three goals and the three phases of the generic methodology. While clarifications of each of the three goal dimensions can and should go on,[26] the holistic methodology would provide the practical expression of their relationship to each other. It holds together the two of the triad of goals, curriculum, and method which is a prerequisite of any well rounded conception of teaching.

CSI, in choosing its three interacting goals, drew heavily on a previous document. There the interconnections between what has here been called the consider, choose, and commit phases were already suggested in the following, with the emphasis editorially added:

> Teachers should also ask how they can guide young persons by means of their growing *understanding* of life toward a deeper *commitment* to the way things ought to be, to the true and the good;. . . how, through the learner's expanding awareness of the moral options that life presents, they can guide him to *choose* Christian options, based on Christian commitment.[27]

Goal talk in that document was never translated into a methodology that would be consistent with such rhetoric. That is what the holistic methodology here proposed does. It rescues such rhetoric from abstraction, puts methodological flesh on the distinctiveness of the goals. It still allows the classroom teacher considerable flexibility in the selection of specific techniques and strategies in each of the phases, while ensuring that the techniques fit into a larger flow of learning, of coming to know Christianly conceived.

What remains is to indicate briefly what the holistic view of man, the holistic view of knowing, and the holistic view of classroom method require about curriculum content and organization.

Holistic Curriculum

Curriculum materials can be and have been packaged in various ways. From the trivium and quadrivium of the Greeks and the Romans to the seven liberal arts of the Middle Ages, and down to the proliferation of disciplines and subjects of today's curriculum, revisionists have all tried to divide the encyclopedia of possible knowledge into a given number of packages or subjects for learning in schools.

The curriculum of today's school is by now a curious mixture of the old and the new, with contenders always jostling for a more prominent place in the school day. Those who seek "basic education" want to reduce the multiplicity of possibilities to a limited number of generative subjects. Those who seek "relevant education" seek to add to or alter these basics. What actually exists is the result of this cacophony of voices seeking to be heard for their view of both the number and kind of subjects which will best produce the educated citizen.

What is a Christian educator, who wishes to think Christianly, to make of such a discordant symphony? What can be used to sift out the faddish from the truly fruitful for Christian knowing? In the search for a curriculum that is distinctly Christian, the educator runs the risk again of being merely imitative, and in so doing inviting into the City of God the Trojan horse of secularism, idealism, or pragmatism. None of these will do.

What many attempts at making curriculum distinctly Christian suggest is that the Christian view of life is to be integrated into the curriculum. Both publicity brochures and serious essays speak of giving a Christian perspective on life and learning. All agree that some sort of fusion between Christian values and subject matter is to take place, and that in some sense the Bible is the center of integrated curriculum. However the meanings of integration as it bears on faith and learning differ, sometimes in the same publication.[28]

Meanings Of Integration

In one meaning of integration the academic disciplines are left in place and the teacher, with the assistance of Christian textbook and other resources, adds a Christian interpretation or assessment to such subjects. Locating in God the order and beauty of mathematics and the intricacy and design of the physical world in science are given as the way that the integration takes place. So too in history and social studies Christian assessment of cultural practices or forms of government can occur in teacher resource or textbook talk.[29]

Thus the same academic subjects as in secular education are baptized by sprinkling with evaluations or interpretations, thus effecting an integration of Christian faith and subject matter. A committee of Christian scholars has indicated at least seven "ways in which the biblical revelation may give structure and direction to our work in the disciplines."[30]

Among these ways are that "the biblical revelation can inform the direction of our investigations, the emphases we give and the theses we try to establish" and that "the biblical revelation speaks to what we do with our theoretical knowledge, for what purposes or ends we use it". All seven ways indicate both the extent and the complexity of this interpretation of integrating faith and learning, but they all assume the disciplines to be individually the framework within which such integration takes place.

A quite different view of integration is one in which the subject matter is chosen because it cuts across the academic disciplines.[31] Integration of the various disciplines into a new curriculum topic or subject is achieved by selecting some organizing rubric which by its nature calls for interdisciplinary content. For example the subject would be ecology or environment, but its content would not be limited to biology or botany; it would include political, social, and economic matters, each selected for its relevance to the problem of man and environment. The integration of the Christian perspective would operate at two levels: one in the choice of the organizing topic, and the other in the inclusion of biblical materials as part of the content.

Both of the above meanings given to integration have their proponents and are well intentioned attempts to honor the principle that the Christian faith should be operative in curriculum building.

While this brief description of the two views of integration does not do full justice to either of them, our purpose here is to assess their major thrust in the light of the holistic theory of man, knowing, and classroom method outlined earlier.

To review briefly, such holistic conception would seek a curriculum content and organization that would most likely engage not just the intellect of the learner, but the whole learner. Such content and organization should also make it likely that the knowledge gained is the kind where action and doing are a constant and necessary ingredient. Finally, to honor the holistic methodology the curriculum content should encourage the full range of the phases of consider, choose, and commit to be incorporated again and again in each cycle of learning.

Curriculum of Concerns

The second meaning of integration, in which the focus of units or courses is a perennial human problem and which cuts across the disciplines, is a more likely candidate for fulfilling the demands of a holistic anthropology, epistemology, and methodology of instruction. When the organizing rubric under which content is chosen is a perennial human concern, adjusted to age level, then by its very nature it is value laden, and filled with ambiguities and alternative resolutions. Such resolution points always toward action and life style, even when the school situation does not allow actual life-style follow up. It points toward discipleship and obedience because the curriculum is so organized that the topic cannot be confronted only intellectually, and the learnings cannot be just beliefs that such and such are the facts or theories of the matter. Moreover the Christian , perspective is a central and not tangential concern, or a footnote addition to an otherwise self-contained discipline. The material is not baptized by sprinkling but by immersion in a Christian concern.

A full description and defense, both pedagogically and psychologically, cannot be given here, as the case being made is that it comports best with a philosophical perspective, a Christian one. Such psychological evidence would point toward its greater motivation and retention possibilities, toward a more likely adoption of a Christian perspective on life by the learner. Such evidence would also point to the power of teacher modeling Christian concern as well as modeling how Christians come to know.

Before proceeding with a sketch of the preferred curriculum it should be pointed out that the case being made is for the required, common learnings in the curriculum and not the whole curriculum. Electives and enrichment curriculum, and specialized knowledges also are part of the total school day. The academic disciplines have their place, particularly at upper levels of schooling, but their status is that of electives. Specialized knowledges, like algebra and foreign language, and specialized skills like music have a similar place, but not in the required, common learnings of elementary and secondary education. Within this model time in elementary school also can be devoted directly to word attack skills in reading and computational skills in mathematics. Whether these subjects are separated into a special period in the day or incorporated, as needed, into the major units in a curriculum of concerns, can be left to the discretion of a local teaching staff.

Whatever specific form the school day would take, the curriculum model here proposed would require that large segments of the common learnings in the required curriculum would be organized around a series of enduring (through the grade levels) and perennial (through the ages) human concerns rather than the disciplines.

To assist those who find the total argument convincing, but who need some examples in order to see its possibilities, the following are suggestive, but obviously not a complete set of subjects.

Human sexuality is one such enduring life concern, for any age level and common to all. Data and principles from biology, psychology, sociology, and theology or religion are the minimum essentials of the Christian conception of sex, sex roles, and sexual life styles, both inside and outside marriage and family.[32] While the secular school can find no responsible way to handle this value-laden subject, the Christian view of the school here defended can, and can do so confidently and distinctively. Handling the same topic within any one discipline inevitably leads to reductionism and less than a responsible grasp of sexuality, Christianly conceived.

Career education, from kindergarten through high school, is another area of human concern, one which no academic subject by itself can address, except abstractly. When the Christian concept of calling is joined with social studies, economics, and others, we have the possibility that each learner will be confronted with and assisted in acting on this important choice facing every young person.

Hunger, in both its personal and social dimension, is everywhere present. It involves not only understanding and action on personal diet and nutrition, but understanding and action in political and social dimensions as well. While some attempts have been made to incorporate this human concern into curriculum materials,[33] much expansion and elaboration at several grade levels remain as a challenge to extend this kind of curriculum of concerns.

Finally, and even more briefly, Christian perceptions of and strategies for dealing with such issues as warfare, prisons, poverty, pollution, etc. are prime subjects for elaboration into full-fledged and properly graded materials, K-12. The possible list of Christian concerns that would or could be included is a long one, and variations on all are conceivable for different grade levels.

Curriculum materials based on this model will be produced, however, if (and likely only if) a significant number of Christian educators both begin in small ways on their own and ask Christian publishing houses and service organizations to provide them with textbooks and other teaching resources which exemplify this conception of curriculum, and this meaning of integration of faith and learning.

This extended essay has had as its purpose the providing of a case for a holistic view of man and knowing, seen in biblical perspective. The curriculum and classroom method counterparts have been included to show that all aspects of schooling are affected by such a theory. It is given to encourage Christian educators who have made a professional commitment to making their teaching ever more distinctly and consistently rooted in Christian philosophical commitments.

Notes

1. N.H. Beversluis. *Toward a Theology of Education* . Grand Rapids, Michigan: Calvin College Occasional Paper No. 1, February, 1981, pp. 20-27.

2. See John Cooper "Dualism and the biblical view of human beings," *The Reformed Journal*, September and October, 1982. For earlier writings which argue rather explicitly for a form of dualism in human nature see Henry Zylstra, "Modern Philosophy of Education," in *Testament* of *Vision* (Grand Rapids, Michigan: Eerdmans Publishing Co., 1961) in which he asserts, "Man is an horizon in which two worlds meet, the natural and the spiritual" and, "He lives in two orders," p. 84.

3. In addition to those cited as illustrative the following reflect a similar holistic view, with variations. Geraldine Steensma, "The First Key," in To *Those Who Teach* (Terre Haute, Indiana: Signal Publishing Co., 1971); G. C. Berkouwer. *Man, The Image* of *God* (Grand Rapids, Mich.: Eerdmans Publishing Co., 1962) pp. 194-107. Such a view is also evident in Paul Ramsey, *Basic Christian Ethics* (New York: Charles Scribners, 1952) pp. 249-259 where he rejects any definition of "image of God" as that which belongs to any given faculty and holds that image resides in the reflection (relationship with God).

4. *Human Development, Learning and Teaching* (Grand Rapids, Michigan: Eerdmans publishing Co., 1961), p. 43.

5. Arnold De Graaff and James Olthuis (eds.) *Toward a Biblical View of Man.* (Toronto, Ontario: Institute For Christian Studies, 1978), p. 1.

6. *Curriculum: By What Standard?* (Grand Rapids, Mich: National Union of Christian Schools, 1966), p.8.

7. *Ibid,* p.8

8. See for example Norman DeJong, *Education in the Truth* (Nutley, New Jersey: Presbyterian and Reformed Publishing Comany, 1969), chapter 11 "The Organic Unity of Man." Also G. C. Berkouwer, *Man, The Image* of *God* (Grand Rapids, Mich.: Eerdmans Publishing Company, 1962), chapter on "The Whole Man," pp. 194-207.

9. See John Brubacher, *Modern Philosophies of Education* (New York: McGraw-Hill Book Company, 1962), pp. 74-86 and 89-95 for a discussion of disputes between coherence and correspondence theories.

10. See Philip Holtrop, "Toward a Biblical Conception of Truth and a New Mood for Doing Reformed Theology," *Theological Forum* (of the Reformed Ecumenical Synod) Vol. V, No. 2 (June, 1977). A condensed version appeared in *The Reformed Joumal*, February, 1977, pp. 9-13.

11. Nicholas Wolterstorff. *Reason Within the Bounds of Religion* (Grand Rapids, Michigan: Eerdmans Publishing Company, 1976). He has argued the case against what he calls "foundationalism", a form of what is in this essay called coherence theory. See especially chapter 4.

12. For a general critique of foundationalism and its inadequacies from a Reformed perspective see Alvin Plantinga, "On Reformed Epistemology," in *The Reformed Journal*, January, 1982, pp. 13-16; see also his "The Reformed Objection to Natural Theology," in *Christian Scholar's Review*, Vol XI, No. 3 (1982). See especially his "Is Belief in God Rational?" in *Religion and Rationality*, C. Delaney (ed.). (South Bend: University of Notre Dame Press, 1979). pp. 7-27. For latest reflection of such ferment in epistemology see *Rationality in the Calvinian Tradition*, H. Hart et al. (eds.). (Lanham, MD: University Press of America, 1983).

13. Jerry Gill. *The Possibility of Religious Knowledge* (Grand Rapids, Michigan: Eerdmans Publishing Company, 1971), p. 121. See also his *On Knowing God* (Philadelphia, Penn.: The Westminister Press, 1981) in which in a chapter called "Knowledge Through Participation" he argues that "it is necessary to view bodily activity as a form of cognitive judgment" (p. 95), and using Polanyi's concept of "indwelling" says that "indwelling is an important aspect of every cognitive situation. There is always a sense in which the process of coming to know anything, be it object or persons, is dependent upon empathetic indwelling" (p. 95).

14. See, for elaboration of this point Philip Holtrop, "A Strange Language: Toward a Biblical Conception of Truth," *The Reformed Journal*, February, 1977, pp. 9-13.

15. H. H. Price, "Belief 'In' and Belief 'That'," *Religious Studies*, October, 1965, pp. 5-27.

16. Nicholas Wolterstorff. *Curriculum By What Standard?* (Grand Rapids, Michigan: National Union of Christian Schools, 1966) p. 10.

17. See, for the best treatment of such a theologian, Steve Prediger, *Truth and Knowledge in G. C. Berkouwer: The Contours of His Epistemology* (Toronto, Ontario: Institute for Christian Studies, 1982).

18. Thomas H. Groome, *Christian Religious Education* (San Francisco, CA: Harper and Row, 1980). See especially Chapter Seven, "In Search of a 'way of knowing' for Christian Religious Education."

19. For a simplified summary of this doctrine see Louis Berkhof, *Manual* of *Reformed Doctrine* (Grand Rapids, Michigan: Eerdmans Publishing Company, 1933), pp. 23-26. For a more elaborate treatment of general revelation see G. C. Berkouwer, *General Revelation* (Grand Rapids, Michigan: Eerdmans Publishing Company, 1955).

20. *Nature, Man, and God*, (New York: Macmillan, 1956) p. 314. In *The Self*

As Agent by John Macmurray (London: Faber and Faber, 1957) a similar argument is given. See especially Chapter Four, "Agent and Subject."

21. Stuart Fowler in *No Icing on the Cake*, edited by Jack Mechielsen (Melbourne, Australia: Brookes-Hall Publishing Foundation, 1980) p. 29.

22. Douglas Blomberg,Ibid, p. 51.

23. G. Steensma and H. Van Brummelen (eds.) *Shaping School Curriculum: A Biblical* View (Terre Haute, Indiana: Signal Publishing Co., 1977) p. 5.

24. "Are Classroom Practices and Philosophy Married?" *Christian Educators Journal,* April, 1983, p. 10 and 12.

25. *Principles to Practice* (Grand Rapids, Michigan: Christian Schools International, 1979) p. 1.

26. See Henry Triezenberg, "Up With Decisional Learning," *Christian Educators Journal,* November, 1976, pp. 23 ff. For further proposed clarification and revision of the taxonomy see Nicholas Wolterstorff, *Educating for Responsible Action* (Grand Rapids, Michigan: Eerdmans Publishing Company, 1982).

27. N. H. Beversluis, *Christian Philosophy of Education* (Grand Rapids, Michigan: National Union of Christian Schools (now Christian Schools International), 1971 p. 39.

28. See *Christian Home and School,* March 1982, p. 15 ff. In this special issue the curriculum theory and its application to textbook production is outlined.

29. For concrete application of this meaning of integration see the Christian Perspective on History series, published by Christian Schools International from 1973-76. For its application to the subject of civics see William Hendricks *Under God* (Grand Rapids, Michigan: CSI Publications, Fourth edition, 1981). In this latter text there is persistence assessment of social policy from a Christian perspective, usually in the form of raising questions.

30. Calvin College Curriculum Study Committee, *Christian Liberal Arts Education* (Grand Rapids, Michigan: Calvin College, Eerdmans Publishing Company, 1970) p.59-60.

31. G. Steensma and H. Van Brummelen, *Shaping School Curriculum: A Biblical* View (Terre Haute, Indiana: Signal Publishing Company, 1977), especially chapter 6, "A Design for Elementary and Secondary Curriculum." See also Norman DeJong, *Education in the Truth* (Nutley, New Jersey: Presbyterian and Reformed Publishing Company, 1969), Chapter 11. For textbook application of this interdisciplinary approach see *Man in Society: A Study in Hope.* Ary De Moor et *al.* (Grand Rapids, Mich.: Christian Schools International, 1980.) It is designed for secondary schools.

32. See, for example, William Hendricks. *Toward Christian Maturity, K-6: Guide For Teaching Human Sexuality,* (Grand Rapids, Michigan: Christian Schools International, 1981;) See also, for middle school, by the same author, *God's Temples,* second edition, 1983, with accompanying Teacher's Edition.

33. Yvonne Van Ee, *5 Days* of *World Hunger Awareness* (Grand Rapids, Michigan: Christian Schools International, 1982), a one-week study for grades 4, 5, and 6.

Index

About the Editor

Dr. Donald Oppewal is Professor of Education, Emeritus at Calvin College, Grand Rapids, Michigan. He taught philosophy of education and curriculum in both the undergraduate and graduate courses for thirty years.

His professional activities included being a founder and Editor of the *Christian Educators Journal,* a quarterly journal of, by, and for the Christian educator. He compiled several Departmental and College readers for different courses. He also edited or authored eight monographs in the Calvin College Monograph Series.

He has published extensively, both by himself and in collaboration with others, in education journals and books. His monograph, *Biblical Knowing and Teaching,* and one of his journal articles, "American Calvinist Day Schools," are included in this collection.

Other collaborations in publications include *Society, State, and Schools: A Case For Structural and Confessional Pluralism*, 1981, and *Censorship: Evidence of Bias in Our Children's Textbooks*, 1986.